In Praise of Faery Healing

Margie McArthur has woven together a bright tapestry of wisdom as ancient as the northern hills, yet sparkling fresh in its relevance to our lives today. The first half of the book is a veritable treasury of faery lore from the Celtic lands, including historical accounts of faery healers and a fascinating compendium of magical plants, trees and stones. The second half is a practical manual for contacting the faeries today, full of skillfully-wrought exercises and meditations. Margie speaks with an authentic voice that rings with the truth of lived experience, and she writes in a lucid style that seeks ever to clarify, rather than speak in veiled hints, as has often been the case in works on this subject. At a time when we need more than ever to seek the lost connection with our invisible allies for healing ourselves and our planet, this book serves as an inspiring and invaluable resource.

—Mara Freeman, author of *Kindling the Celtic Spirit*

Faery Healing is an indispensable exploration of the once-lost indigenous healing practices of the ancient Celts…a clear, contemporary and insightful guide for readers, healers and mystics. *Faery Healing* is one of the most unique spirituality books ever published and it represents a major contribution to the reconstruction of contemporary pagan traditions. You will read this book and use it again and again!

—Timothy Roderick, author of *Dark Moon Mysteries* and *Apprentice to Power*

Faery Healing is a marvelous look into the history, lore, and magic of the faerie realm. This well-researched and lyrical volume is filled with fascinating tidbits from legend and myth. From this painstakingly researched material, McArthur has created practical and useful applications for the modern day practitioner of metaphysics and magic. *Faery Healing: The Lore and the Legacy* is one of the few serious works on faerie magic that I have come across, and will be on my bookshelf for years to come.

—Yasmine Galenorn, author of *Embracing the Moon*, *Crafting the Body Divine*, and *Ghost of a Chance*

This book is packed with useful and fascinating lore about faeries and faery healing, but the thing I like best about it is the way it gently leads you into discovering faery information for yourself. Personal experience is the most useful experience of all, specific and individual faery treatment is better than book lore, and information from the true source is the most relevant. The paths Margie McArthur shows us to the Otherworld are paved with the priceless gems of faery healing, faery magic, and faery fun. She takes us by the hand and guides us there and back safely and joyfully. You'll love the journey!

—Jessica Macbeth, author of *The Faeries' Oracle*

This enjoyable, well-written, thoroughly researched, information- and idea-intensive book may surprise some readers with what an extensive body of health practices is associated with the faery faith. Margie McArthur's *Faery Healing* shows us how ancient therapies, which accessed the Powers of the Living Land and the Celtic Otherworlds illustrates theories of modern energy medicine. In sections on "Faery Healing for Today," Margie also provides numerous suggestions for making relationship with the different orders of life and activating "the part within ourselves that is faery" as a means of achieving wholeness.

—Janina Renee, author of *Playful Magic, Tarot for a New Generation, By Candlelight: Rituals for Celebration, Blessing, and Prayer*

This is, quite simply, one of the best books on faery tradition I have ever read. Margie McArthur has skillfully woven many threads together to create a straightforward narrative that cannot fail to both inform and delight anyone who has an interest in the traditional healing practices of our Celtic ancestors. Not satisfied to simply rehash the same old material, McArthur has produced a comprehensive book, containing a unique and intelligent point of view. I predict *Faery Healing: The Lore and the Legacy* is going to become a classic reference in field of study, and will be treasured by many, now and in years to come.

—Tira Brandon Evans, founder of the Society of Celtic Shamans and author of *The Green and Burning Tree, The Labyrinthine Way,* and *Healing Waters*

Margie meticulously examines healing folklore of the British Isles, tracks its connections to Celtic beliefs and has written a usable and useful approach to the healing of mind, body and spirit.

—Grey Cat, author of *Deepening Witchcraft* and co-author of *American Indian Ceremonies*

If it's authentic lore about the Celtic faery folk and human faery doctors you're wanting, this is the book to read. It's not made-up nonsense but well researched information drawn from pre-Christian and folkloric sources. If you want to know about the Good Neighbors, this book is the real thing.

—Barbara Ardinger, Ph.D., author of *Finding New Goddesses, Quicksilver Moon, Goddess Meditations,* and *Practicing the Presence of the Goddess*

Faery Healing
The Lore and the Legacy

Margie McArthur

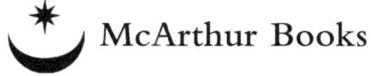
McArthur Books

Copyright © 2003, 2006, 2020, Margie McArthur
Cover art © 2003 Margaret Walty
Interior design by Victoria May

McArthur Books, 2020
New Brighton Books, 2003
Printed in the U.S.A.

About the Cover:
"The Tree of Life in the illustration is at once an apple tree, a rose tree, and a hawthorn tree, bearing both blossom and fruit. The Faery Queen/Goddess is before it, radiating the green fire of life and healing. Fire rises to meet her from the bowl below, and the reflection in the water is not hers but that of her male counterpart. The plants and herbs of healing grow out of her dress. I've also suggested the green diamond of the world (in the shape of the light behind her) and red heart of the Glen below. Various faery creatures hide in the Tree's roots, among foxgloves and the fungi that open out of decay into life." —Margaret Walty

No part of this publication may be reproduced or transmitted in any form or by any means, electric or mechanical, including photocopy, recording, or any information storage and retrieval system now known or to be invented, without permission in writing from the publisher, except by a reviewer who wishes to quote brief passages in connection with a review written for inclusion in a magazine, newspaper, or broadcast. Contact McArthur Books, Santa Cruz, California, www.faeryhealing.com. All rights reserved.

Library of Congress Cataloging-in-Publication Data
McArthur, Margie.
    Faery healing : the lore and the legacy / Margie McArthur.
p. cm.
Includes bibliographical references and index.
ISBN 978-0-9994702-0-6
    1. Fairies--Great Britain. 2. Healing--Great Britain--Miscellanea. I. Title.

BF1552.M36 2003
398'.45'089916041--dc22

2003061553

DEDICATION

To the Faeries!
May all beings realize their kinship again!

BLESSING

Blessed Brigid, Flame of Delight in the many worlds,
May the fires of your Sacred Hearth be rekindled.
May they burn brightly, their flames bridging the many worlds,
Bringing the starpower of the Heavens down to enliven
The stars that live deep within the heart of Mother Earth.

Grant us the gift of your brightness and warmth:
The fire that is inspiration.
Let us draw sustenance from your Well of Deep Peace,
That nourishes all of Life.

Enfold us in your mantle of protection and healing.
Guide us as we heal, and in our creative endeavors.
Grant us the inspiration that enables
The creation of True Beauty and Harmony.

Blessed One, Fair One,
This do we ask of you,
As we offer you the Inextinguishable Light
Of our love and homage.

Table of Contents

Foreword viii
Acknowledgments xi
Introduction xii

Part I	Origins of the Celtic Faery Healing Tradition 1	
Chapter 1	Faeries, Druids, and Deities 2	
Chapter 2	The Living World 23	
Chapter 3	Elements of the Living World 34	
Chapter 4	Elements of the Celtic Healing Tradition 46	
Chapter 5	The Irish Traditions 77	
Chapter 6	Evidence of Faery Healing Traditions in England, Scotland, Wales, and the Isle of Man 93	
Chapter 7	Faeries and Witches 102	
Part II	Making the Cure 111	
Chapter 8	Faery-Induced Ailments and Their Cures 112	
Chapter 9	Faery Herbs: Materia Magic, Materia Medica 123	
Chapter 10	Faery Stones: Materia Magic, Materia Medica 153	
Part III	Faery Healing for Today 159	
Chapter 11	Standing on the Threshold of a New Era 160	
Chapter 12	Sacred Earth: The Living Land, and the Web of Life 167	
Chapter 13	Yesterday's Faery Healing: Assessing the Past 174	
Part IV	A Practical Manual for Faery Healing 181	
Chapter 14	Faery Healing 182	
Chapter 15	The Tools of Healing: Some Foundational Techniques 190	
Chapter 16	The Cosmology of the Faery Realm 220	
Chapter 17	Traveling within the Faery Realm 228	
Chapter 18	Practical Work within the Faery Realm 256	
Chapter 19	Coming from a Place of Love 282	
Chapter 20	Brigid's Mantle, Airmid's Cloak 290

Chapter 21	Empowering Yourself to Heal	312
Chapter 22	Faery Medicines	329
Chapter 23	Reweaving Brigid's Mantle, Restoring Airmid's Cloak	339

Part V	**Appendices and Bibliography**	**355**
Appendix A	The Festivals	356
Appendix B	Fiona Macleod and William Sharp	358
Appendix C	Suggested Readings	359
Bibliography		362

Index 365

Journeys

Grounding 101- Beginning Level	194-196
Grounding 101 - Intermediate Level	196-197
Grounding 102 - Advanced Level	198, 199
Feeling the Directions and Their Powers	203, 204
On the Great Tree	230-233
To the Glen of the Precious Stones	241-242
To Finias,	242-245
To Gorias	244-246
To Murias	247-249
To Falias	249-251
To Find Faery Healing Allies	257-258
Into the Stars Within the Earth	260-262
Seasonal Journey #1	264-266
Seasonal Journey #2	266-268
Empowerment Journey to Falias	276-279
Empowerment Journey to Finias	269-272
Empowerment Journey to Gorias	272-274
Empowerment Journey to Murias	274-276
To the Faery Healing Grove	291-294
There Is One River	325-327
Self Healing	340-341
Reweaving Brigid's Mantle	345-347
Carrying the Forest Through Time	350-352

Foreword

*P*ixies dance. They say that it is the patter of their feet that keeps the planets spinning. They tell me Centrifugal Force is the name of a set of pixy dances. They work/play hard to keep everything turning properly. Like the pixies, we each have our own bit to do in keeping the Earth and ourselves dancing in harmony and good order.

We live in exciting times. After a long separation, the Otherworld of Faery is rapidly coming back into synchronization with Earthmother. The two worlds (or sets of dimensions) are swirling back together in the natural tides and currents of the universe. This is a part of the great dance of all the worlds and galaxies, and it means that once again, we have increasingly closer access to the wisdom and wit and joyfulness of Faery.

The Fae Folk are a little unnerved by the mess we've been making since they were last close—too much cement, too few trees! This is harmful to us and to Earthmother. They say we need to remember that we are her children. It is time, they tell us, for healing. It is time for us to re-learn how to regenerate ourselves and the world around us through subtle healing energies and the use of natural healing techniques. This book is a copious compendium of remarkable remedies, powerful potions, rare rites, and inventive ideas. Margie's wisdom and experience shine through these pages. She is a natural healer. We all are natural healers, of course, but some of us have forgotten just how we go about doing it. Margie and the Fae remind us here of many of the historical, practical, and once-everyday-but-now-mostly-forgotten facets of natural healing. Modern scientific medicine is very useful in its way, but it isn't always the best thing for every problem we might have. Nor is it the only kind of healing available to us. For example, if you break a leg you need a doctor to set it and put it in a cast. You need a healer to soothe the traumatized tissues and energies and accelerate healing. Some comfrey tea could promote the healing of bones. And a few prayers to the deity of your choice for patience, for healing, and for insight would not come amiss.

Some of these require skilled help, but many of them we can do for ourselves—and for others. We discovered many natural healing techniques through simple experimentation long ago, and we are still discovering more. However, another very important source was, and still is, inspiration—inspiration from Spirit, and from nature spirits. This inspiration is still available to us, and in these pages you will find ideas and techniques to help you access it, just as did the Faery Doctors of old.

There are a million techniques for using the natural energies and objects in our environment for healing. The Fae know them all and are willing to share. We just have to learn to listen, and the teachings in this book can help you to do so. It isn't hard; it just takes willingness and practice.

I remember when once I woke up on Beltaine morning quite ill. I lay in bed wondering what to do, and a friendly gnome said, "Go outside."

"I don't feel like going outside," I moaned.

Suillean rolled her eyes and asked, "Will you ever learn to listen?"

I dragged myself out of bed, muttering unhappily. When I finally got outdoors, I asked, "Now what?"

"Look and listen," she advised tersely.

I did. It took a while to get out of my absorption in how miserable I felt and to notice that this first of May was a truly lovely one—sunshine, a cool breeze through the trees. I felt better already—but not enough better. I kept looking at the bright sky, at the whispering trees, at the soaring birds. Suillean sighed.

"TOES!" she shouted.

I jumped. Then I looked at my feet—and looked more closely. Surrounding my toes were very tiny blue flowers, hidden in the grass. Dozens, hundreds, thousands of them. I sat down in the grass to look at them. "What are they?" I asked.

"You know what they are. These are miniatures of the ones you knew in Scotland."

I lay on my stomach to look more closely. "Speedwell?" I wondered.

She grinned and nodded. "Pixy speedwell we call them, because they are so small."

I knew better than to ask Suillean how to heal with the flowers, and simply asked the speedwell instead. "Drink our light," they whispered.

I puzzled over that for a bit, and finally got it. Flower essence remedy. I placed a glass of spring water among the flowers in the sun, and waited until it was charged. Like many faery medicines, it fizzed inside me after I drank it and the fizzing made me feel lighter right away.

I went back to bed and slept soundly for three hours. When I woke, feeling somewhat better, Suillean was sitting in the sun by my bed. "You aren't well yet," she said firmly, "so don't even think about getting up. I'll be back tonight."

I rolled over, and to my surprise promptly went deeply into a dreamless sleep. About midnight, Suillean returned and suggested we go outside again. The moon was up and the night was crisp and clear, the snow on the mountains gleaming in the distance. I made another glass of the essence of speedwell, infused with moonlight this time, and drank it down. When I woke up in the morning I couldn't tell I'd even been sick. I felt better than I had in weeks. For no reason at all, I burst into laughter—and heard faery (and gnome) laughter all around me.

And of course, the greatest healing technique of all is laughter—faery laughter, the Earthmother's laughter, the laughter of the birds, the trees, you, me—all of us together, sharing and laughing. Giggles are good, too. Remember the old saying, "An apple a day keeps the doctor away"? Well, the faery version is "Giggles keep us gladsome—a merry spirit needs no cure!" Laughter changes the entire universe for the better whenever it is heard. Does this mean that laughter alone will keep us well? No. Well…maybe. Sometimes. Does it mean that it will make us feel better? Absolutely! And laughing with the faeries is the very best and most healing laughter of all.

We can all learn to listen to the Fae. Read this book. Follow the directions. Listen. And laugh with the faeries. It will transform your world.

—Jessica Macbeth
An Lios
Midsummer 2003

Acknowledgments

This book was aided, abetted, assisted and encouraged, both directly and indirectly by many dear teachers, friends and family members. My thanks and love go out to all of them: Jo Ann Aelfwine, Linda Boyer, Rosalyn Bruyere, Josephine Dunne, Rosemary Gladstar, Richard Gordon, Alana Graham, Mara Freeman, Greg Harbert, Christopher Hobbs, John Hock, Ishana Ingerman, Gabrielle Laney, Jessica Macbeth, Jeanine Pollak, Jeanine Sande, Bob Stewart, Kris Thoeni, Michael and Lesley Tierra, Maia Whitemare, Andrea Wilson, Joseph Woods, all of my own "Clan McArthur"—Bran, Althea, Sunflower, Dylan, Emrys, Henry—and of course, and most especially, the faeries…

WARNING

The material in this book is offered for historical, folkloric, and informational purposes only. If you are ill, please remember that your physical body needs physical care; seek out a competent healthcare practitioner.

NOTE

I would like to note that although this book is written from a Pagan perspective, complete with references to gods and goddesses, one does not have to be Pagan to make use of the Faery Healing information contained herein. Indeed, our Catholic Celtic ancestors did very well working with Christ, his Mother, his saints, angels and apostles.

Although names and definitions of deity vary from place to place and culture to culture, deity itself is beyond name and definition; the names are strictly for our convenience, and definitions can cover only part of what is so vast. The Celtic peoples referred to in this book believed a wide variety of things; there was certainly no one Celtic religion, though similar deities were found throughout the Pagan Celtic world. It is for you, the reader, to apply your own religious perspectives and definitions to the information found in this book.

Introduction

This book is about the traditions of Faery Healing among the Celtic peoples of the British Isles as evidenced in their faery lore and folk healing customs. It will focus specifically, though not exclusively, on healing beliefs, traditions, and practices associated with the faery folk.

In the old Celtic traditions, interaction between the race of men and the race of gods and Spirit Beings was not an unusual occurrence. Even in more recent, historic times interaction between the realms of human and faery was not a rare event. In cases of particularly profound interaction the result was often a gift of some kind bestowed upon the human. This gift was usually that of healing or prophecy, such as with the famed Thomas the Rhymer of medieval Scotland whose service to the Faery Queen was rewarded with the gift of "The Tongue That Could Not Lie." In other words, it was the gift of prophecy that he was given.

The ancient ways of curing, as preserved in the Irish folk traditions and written about by such scholars and folklorists of the late 1800s and early 1900s as Lady Francesca Wilde, William Butler Yeats, and Walter Y. Evans Wentz, were full of charms and incantations, mysticism and magic. All of these show knowledge of and reverence for Greater Beings and Greater Powers.

Indeed, all Celtic healing lore wherever we find traces of it is full of magic and mysticism, demonstrating faith in and often fear of these Greater Powers.

The Irish Celtic traditions of healing were said to come from the Tuatha De Danann and/or the faeries. Since the Tuatha in a sense *became* the Faery, it is not surprising that healers were referred to as Faery Doctors and are reputed to have learned their secrets and gotten their healing powers from the faeries.

Lady Wilde says, "Every act of the Irish peasant's life has always been connected with the belief in unseen spiritual agencies. The people live in an atmosphere of the supernatural, and nothing would induce them to slight an ancient form or break through a traditional usage. They believe that the result would be something awful; too terrible to be spoken of save in a whisper, should the customs of their forefathers be lightly interfered with."[1] She adds that change comes slowly to such remote places, unlike the large cities and centers of civilization, and that it is in the remote distant reaches of Ireland, particularly western Ireland, that the most ancient customs and ways were still, in her day, to be found.

Therefore, the folklore of Irish healing includes charms for love, charms for the bite of a dog, charms for toothaches, fevers, sprains, rashes, pains, poisonings, and all the other ills to which humanity is heir. Many of them are simply charms and incantations, but in some cases the prayer is accompanied by a ritual action such as binding a sprain with a strand of black wool, or burying nail parings and hair to "bury" the Falling Sickness.

Some cures, such as making a burn-healing, scar-preventing ointment from sheep suet and the bark of the elder tree, would seem to be more materially based than magically based, though the sanctity in which elder was held would most likely have been part of the magic of this cure.

In Welsh lore, one of the surviving, most well-known connections between the faeries and the healing arts is the tradition of the *Physicians of Myddfai*. This family of physicians is said to be descended from a faery woman who fell in love with a shepherd and came out of her magical lake to live on land and marry him. She bore him children, but ultimately—he having broken the terms of their agreement as is often the case in stories of this nature—went back to her lake. However, she did return, briefly, to gift her human children with knowledge of the healing arts.

This story is similar to other "Ladies of the Lake" of Celtic tradition who emerged from their watery depths long enough to bestow important gifts from the Otherworlds upon those in this one. It is also reminiscent of stories of the selkies or seal-people, whose sealskins, shed when they come ashore to play, are occasionally stolen by young men entranced by selkie beauty. This leaves the selkie stranded on land till she somehow can regain the skin and return to the sea. In each case the story is one of interaction and sharing between the different orders of life. This sharing usually produces offspring who then carry within them the gifts of both human and nonhuman parents. They are frequently gifted healers or seers.

This book will, for the most part, focus on the more mystical and magical aspects of the Faery Healing Tradition rather than the strictly medicinal ones which are covered well in other books, though there will be some overlap.

The magic and mysticism of these healing traditions has been seen by some as mere superstition. Indeed, many aspects of the old folk healing tradition would seem bizarre and repulsive to us today. It should be noted, however, that superstition inevitably grows up around strongly held beliefs when the rationale behind them is no longer clear or understood. Any and all beliefs, when uninformed or misunderstood, are capable of turning into superstitious nonsense over time, thus allowing strange and occasionally grotesque elements to arise.

A more informed and comprehensive view of the Faery Healing Tradition allows us to see how these mystical and magical traditions and beliefs demonstrate the deeply religious nature of the Celts from ancient times right into more historical times. They serve as a link between past and present and as a bridge to understanding the old Pagan religious worldview that preceded the rise of Christianity. The beliefs standing behind some of these healing traditions and practices are, indeed, very old and deep-rooted. This glimpse into ancient ideologies and practices shows us the remarkable continuity of spiritual beliefs no matter in which religious garbs they may be cloaked.

END NOTES

1   Wilde, Lady, *Ancient Legends, Mystic Charms & Superstitions of Ireland*, Chatto & Windus, London, 1919, p. 188.

PART I

Origins of the Celtic Faery Healing Tradition

CHAPTER 1

Faeries, Druids, and Deities

CELTIC HEALING TRADITIONS AND THE FAERY FOLK

Celtic healing traditions, wherever we find them, are intimately bound up with invisible and otherworldly powers and most especially with the invisible beings known as the faery folk. We have evidence of this from virtually all of the folklore collected at the end of the 19th century by scholars and folklorists such as W. Y. Evans Wentz, Lady Wilde, Lady Gregory, William Butler Yeats, and many others as well. In addition, we have the evidence of texts such as the *Physicians of Myddfai*, first translated into English in 1861, which concerns old Welsh healing traditions that date from at least the 13th century.

In understanding the Celtic Faery Healing Tradition it is essential to have an understanding of the worldview of the Celtic peoples, especially as it concerns the faery folk and their role in illness and health. Much of the evidence preserved concerning Faery Healing is found in Irish sources; therefore, much of what is covered in this book will pertain to Ireland.

Before we begin with our faery lore, a few words must be said about the Celts themselves. In this day and age when we hear the word *Celt* or *Celtic*, we think of the British Isles, particularly Ireland and Scotland. However, at present there are six, possibly seven, areas of the world that consider themselves to be the *Celtic Nations*: Ireland, Scotland, Wales, Cornwall, Brittany, Isle of Man, and the region of Galicia, in northern Spain.

Historically speaking, the people we think of as Celts were not a tribe of people bound together by common racial characteristics, linguistic identity, or a common lifestyle. They were not even all from one particular locality though their origins seem to lie in the specific geographic region of central and eastern Europe. They were, in fact, several tribes of people, whose cultural similarities and continuities, including those of values, beliefs, and institutions, bound them together. They were fierce warriors; they were boastful; they loved feasting, poetry, music, storytelling, and adorning their bodies with beautiful clothing and jewelry. They were superb metalworkers, and many fine pieces of their metal work survive today in testament of this fact. They were hospitable, loyal, and family-oriented. They did not refer to themselves as *Celts*, but by the various names of their individual tribes.

They also shared religious philosophies and beliefs, including belief in the existence of the worlds of Spirit and the immortality of the soul. They had a strong streak of mysticism and a similarity of spiritual and ritual practices born, perhaps, from the deep forests and sparkling lakes and rivers of the lands in which they lived.

Over the course of time the Celts migrated and warred their way westward—influencing cultures as they went—from their conjectured beginnings in the steppes of Russia all the way to the furthest westward reaches of Atlantic seaboard in Ireland. One might even argue that they didn't stop there since so many of their descendants now reside in America! In addition, the story of the sixth-century voyage of St. Brendan the Navigator suggests they may well have traveled as far as the North American continent well before the time of the Viking Leif Erikson whose 10th century voyage predated Columbus by almost 500 years. Unlike the Vikings and Columbus, they appear to have left no settlements in their wake.

But if evidence in the surviving Celtic lore is any indication, there was always something special about the direction of West. The Irish Otherworld of *Tir na nOg* was in the West and was one of many magical islands in the Western Sea. These islands were visited by Maelduin on his famous *immrama*, or mystical voyage, as recounted in the Irish poem *The Voyage of Maelduin's Boat* (transcribed in the eighth–ninth century, though probably much earlier in origin). Celtic scholar Caitlin Matthews has argued convincingly that these poetic *immramas* were, in actuality, Celtic "Books of the Dead," that is, guides to the afterlife recounting specific states of awareness, functions, duties, guides, and threshold guardians to be met up with in the life after death.[1]

West was also the direction of the Otherworld in certain Breton legends, which mention the dead being taken by ship to the Land of the Dead located in the Western Sea. This is an instance where realities overlap because West meant not only the physical reality of the Western Sea itself, right off the coast of Brittany, but the mythical reality of the invisible but very real Otherworlds of Celtic tradition. There are many such instances of overlapping realities, since our tendency to partition aspects of life into tidy little compartments is really a rather modern way of looking at things.

As can be seen, in Celtic tradition there is a close association between death, the sea, and the West, which is, in the Celtic lands, the direction of the sea.

It is interesting to note that these Otherworlds are generally located "in the West," direction of the setting sun, or below the surface of the Earth, as we will see later.

Faeries

Belief in the faeries was an integral and accepted part of the Celtic worldview. Though there were several theories as to exactly *what* faeries were, everyone knew *that* they were. Faeries existed. Even the Christian clergy did not dispute their existence—faeries were part of everyday life.

Faeries were considered powerful and frequently unfriendly beings. Measures were taken to assure they were not offended, to placate them, and to protect man and beast against their trickery and wrath. They were thought to steal the *toradh*, or essence, of the butter, the milk, and sometimes the crops unless suitable protections were in place. They were thought to be fond of stealing human children leaving their own wizened, ugly little children (referred to as changelings) in their place.

They often took *people*, leaving *something* in their place. This *something* occasionally resembled the person, but sometimes it did not. Young and beautiful children and women were in particular danger of being taken, and when it was a young mother who was taken it was thought that she was taken to the Faery Realm to nurse faery children. Sometimes those taken would be returned to the human world, frequently with interesting stories to share about their time "away." Often, these people were never quite the same again.

Yet the faery folk were not considered to be invariably antagonistic to humankind. They were also known to demonstrate good will toward humans, providing assistance and gifts. One of the gifts was that of healing. Occasionally, the faeries would gift a human, usually one who they had taken away for a while, with remarkable healing information, techniques, and powers. These people, greatly sought after and much respected for their gifts, were known as Faery Doctors or Faery Healers. The majority of Faery Doctors were women. Women Faery Doctors were also referred to as Faery Women, a confusing term as it was also used to refer to women of the faery folk themselves. The term itself is a literal translation of the Irish word "bansidhe" (pronounced *banshee*) which in Irish lore is a particular type of faery woman most often associated with death.

THEORIES AND EXPERIENCES OF THE FAERIES

But who and what are the faeries? This is a question that has been under discussion for a long time, and is one for which various answers, scholarly, scientific, and religious, have been proposed.

According to W. Y. Evans Wentz in his monumental work, *The Fairy Faith in Celtic Countries*, there have been four basic scholarly theories advanced to explain the phenomena of the (mostly invisible) beings we know as faeries. The first of these is the Naturalistic Theory which posits that humankind's belief in faeries, ghosts, and spirits is the direct result of its attempts to rationalize and explain natural phenomena. Thus, benevolent faeries and spirits may be found in gentle, beautiful landscapes, and fierce and terrible faeries and spirits are likely to be found where the landscapes and conditions are stark and harsh.

The second theory is called the Pygmy Theory and holds that belief in the faeries has arisen from a folk memory of an actual prehistoric race of small or "pygmy" peoples. According to this theory, these people were perhaps the indigenous inhabitants of Western Europe, including the British Isles, and were driven into the mountains and other inaccessible places by the arrival of invading tribes such as the Celts. They survived for a long time in their hidden places, occasionally and often accidentally showing themselves to the new inhabitants. Because of their shyness, small size, and their ability to seemingly disappear, the Pygmy Theory held that these people were what have come to be known as the faery folk.

The third theory, called the Druid Theory, suggests that belief in the faeries and their magical ways, often referred to as the Faery Faith, is a folk memory of the legendary Druids and their magical practices. According to Evans Wentz, this theory, along with the second theory, although they may sound plausible are inadequate in explaining all the facets of the Faery Faith because they take into account only the outward aspects of the belief and not the inner, more subtle aspects. The first, or Naturalistic Theory, illuminates the issue a bit better but still misses the mark, positing that the outside (i.e., landscape) gave rise to the inside (i.e., the Faeries/Spirit Beings) rather than the reverse of this.

The fourth theory is called the Mythological Theory and Evans Wentz finds this one to be of great significance. This theory holds that the beings now referred to as faeries are, in reality, the old Pagan Celtic deities diminished by the passage of time into smaller and less powerful versions of themselves. While this theory has some merit, it still does not explain the origins of the faeries. It simply moves the question back a step so that it becomes, instead, a question of the origins of these Pagan deities.

Evans Wentz takes this theory a step further with one of his own called the Psychological Theory in which he attempts to create a root theory of which the others can be shown to be contributory branches. As such, the Psychological Theory contains elements of the other four theories but goes deeper.

Evans Wentz's Psychological Theory comes at the issue from a different direction. It begins with the experienced reality: Since faeries and other invisible beings have been seen, communicated with, and experienced by many people for many centuries, they therefore exist. What most, though not all, of those experiencing the faery folk share in common is that they have lived very close to nature and therefore outside of the hypnotic influence of civilization's materialistic, rationalistic, and reductionist philosophies. They have seen, and have no need to rationalize away what they have seen or experienced.

Evans Wentz reminds us that all of us have this most human capacity to experience and interact with beings of the subtle realms, but have quite likely been "civilized" or "educated" out of it. Those who live close to nature are open to the stirrings of soul created by nature's beauties and elemental realities. These soul stirrings open an innate ability to perceive and experience realities which are ordinarily invisible to common vision. Thus, trying to describe the origins of the faery folk as rationalizations of weather and landscape or calling them folk memories of pygmy tribes may explain, at best, only the external, physical presentation of faeries, but does not approach the internal, psychic, experiential one, the "soul" aspect of the experience, so to speak. To describe faeries as diminished versions of the Pagan deities comes a bit closer as the deities themselves may be defined as personifications of vast, archetypal powers which manifest in the world in various ways. But still, the emphasis here is on rational explanation rather than on soul experience.

So again, who and what are the faeries? Experiences, both those recounted in the folklore as well as the more contemporary accounts, lead to the conclusion that faeries are simply one type, a very specific type, of the many orders of beings that exist within the vast web of life-forms that make up the world of nature; in this case, the etheric, subtle, non-physical aspect of nature. More specifically, faeries are the Spirit Beings who enliven nature; they live in a reality that mirrors our own, but it is a pure, primal, pristine, and subtle version of our reality.

As such, they are separate from—though closely related to—other orders of beings within nature's Web of Life such as plant spirits, tree spirits, and Elemental spirits. There is in particular somewhat of an overlap between faeries and plant and tree spirits as found in such stories as that of the Elder Mother, the Apple Tree Man and the Oak Men, all of which we will touch on in later chapters. In a sense, the word faery may be used to describe these beings as well, though I often choose to use the alternate spelling *fairy* when referring to them, to distinguish them from each other.

TESTIMONY OF THE REVEREND KIRK

One of the most intriguing accounts of the world of Faery was written by the Reverend Robert Kirk, a 17th century Scottish Episcopalian minister and scholar. His small handwritten book, *The Secret Commonwealth of Elves, Fauns, and Faeries*, is a detailed survey of the beliefs of his Gaelic-speaking parishioners with regard to the faery folk, the Otherworld, and seership. As such, it provides a first-hand account of the Faery Faith as it existed among his congregation in the Scotland of his era. Much of the same beliefs were still common two centuries later when Evans Wentz, Lady Wilde, and W. B. Yeats were collecting their information.

The Secret Commonwealth of Elves, Fauns, and Faeries was privately circulated and apparently caused quite a stir, containing, as it did, quite curious material concerning the interaction of our physical realm with the invisible realm of the faery folk. Kirk himself held that the belief in these Otherworlds and in faeries was in every way compatible with Christianity, and indeed, constituted a good defense against atheism.

Reverend Kirk contends that since there is no such thing as complete emptiness or void in the universe, every space and place has its inhabitants, and the faery folk may be counted among Earth's invisible inhabitants. Kirk describes the Faery Beings as "of a middle nature betwixt man and Angel," and as having "light, changeable bodies, like those called Astral, somewhat of the nature of a condensed cloud, and best seen at Twilight." He also refers to them as "chameleon like," indicating that their bodies can change color. These bodies of "congealed Air" are so "pliable," according to Kirk, that the spirits inhabiting them can make them appear or disappear as they please. Some faeries have bodies so delicate that they feed only on a "fine spirituous liquor (essence)" while others feed on the more solid core "essence" of actual physical foods, which they were known to steal away from time to time.

Kirk tells us much of interest about the faery world. He maintains that it is located within the land itself and is a mirror image, or polarized image, of our own world, especially with regard to how time works. Their time, whether time of day or season of the year, seems to be the reverse of our own.

He tells us that the faeries change their lodgings at each quarter (Imbolc, Beltaine, Lughnasadh, Samhain—see *Appendix A*), swarming through the air with their bags and baggage. This was so widely known to be true that Gaelic seers often kept from the highways on these days to avoid meeting up with them. Instead, they spent the day at church or doing blessings and protections upon themselves, their cattle, and their corn.

Certain people, often but not always seventh sons, were thought to have the ability to heal and cure disease using traditional methods, prayers, and incantations. Of these healers Kirk says that "the virtue goes out from them due to spirituous effluxes." This is what we today would term *vital energy* or *psychic energy*. These healers had an abundance of this energy and possessed the ability to transmit it to the patient by touch and prayer. This is key to working with Faery Healing, and we will come back to it in later chapters.

Kirk tells us that frequently these people had the gift to see Faery Beings and communicate with them. The faeries might communicate to these seers by means of signs or "dramatic action," but the seer himself had to develop ways to correctly understand and interpret what had been given to him. This is another important key to Faery Healing—without the correct understanding of what is being given, the healing work suffers.

Kirk's account, therefore, informs us that certain people, often seventh sons (and with the help of other accounts we may infer seventh daughters as well) are often gifted as both seers and healers, and that these gifts allow interaction with the Faery Realm.

FALLEN ANGELS

The most widespread belief of faery origins held by the country people interviewed by Lady Wilde was that the faeries were fallen angels. God cast them out, it was thought, at the same time that he cast out Lucifer for the sin of pride. These angels literally fell out of heaven. Some fell to the Earth and "dwelt there as the first gods of the Earth long before humans were created." These small, beautiful faeries lived in great comfort and luxury in their magnificent palaces under the hills and in deep mountain caves. Their strong magical power enabled them to obtain whatever they wanted or needed for their homes, and they had the ability to shape-change into any form they wished. It was held that they would not die till the last day of the world, at which time they would be forever annihilated, a fact which they knew and which caused them great distress.

Because of their mortality they were very jealous of the immortality promised humans. Because of their small size they were jealous of the size and strength of humans. Loving beauty, they were very tempted by beautiful humans and loved to steal them away as wives, husbands, or children. The children of these unions were strange and mystic creatures, passionate, bold, reckless, vengeful, difficult to live with, and often became famous for their musical gifts. Their beautiful eyes gave away the fact that they were not completely human but also of the race of the Sidhe.

Other angels cast from heaven fell into the sea where they created beautiful palaces of crystal and pearl for themselves. It was said that on moonlit nights they frequently came up from the depths of the sea, riding their white horses onto the land, to hold celebrations with their Earth kin who lived in the hollow hills. On these occasions, faeries of both Earth and sea danced together under the ancient trees and drank their "faery wine," which was nectar, from the cups of flowers. These faeries were said to be beautiful, gentle, and harmless (though given to occasional mischief) if they were left alone and allowed to dance without interference from mortals on their faery raths, or forts on moonlit nights.

Still other fallen angels were thought to be demonic. At the end of their fall from heaven, they found themselves in hell and the devil gained control over them. Ever since then, it was thought, he has sent them forth on his missions of evil. They went forth tempting people to sin by means of glitter and false pleasures in hopes that people would lose their souls in the pursuit of such things. These faeries dwelt under the Earth and taught their secrets only to those chosen by the devil such as the "witch women." To such as these they taught the art of making incantations and love potions, the power to work wicked spells, the knowledge of how to change their shapes using their powers and certain magical herbs. They taught these women all the secret knowledge, including the power of times and days, of herbs and evil spells, all of which these faeries had learned from the devil. Thus, the "witch women" were very much feared whether they did good or ill, because they were thought to have all the power of the faeries, and all the malice of the devil.

This interesting distinction is similar to the two *courts* of Faery referred to in Scottish lore, the *Seeley* or blessed, hallowed (i.e., kind and good) Court, and the *Unseeley* or unhallowed, unblessed (i.e., wicked and inimical) Court. In general, much folklore tends to separate the faeries into two categories: sociable/solitary, helpful/unhelpful, friendly-to-humans/unfriendly-to-humans, and so on.

It might also be noted here that by the 17th century the way faeries were perceived and experienced had begun to vary somewhat from country to country. In England, faeries had begun to diminish in stature, become mischievous and sprightly, and were finding their way into the literature of the day. In Scotland, the rise of Protestant Presbyterianism had affected the Scots view of witches, faeries, ghosts, and goblins; and as Yeats rather humorously put it, "In Scotland you are too theological, too gloomy....You denounce them (the faeries) from the pulpit....You have soured the naturally excellent disposition of ghosts and goblins."[2] But in Ireland the old faery tradition remained strong although the ongoing centuries of Christianity continued to leave their mark upon it. In Ireland, faeries were accepted as part of the natural order; they were still beings to be lived with and reckoned with. As Yeats put it, "For their gay and graceful doings you must go to Ireland; for their deeds of terror to Scotland."[3]

Lady Wilde added that in spite of the dread, awe, and respect that people had for the faeries, and in spite of how they tried to never offend them, people did not *worship* the faeries because they considered them inferior to humans. This is a significant point, implying as it does a kinship type relationship between humans and faeries rather than a worshipper-to-deity one. We will come back to this in later chapters.

THE VISIONS OF A. E.

Nineteenth century visionary writer and artist George Russell, who was known as A. E., has given us an account of his visions of the faery folk and has left us his paintings of them as well. In his description of the beings he had seen, he indicates that they seem to fall into two great categories or classes: those who are Shining and those who are Opalescent.

The Shining Ones appear to be shining, luminous, and colorful, of human height or a bit taller, and to be of a collective, or hive-like consciousness. A. E. associates them with the Middleworld rather than the Earth-world or Heaven-world. The Opalescent Ones appear to be of great height, fourteen feet or so, and seem to shine with a light that comes from within, radiating from their heart center. They are surrounded by flaming, wing-like auras of light, which radiate outward in all directions. A. E. felt that these beings corresponded in a general way to the old Irish gods, the Tuatha De Danaan, but he hesitated to attribute a personal identity to any of them, since all seemed to be such great and kingly beings.

Legends of the Gods

Cliodna, Rhiannon, Dian Cecht, Miach and Airmid

In spite of A. E.'s reluctance to precisely correlate the beings he saw with specific members of the Tuatha De Danaan, learning the legends associated with various of the Irish Tuatha De Danaan, the Welsh Children of Don, and other gods and goddesses can be useful when working with them, as the legends give us the attributes, characteristics, and powers of these beings. These in turn help us to understand the flavor and frequency of their energy as unique and individual beings.

An example is found in legends of the beautiful Irish Faery Queen Cliodna who was associated with South Munster. She possessed three magical birds with bright lovely plumage, who fed upon the fruit of the Otherworld tree. Her birds sang so exquisitely that they lulled the sick and infirm into a healing slumber.[4] This is reminiscent of the

Welsh Goddess Rhiannon who also possessed sweet-singing magical birds.

Another example is found in the story of the Tuatha physician Dian Cecht and two of his children, his daughter Airmid, and his son Miach, both also healers. Their legend, recounted in the Irish *Book of Invasions*, tells the story of Dian Cecht's jealousy of his son Miach who was able to successfully restore Nuada's hand which Dian Cecht had been unable to do, creating instead a silver hand as replacement. Dian Cecht's jealousy caused him to strike his son four blows, the fourth one killing him. Airmid was grief stricken, but while tending her brother's grave discovered that 365 herbs had grown upon it. She gathered these in her cloak, one herb to cure illnesses of each of the 365 nerves of the human body as well as one for each and every day of the year.

This story informs us that Dian Cecht, Miach, and Airmid are all deities of healing. It further informs us that Airmid is particularly connected with herbal healing. It tells us that Miach is the wielder of powers that have to do with almost miraculous restoration and regeneration of the physical body, and his powers transcend death as is evidenced by the healing herbs that sprang up on his grave. It also informs us that Dian Cecht's skill was not as great as that of his son, and that he was, in addition, subject to fits of jealous rage reminiscent of the all-too-human behavior of the Olympian deities of ancient Greece.

Brigid
Yet another example is Brigid, beloved Celtic goddess well-known throughout the British Isles as the triple-aspected goddess of poetry, smithcraft, and healing. Occasionally the three aspects were portrayed as three sisters, all named Brigid, an example of the triple form so beloved of the Celts. She was sometimes said to be the daughter of the Dagda, the "All-Father" of the Tuatha De Danaans. In Ireland she was known as Brigid, in Scotland as Brigid or Bride, and in Britain she was known as Brigantia, goddess of the Brigantes of Northern England. In spite of the fact that not many tales seem to have survived about her, she loomed larger than life in the psyche of the Celts of the British Isles, and it is likely that her legends were juxtaposed onto those of the early Irish Christian saint of the same name, who in Wales was known as St. Ffraid.

She was, and is, the goddess of poetry, smithcraft, and healing and the fire that is behind them all: the fire of the mind and mind's inspiration that sparks and ignites the poet's creativity; the fire of the forge and skill of the craftsman/woman; and the fires of life that must burn properly so that life may continue and healing occur. Each of these shows itself to be the fire of creation and transformation. Thus, she is the pre-eminent deity/saint of Celtic healing, and with her fires that span the Three Worlds and unites them, she may also be considered the matron deity/saint of Faery Healing.

Her cult center was in Kildare, Ireland, where in Christian times a perpetual fire dedicated to St. Brigid burned within a sacred precinct and was tended by nineteen nuns. It is said that this sanctuary predated Christianity and was originally a Pagan site dedicated to the Goddess Brigid, the fire there tended by nineteen priestesses. The remnants of this sacred enclosure may still be seen today in Kildare. Remnants of other similar fire temples have been found in other areas of Ireland.

Brigid's connection with yet another of the Four Elements, Water, is very strong. Many wells were dedicated to her. Fire and Water—heat and moisture—are the elements that make life possible. It becomes evident, therefore, that Brigid is above all a goddess of the elements that create life and allow it to exist and endure: Fire and Water. As such, she is a goddess of fertility, and it is not surprising to discover that she was the special goddess/saint of women in childbirth, nor that in her Christian form of St. Brigid she was said to be the midwife, wetnurse, and fostermother of the Christ Child.

Her feast day, which was known as La Feile Bride (the Festival of Brigid), Imbolc, and later still as Candlemas, falls on February 1st which was during the lambing season. This timing further affirms her connections with fertility, life, birth, and even with the mother's milk that sustains life. The Christian name for it, Candlemas, referred to the fact that candles for the new year were blessed on this day, another connection with Brigid's Fire aspect.

The stories, but particularly the customs and lore about Brigid in both her Pagan or Christian guise, inform us that we are dealing with a very powerful being, one of the "Old Ones" deeply connected with the primal powers of life itself—Air, Fire, Water, Earth—origination, creation, formation, and manifestation, as well as fertility and abundance.

Both Brigid and Airmid are deities of the Tuatha De Danaan or People of the Goddess Dana—known as Danu on the continent and Don in Wales—to whom we now turn our attention.

Dana

Standing behind all of the Tuatha De Danaan deities is the shadowy and mysterious figure of their Mother, the Goddess Dana. References to her are scant in Irish lore, but she is thought to be cognate with the Welsh Mother Goddess Don and related to Domnu, the Mother Goddess of the Fomorians who were in Ireland before the Tuatha arrived. Dana, Don, and Domnu are most likely cognate with the European Danu, who gave her name to many rivers on the continent. Dana's original name may have been Anu or Ana, with the "d" coming into being later; the important Irish Goddess Aine of Munster is thought to be a later version of Anu/Ana. Dana/Ana may well be related to the Greek Danae, but this has not yet been determined for certain.

Morgen
Mention of Celtic deities connected with healing would not be complete without mention of Morgen, the British goddess whose Otherworldly island realm may have been the prototype for legends of Avalon, the mystic Isle of Apples. Morgen was the ruler of this realm, which was reached only by sailing on the Otherworld Sea. She dwelt there practicing the arts of healing along with her eight sisters, she herself making the ninth. Nine was a very sacred number in Celtic lore as it was three times the sacred number three. Morgen has also come down to us in somewhat altered form as the Morgan le Fay of the Arthurian tales. This name means "Morgan of the Faeries," or "Morgan the Faery Woman," which provides an interesting link back into her Otherworldly/Faery Realm origins. The name *Morgen* itself is thought by some to mean *sea-borne*, as in one who comes from the sea.

Morgen is one of the three Faery Queens or Faery Women who comes to fetch King Arthur after his last battle, taking him off to her island realm to be healed of his grievous wounds. She promises that if he stays with her a suitable length of time he will be made whole again. In this, she shows herself to be a goddess of regeneration.

The nine maidens who, as described in the Welsh poem *The Spoils of Annwn*, tend the Underworld Cauldron of Pen Annwn, warming it with their breath, may well be related to Morgen and her sisters.[5] From the *Vita Merlini*, or *Mystic Life of Merlin*, and concurrent medieval texts by Chretien de Troyes, Morgen emerges as a goddess skillful in the arts of herbal healing.[6]

THE TUATHA DE DANAAN

When speaking of the Tuatha De Danaan, it is important to realize that we are referring to a time period that is considered to be pre-Celtic. It is only when the Milesian invaders enter the Irish scene that we finally encounter what is considered truly Celtic, or more correctly, *Gaelic*. Yet the Milesians make their first appearance in tales concerning the Tuatha De Danaan so the two are inextricably linked in this particular, very early, mytho-historic period of time.

One important thing to keep in mind is that the deep roots of the Faery Faith most likely predated the arrival of the Celts to the lands in question. The beliefs the Celts encountered were simply absorbed into their own pre-existing belief system, which may well have had its own form of faery beliefs.

The *Lebor Gabala Erenn*, or *The Book of the Invasions of Ireland*, tells us that the divine race that we know as the Tuatha De Danaan—the People of the Goddess Dana—arrived in Ireland, coming "in dark clouds through the air." They conjured a magical mist and stayed hidden in it for three days. They came from the "Four Cities of the North" where they had become wise and skillful in the arts of magic. From these Four Cities also came, perhaps brought by the Tuatha De Danaan, the *Four Treasures*. From Finias in the East came the Sword of Nuada, from which none could escape; and from Gorias in the South came the Spear of Lugh, which assured victory in battle. From Murias in the West came the Cauldron of the Dagda, from which none went away unsatisfied; and from Falias in the North came the Stone of Fal, which shrieked when a lawful king was upon it.

They landed in Ireland on the feast of Beltaine (May 1st, one of the Quarter Days, traditionally the beginning of summer, the pastoral season, and the time of light and warmth), and engaged the inhabitants in battle for possession of the land. Upon winning this battle, and later a second one, they became the undisputed rulers of Ireland, bringing culture, arts, and sciences to the people. Later they were defeated by the invading Milesians. After the battle, an agreement was reached. The Milesians took possession of the "upper half" of the land, while the Tuatha De Danaan were given possession of the "lower half" of the land.

This taking of the "lower half" of the land is highly significant as it tells us that the Tuatha De Danaan then retired to live *within* the Earth, within the mounds and hills which became known as the *sidhe*, a name which later became synonymous with the faery folk.

In this legend, we are shown that there is a link between the divine mythical race of the Tuatha De Danaan and the beings later known as the faery folk. Therefore, we can expect that the faeries will be credited with some of the same powers attributed to the Old Gods, the Tuatha De Danaan; though as one might expect, those powers have diminished in both scope and grandeur over the course of time. The Tuatha were capable of great and glorious deeds, impressive feats of magic both good and ill. The faeries are capable of smaller, less extraordinary magics, but still clearly possessive of powers beyond human ken.

Whatever one chooses to believe about the faeries or about the Tuatha De Danaan, it is clear from the faery lore collected over the last few centuries that we are dealing with a very real phenomena, and very real, rather than imaginary, beings.

The *below-the-surface* residence of the Tuatha De Danaan has additional significance in that the Underworld is traditionally a place of great power, associated with the deep powers of the Earth. Setting aside for the moment the prevalent conception of the Underworld as a "hell" type world, full of pain, torture, and nasty demons, a much older stratum of belief tells us that the Underworld is a place of great power. It is the place of the deep powers that give rise to life on Earth and is the abode of many beings, including the faeries, the dead (i.e., the ancestors), and powerful InnerEarth Beings having to do with the life processes of the Earth. Therefore, the InnerEarth, the Underworld, is associated with life and death, regeneration, healing, and transformation at their most primal levels. As dwellers in this realm, the faery folk partake of these powers.

Thus, in working with Faery Healing one is working with the powers of the InnerEarth, from the deep, primal titanic forces of the very oldest of the gods, to the archetypal realm of the Old Gods of the Tuatha de Danaan and Children of Don, to the realm of the faeries, the nature spirits, and plant devas. All of these may be drawn upon, worked with, and mediated in this form of healing, and their powers of life, death, regeneration, healing, and transformation brought to bear.

A brief note on the meaning of the word *sidhe* (pronounced "she") seems appropriate here. Originally, this Irish word referred to the rounded hills or mounds, also called faery mounds, which were said to be the home of the faery folk. Later, the word came to refer to the faery folk themselves. It also has associations with the Gaelic word for wind or blasts of air, possibly referring to the fact that faeries were thought to travel in the whirling winds. The word also has associations with the old Irish word for peace, the faery folk being sometimes known as the People of Peace (which some think may have referred to the silence of their movements and actions). Interestingly, the word may also be related to the *Sanscrit* word *Siddhi*, which refers to the almost supernatural powers resulting from intense spiritual development and self-realization of those on the Yogic path.

It is interesting to see how each of these definitions adds a layer and dimension of meaning to our understanding of the faery folk. The faery folk, when considered by these understandings of the word sidhe, are seen to be the *Powers of the Living Land*—the powers of the sacred mounds, high places, and hollow hills—powers who move on the whirling, spiraling winds, bringing changes, flux, and transformation. One is never quite the same after an encounter with them, but the knowledge of how to dance with their rhythms and respect their ways can bring harmony and, eventually, peace.

The Druids

More could be said about the Tuatha, but let us move on to the subject of the Druids. The Druids were the poets, magicians, healers, astronomers, genealogists, lawgivers, and perhaps even priests of the ancient Celts. They held a powerful place in Celtic society, second in importance only to the king. They officiated at religious ceremonies, and kings sought their advice. By their emphasis on poetry and genealogy, they were able to hold the history and memory of their tribes. With their training in Starlore, they knew the wisdom, mysteries, and influences of the stars. By the virtue of their training in magic, they had access to the gods and the Otherworldly powers, as well as having the power to see the future and influence events. Their training in natural science gave them the wisdom of the trees and the plants, and therefore, knowledge of healing.

It was the Druids' skill in the healing arts, as much as their magic and wisdom, which connected them to the later Faery Healing Traditions.

They were known to be very skillful healers. Indeed, the literary and archaeological evidence demonstrates that ancient Celtic Druidic healers were impressively knowledgeable about herbal healing, carrying their herbal medicaments with them in a bag which was called a *les*. They were acquainted with such advanced medical techniques as trephining, cupping, cauterization, several kinds of surgeries including amputations, brain surgeries, and Caesarian sections, and the knowledge of how to set broken bones.[7]

The Roman writer Pliny speaks admiringly of the Gaulish healers a few decades before the Roman conquest of Gaul, saying that they mixed astrology and medicine in their practice and that they had such exceptional reputations that many went to study with them.[8]

It was said that the Druids had power over the very Elements themselves and could conjure blinding mists and terrifying storms of fire, rain, or snow. They knew the power of *sound*, and with their singing and chanting could cause physical manifestations of many kinds. In actuality, the power of sound, as well as the patterns of sound (i.e., poetry, rhythms of sound), are prominent in Druidic lore, and most definitely play their part in the later, Celtic healing traditions as well.

To have power over something one must be in a certain kind of relationship with it. One must be *attuned* to it. To be attuned is to be *tuned*, i.e. to be vibrating at the same frequency. When this occurs, one is in alignment with the Element, the plant, the being, the sickness, or wholeness, and can therefore partake of and utilize its power. This is the basis of true magical power, and is as true for us now as it was for the Druids of the past.

Amergin, chief bard of the invading Milesians, the ancestors of the Irish Gaels, expressed this kind of consciousness well when he said on first setting foot on the holy earth of Ireland:

> *I am a wind on the sea,*
> *I am a wave of the ocean,*
> *I am the roar of the sea,*
> *I am a powerful ox,*
> *I am a hawk on a cliff,*
> *I am a dewdrop in the sunshine,*
> *I am a boar for valor,*
> *I am a salmon in pools,*
> *I am a lake in a plain,*
> *I am the strength of art,*
> *I am a spear with spoils that wages battle,*
> *I am a man that shapes fire for a head.*

As chief bard of the Milesians who were attempting to take possession of Ireland, Amergin had invoked the land of Ireland, had attuned himself to it, and was expressing this in his magical incantation. This shows us that, as a Druid, he was schooled and skilled in using the power of attunement and the power of sound.

This power of attunement is the basis of the way in which we, today, can make contact and have relationship with the faery folk, and hopefully, create a relationship of mutual respect, trust, assistance, and healing.

The fairies

There is another thread in this weaving that we must consider here. The word *faeries* is often used in an almost generic way to refer not just to the People of the Sidhe, but to many other beings as well, who, if we were describing them by function, might better be described in our modern parlance as elemental spirits, nature spirits, and devas. As might be expected, the old lore has its own ways of describing them.

Greek tradition refers to many such beings under the general designation of *nymph*. But within that large general designation existed many smaller classifications of beings. Spirits inhabiting forests were known as *dryads*, whereas the spirits of the individual trees were often referred to as *hamadryads*. Water spirits were divided into those of the fresh waters of rivers and streams known as *naiads*, of the Mediterranean called *nereids*, and in the great sea that lay beyond the Mediterranean they were known as the *oceanids*. Spirits known as *limniads* presided over lakes, marshes and swamps. The *oreades* were the mountain spirits, the valley spirits were the *napaea*, and the *limoniads* were the spirits of the meadows.

In addition, Greek tradition refers to two distinct classes of gods: the Titans, who were the Elder Gods most akin to the primordial, gigantic forces which formed and comprise the planet, and their children, the more familiar Olympian gods who dwelt on Mt. Olympus. The Olympians seemed to have a somewhat human aspect—their loves, hates, jealousies, and spats were legendary—while still displaying enormous godlike powers over major areas of life and nature.

The folk traditions of the British Isles have their own versions of these. See the works of Katherine Briggs (listed in the Bibliography) for a more detailed account of Bristish faery folk.

Teutonic tradition, which came to the British Isles with invading tribes of Saxons, Angles, Jutes, and Danes, is rich in the lore of Faery Beings of all sorts. The higher order of beings, comparable to the Tuatha De Danaan, were the Old Gods and Goddesses commonly known as the Vanir and Aesir, the Vanir being the older strata. But we also hear much about the lower orders of beings referred to as *wights*, more commonly known as *elves*, and sometimes referred to as the *Underground People*. There are many subdivisions of these beings and regional names for them. According to *Teutonic Mythology,* the masterwork by Jacob Grimm, elves are roughly divisible into at least three categories:

Light Elves are associated with lightness and brightness; their residence corresponds with the Upperworlds.

Pale Elves are sometimes referred to as grey elves and are associated with this world—the Middleworld. They are thought to perhaps be the souls of the dead, and their residence is in the Teutonic Underworld of Hel, home of the great Underworld Goddess Hela whose name means *light.*

Dark Elves are sometimes referred to as brown elves or dusky elves. These elves are associated with darkness, coarseness, mountains, caves, and mines. Their residence is also in Hela's realm, Hel. This category contains yet another subdivision known as Black Elves who may be closer in nature to dwarves.[9]

This categorization illustrates an interesting variation on the concept of the Three Worlds which we find deeply embedded in much Northern European lore, and which is found also in the Celtic worldview in the form of the Three Realms of Earth, Sea and Sky. The Underworld was a world of spirits: faeries, elves, dragons, ancestors, and some deities. The Upperworld was also a world of spirits: the sun, moon, and stars (which included the planetary bodies) representing the high gods. The Middleworld was, of course, our earthly plane, and comprised of both material and Spirit Beings.

The word *elf* comes from an Indo-European root meaning *white*, from which evolved the Germanic *albiz* and *albaz* meaning "white ghostly apparitions." Unquestionably, elves, like faeries, are known to be beings of light—they are Shining Ones. From the same root word comes *Albion*, an old name for Britain that means "White Island." In Greek myth, Albion was a son of the sea god, Poseidon. Again, we see the relationship between the sea and the magical Otherworld whose inhabitants were Shining Ones often depicted as *white*.

It is interestingly ironic that Hela's Underworld realm, Hel, has become known in our age as a place of infernal, demonic, tormenting fire rather than as a place of the hidden but regenerative and transformative fire and light of the Underworld—the *Earth Light,* as contemporary author R. J. Stewart refers to it.

No less an authority than Fiona Macleod, one of the most prominent figures of the Celtic Renaissance of the late 19th century, draws a distinction between the different orders of beings which I herein refer to as faeries and fairies:

> *...I was also told of the Sidhe, often so rashly and ignorantly alluded to as the fairies in the sense of a pretty, diminutive, harmless, natural folk; and by my nurse Barabal instructed in some of the ways, spells, influences, and even appearances of these powerful and mysterious clans....I do not think, unless, as a very young child, I even confused them....But the Sidhe are very different than the small clans of earth's delight.*[10]

Elemental Beings, Nature Spirits, and Devas

Using more modern terminology, let's take a brief look at Elemental spirits, nature spirits, and devas, especially as they have been regarded within recent Celtic lore.

Elemental spirits are the spirits of each of the Four Elements—Air, Fire, Water, and Earth —who participate in the construction process of nature by acting as building blocks for matter. They are small subtle units of consciousness having specific energetic frequencies. These spirits/frequencies comprise the subtle, ethereal, invisible aspect of what eventually manifests physically and materially as an *Element* in nature: Air, Fire, Water, Earth.

Nature spirits are the spirits of the plants, trees, waves, and such, both as families and species and as individuals. They are akin to the Greek dryads and nereids. These spirits possess consciousness although the consciousness of the individual plants and trees is often more hive-like than individual. Consciousness seems to work on an incremental level: the degree of individuality and self-awareness seems to increase incrementally with the size of the being. That is, the being that is a forest, for instance, has a greater degree of consciousness, awareness, and individuality than does a specific tree in that forest.

This brings us to the devas, the great, shining, over-lighting spirit beings of the natural world. And it is here that we find much more individuality, as devas are the consciousness of a group of plants or trees rather than the consciousness of an individual plant or tree. As such, they are larger, greater beings/consciousnesses and are composed of all the smaller, individual beings/consciousnesses that comprise their particular species in that locale. There are yet larger devas who are the devas of an entire species.

In addition, there are beings who are forests, mountains, clouds, hurricanes, and just about any other natural phenomena of which one can conceive.

A. E. describes seeing in vision some beings living within a lake. These beings, whom he took to be Elemental Beings, were luminous and full of color, close to human stature in size, and seemed to possess a collective, hivetype consciousness as their actions all seemed to be in accord with one another. One of them was larger than the others, seated on a throne, and seemed to be their king. He shone brightly, silvery-blue and gold, with the gold seeming to predominate and shine through the blueness. A "lustrous air" seemed to fountain up from beneath the king, and when he breathed it in he grew in power. The smaller Elemental Beings, their shining "dimmed to a kind of greyness," seemed to descend through the lake toward the king on the right side. When they reached the throne they went up to the king, bent, and kissed his heart. This seemed to renew and enliven the spark of their being, causing them to blaze up becoming more radiant and colorful, and shoot upward and away to the left side.

In this description it is possible to discern within this watery realm the workings of a hierarchy of beings. The fountain, arising from within the lakebed, channels power out from within the Earth. The largest of the beings present seemed to be the king; his essence was fed by the luminous fountain beneath him. In turn, it was the king's function to feed and renew the smaller, lesser beings who, depleted into dimness, descended toward him through the waters. In other words, as the king himself was fed by the energy forces which fountained up from the lakebed beneath him, his power increased till he was sufficiently filled so that the power could flow through him, out through his heart and into the dimmer beings who kissed his heart. As they were renewed they shot up and away from him re-energized, at least for the moment. The king, larger and brighter and able to directly access the power of the fountain, was a "larger" more individualized being than the smaller, dimmer beings who had to access it through him.

These are fairy folk too, according to common parlance, but as I have stated previously, I refer to them as "fairies" with an "i" rather than an "e" to distinguish them from the class of beings we have been discussing as the Tuatha, the Old Gods, the Shining Ones. They are functionally different and have a different level and type of consciousness, awareness, and intelligence. But when we move into the actual, practical Faery Healing section of this book, remember that they, too, have their part to play.

Summary

Let us attempt to draw some of these threads together that we may look at the pattern of the weaving that they create.

There are several legends as to the origin of the faery folk and several theories as to their nature. Some people believe the faery folk are synonymous with the ancestors, some of whom are buried within the old mounds and hills. Others believe the faery folk are fallen angels. But all agree that they live, to one extent or another, within the Earth, whether it be in hollow hills and caves or in their palaces under the sea or on the far islands of the sea.

The magical Otherworldly isles in the Western Sea, which are also known to be home to the Tuatha De Danaan, bear quite mystic-sounding names such as *Tir na nOg*, meaning Land of the Ever Young, *Tir na mBeo*, Land of the Ever Living, *Tir Tairngaire*, the Land of Promise, *Tir fo Thuinn*, Land Under the Waves, *Tir na mBan*, Island of Women, and *Tir na Sorcha*, Land of Brightness. And, as mentioned earlier, the West is also the place of the dead. All of this suggests a relationship between the ancestral dead, the faeries, and the Tuatha De Danaan.

Perhaps this is telling us that the Tuatha De Danaan *are* the ancestors, a theory given credence by the fact that the gods are seen as the First Ancestors in many tribal cultures, including the Celtic, and genealogies are drawn based upon this fact. Since we have already established that there is a relationship between the faery folk and the Tuatha, this theoretical familial relationship between our human ancestors and our Tuatha ancestors would imply that there is a familial relationship between the faery folk and humans.

So when we enlist the assistance of the faery folk in our healing work, we are enlisting the aid of other members of our own family. This is an important point because it indicates that in order to correctly attune ourselves to the Faery World and access communications and assistance, we may use the Principle of Resonance; that is, finding the part within ourselves that *is* Faery, attuning ourselves to it, and allowing it to open a gateway for us.

Of course, by virtue of being alive on the Living Earth, we are related to ALL forms of earthly life, including the Elemental Beings of whose very nature our bodies partake, and this fact is also important to our healing work. We will go more deeply into this subject in *Part III* and *Part IV* of this book.

The relationship between human and Faery, however, would seem closer than relationships with some other orders of being. This is not to say that we are Faery. We are quite clearly human. Yet, these complex, subtle interrelationships indicates that the edges are not completely sharp and well-defined. Rather, the issue is one of moving and flowing between states of being and consciousness while retaining as one's primary identity, the *form* into which one was born.

A. E. also beheld a vision wherein he saw several shining and silvery figures rise up from the waters and display to him, one at a time, the Four Treasures of the Tuatha De Danaan: the Stone, the Cauldron, the Sword, and Spear (we will learn more about these treasures in subsequent chapters). This vision, somewhat reminiscent of that of the hand of the Lady of the Lake rising from the lake to give King Arthur his sword, may have been an illustration of the connection between the Old Gods and the *Primal Elemental Powers* which these treasures represent, as held in the memory of the land.

This web of relationships links together the land and its memory, the Tuatha as the Old Gods, and all beings who live on and in the land.

So the search for the "who and what is faery" takes us right into our own family tree, the Great Tree of Life of which all others are branches, and the Sacred Living Land from which it springs and is nourished.

END NOTES

1 Matthews, Caitlín, *The Celtic Book of the Dead*, St. Martin's Press, NY, NY, 1992, pp. 5–6.
2 Yeats, W. B., Ò*The Scots and Irish Fairies,*Ó *Scots Observer*, 1889.
3 Ibid.
4 Green, Miranda, *Dictionary of Celtic Myth and Legend*, Thames and Hudson, London & NY, 1992, p. 62.
5 Stewart, R. J., *Mystic Life of Merlin*, Routledge, & Kegan Paul Ltd, London, 1986, p. 128.
6 Matthews, Caitlín, *Ladies of the Lake*, Aquarian Press, an imprint of Harper Collins, London, 1992, p. 58.
7 Ellis, Peter Berresford, *The Druids*, William B. Eerdmans Publishing Co., Grand Rapids, MI., 1994, pp. 213–215.
8 Ibid.
9 Grimm, Jacob, *Teutonic Mythology*, James Stallybrass (translator), George Bell and Sons, London, 1883, 1888, pp. 442–448.
10 Macleod, Fiona (William Sharp), *The Works of Fiona Macleod, Vol. IV, Iona,* William Heineman, Ltd., London, 1927, pp. 197, 199.

CHAPTER 2

The Living World

The ancient Celts were people of the Earth. Like all early peoples, they lived in close constant interaction with the Earth and were acutely aware of her seasons, moods, and weather patterns, which directly impacted their lives in a way hard for us modern folk to imagine. They were aware of the many elements that made up the world, and the plethora of beings which inhabited Earth's body. They were aware of subtle, invisible dimensions of life, and of the constant interaction of the physical world with the unseen Otherworlds in which they implicitly believed. These basic everyday realities transcended any particular theology, finding expression equally, over time, in both Pagan and Christian terms.

The sun rose in the morning, bringing light and heat; it set in the evening, bringing the beauties of the sunset which gladden the heart. The moon rose in the night sky, bringing beauty and giving a sense of structure and order to the passage of the days and nights. The stars, wheeling their sparkling way through the vast deep of the night, imparted order to the seasons as they traveled the sky during the course of the year. The homely fire kindled in the hearth brought light and warmth to the household and cooked the food of warriors, kings, and peasants, while it cast shadows in the room, shadows which were alive with hosts of unseen beings.

Theirs was a world filled with life—a Living Earth, a Living World—inhabited by hosts of visible and invisible Beings of all kinds, some friendly to humankind, some unfriendly, some indifferent, some malicious. Even though some of the beings were invisible, they still could and did cause things to happen. Therefore, they must be reckoned with, acknowledged, and related to in some fashion.

Consequently, not only sun and moon were greeted when they arose, as one would greet beloved friends, but offerings were made to faeries as well as to trees, rivers, lakes, and other natural entities. Over time, prayers and protocols of behavior came into being concerning interaction with the various kinds and orders of beings. The theological change from Paganism to Christianity caused a gradual evolution in how these beings were seen, but did not alter belief in them or the necessity for interaction.

Many of these prayers, charms, and customs are apparent in the folklore collections, particularly the *Carmina Gadelica* of Alexander Carmichael collected in the late 1800s and early 1900s. Indeed, one of those interviewed told Mr. Carmichael:

> *The old people had runes which they sang to the spirits dwelling in the sea and in the mountain, in the wind, and in the whirlwind, in the lightning and in the thunder, in the sun and in the moon, and in the stars of heaven.*[1]

The Sun

The sun was regarded as a great beneficent power. In Wales, when the sun rose on the great festival days, it was said that he was "dancing." (Note, however, the references to the sun as feminine in the Scottish prayers below.) The sun was also often said to be laughing or joyous. There was an old expression in Wales concerning sunset and sunrise:

> *He is going to rest, and he is awaking.*[2]

The power of the time of sunrise granted virtue to magical herbs and healing waters, both of which had to be gathered just before the sun rose.

The sun's path around the Earth marked out the circle of the seasons and thus represented the *wholeness* of the year. When performing sacred ceremonies, including the visiting of holy wells, it was customary and auspicious to walk or crawl on hands and knees three times deosil, that is, sunwise (always turning to the right), around whatever sacred object (i.e., bonfire, holy well, cairn, sacred stone) marked the center of the ceremony. This action, which mimicked the sun's path, called in the power of the sun to the ceremony being enacted.

As one might expect, to move against or contrary to the direction of the sun (toward the left) was held to be unlucky and often malicious. However, this normally unlucky movement could be put to good use in healing when banishing an ailment.

Here are two beautiful prayers to the sun from the *Carmina Gadelica*.

The Sun
The eye of the great God,
The eye of the God of glory,
The eye of the King of hosts,

The eye of the King of the living,
Pouring upon us
At each time and season,
Pouring upon us
Gently and generously.
Glory to thee,
Thou glorious sun.
Glory to thee, thou sun,
Face of the God of life.[3]

The Sun
Hail to thee, thou sun of the seasons,
As thou traverses the skies aloft;
Thy steps are strong on the wing of the heavens,
Thou art the glorious mother of the stars.
Thou liest down in the destructive ocean
Without impairment and without fear;
Thou risest up on the peaceful wave-crest
Like a queenly maiden in bloom.[4]

THE MOON

The moon was the beloved companion of the night who rendered "guidance and leading to the night," and to whom the knee was bent and the head was bowed in reverence. Notice was taken of the moon in all its phases, and each of the phases had its special powers and uses. For it was thought better to work with the powers of the moon than contrary to them.

The new moon was considered auspicious for all new undertakings; thus, moving house at the new moon would insure abundance and success in the new residence. Healing herbs and dew were gathered at the new moon; their fresh and vibrant power was thought to grow as the moon grew. Gazing at the new moon was not done through glass or with trees in the way, for that took away the luck in it.

All activities having to do with completion or severance were better begun at the full moon whose energy would aid these things as it waned. Grass mowed at this time dried rapidly into hay without much danger of molding. In general, crops were sown and harvested in accordance with the cycles of the moon.

The moon was held to be quite powerful, and as with all powerful things and beings, care must be taken. It was considered dangerous to sleep in the moonlight and especially for the rays of the moon to fall on the face of a sleeping child. It was thought that moonlight falling on the eyes of any sleeping person might cause blindness. An even worse possibility was that it would cause the person to become moonstruck, in other words, a lunatic.

Here is a lovely prayer to the new moon, from Alexander Carmichael's *Carmina Gadelica*.

New Moon
I am lifting to thee my hands,
I am bowing to thee my head,
I am giving thee my love,
Thou glorious jewel of all the ages.
I am raising to thee mine eye,
I am bending to thee my head,
I am offering thee my love,
Thou new moon of all the ages.[5]

As can be seen from these prayers, the prevailing theological particulars did not matter. Whether the people professed Paganism or Christianity, the sun and moon were seen as worthy of being addressed and acknowledged, loved and praised for their beauty.

The Stars

In the ancient world, the Druids had been known and well respected for both their knowledge of the stars and for their ability to divine by the stars. This knowledge seems to have preceded the incursion of our now familiar Arabic-based astrological system into the Celtic lands, which occurred after the start of the Christian era.[6]

When we look up at the sky, the stars seem to form patterns and images. Every culture in the world has noticed star patterns and has created stories about them. So it should come as no surprise that the Celts did likewise, stories of the great ones—heroes, giants, gods, and saints—becoming associated with the stars.

Thus, the Milky Way, known in Wales as *Caer Gwydion* (stronghold or castle of Gwydion), was thought to be inhabited by the souls of heroes, kings, and other persons of honor and renown, while in Britain, the Big Dipper was *Arthur's Plough-tail*, Orion was *Arthur's Yard*, and the Lyre was *Arthur's Harp*. The circumpolar constellation of the Northern Crown, Corona Borealis, was known in Wales as *Caer Arianrhod*,[7] the spiral castle of the Welsh Goddess Arianrhod. She was a goddess of the moon, the stars, and possibly of initiation and reincarnation as her castle was where the dead were thought to go between lives. Cassiopeia's Chair was known as the *Circle of Don*, Don being the name of the mysterious and seldom mentioned mother of the Welsh deities.

In Ireland, the Milky Way was known as *Beachlachna Bó Finne*, the Way of the White Cow, the white cow being a personification of the Goddess Dana, who was the Irish form of the great Earth and celestial Goddess Danu of the continental Celts. Her personification in the form of rivers was found all over Europe, making it seem likely that the Milky Way was considered a life-giving celestial river of sorts as well. The image of Dana, mother of the gods, as the White Cow whose milk is a river of stars, is one both cosmic and endearingly personal since cattle were beloved of the insular Celts and played such an integral part of their life for so many centuries.

During the Christian era, the beings for whom these star groupings were named were recalled more as ancient heroes rather than as gods and goddesses, but their stories were important to the people nonetheless—a part of the culture and as familiar as yesterday.

The Colors of the Winds

In the 11th century poem *Saltair na Ran* (the psaltery or songbook of Ran), reference is made to the qualities of the winds originating from the twelve directions, including their colors, temperatures, and the influences they carried—all of which together might also be described as their *personalities*. These descriptions had immense practical applications relative to hunting, fishing, farming, and life in general. In Scotland, for instance, it was thought that the *Cailleach Bheara* (the Old Woman or Hag Goddess) sent her minions—the fierce winter winds—to blast the land with the ferocious winter storms.

These winds were divided into four chief winds, four winds below them, and four subordinate winds, twelve in all. The four chief winds were the winds of the four cardinal directions of East, South, West, and North. Further information on the winds is found scattered throughout folkloric sources.

The Winds and Their Colors
as given in the *Saltair na Ran*[8]

	North　black	
	North Northeast　speckled	
	Northeast　dark	
West　pale or dun		East　purple
West Northwest　dark brown		Southeast　red
Northwest　brown		South Southeast　yellow
	South　white	
	South Southwest　grey green	
	Southwest　green	

The royal purple East wind (which in some Irish lore was instead considered red) was said to be beneficial, the East being the place "from which all good things come." The East wind brought the best luck possible. The white South wind was also considered a fortunate wind, the herald of good luck and longevity. The dun-colored West wind was not a very fortunate one; it was said that death was carried on this wind. The black North wind was thought to bring ill luck and misfortune.

Since the sun, always considered a beneficial influence, rose in the East and set in the West, the correspondences above are understandable as it was probably thought that the winds from those directions carried the attributes of the rising and setting sun, life and death, respectively. Since the bitterly cold winter winds came from the North, it is understandable that misfortune was associated with the North, whereas winds from its opposite, the South, would bring the opposite qualities, i.e., good fortune.

Plants and Animals

It is clear from prayers and invocations found in the folklore collections that what we refer to as *plant spirits* were undoubtedly recognized by the Celtic peoples, although through the years of Christianization this concept may have evolved into one of simply recognizing the plant's unique, God-given properties. Nevertheless, the plant was often spoken to and addressed as a sentient being while being plucked, as in the example below.

I am plucking thee,
Thou gracious red myrtle,
In the name of the Father of virtues,

In the name of the Son Whom I love,
In the name of God's eternal Spirit.[9]

Our chapter on faery plants will contain further information on this aspect of the Celtic traditions.

There was also a vibrant lore concerning the characteristics and personalities of the different animals. These comrades on life's path were looked upon with love and kindliness, their virtues admired, and often "wished upon" others as a blessing or gift.

Wisdom of serpent be thine,
Wisdom of raven be thine,
Wisdom of eagle.
Voice of swan, be thine,
Voice of honey, be thine.
Voice of the Son of the stars.[10]

Often, omens were taken from the appearance, behavior, or movement of certain animals at certain time of day or times of life. It is said that these may well be remnants of a much larger body of animal lore that was known in ancient times.

A CHANGE OF THEOLOGIES

When the British Isles became Christianized, which was a rather gradual process, belief in the gods and goddesses and various other spirits became belief in God, his angels and saints and his Mother, as well as the devil, his demons, and fallen angels. In some cases, there was a direct crossover and a deity became a saint, such as with the Irish Goddess Brigid whose legends became firmly attached to the life of a saintly and virtuous holy woman, St. Brigid of Kildare, and the Irish Goddess Anu (her British form was Ana), mother of the gods, who became associated with St. Ann, mother of the Virgin Mary. In other cases, deities became folk heroes, while nature spirits, land spirits, and faeries sometimes became demons, major or minor. Some places sacred to the Pagan gods and goddesses became associated with the Christian devil, while others were reconsecrated to the Christian God, his Mother, or the various saints.

In spite of these changes, it appears that, to a certain extent, a basic animistic worldview remained as did the ease of relationship with nature and the beings of nature.

A few definitions may be in order here. *Webster's Dictionary* defines *animism* as "(1) the doctrine that the soul is the vital principle of organic development; (2) the attribution of conscious life to nature or natural objects; (3) the belief in spirits separate from bodies."

The word *pantheism* is defined as, "a doctrine that equates God with the forces and laws of nature."[11]

As can be seen by these definitions, the practical, everyday theology of the Celtic people, whether they professed to Christianity or Paganism, was essentially animistic and pantheistic. God was not separate from his creation, but expressed his multifaceted Divine Nature in the great multiplicities of life-forms he had created. All of these created forms partook of the Divine Nature to some extent. Another, more Christian way of expressing this was to say that all forms of life *glorified* God simply by being who and what they had been created to be. Thus, the trailing pearlwort plant gave glory to God by being the healing plant that it was and allowing humans to partake of its powers; and the moon, by giving its light and guidance by night, also glorified God.

During the course of my own Catholic childhood I recall being taught that according to our doctrines worship must be given to God only; what was offered to his Holy Mother and the saints was to be classified as loving veneration. Yet, as I observed and participated in the honoring of the Mother and the saints during my upbringing, I failed to see any real, significant difference between what was being done and referred to as worship and what was being done and referred to as veneration, particularly with regard to the Holy Mother. It seemed the important difference was in the semantics, though my dear departed Catholic mother would probably disagree!

Saints and Angels

The Christian conception of the roles of saints and angels provide an interesting comparison with the older Celtic Pagan theologies. Angels were considered to be the messengers of God, shining and powerful beings conveying the words, will, and messages of God from his High Throne to the human realm. The saints were exalted and glorified humans whose good deeds and honorable lives had earned them a special grace and place in the heart of God. As such, it was believed they were just a bit closer to God's ear than the average human. Because of this, they functioned as intermediary, intercessory beings, for certainly God would be willing to listen a little more closely to what his good friends had to ask him!

In a similar way, the Celtic divinities and Faery Beings functioned as intermediary, intercessory beings to a Greater Power. They, too, were and are links in the great chain of life-forms.

They perform this function by operating as matrices of power, allowing access to specific frequencies of that greater power or allowing the power to flow from one level of being to another. For example, the Goddess Brigid was a goddess of poetry, smithcraft, and healing. To work with her allowed one to access these specific frequencies of energy in exactly the same way as a Catholic praying to a patron saint of these things could access these same frequencies. It is a matter of *tuning*, similar to tuning a radio to the correct station.

In any case, the Celtic people enjoyed a close, friendly, and intimate relationship with the orders of nature, as well as with God, his Mother, saints, and angels, which would seem to imply that their earlier, pre-Christian relationship with the Divine Forces by other names had been similarly cordial.

The Many Orders of Beings

Behind all the prayers, invocations, customs, and practices was the belief, the knowledge, that the world was a Living World, and full of beings with whom one was involved in a relationship. This relationship entailed, as do all relationships, an interaction and an exchange of energies, hopefully reciprocal, with these beings. One prayed, sending forth energy in the form of prayer or praise; the beings responded, sending their energy back in some form. As energies flowed back and forth this way a circuit was formed, and a reciprocal relationship was born and grew.

To summarize, the Celts lived in a Living World, a world populated with beings visible and invisible. This was as true of the Celts living during the last 2,000 years of the Christian era as it was of their forebearers, though the beings were most likely known by differing names throughout this long period of time. Interaction with these beings, including the faeries, was an everyday affair.

We will come back to this concept and expand on it in *Part III* of this book, taking a more in-depth look at—while using more contemporary terminology—the Web of Life and the many orders of beings that exist within that Web, as well as the Sacred and Living Land which is the heart and matrix of it all.

Some Elemental Clarifications

A note of clarification: In this book I will use the word *Elements* to refer primarily to the Four Classical Elements of Air, Fire, Water, and Earth. Some Pagan scholars today argue that these four, originating as they do in ancient Greece, are alien to the Celtic culture and that the Celts had more than four elements in their own system of elements. They suggest that the Celts acknowledged perhaps as many as nine elements, including land, sea, sky, sun, moon, wind, clouds, mountains, trees, plants, and stones.

Aside from the fact that there was most definitely interaction and possibly exchange of concepts between the Celts and the Greek during early phases of history (i.e., the Greeks were trading with the continental Celts by 600 B.C., and the Celts had sacked Delphi by 279 A.D.), this argument is, in my opinion, largely a matter of semantics. I use the word "Elements" (note the upper case "E") to refer to the primal *Four Elements* or fundamental movements of the energy that allowed creation to come into manifestation, rather than as the gigantic *Powers* acknowledged by the ancient Celts and many other ancient peoples. These latter *Powers* may well have included such things as lightning, thunder, the moon, the sun, earthquakes, mountains, trees, wind, and so on.

Very often even these powerful forces were seen as entities, and gigantic ones at that. The personification of these great primal or elemental forces was prevalent in the legends of the Celtic world. Although I will not refer to them as Elements, it is important to understand that the very personification of these forces enabled the people to relate to them with the familiarity of a relative.

By way of example, in Ireland and Scotland we have stories of the Old Woman of Beare, the *Cailleach Bheara,* who created lakes, islands, mountains, and cairns by dropping stones from her apron as she flew and traveled across the land. In Scotland tales are told of the *Cailleachan*, or storm hags, who brought the terrible and destructive storms. The brilliantly colored ribbons of light which streamed across the night skies and which we know as Aurora Borealis were known as the *Merry Dancers* and the *Nimble Men*.[12] In Wales, we have stories of the giant Bran the Blessed, who being far too large for any boat to hold him, waded across the waters from Wales to Ireland. When seen by those on the far shore, the sight of his head above the waters appeared to be a mountain with two lakes upon it, traveling across the sea. In Scotland there are many stories of giants whose exploits, endeavors, and even arguments were the cause of various mountains and rock formations.

These are the *Titans* of Celtic mythology, the Earth-Powers and Earth-Shapers, who shaped and molded and built the Earth. In author Ella Young's rendering of Celtic tales in *The Earthshapers*, we find the Tuatha De Danaan scooping out hollows of land to create the lakes and hills of Ireland.

Similarly, in Teutonic tradition, whose influence was brought to England with the invading Angles, Saxons, and Jutes, we find the powerful Goddess Frau Holle, also called Mother Holle, Holda, or Hulda, who causes snow to fly on Earth when she shakes out her feather comforter; while in Russia there is King Frost, who brings the snow and spins the ice from tree to tree. And we cannot forget the Teutonic Primal Giant Ymir who was the first being to emerge from the Ice of the Primal Void, and from whose body the entire world was later formed.

The Four Elements are representative of what I refer to as the *horizontal* worldview: the earthly plane and its subtle counterparts. The Celtic realms of Sky, Land, and Sea—even when given Elemental correspondences of Air, Earth, and Water respectively—refer to a *vertical* worldview. This perspective is linked to and often represented by a World Tree with its roots as the Underworld, its trunk as the Middleworld, and its branches as the Upperworld. Such a tree, allowing access between the Three Realms, is not unique to the early Celts but is found in many cultures throughout the world.

Each of these ways of studying the Celtic worldview will be helpful to us, and we will use them both in this book.

END NOTES

1. Carmichael, Alexander, *Carmina Gadelica, Vol. 3*, Oliver and Boyd, Edinburgh & London, 1928, p. 271.
2. Trevelyan, Marie, *Folklore and Folk-tales of Wales*, Elliot Stock, London, 1909, Chapter 3.
3. Carmichael, Alexander, *Carmina Gadelica, Vol. 3*, Oliver and Boyd, Edinburgh & London, 1928, p. 307.
4. Ibid, p. 311.
5. Ibid, p. 291.
6. Ellis, Peter Berresford, *The Druids*, William B. Eerdmans Publishing Co., Grand Rapids, MI, 1994, p. 237.
7. Trevelyan, Marie, *Folklore and Folk-tales of Wales*, Elliot Stock, London, 1909, Chapter 3.
8. Matthews, Caitlin, *Elements of the Celtic Tradition*, Element Books Ltd, Dorset, 1989, p. 11.
9. Carmichael, Alexander, *Carmina Gadelica, Vol. 4*, Oliver and Boyd, Edinburgh & London, 1928, p. 137.
10. Ibid, *Vol. 3*, p. 241.
11. *WebsterÕs Seventh New Collegiate Dictionary*, G. & C. Merriam Company, Publishers, Springfield, MA, 1967.
12. McNeil, F. Marian, *The Silver Bough, Vol. 1*, William MacLellan, 1956, Canongate Classics, Edinburgh, 1989.

CHAPTER 3

Elements of the Living World

Sacred Fire, Sacred Water

The Four Classical Elements of Fire, Water, Earth, and Air are essential to life. The Air surrounds us and is a given, although our recent industrial-age ability to effectively pollute it makes it less of a given than it was in the past. The Earth beneath us is a given, though its quality and ability to sustain life varies from location to location. Water, however, is another story, as is Fire. Humans have always sought fresh potable water sources by which to build their habitations, and have frequently depended upon the bounty of river and sea for some part of their food sources. Equally important has been, and still is today, the fire that warms and cooks. Before the advent of safety matches, people were dependent on obtaining fire from pre-existing sources such as lightning-caused fire, or else had to create it by friction. Several implements for doing this have come into being through the years, but all depend upon the basic element of a friction-created spark, which was captured and carefully tended. Some scholars hold that the spirits of wood and stone were invoked by the use of these implements.

There's a certain inherent magic to fire and to our ability to create it. Fire—by whatever means we kindle and spark it—seems to just *spring* into being. One moment it's not fire, then there's warmth, a bit of heat and smoke, and then, amazingly, there's that magic spark, which must be captured, and tended.

Because it was not easy to create fire, the care and tending of it was a matter of extreme importance in times past. And Fire itself—that great and powerful being who can both create and destroy—was honored and respected, and seen to symbolize the very spark of life itself.

In one sense, the primacy of the Elements of Fire and Water in the Celtic tradition speaks of the practical aspects of life, and the urgent necessity/importance of both fire and water for the functions of life. In another sense, it bespeaks the blazing, life-engendering sun and the moist, life-birthing Earth with its primordial womb, the sea. In yet another sense, it symbolizes the life-giving attributes of the Divine Being or Beings, who created the world.

There are many customs that attest to the importance of both fire and water to the Celtic people of the British Isles.

FIRE

Lady Wilde tells us that the Irish people believed that evil power could only exist in darkness, therefore, light—sun, fire, and candle—were all protection against it.[1]

Fire was said to be the greatest protection against faery magic, since it was the most sacred of all created things, and none of the created things save humankind had power over it. Only humans attained the knowledge of how to draw the Spirit of Fire from its dwelling place in stone and wood. Therefore Fire—as the "visible symbol of the invisible God"—could be used by humankind to bless and protect, and to guard against faeries and their magic.

Fire's bright tongue of flame, rising upward toward the heavens, was thought to be the visible form of a divine spirit dwelling in the substance which had been ignited. Fire was thought to be endowed with mysterious and magical cleansing powers, which was why the people made circles of fire, or sometimes two fires, and walked their children and cattle between or around them as a protection against evil and illness.[2]

Ancient Ireland's sacred fire at Tara was lit only every three years and then with much ceremony. A lens was used to concentrate the sun's rays on pieces of dried wood until sparks arose and ignited the wood. From this fire, all the sacred fires of Ireland were then kindled. Sacred fire was also acquired by the friction of wood or the striking of stone. It was thought that by these actions the priests invoked the spirits of fire who dwelt in wood and stone.[3]

There were many fire-related customs and rituals, some for every day, some only to be done on special occasions, and some for when there was a special need.

It was considered unlucky to give away a coal of fire from the house before a child had been baptized. Because of Fire's protective power, giving it away would be to give away the household's protection and thus its luck.

Indeed, there were several occasions upon which it was unlucky to give away a lighted sod or hot coal, May Day being the most important one but butter churning days being important as well.[4]

Fire was thought of as purifying, healing, and sacred, and it was thought that while a fire burned on the hearth, lightning could not strike the house.

In Wales, when country people were distressed and troubled about a problem, they would whisper the problem into the oven, or touch the stone over the chimney, throw a handful of dry earth into the hearthfire, and whisper their problem to the flames as the dry earth burned. This was presumed to deflect any evil that threatened.[5]

When baking the family's bread, the old women were careful to leave some of the wood chunks and ashes from the previous fire inside and use them to ignite the new fire for the new baking. This had been done for generations and is related to similar customs of saving some of the old fire to use in beginning the new, thus carrying forward the luck and blessing of the fire.[6]

Since Fire was representative of the Spirit, to put out the light or candle at the table while people were still eating supper meant that there would be one less person at the table before a year had passed.[7]

Large community fires were held on May Day (Beltaine) and also on St. John's Eve (Midsummer). From these large fires the smaller household fires were relit. Often two fires were lit and cattle were paraded between them in order to partake of their blessing and protective power. Three or nine different kinds of wood were necessary to build the Midsummer fires; often the charred remains of a log from the previous Midsummer fire was used as well. Girls held bunches of three or nine different kinds of flowers, while boys wore them in their buttonholes. Holding hands, they jumped the fire for luck and blessings.

Fire's blessing and protection this time of year was crucial since it was also the time when the faeries most frequently stole away beautiful women and children (a fact interestingly coincidental with July's reputation as the "Hungry Month," coming as it did just before the year's first harvest in August).

The Midwinter time of Christmas had its fires as well. It was customary in many areas of Wales to keep a portion of the Yule log until the following Christmas Eve when it was placed into the fireplace along with the new Yule log, and the old and new were then burned together. It was said this was done for luck, but in the past it was known that such a custom was protective against evil influences. This custom is clearly another example of carrying over the luck of the fire from the old year into the new year.

One of the most sacred and significant forms of the sacred fire was the need-fire. This was a fire produced by the friction of two pieces of wood. Not only did the ritual kindling of the need-fire play a prominent part at the Fire Festivals of Imbolc, Beltaine, Lughnasadh, and Samhain, but a need-fire was considered to be the most powerful charm possible for dealing with evil spirits of all kinds.

In Scotland, a need-fire or *tinegin* (forced fire, or fire of necessity) was constructed at times of great trouble, such as during an outbreak of plague or as a corrective to the murrain in cattle. This fire had some very specific construction parameters including the fact that there must be 81 married men (nine times nine) involved in the ritual of its construction. First, all the fires in the parish must be extinguished. Then two huge planks were rubbed together by the men, who took turns working in groups of nine till fire was produced. Each family was then supplied with a flame from this *forced fire* which was then used to light the fires in their homes. Immediately thereafter, a kettle of water was put on the fire. The water was afterwards sprinkled upon the cattle or people who were ill.[8]

That the men in this ceremony must be married (thus presumably proven virile) is highly significant. The married men, the sexual friction of the planks rubbed together to produce the spark of fire, the sprinkling of water thereafter, and the use of multiples of the sacred number three (3 x 3 = 9, 9 x 3 = 27, 27 x 3 = 81) are significant signals that this interesting rite embodies some very primal elements of belief.

Also in Scotland, there was an interesting fire ritual performed for sick children thought to be under the influence of the Evil Eye. The custom was known as *Beannachadh na Cuairte*, which means the Blessing of the Circle. It involved passing a sick child through an iron hoop wound around with a blazing paraffin saturated straw rope. Spaces had been left on the hoop for women to hold it, and the child was passed quickly through the hoop by the wise woman of the district while an appropriate incantation was recited.[9]

Another practice which demonstrated the sanctity of fire was *saining*, or blessing with fire. Crops, children, cattle, and boats were sained by people carrying torches around them in a sunwise direction. This practice persisted till early in the 20th century.[10]

The hearth-fire, that crucial and central part of the home, was routinely banked down or *smoored* for the night, and there were specific incantations/prayers to accompany this.

I am smooring the fire
As the Son of Mary would smoor;
Blest be the house, blest be the fire,
Blest be the people all.[11]

And in the morning, the hearth-fire was ritually awakened, also with accompanying prayers.

I will raise the hearth-fire
As Mary would.
The encirclement of Bride and of Mary

On the fire, and on the floor
And on the household all.[12]

These two examples, like the ones in the previous chapter, are from Alexander Carmichael's wonderful Scottish folklore collection, the *Carmina Gadelica*.

WATER

Where there is water, life can exist. Water, with its inherent abilities to dissolve, cleanse, soothe, cool, and nourish, has long been held blessed and sacred in many lands. The upwelling of water from the heart of the Earth was appreciated as the miraculous thing that it truly is, and was seen to bring with it virtue and power from the heart of the Earth. For these reasons, lakes, wells, pools, streams, and springs, seen as gateways to the Inner-Earth and the Otherworlds, have been honored and venerated. There have been many customs and traditions attached to this veneration.

Yet those who live closely with Mother Nature cannot help but be acutely aware of her double-aspected character. They cannot afford the luxury of the cute and cozy beliefs we sometimes find ourselves entertaining in our own culture, far removed from day-to-day interaction with nature as it is. People who live closely with nature are quite aware that nature destroys as well as creates, and this is as vividly true of water as it is of fire. Storms rage, floods arise, rivers overflow, boats sink, life is lost. All of these are as much a part of water's disposition as are its more beneficent aspects.

Being careless with water was considered dangerous in the Celtic lands. It was believed that to thoughtlessly or frivolously scatter water while washing hands in the morning would scatter the luck for the day. To spill water while carrying it from the spring or brook foreshadowed sorrow; again, it was like "spilling" one's luck.

It was considered unlucky to take any payment for water given to others. Those who took money for water would, it was thought, someday themselves suffer the torments of great thirst.

There was a belief that the ceremonial pouring out of water during drought times would bring the rain. This was known to be so effective that there was a common expression among the Welsh peasants, "Don't spill the water about unless you wish for rain." During rainy weather, people were careful to not spill water lest they bring on even more rain, or perhaps a storm. This carefulness with water was even true with regard to rivers and lakes. It is said that the older people, in particular, were always upset to see children stirring up the waters of rivers or wells by tossing in stones.

Dew

The sanctity in which water was held extended even to dew. In Ireland, dew acquired just at sunrise on May Morning was called "May Dew" and was used to wash the face as it was thought to guarantee beauty.[13]

On the eve of the Feast of Brigid, February Eve, the '*Brat Bride*' was placed outside by the women of the house. This cloth was laid over a bush and left there all day and all night, for it was thought that during the night Brigid passed by and touched it, bestowing her many blessings upon it. The cloth was brought in the next evening, and a piece of it was given to every female in the house for blessings and protection. Sometimes the *brat*, which could be any cloth though sometimes it was a shawl or length of ribbon, was thought to encourage fertility in women and cattle and to assist in difficult births. It was also used for healing and protection. Lying outdoors all night the *brat* absorbed the dew of the night, which, being Brigid's special night, held her power and blessings. Leaving the cloth outdoors on Brigid's night the following year could renew this power.

The Sea

The sea, now known to be the womb of life on this planet, was a nearly constant presence in the lives of many of the Celtic peoples of the British Isles and Brittany. The lives of coast-dwelling people of the past were, by nature, closely bound up with fishing and with the collection of seaweeds for food and fertilizer. Because of these things, the sea was intimately experienced in everyday life, and consequently, known and respected for her immense power to both nourish and destroy, as loss of life to the sea is another constant in the experience of those whose lives are bound up with her.

In Wales, the white waves of the sea were regarded with awe and considered to be the spirits of those who had drowned. The drowned also came riding in over the waves on their white horses at the times of Christmas, Easter, and All Hallows Eve, the times at which they held their revels.

In Ireland, sea water itself was held to have great health-giving properties. To bathe in it nine mornings in succession was considered a good healing practice. To take nine plunges into the sea in succession on one morning was thought to be good for nervous people, and for a child to take a small dose of sea water each morning upon arising from bed guaranteed a long life. Placing a sick, feverish person on the seashore when the tide was coming in was believed to cause the disease to be carried out on the tide.[14]

Wells

Wells of all kinds were greatly venerated. Offerings were made to wells, just as in the distant past the Celts were known to have made offerings to lakes and other water sources. From the common household well at which, in Wales, it was the custom for a new wife to make an offering of pins when she entered her new home for the first time, to the more sacred and special wells known for their magical and healing waters, the sacredness of water was recognized.

Some wells were known to be especially good for the leaving of offerings such as pins or rags. To pass such a well and not drop in a pin was to court bad luck. These pins or rags were left as wish offerings or as thanks offerings, for what was requested must be properly appreciated and thanks be given.

To offend a spring or well by ill-mannered behavior, by quarreling, or by lack of appreciation for its gifts was to possibly invoke the wrath of the well's guardian or indwelling spirit being, who was often thought to be in the form of a serpent or dragon. Such offenses could result in epidemics, flooding, or loss of the well's potency, which might affect the fertility of the neighboring lands and rivers.

One of the most common traditions associated with wells was that of well-dressing. On certain days it was customary for people to decorate wells with flowers and ribbons in thanksgiving and appreciation for the healing and cleansing powers of water.

Wells were sometimes used for divination. In Wales, certain wells were thought to have oracular powers, and people visited them to ascertain, for instance, the name of the person who had stolen their property. In order to determine the guilty party, a person tossed a piece of bread into the well and recited the names of the suspects. The bread would sink at the mention of the thief's name. If it did not sink but gradually dissolved, the thief would not be caught.

Girls would go to certain wells and cast a branch upon its waters to test the fidelity of their sweethearts. Likewise, people would cast the garment of a sick person into certain wells to determine the outcome of the illness by whether the garment sank to the right or left side of the well.

One of the most fascinating and widespread traditions was that of healing wells, of which, even today, there are a great number still in use. Wells are frequently dedicated to saints (the most popular seeming to be St. Ann and St. Brigid), especially in Catholic Ireland, and the dedication of wells to a holy being is a hold-over from earlier Pagan times when the wells were dedicated to various deities.

In *The Silver Bough*, F. Marian McNeill tells us that, in the Scotland of her time (early to mid 20th century), there were reputed to be over 600 holy wells scattered over the countryside, some still visited, but most of them no longer maintained or used.

Some of the healing wells were simply wells whose sacred waters were said to improve health and well-being in a general way. Many of the wells, however, had very specific healing associations and abilities. There were wells reputed to help toothaches, arthritis, eye problems, heart problems, bone problems, chest maladies, and many other things. *Tobar Maire* (Mary's Well) near Dundalk in Ireland, for example, was visited by thousands for relief from heart problems and poor eyesight. In addition, some wells were said to not only cure physical problems but to absolve sins as well.

The usual procedure at a holy well was to go sunwise around the well on the knees a number of times, often nine, but always in multiples of the sacred three. Then some of the well water was consumed. This was always accompanied by prayers. Sometimes it was customary to build up little piles of the white stones which were often nearby, using them to pray in a manner similar to how a rosary or other types of prayer beads are used to count prayers; or perhaps the stones were used to count the circuits made around the well. It was thought that the angels would count these stones—and thus the prayers—on the Last Day. It is quite likely that these white stones contained quartz, and this becomes interesting when we remember that stone amplifies power, and that quartz-containing stone is known to hold a piezo-electric (i.e., electro-magnetic) charge. So perhaps these stones were used as more than simply prayer counting devices. Perhaps the stones were used to *hold* the power of the prayers.

And where there are wells there are inevitably well offerings, as people brought things to offer as thanksgiving for the cures they received. Even today objects of offering, such as stones, flowers, and coins are likely to be found in the vicinity of holy wells. On a recent trip to a holy well in Cornwall, a friend observed the well's overhanging tree hung with shoelaces, hair-ties, and bits of handkerchiefs.

In Ireland, the first water drawn from a sacred well after midnight on May Eve was called *Sgaith-an-Tobar*, meaning the purity of the well. This water was considered especially potent and a sure antidote to witchcraft and other evil powers. It was sprinkled on the cattle on May Day. After the *Sgaith* had been drawn from a well, a small tuft of grass was thrown into the well to show others that the first water had already been taken from it.[15]

What is the source of healing power in the water of these wells? Sometimes, the waters may be rich in minerals, and these minerals provide important nutrients and substances that improve health when consumed or absorbed through the skin. Mineral waters have long been used for healing purposes. But often, there may be no known scientific explanation for the power of the well waters, yet the cures seem to occur nonetheless.

A factor to consider concerning the efficacy of holy wells is the Power of Place, the particular geomantic energy of the land itself, the energy that marks it as a place specific and different from other places. This has to do with not just the well itself, but how it is placed on the land, what is around it, and features of the land. Often sacred stones or special trees, such as hazels or hawthorns are located near holy wells. All of these contribute to the uniqueness of each site, the power it generates, and the veneration in which it was held.

Another factor may be that a place which has been venerated and at which prayers have been said for many years builds up a distinct energetic charge, if, indeed, there was not already a naturally occurring one there to begin with. All of these factors contribute, on both physical and psychological levels, to the healing powers of these holy wells.

The holy wells were thought to be especially powerful on the Quarter Days and were visited then, if possible. They were also visited on the feast day of the saint to whom the well was dedicated, and sometimes on the first Sundays and Mondays of May and during Whitsuntide.[16] In England, well-visiting season began in May, peaked at Midsummer, and began winding to a close in mid-September.[17]

When people received healing at healing wells, they often left not only pins and rags but crutches and walking sticks as evidence of their now-healed ailment.

Because power is power and tends to be neutral in nature, what can be used for good can often also be used for evil. Wells known to have power were sometimes used for evil purposes, too. Near Llanudo, Wales, was a spring called *Ffynon Elian*, to which some people would come to take the waters under the pretense of using them for healing, but in reality intending to use them to work harmful magic on their enemies. In times past, this particular well was referred to as the "well of evil." There was a man living near it who was known as the "clerk of the well," and people wishing to harm others by the power of the waters would come to him for assistance. If paid handsomely, the clerk would enter the victim's name in his book, and then work magic on the name by means of pinpricking it or inscribing it on a stone which was then thrown or lowered into the well. Sometimes, instead of the stone an image of the victim was made of wax or dough and pins were stuck into it. In order to remove the curse, the stone or other object had to be retrieved from the well and the victim's name erased from the book.

In their lovely book on the holy wells of Ireland, Walter and Mary Brennemen hypothesize that the holy wells are representative of the *Sacred Center* of a particular area. The Center had to do with the holy being/saint or deity of the place, who was, in essence, a personification of the Power of Place. Through the healing and transformative power of the waters of the healing well, the holy being, saint, or deity makes life possible and must therefore be thanked and honored.[18]

Springs

Closely related to wells are natural springs. There is much folklore regarding the magical efficacy of spring water. When drawn between 11 and 12 P.M. on Christmas or Easter night, it was said to turn into wine and was considered good for digestive and abdominal disorders. For protection against evil spirits, water was silently drawn down stream on Easter morning. Often young men and women would walk to the nearest significant spring on Easter Monday, fill their water jugs, and sprinkle flowers around the surrounding area, as offerings of thanks. This was thought to bring good luck for the coming year. Any water drawn before sunrise on Sundays had magical properties, provided it was taken from three separate springs but drawn into one jug. Water drawn from any important spring at midnight on St. John's Eve would remain pure and fresh for the entire year.[19]

Girls used spring water on May Morning to tell fortunes. Also, there were particular springs in which the flow of water was carefully watched on May Morning, because this flow was thought to determine how the crops and sheep would do that year. If the spring flowed quickly and abundantly, the people felt that things would be scarce; if the spring flowed slowly, it would be a year of plenty.

As we have already mentioned, and as can be seen from the lore above, water sources such as springs and wells were often seen as portals opening into the Otherworlds, particularly the Underworld with its mysterious powers. Since plants and trees spring up out of the Earth, the Underworld powers were seen to be the source that empowered this mysterious power of growth, and therefore, life. Water springing up from deep within the Underworld carried not only the rich minerals from its travels through the layers of the Earth, but also the very energy of creation itself.

Sacred Earth, Sacred Air

Although Fire and Water were the pre-eminently important Elements, this does not imply that the Elements of Air and Earth were not recognized and valued.

AIR

For a culture whose livelihood was so very involved with the sea and with fishing, the correct winds were always of paramount importance.

The Northern winter brought its fierce gales and terrific storms. It is said that there were many Gaelic words for wind, describing every possible variation of wind that existed, a fact which also attests to the importance and significance of wind. As was discussed in the previous chapter, in early Ireland the winds were known not only from their twelve directions of origin, but by their colors, characteristics, and by the influences they brought to bear. Lady Wilde tells us that in some cases auguries were obtained by consideration of the motion of the winds.[20]

In Ireland, a whirlwind sometimes was thought to indicate that a devil was dancing with a witch. It was also believed that the fairies were rushing by in the whirlwind with the intention of carrying off some mortal to their faery palaces or mounds. The only help for this was to throw clay, or sometimes a shoe, at the passing whirlwind. This would cause the faeries to drop their victim.

It was also believed that if a bride steered a boat on her wedding day, the winds and the waves would have no power over it. All brides are, of course, on a very deep level a representation of the Goddess Brigid, who had similar powers, of which the human brides partook.

EARTH

With regard to the Element of Earth, people living on the land are keenly aware how their life is bound up with Earth's bounty and beneficence. They know the power and practical magics of land, of earth, of soil, and of rock. The Earth was honored, loved, and respected for its beauty as well as its bounty. Many customs and practices recorded attest to this, including offerings left for the Earth, harvest festivals, and the making of corn dollies to represent the spirit of the harvest.

As W. G. Wood-Martin says in his book *Traces of the Elder Faiths of Ireland*:

The earth they doubtless regarded as the great power that produces all things, from which all life springs, and to which all life returns. In nothing is the idea more noticeable than in the numerous charms and superstitious observances still in use amongst the peasantry with regard to the burying of objects, animate or inanimate, in mother earth.[21]

The use of clay to make faeries to drop their victims, and the use of iron or salt as protection against the evil influences of faeries and witches demonstrate that the magical "grounding" and "solid" powers of Earth were recognized and utilized in daily life.

END NOTES

1 Wilde, Lady, *Ancient Legends, Mystic Charms & Superstitions of Ireland*, Chatto & Windus, London, 1919, p. 89.

2 Ibid, p. 125.

3 Ibid.

4 Ibid, p. 211.

5 Trevelyan, Marie, *Folklore and Folk-tales of Wales*, Elliot Stock, London, 1909, Chapter 2.

6 Ibid.

7 Wilde, Lady, *Ancient Legends, Mystic Charms & Superstitions of Ireland*, Chatto & Windus, London, 1919, p. 211.

8 McNeil, F. Marian, *The Silver Bough, Vol. 1*. William MacLellan, 1956, Canongate Classics, Edinburgh, 1989, p. 61.

9 Ibid, p. 62.

10 Ibid.

11 Carmichael, Alexander, *Carmina Gadelica, Vol. 1*, Oliver and Boyd, Edinburgh & London, 1928, p. 239.

12 Ibid, p. 233.

13 Wilde, Lady, *Ancient Legends, Mystic Charms & Superstitions of Ireland*, Chatto & Windus, London, 1919, p. 206.

14 Ibid, p. 206.

15 Ibid, p. 124.

16 McNeil, F. Marian, *The Silver Bough, Vol. 1*, William MacLellan, 1956, Canongate Classics, Edinburgh, 1989, p. 64.

17 Clarke, David, with Andy Roberts, *Twilight of the Celtic Gods*, Blandford, Cassell PLC, London, 1996, p. 99.

18 Brenneman, Walter L., Jr., and Mary G., *Crossing the Circle at the Holy Wells of Ireland*, University Press of Virginia, Charlottesville and London, 1995, p. 67.

19 Trevelyan, Marie, *Folklore and Folk-tales of Wales*, Elliot Stock, London, 1909, Chapter 1.

20 Wilde, Lady, *Ancient Legends, Mystic Charms & Superstitions of Ireland*, Chatto & Windus, London, 1919, p. 211.

21 Wood-Martin, W. G., *Traces of the Elder Faiths of Ireland: A Handbook of Irish Pre-Christian Traditions, Vol. I*, Longmans, Greens, and Co., NY and Bombay, 1902, p. 284.

CHAPTER 4

Elements of the Celtic Healing Tradition

The many beliefs and practices associated with faeries and Faery Healing were part of the fabric of the daily lives of the people, inherited from their ancestors. Our study of Faery Healing must be put in a context, so it is important to look at some of these beliefs.

The natural world was full of omens to the Celts. Bird flights and calls, animal movements, the clouds, the whisper of leaves in the wind, the movements of the stars—all these things had meaning and importance. This was the way the gods communicated with humanity. These things revealed the will of the gods, therefore a correct interpretation of them was vital. It was important to be in alignment with the powers of the universe and to not cause offense to the gods. The Druids had been knowledgeable about these things, of course, and had known how to observe and interpret the signs and omens. Later in time, with the coming of the new religions, the same basic belief was held. God communicated to humans through nature as well as through priests and Scripture. Some of the remnants of these ways of communication have survived down into our times and are recorded in the folkloric sources.

In discussing the Faery Healing Tradition we will be focusing on the folkloric material gathered over the last few centuries from Ireland, Scotland, Wales, Isle of Man, and England. By isolating what seem to be key elements that repeatedly appear in the folk healing traditions of these countries, we can learn much about the prevailing practices, and more importantly, discern the beliefs which underlie them.

Like all traditional cultures, the Celts made use of nature's offerings in their healing practice. They used the plants, trees, animals, and stones found around them for healing purposes. However, since they lived in such close relationship with the natural world and because they were an intensely spiritual people, the plants, trees, animals, and stones were used not only for their physical properties but quite often with an awareness of their metaphysical properties as well. By and large, this knowledge was the province of specialists: first, the Druids, and later on, the folk healers—the Wise Women, Cunning

Men, and of course, the Faery Doctors. Over the course of time some of this passed down into "common knowledge," though the folklore tells us that the Faery Doctors held many healing secrets unknown to the common man or woman. We will discuss this in more depth in *Chapter 5*.

This chapter will look at the various elements that make up the Faery Healing Tradition. These include the healing uses made of plants, trees, animals, stones, colors, and numbers.

In addition, we will examine some of the more mystical practices within the Celtic healing traditions such as the importance of light and darkness, the significance of silence and secrecy, and the use of sound, especially in the form of charms and incantations. These practices, which might be termed magical or mystical, were particularly important as they worked at a mental-psychological level, an energetic level, and even on spiritual levels, thus enhancing the efficacy of other, more physically based healing practices.

We will also look at the use of mind-emotion-power, or what was called *mesmerism* in the 19th and early 20th centuries. Mesmerism is related to (though not the same as) what we now would call hypnotism, and to the states of consciousness capable of being induced by trance or journey work.

As we look at all of these facets of the healing tradition, we will see how things work together in a magnificent holism of mind and body and spirit.

The Many Aspects of a Cure

Just as there are many aspects to a human being, there are many aspects to a cure. A good and effective cure is one in which many of those human aspects are engaged. Mind, beliefs, emotions, body, spirit—all these play their very necessary and important parts.

The many aspects of a cure can be divided into the rough categories of physical, magical, psychological, and spiritual, all of which we will look at in turn. In Celtic and Faery Healing Traditions, these aspects, particularly the physical and magical-spiritual aspects, are so interwoven as to be almost inseparable. Nevertheless, I will attempt to tease them apart, albeit briefly, just enough to catalog them before allowing them to flow together once again in my descriptions of their uses. In later chapters we will focus more on the specifics of the various plants, herbs, and trees.

In brief, the physical elements of the cures involved the use of such physical substances as plants, trees, animals, iron, stones, crystals, milk, butter, salt, teas, salves, saliva, water, and fire. The magical elements of the cures involved spiritual beliefs and practices, charms, amulets, and incantations, attention to time, tide, and season, sun and moon, light and dark. The psychological elements of the cures involved certain beliefs relative to the omens, indicators, transference, charms, and the incantations which were used as part of the process.

Physical Aspects of a Cure
The Green World

As stated above, all traditional cultures have a good knowledge of the healing virtue of the plants and trees that surround them. Upon this knowledge, their very survival depends.

Herbs

Lady Wilde informs us that it was from their advanced knowledge of herbs that the Tuatha De Danaan gained their reputation as great sorcerers.[1] Dian Cecht, during the Battle of Moytura, prepared a bath of healing herbs into which the dead and wounded were placed, and they emerged healed and whole. The bath could not heal the king's battle-severed hand, however, so Dian Cecht made him a silver hand and the king was known thereafter as Nuada Argentlam (*Nuad Airgeat lamh*) or Nuada of the Silver Hand.

Dian Cecht's daughter Airmid was also known to be a healer. When her brother Miach was killed by their jealous father, Airmid tended Miach's grave. To her surprise, she found that many healing herbs had grown upon it—one herb for each day of the year and each nerve of the body. She gathered them up in her cloak. Later, possibly in his envy at her knowledge, Dian Cecht mixed them up so she would not know their correct properties.

This rather extraordinary story indicates that the ancients were extremely conversant with the healing powers of herbs and knew a great deal about treating a good many human ills, a position lent credence by what we have already mentioned about the reputation of the Druids as healers.

As time passed and religions changed, and Druidism lost its power and influence to the Christian influx, at least some of the medical knowledge and practices of the Druids seems to have passed into the keeping of certain *physician families*. These families carried the knowledge for many years. Although some of the physician families were still extant in the 19th century when the folklore was being collected, much of the herbal healing tradition had trickled down into the hands of the folk healers known as Faery Doctors, who were said to have obtained their knowledge of herbal healing from the faeries.

Medicines from plants and trees were used for healing both faery-induced ills and the more mundane physical ills. When used to treat faery-induced diseases, the various plant medicines used were often tied onto the body or carried in pockets or pouches, or used in the form of teas or baths. Because magic and medicine were so intertwined, charms and ceremonies were used along with the plants for both kinds of ailments. Sometimes the charms themselves made use of plants, such as the use of rowan twigs bound with red thread to create a cross-shaped amulet protective against evil spirits, faeries, and witches.

Faery Doctors were sent for when people became seriously ill. Female Faery Doctors, often called Faery Women, were especially called upon when a child became ill as it was thought that only they had the secret herbal knowledge necessary to heal the child. The treatment usually consisted of the child consuming an herbal drink which had been prepared by the Faery Woman. The drink was, of course, prepared with the usual charms and chants.

A childless woman was thought to have the strongest power over the secrets of herbs, particularly herbs used to cure children's sicknesses.

Faery Doctors both male and female knew the secrets of when and how to pull the plants for healing purposes, and the correct charms and incantations to say while pulling them. The time of the year and day, and the phase of the moon made a difference; and different plants had different requirements. The Faery Healers knew *all* of these things, whilst the average person knew only some of them.

It was common knowledge, for instance, that herbs picked on May Eve had a special, sacred, and mystical healing power, but only if pulled in the name of the Trinity. If pulled in the name of the devil, their power was then diverted to evil purpose. These special May Eve herbs could be made by the Faery Doctors into powerful potions which no sickness could resist. One of the chief herbs used thus was yarrow, known to have so many virtues and uses that in Ireland it was called "the herb of seven needs or cures."

Other herbs, such as St. Johns Wort, attained their maximum virtue if pulled on the feast day of St. John, June 24th, at midday, the time of the sun's greatest power.

Some herbs could not be harvested by human hand lest their power turn to ill and therefore various measures were devised to harvest them. One of these was to tie the plant to a dog's foot and then cause the dog to run away. This would pull up the plant, now quite safe for human use.

In *Part II* we will delve more deeply into the magical and medicinal uses of plants.

ANIMALS AND INSECTS

Various animals and insect parts were often part of the cures. Crushed and burned snail shells were boiled and served up to cure consumption cases, and it is probable that the high mineral content of the shells was of benefit for such a wasting type of disease because minerals help repair body tissue. Snails themselves were boiled up along with barley, and the resulting liquid was given to cure consumption.

Spiders were often gulped down, eaten web and all in a lump of butter, or worn suspended in a cloth sack around the neck to cure a variety of ailments ranging from chronic cough to consumption.

Though it seems repulsive and hard for us to understand today, animal dung was thought to have healing power and was used in several types of cures. In Ireland, goose dung boiled in milk was a specific for jaundice. An ointment made from goose dung and hog lard was used for ringworm, and a poultice of fresh cow dung was used to heal a bacterial skin infection known as erysipelas or St. Anthony's Fire. While many of the old cures have value today, it does seem best to leave these particular ones in the past!

THE MINERAL WORLD

Iron

Throughout faerylore, we continually run into the information that the faery folk detested iron. To this day no one quite knows why this is so, though there is much speculation—historical, anthropological, and chemical. (For my own speculations on this subject see *Chapter 10*.)

One of the speculations is that iron's magnetic properties cause it to block or redirect energy, thus interrupting and interfering with natural energy flow patterns. We see evidence of this as metal (i.e., iron) stakes have been sometimes driven into the Earth at "power places" to redirect the flow of Earth energies. The current term for these powerful places is "leylines," and some currently term this practice "Earth Acupuncture."

Whether contemporary speculations about iron are correct or not, the people used iron as a protective charm against faeries because the people judged from accumulated folk wisdom and their own experiences that it worked.

Therefore, a piece of iron was often sewn into a baby's clothes before baptism to protect it from being stolen by the faeries before this sacred protective rite could occur.

An iron ring worn on the fourth finger was considered effective against rheumatism, indicating that rheumatism may have been considered to be a faery-caused disease.

Crystals

Lady Wilde says that the use of crystals for charms is of great antiquity in Ireland, and was, perhaps, a mode of divination brought in by an early wandering tribe from the East. Many of these crystal charms have been found throughout the countryside of Ireland. Generally they are globular in shape, and appear to have once been set in royal scepters or sacred shrines.

At Currahmore, the seat of the Marquis of Waterford, one such stone was to be found. Known as the Curraghmore Crystal, it was said to have miraculous curative powers. It was thought to have been brought from the Holy Land by a member of the Irish Le Poer family who received it as a gift from the famous medieval crusader Godrey De Bouillon. As of the 19th century it was still in the possession of the Marquis, who generously loaned it out to people in need. It was a ball-shaped rock crystal, a bit larger than an orange, with a circular band of silver around the middle. People used it to cure sick cattle by placing the ball in a running stream and driving the cattle back and forth across the stream several times. This ball was famous, and people came from all over Ireland to borrow it. It was always returned safe and sound, so greatly was it respected.

Stones

Stones have a widespread use in the Celtic healing traditions. Elf-stones, now thought to be ancient arrowheads, were used as charms to guard cattle. Often, stones used for healing were blessed or charmed by a Faery Doctor, and then cast, or simply rubbed upon the body as part of a healing ceremony.

Three stones were used to cure the Mad Fever. They were charmed by a Faery Doctor who then cast them saying:

The first stone I cast is for the head in the mad fever; the second stone I cast is for the heart in the mad fever; the third stone I cast is for the back in the mad fever. In the name of the Trinity, let peace come. Amen.[2]

Three green stones were used to cure hip disease. These stones had to be gathered in silence from a running brook between midnight and morning. The afflicted leg was then uncovered and each stone was rubbed from hip down to toe several times while saying: "Wear away, wear away, There you shall not stay, Cruel pain—away, away."[3] In this case, the green color of the stones may have represented health and vitality. Such stroking would, of course, put pressure on various acupuncture points along the meridians (energy pathways) which run down the leg, and would actually constitute a form of acupressure.

Nine smooth river stones were used to determine if a sick person would recover from his or her illness. These stones were flung over one's right shoulder and then laid in a turf fire, remaining there untouched for one night. If when struck together the next morning the stones emitted a clear, bell-like sound, the person was destined to die, as this sound was held to be the sound of the church bell being rung for his or her funeral.

Nine black stones gathered before sunrise was a cure used for mumps. The patient was taken, in total silence and with a rope around his neck, to a holy well before sunrise. Then three stones were cast into the well in the name of God, three were cast in the name of Christ, and three were cast in the name of Mary. If this was done three mornings in a row, the person would be healed.[4] In another version of this cure, the person was rubbed with the stones similar to the hip-disease cure given above.[5]

These were very powerful cures as they incorporated the number nine, which is three times the sacred number three. This particular cure incorporates several powerful elements: darkness, silence, the holy well, the stones, and the power of three and nine. The power of the Underworld is here as well with the use of the well, traditionally a portal to the Underworld. The stones carry the magical command down the well and into the Underworld, so that the Underworld's power can bring the wish into being. The fact that the stones must be dark (i.e., black) is also of significance.

A widely used form of healing stone was the bullaun. These were also referred to as cup-marked stones or as "cup and ring" stones. Bullauns are fairly large stones with indentations which collect water. The water was considered very precious and potent for healing and was used for healing everything from rheumatism to eye disorders, and for ensuring fertility as well as safe delivery of children.

Evans Wentz tells us that bullauns were associated with the faeries, and the people would often leave libations of milk for the faeries in them.

In Ireland, very old stone spindle whorls, used in ancient times for spinning fibers, were referred to as "fairy millstones" and were used to cure wounds.[6]

OBJECTS OF MAGIC AND POWER

Salt, Milk, and Fire

One of the most powerful charms against evil was a properly prepared drink of salt and water. In order to be effective, it must be prepared by a Faery Doctor in a specific magical way that included the saying of appropriate magical words over the drink. Since salt is known to kill germs, this would have seemed a rather sensible remedy for the illness of evil.

A small amount of salt tied up in a child's dress when the child was laid in its cradle was used as a charm against the child being stolen by the faeries.[7]

It was considered unwise to ever give away any fire or salt while the butterchurning was going on. Both fire and salt were considered lucky and protective, so to give them away would be to give away your luck and protection. To avert evil one gathered up salt with the left hand and flung it over the right shoulder into the fire.

As such a vital part of most people's diets, milk was a sacred thing. It was poured on the threshold as a protection, but it was considered unlucky to give away, just as with fire and salt.[8]

THREAD MAGIC

Thread is used to sew, bind, tie, and secure things into place. It is not surprising to find that it was used magically for the same purposes. Since sheep were commonly raised, wool thread was frequently used in this kind of magic. Sometimes certain colors of wool thread were required for certain kinds of magic.

Red thread was widely believed to have the ability to prevent faery magic and mischief or to stop it if it was already in progress. As the old Scottish rhyme said:

Rowan bead and red thread
Put witches to their speed…

Or alternately:

Rowan, lammer (amber), and red threid
Pits witches to their speed.

This charm thus combined the protective potencies of both the highly esteemed rowan berry and color red, as well as that of amber, whose golden color linked it with the sun.

Red thread tied across doorways was said to prevent malicious faeries from coming in to carry people away.

Black woolen thread was used as part of a charm to heal sprains. The sprain was bound with the thread while the healer recited a charm stating that the joints, bones, and sinews were now also bound together, and healed by the power of God, the saints, and Mary.

Blue thread was used as a charm in Scotland. It was worn to prevent fevers in nursing mothers, and these valuable thread amulets were handed down from mother to daughter through the generations. Blue thread or yarn was also used for purposes of divination, particularly having to do with marriage partners, such as in the Scottish Halloween rite of "winning the blue clew."

Binding things together with a thread, such as in the example above, was done to cause two things to come together and affect each other, the stronger affecting the weaker, the good affecting the bad. It is, in essence, a *retuning* mechanism of sorts, as it was expected that the "good" (God, his mother, the saints, the angels) would overpower the "bad" (the sprain).

Alexander Carmichael records that in Scotland there was a charm referred to as the "Charm of the Three Threads" that was used to help sick animals, usually cattle. For this charm, a three-ply cord was made, one ply being black, one red, and one white. This "three" was held to relate to the Trinity, but as we have seen three was a sacred number long before Christianity took hold. The black thread represented the condemnation of God on the sickness, the red thread represented the crucifixion of Christ (for blessing and healing), and the white thread represented the purification power of the Holy Spirit. Thus each member of the Trinity lent its special power to the charm: the sickness was condemned, and purification and healing blessings were brought to bear. The three threads were plaited together to form a cord which was then wrapped three times and tied around the animal's tail in the shape of a trefoil loop. As it was wrapped, the cord was spat upon three times, once for each member of the Holy Trinity.[9] This cure, with the appropriate prayers, could also be used for animals afflicted with the Evil Eye.

Interestingly, white, red, and black are the colors traditionally associated with the Triple Goddess—white for the youthful maiden Goddess, red for the fruitful Mother, black for the Old Woman, the Cailleach.

In Ireland, thread or string was often tied around the head to cure headache.[10]

SALIVA, HAIR, AND NAIL PARINGS

There was great belief in the efficacy of saliva, which was seen as sacred, and spitting was used for magical purposes including scaring away the faeries. Saliva was thought to contain the essence of a person because it came from the mouth as did the person's "breath of life." Spitting on wounds was considered to be useful in helping to cleanse them and expedite their healing. The spittle of a fasting person was considered to be very powerful. The people held that there was a blessing in saliva, particularly in the saliva of someone who had been fasting, and that to spit on or *for* something, was like saying, "God bless it."

Care was taken with the proper disposal of hair clippings and nail parings. Both of these things were considered to be an intrinsic and important part of a person. The hair was thought to hold the person's strength and power, and the nails, since they seemed to grow outward from within, were akin to the person's essence in externalized form. Because of this they were considered to function magically as a connection to that person. Therefore, care must be taken that they did not fall into the wrong hands as they could then be used to cause harm to the person by use of the energetic link. Often windows and doors were kept closed while these hygienic trimming exercises were underway lest a stray hair or nail find its way out a window or door. Generally, hair clippings and nail parings were carefully swept up and disposed of by burying them in the ground. Occasionally they were burned, though in some places this was not done as it was thought that the person would be weakened as the fire consumed the hair or nails.[11]

These beliefs were based on the magical concepts of *Sympathy* and *Transference*, which hold that there is a link that exists between an original and its image or a substitute of its image. In other words, there is a *sympathy* between them. Therefore, the image or substitute may be used in place of the original for whatever magical working is desired. See the section on *Magical Beliefs*, on page 66.

Similarly, the belief in spitting seems to have been based on this concept of *sympathy*. To spit on something as a blessing was to put forth this part of one's own substance (the saliva), as well as one's energy and intention, for a specific purpose; a magical act indeed.

The Mystical and Magical Aspects of a Cure
The Power of Color

Green was a color associated with the faeries, and of course, with the plant world and its powers of healing and vitality as well. Because of its association with the faeries, it was considered an unlucky color for humans to wear, as it was thought to call up the faeries or offend them, and thereby increase one's risk of being taken by them. In Britain and in some parts of Ireland faeries were thought to wear various shades of green clothing, but in most of Ireland faeries wore other colors. Green stones were used in various cures.

Red was a color of power and vitality. The protective power of rowan berries was due at least in part to their brilliant red-orange hue. The above-mentioned charm that contained both rowan "bead" and red thread was, therefore, especially potent.

As described above, red was sometimes associated with the faeries since occasionally faeries were reputed to wear red, particularly red caps. This was particularly the case in Ireland where faeries were more often seen in red and white than in green.

Yet red could also be fierce and destructive. According to Lady Wilde, the Irish referred to the East wind as the Red Wind: a demonic wind of accursed and destructive power that blasted and withered trees, land, and people.[12]

Red, being the color of blood, is also the color of vitality, or excitability as Lady Wilde puts it. At Samhain it was believed that the dead could be made to answer questions, but only if blood was sprinkled on the dead body. It was thought spirits loved blood, that it excited them and gave them the power and pretense of life, if only for a brief time.[13]

This belief demonstrates a knowledge of the Life Force as carried by the blood, a knowledge somewhat common to the ancient and medieval worldview.

Red's power to stir things up was sometimes used for healing purposes. In Ireland and Wales, red flannel on the chest was used as a remedy for clearing up chest ailments. Sometimes this flannel was coated with a mixture of herbs and thus acted as a poultice to the lungs. Red was thought to bring in its healing warmth; its expansive nature loosened up tight, contracted places.

Yellow things were thought to cure jaundice. Saffron, bastard saffron, buttercups, yellow iris flowers, and certain of the marigolds were used.[14] Jaundice is a problem of the liver, often stemming from a blocked bile duct or from hepatitis. One of the prime symptoms of jaundice is a yellowing of the skin and the whites of the eyes. It seems to have been a matter of "like cures like" (i.e., sympathy) to use yellow things to cure it. However, it is interesting to note that some yellow plants, dandelion and yellow dock root for instance, are very good liver cleansers, so perhaps there is a bit of folk wisdom here.

Yellow-colored flowers such as cowslip, dandelion, gorse, marigold, primrose, and the like were seen as related to the sun, and thus held the same or similar magical powers as the sun, that of warming, blessing, protecting, casting out evil, and the like. As such, they would have been useful against ill-intentioned faeries and witches.

Blue was occasionally worn by Irish faeries and the faeries in some of the northern isles were seen to wear blue caps. Blue-colored flowers were held to be cooling and soothing medicinally. In Scotland, blue threads were used as charms, and a ball of blue yarn—which was called a clew—was used by witches and other mortals to commune with spirits for the purpose of foretelling the future.

Black seems to have been connected with banishing and destroying. Black stones were used to cure mumps and hip diseases. Black threads were used to bind injuries, the combination of the binding together and the black causing the injury to be banished and healing to occur.

White was a color of purity, often associated with the Otherworlds. The Faery Queen seen by Isobel Gowdie of Scotland in the 1600s was clothed in white linen. Sometimes the *bansidhe* or Irish death messenger was seen dressed in white.

Bracket (Gaelic is *breacan*) may not be thought of as a color, but the Irish frequently used this word to describe the clothing worn by the faery folk. By this term, they meant something variegated in color such as an item with stripes. Although the term bracket actually indicates a combination of colors and perhaps patterns in clothing rather than an actual, single color, the term was a quite important one to the Irish country folk, especially with regard to the description of faery attire.[15]

THE IMPORTANCE OF NUMBER

For the Celts, the number three was sacred from time out of mind. It represented the inherent triplicities of life: earth, sea, and sky; beginning, middle, and end; and many others as well. The Celts viewed many of their deities in this way, Ireland itself being represented by a triune goddess—Banba, Fotla, and Eire, the latter giving her name to Ireland. When the Christian doctrine of the Holy Trinity entered Ireland and other Celtic lands, it did not find difficult acceptance. The sanctity of the number three is found in all Celtic nations, in folklore, and in such widely differing traditions as the Pagan Triple Goddess Brigid, and the Christian Holy Trinity. The latter was supposedly explained to the Irish Pagans by St. Patrick by the use of the three-leafed shamrock. The concept was, however, nothing new to the Irish.

It is not surprising to find that the number three and its multiples, especially nine, appear often in the Celtic healing traditions. Holy wells are circuited three times, sometimes nine. A session with a Faery Doctor might involve three visits within a week.

If three was sacred, nine was triply so, and twenty-seven, being three times nine, very sacred indeed. In traditional numerology, the number nine is about completion. Its use in cures is obviously to bring the illness to completion.

Five was also a number of significance, though not as important as three. There were five pre-Gaelic invasions of Ireland, Ireland was divided into five provinces (four and the center), and had five great roads. Interestingly, it was said that faeries counted by fives.[16]

Aside from the mystical significance of these numbers, when actions are performed or charms recited more than once or even twice, a pattern is created, and the actions or words begin to assume a magical importance and significance (Catholics accustomed to reciting the rosary are well aware of this fact). It is as if their importance is emphasized with each repetition, the magical message of the actions or words sinking deeper into the psyche of the reciter and listener until the subconscious levels become involved. The words or actions need to occur more than once or twice, as there is something very different, very *complete* about the number three, representing, as it would seem, a complete *cycle*: the resultant offspring of the marriage of one and two. So it's not surprising in a way, to recall that "the third time is the charm!"

TIME AND TIDE, LIGHT AND DARK

Traditionally, encounters with faeries have taken place at times and places that are, in some way, *borderlands*, that is, times and places which are thresholds where one reality gives way to another. This can be a place such as where cultivated lands meet up with the wild lands; or at the seashore, which is not sea but not really land either; or at places where springs emerge from the Earth; places where two rivers or springs meet; or often even boundaries between properties. A borderland can also be a time such as twilight, which is neither light nor dark. In the cycle of the year these twilights or borderlands are represented by Samhain, when summer gives way to winter, and Beltaine, when winter becomes summer. They are also represented by the equinoxes, times of twilight, and the solstices, times where light gives way to darkness and darkness to light, and midnight, when one day becomes another. On an archetypal level, all these represent the borderland between normal consciousness and paranormal consciousness. This concept is also referred to as *liminality*.

Faery Time

Time itself was said to run differently within the Faery Realm. Those who had been in the Faery Realm or interacted with it in some way always stated that what seemed a brief time while they were there proved to have been a long time once they'd returned; or that what had seemed a long time in Faery had proven to be a short time in the outer world. Sometimes it was said that time in the Faery Realm was the reverse of our time, with the actual seasonal pattern reversed so that when it was summer there was winter here, and so on. But this is simply a way of stating that the time perceptions there were completely different than our normal human time perceptions, and seemed, in fact, to be the complete opposite.

The truth of the matter is that because the Land of Faery lies within the subtle Otherworlds of our planet, it is subject to the timescales which apply there. The planet is huge and very old. The beings who are the spirits of mountains, valleys, plains, canyons, deserts, rocks, and even some trees, as well as the beings who live deep within the land, are ancient. They have a different yesterday and tomorrow than we do. Their time is not about the rising and setting of the sun, it is about the rising and falling of mountain ranges and ocean levels. Theirs is geologic time, not solar time. Time is very different to them than it is to us, and when we are in their realm we will experience time from their perspective rather than from our own. Sometimes this feels very slow; often, it may feel almost timeless, which may be closest to the actual truth of the thing.

This difference in time is very important as it is a key to understanding how it is possible, in faery work, to work across time—moving within past, present, and future. Time is a factor of materiality. When we step out of materiality, out of form and into Spirit, we step out of time. When we step into the Faery Realm we are in the subtle, non-material world, and may therefore move around in time by our intention and imagination, traveling by way of the spiral of time, which is akin to the spiraling of the stars.

This awareness is helpful because it can be used in Faery Healing work, during which we may need to work beyond time, or beyond our "side" of time, sending healing energy to what is, in our small human perception, past, present, or future.

Days of the Week

The days of the week had significance with regard to the faery folk, although the significance varied a bit from country to country.

Sunday—even the very mention of it was taboo to faeries, presumably because it was the Christian holy day. Sunday is of course the day of the sun, which symbolizes all that is—to human sensibilities—bright, warm, and blessed.

Some said that Sunday, particularly the evening, was considered a good day to pull herbs for healing, but others said it was not a good day. "A Sunday cure is no cure," said Mrs. Quaid, one of the women Yeats spoke with on this issue.

Monday was good for working charms to protect against faery wiles. It was a safe day and could be used for cures, except for the first Monday of a quarter. Monday was considered a good day to pick herbs for healing and for Faery Doctors to do their healing.

Tuesday was considered a good day to pick herbs for healing.

Wednesday was regarded as a day of danger in both Ireland and Wales, almost as bad as Friday.

Thursday was thought to be a safe day. On Thursday, the faeries could hear nothing that was said of them. This belief was local to the Scottish Highlands and relates to the holiness of St. Columba's Day. To say *Thursday*, or even refer to it, was a charm against being overheard by "them." Thursday was a good day for Faery Doctors to do their healing. Often they did three-day sessions on either Monday-Thursday-Monday or Thursday-Monday-Thursday.

Friday in Ireland was the day when faeries were thought to have the most power to work evil, therefore Friday was considered a bad day to begin projects, journeys, or have weddings. On Fridays the spirits were thought to be present everywhere, and able to see and hear everything that was going on and to spoil it if they chose, "just out of malice and jealousy of the mortal race."[17] Friday was the day they struck cattle with elf bolts, lamed horses, stole milk, and carried off beautiful children, leaving changelings in their stead. Friday was considered the most unlucky day of all the week.[18]

Often people seeking healing took an oath never to comb their hair on a Friday so that the memory of the grace of healing received would remain till their death (this will be discussed in depth below).[19]

In parts of Scotland, Friday was considered a dangerous day, a day when the faeries could enter homes and behave in an impudent, menacing manner. But in the Scottish Highlands, Friday was considered a safe day, to which "thanks and memory" were associated.

Saturday was considered to be Mary's Day. It was considered a safe day and one on which cures could be done.

Monday, Tuesday, Thursday, and Saturday were generally considered the best days to gather herbs for Faery Healing, though some people thought Sunday was all right too.

The First Monday of the Quarter
This first Monday after one of the Quarter Days of Imbolc, Beltaine, Lughnasadh, and Samhain was considered an auspicious day in many ways. People arose quite early and began the day by being blessed with water which had been obtained by a wise woman, or with water obtained from a woman who had the bridle of the water-horse (a dangerous water-dwelling Faery Being; thus a woman holding its bridle is powerful). It was a good day for lovers to both draw together and to part.

This was a favorite day for people of the Evil Eye to practice their evil art, so everyone had to be careful of it. Cattle had to be protected the whole day. In fact, sometimes the owner kept them inside and made sure his was the only eye that saw them all day long. It was also the day when, supposedly, witches spirited away the milk. It was considered a bad day to lend anyone anything, for it was thought that the luck of the house went with it.

But it was also the day for the men and women who practiced the *frith* or augury to ask for their visions. This was done in a very specific way which will be described later in this chapter.

Times of the Day and Night
Noon was the time of the brightest, strongest sun and was therefore considered a benevolent time.

Twilight was a "borderlands" or faery time, and was one of the times when the veil between the worlds was thin. Dawn and dusk are faery times, when the Faery Realm is more accessible, and faeries are more active and likely to be seen.

Between sunset and midnight evil spirits were thought to be at their strongest.

Times of the Moon
The time of the full moon, as well as just before and just after it, was associated with faeries and their power. They were said to hold their revels under the full moon.[20]

Seasons of the Year
The faeries were most active around the times of the four great festivals, but especially around May Day and All Hallows Eve. May Day is, of course, the old feast of Beltaine, the beginning of summer and the Tide of Life, while All Hallows, the old Celtic feast of Samhain, occurred at the close of the season. Interestingly, faeries were said to be very active around the last day of the year. In our era this is December 31, but by the older Celtic reckoning it was October 31, the festival of Samhain.

The faeries were also very active around St. John's Day, which is equivalent to the Summer Solstice and near the Catholic feast of Whitsunday. St. John's Day fell within the peak of the Tide of Life. Since the power of the sun was at its highest and strongest, St. John's Day was the best time for picking the wonderfully protective St. John's Wort, while May Eve was best for picking yarrow, so that both of these herbs would have their maximum potency.

Midsummer was the time of year at which the faeries were most likely to steal beautiful young women, so it was quite helpful that the flowers and plants most useful in protecting against faeries were also at their strongest.

MAGICAL PRACTICES
SOUND, SILENCE, AND SECRECY
Rhymes, songs, incantations, prayers, and charms are part of magical practice worldwide, and the Celtic countries were no exception. Considering the rich Bardic tradition that was part of the history of these lands, it would be surprising had it been otherwise.

Charms, incantations, and prayers were a very important part of the healing process. These were, in fact, such an integral part of the process that the efficacy of any given remedy would have been questioned had it not been accompanied by the proper incantation or charm. This gives us a clear illustration of the value attributed to the power of sound, in this case, in the form of the power of the spoken or chanted word.

Equally important was the value of silence and secrecy. Faery Doctors often advised those they treated to travel home in complete silence, speaking to no one till they had completed their course of treatment. This silence conserved the magical power of the cure, which would have *flowed out* with the sound had the person broken the spell by speaking. Secrecy was similar; it likewise conserved the power which speech would have spilled outward. Faery Doctors were required to keep their magics, charms, and mysteries secret so that the power of these magics would not be misused, or worse, lost entirely.

CROSSES AND CIRCLES

Crosses and circles were both considered to be very powerfully protective symbols. For Catholics (and Catholicism was the dominant religion in Europe for over 1,000 years), the sign of the cross was always a meaningful religious symbol, but the use of the four-armed cross as a sacred symbol significantly predates Christianity. The sign of the cross is made by touching the forehead, the heart, and the area just below both shoulders as one says, "In the name of the Father (head), the Son (heart,) and the Holy Ghost (shoulders)." This makes the shape of a cross whose center lies in the area of the throat chakra, an interesting link to the power of word and sound.

Interestingly, the sign of the cross combines the rather solid, balanced power of the Four (the Four Directions, Four Elements) with the sacred power of the Three (the Trinity, the Three Realms, and all the other sacred threes). It is quite a powerful symbol no matter which deities are invoked.

The *caim* is mentioned by Alexander Carmichael as having been used in Scotland, although it may have been used in other areas as well. The word means *encompassing*. The caim is, in essence an encompassing, protective circle. It was made by extending the forefinger and using it to draw a circle around oneself while pivoting around, calling on God, the Blessed Virgin, or one of the saints for protection while doing so. This protective circle was thought to travel and move with the person wherever he or she went. Thus, it was really a technique that, through the power of intention and prayer, protectively strengthened the person's auric field by calling in the higher powers to guard and strengthen it.

AMULETS AND TALISMANS

The making and wearing of magical amulets and talismans was an important part of the healing tradition.

Amulets are magical devices made for purposes of protection. An amulet "contains" magic in some way. Sometimes magical symbols, sigils, or words are written upon it; sometimes the magic is in the form of the amulet having been empowered by a blessing. In Ireland, an amulet against sickness was made of a piece of paper upon which was written the first three verses of the Gospel of St. John, which, not surprisingly, are the verses which equates the "Power of the Word" with God:

> *In the beginning was the Word, and the Word was with God, and the Word was God. The same was in the beginning with God. All things were made by him; and without him, not any thing made that was made.*

Amulets were occasionally used as protection against the Evil Eye. The amulet was rolled or folded up so that it could be placed in a small bag and worn around the neck. This practice is similar to one used in esoteric Judaism where words from the Torah are written upon paper or parchment, rolled up and worn for blessings and protection.

Often, certain herbs were placed in the bag to add to the amulet's power. Incantations and charms of blessing and protection were spoken over the amulet during its preparation as well. The use of herbs and charms as part of the process is characteristic of Celtic healing.

Lady Wilde mentions an amulet used for epilepsy. The amulet was made of an elder twig broken into nine one-inch pieces which were then tied together by a three-ply silk thread. This was worn around the neck next to the skin. If the thread broke and the amulet fell, it had to be buried in the Earth and a new one made, as the charm's power was *earthed* (i.e., lost by contact with the Earth) when it touched the ground. This amulet incorporates the magic of the sacred three and the sacred nine, as well as the magical powers of the elder tree.

Amulets work on several magical principles. One of these principles is that of the power inherent in symbols as sacred patterns of words or images that embody power; another principle has to do with the *Power of Sound* as inherent in the blessings spoken during the amulet's preparation, consecration, and use.

Talismans are magical devices designed to attract beneficial influences. They are often made similarly to amulets, but with the intention to attract a beneficial energy rather than avert an evil one.

BINDING

Binding was another magical procedure. Binding caused two things to come together and affect each other, the stronger affecting the weaker, the good affecting the bad. The binding procedure involved literally binding or tying a sprain with a piece of wool (often black) while reciting a charm to the effect that the joints, bones, and sinews were now bound together and healed by the divine or saintly powers.

Binding used the *Power of Sound* (the charm/incantation) along with the *Principle of Association*, in which two things having elements in common may interact through the power of those shared elements. This is a slight variation on the *Principle of Sympathetic Magic* and the *Law of Similarities*. The variation is that with *Principle of Association* the power of the stronger of the two will affect and "retune" the power of the weaker. Thus, to use the example above, the greater power of God, Mary, and the saints will retune the sprained area, causing the misaligned muscles and sinews to come back into their normal, healthy, and harmonious state of being.

DIVINATIONS, OMENS AND INDICATORS

As can be seen by virtually *all* of this information, divination—the process of trying to look into the future to find an outcome—was an inherent part of Celtic tradition. It dated at least as far back as the Druids who were well known in the ancient world for their skill in augury. As such, it is not surprising to find it in use as part of the healing process, as well as at those liminal or borderlands times of the year, the all-important Quarter Days, and those significant times of day—dawn, dusk, midday, and midnight. These divinations were generally referred to as auguries.

The basis of the auguries was observation of signs presented by nature, a time-honored practice used by the Druids as well as many other cultures. The Divine Voice speaks through nature, so the abilities to see and interpret the signs were, and are, abilities greatly valued. Therefore, divination was done on the flight of birds, the sounds of birds, the movements of animals, and the patterns of clouds, as well as many other natural phenomena.

Several of the old techniques for augury have come down to us in the form of literary references and folk traditions. One of the most interesting ones was called *frith*, which means simply "augury." Alexander Carmichael's *Carmina Gadelica* tells us that it was widely used in the Highlands and Islands of Scotland, an area with strong Scandinavian influence.

Though the description comes from times obviously recent and Christian, the technique itself has a distinctly archaic and Pagan ring to it.

The *frith* was done just before sunrise on the first Monday of the quarter, the Quarter Days being Imbolc (Brigid/Candlemas), Beltaine (May Eve, Roodmas), Lughnasadh (Lammas), Samhain (Halloween/Hallowmas), and was used to divine the omens for the coming quarter. The frith was also used to determine the whereabouts of lost people or animals.

The augurer, fasting, barefooted, and bareheaded, arose before sunrise, and with closed eyes made his way to the doorway that led outside. Placing one hand on each of the door jambs, the augurer mentally "beseeched the God of the unseen" to grant him his augury and show him what he sought (I am using the masculine pronoun, but women also performed auguries). Then he opened his eyes and looked steadfastly straight ahead, carefully observing what was there to be seen. After this he interpreted his observations.

A variation on this technique was for the augurer to create a tube or pipe using the palms of his hands and to look through it at what there was to be seen. Sometimes this augury was referred to as the Augury of Mary (*frith Mhoire*), as it was thought that this was the technique the Virgin Mary had used to find the child Jesus when he was lost but later found in the Temple in Jerusalem. Note the many thresholds or borderlands in this procedure. It was done at dawn, on a Quarter Day, neither indoors nor outdoors, and begun while awake but with eyes closed.

It is interesting to note that this was done on a Monday which is really "Moon Day," the day of the moon. Perhaps this hearkens back to a time when a lunar calendar was in use. Traditionally, the moon has been tied into cycles, particularly women's cycles, and is also linked with things such as intuition, sensitivity, and psychism. It is interesting that the frith was done on the first Monday of each quarter as the four quarters of the year are somewhat analogous to the four phases of the moon, thus providing another link to the various lunar correspondences of cycle, rhythm, intuition, and psychism.

Divinations of various sorts were also done as part of the festivities at Beltaine and Samhain and occasionally at Candlemas, which falls within a day of the Feast of Brigid. On May Eve, the young women used yarrow to divine the identity of their future lover. They danced around it, put a sprig of it under their pillows that night, and hoped for a prophetic dream.[21]

Omens and indicators were used on an everyday basis to determine the outcome of situations. Sometimes an herb such as yarrow was placed in a sick person's hand. If the yarrow withered in the hand after a number of hours (by the next morning for instance), the person would not recover. It the yarrow did not wither the person would recover.[22]

Mentioned in the previous chapter was the method of determining the outcome of sickness by taking take nine smooth stones from running water. These were then flung over one's right shoulder and laid in a turf fire to remain untouched for the night. The next morning they were struck together, and if they emitted a clear, bell-like sound the sick person was doomed to death, as the sound of the stones was thought to represent the sound of the church bell tolling for his or her funeral.

Magical Beliefs

There were several deep-seated beliefs that were part of the healing tradition simply because they were so commonly held. In truth, the *Magical Practices* given above were based on the *Magical Beliefs* given below and elsewhere in this book. I have separated them only for the convenience of writing about them.

The Power of the Priests. As with all technicians of the sacred, priests were believed to be capable of doing cures if they so chose. Sometimes they did so, by use of the rites of the church. But according to Lady Wilde and W. B. Yeats, the Faery Healers and Herb Women were much more popular with the people, although they were not popular with the priests.

Assorted Magical Beliefs. In Ireland, there was a belief that worms of various kinds were responsible for various diseases. In a society that must have seen plenty of worms, maggots, and other small wiggly creatures in the course of life, this is not a surprising belief. When you really think about it, it's not much of a stretch up to our current belief in small, swimming, or wiggling, microbial life-forms as the cause of disease.

Several of the folk practices involve this belief about worms. For instance, there was a belief that when a seventh son was born, if an earthworm was put into the child's hand and kept there till it died, the child would have the power to charm away all diseases. If an earthworm was put into the hand of a soon-to-be-baptized child and kept there till it died, that child would have the power to cure all children's diseases.[23]

Beliefs about seventh sons, and especially seventh sons of sevenths sons, were very prevalent. The seventh son of a seventh son had power over all diseases and could cure them by the laying on of hands. The double sevens were believed to have the Second Sight as well.[24]

A son born after his father's death was held to have power over fevers. A child born in the evening was held to have the ability to see spirits, such as ghosts and faeries, and to have power over ghosts. A child born in the daytime did not possess this talent.[25]

Concerning ghosts, it was believed that neither they nor devils could cross running water, particularly at night, so one could obtain safety from them by crossing it.[26]

Among the very deep-seated beliefs about faeries were concerns about the vengeful nature of faeries, as well as the fear of being trapped in their realms.

Faeries were known to take terrible revenge if offended or slighted by such things as treading on their homes or refusing them entrance into one's own home if they came knocking. Such trespasses incurred no small amount of wrath from them, and the result might be the infliction, temporarily or permanently, of blindness, weakened limbs, or even lameness upon the offender or one of his household. This belief was taken quite seriously and great care was taken to not cause offense.

To partake of food or drink, and in some cases, to hear the faery music, while in the Faery Realm, brought an enchantment which bespoke discontent and/or death. In some cases, the person never returned from Faery. In other cases, the person might return in body, but was never quite as he or she had been before, and often died soon thereafter.

These experiences point to the truth of the Faery Queen's admonition to Thomas Rhymer to not eat the fruit of the trees of the Underworld because they contained "all the plagues of hell." The real message was that the Faery Realm and the human realm are different, having different vibrational frequencies; and what is sustenance to the beings of one realm may not be appropriate for beings of the other. It must be remembered that when faeries took human food, they consumed not the material portion but only the *essence* of the food—that is, its pure, raw, energetic, vibrational essence. Humans, having material physical forms, generally *need* that essence cloaked in material form; otherwise it may be too strong.

Psychological Aspects of a Cure

There are many magical and psychological elements that figure into these cures.

Love is an element that shows up in some of the cures. Sometimes, in order to be effective, a remedy had to be given freely and with love, rather than made or purchased by the sufferer.

Transference occurs when a disease is relocated from the sufferer to another living being, whether it be animal, plant, or insect. Lady Wilde gives a few examples of this. In one instance, a rather nasty-looking insect was imprisoned in a bottle. As it died, the sick person recovered. In another instance, children with mumps were taken to the pigsty and had their head rubbed against the pig's back in an effort to transfer the mumps to the pig.

Contagion is a variation of transference and occurs in situations during which a body part is used to represent the entire body and its disease. Nail parings, for instance, or pieces of hair might be so used. The basis of this belief is that beings and items which have been in contact with each other continue to interact even after they have been separated, a belief which clearly refers to their energetic component rather than the physical. The body part so used was then dealt with magically, such as by being buried in the ground or thrown in the sea, thus taking the disease along with it. The key element here is that "the part represents the whole."

Sympathetic Magic works on the principle of the *Law of Similarities*. It works by using the power of imitation, and "like equals like." Lady Wilde gives several examples of this. For instance, to extract a thorn the healer must possess power over thorns. Therefore, the power of thorns was invoked, usually in the form of reference to Christ's crown of thorns. This granted the power to effectively and safely extract the thorn from the afflicted.

Another instance of sympathetic magic was in the use of graveyard clay from a newly made grave to destroy feelings of love between two lovers. It was shaken between them, thus invoking the power of death it contained, to destroy their love.

Soil walked over by pallbearers at a funeral was applied to warts, which were then *wished away* by the death power contained in the funeral-related soil.

Yet another example of this kind of magic was related to getting rid of toothaches. The person with the toothache would go to a grave, kneel, and say a prayer for the deceased. Then, he would take a handful of grass from the grave, chew it, and spit it out. The power of death, in this case directed at the toothache, was invoked by chewing the grass from the grave. The prayers said previously for the benefit of the deceased protected the person from that same power of death by showing his goodwill and good intention. Therefore, the power of death would work only on the toothache, and work so powerfully that it ensured against any further toothaches during the course of the person's life.

Magical Words and the Power of Sound are amply illustrated in the healing tradition by the fact that the Faery Healers almost always recited or sang incantations and prayers in conjunction with the other treatments they administered. The basis of this is a belief in the *Power of Sound* to alter reality and create change. *'In the beginning was the*

Word,' says the Bible. Although this belief may be looked upon as a simple-minded belief in "magic words," it arose from older, more sophisticated understandings of the power inherent in sound waves and frequencies, and their patterns. Those Bards and Druids of old, with their reputed power to raise boils, cause deformities, induce sleep, and bring about storms with the power of their songs and chants, must have known something!

The Power of Opposites is illustrated in the power attributed to both sound and silence. This is shown in the cures in which Faery Doctors prepared a potion, complete with appropriate prayers and incantation, and then instructed the person to journey home in silence and to take the remedy in silence. The power of sound, the prayers and incantations, bring in the healing power which must be then carefully conserved by the opposite power, that of silence, in order for the remedy to be effective.

Subtle Energy Work may have been the basis of another magical-seeming procedure used by Faery Healers. They called it *stroking*.

A similar technique described but not named by Lady Wilde was one in which the healer would make passes with his hand over the afflicted part of the body, moving very slowly at a slight distance away from the body while indistinctly muttering a chant or incantation in a low voice. This was used for the pains of rheumatism and Lady Wilde compares it to mesmerism.

When I first read of these things, the picture that flashed before my eyes was one of the healer stroking the sick person, either physically or within the person's *aura*, or energy field, with long, gliding motions which followed the body's natural lines, and perhaps the pathways of energy which flow through the body. These pathways are referred to in Chinese medicine as the *meridians* although the ancient Irish most likely had their own beliefs and names for them. Such a stroking motion by one capable of moving energy through their hands could quite effectively loosen stuck energies and get them flowing properly again. Sometimes this was referred to as *the touch*. Curing by laying on of hands is found in many cultures of the world in various forms, and is often accompanied by prayers and incantations. My own mother possessed *the touch*. She used love, compassion, and silent prayer rather than incantations, but her hands would grow hot, and the pain would be relieved.

Combinations of Powerful Things were considered especially powerful and useful. One example of this is the old Gaelic *birth baptism* performed for newborns shortly after birth by the midwife. These involved water, fire, number, circles, sound, and the powers of sun and moon. This baptism was considered very important because it blessed and protected the child from all manner of spiritual evils until the formal church baptism could be performed.

There are a few variants of the birth baptism. Generally speaking, when a child was born he or she was passed over a flame three times from the midwife to the father while the midwife murmured a prayer to the fire-god invoking this god's power and blessing on the little one. The father then carried the child three times around the fire while more words were murmured to the power of the sun-god. The midwife then anointed the child's forehead with three drops of water while invoking for the child the blessings of each member of the Trinity, thus consecrating the child to these three powers and invoking their protection on him or her.

A bath was prepared for the child; a gold coin and a silver coin were placed into this bath. While these coins were said to invoke love of peace, wealth, joyousness, means, good fortune, goodness, and victory, the sun/moon symbolism is quite obvious. The bathwater itself was quite possibly drawn from a spring water source. The midwife held the child over the bath and poured nine handfuls of water over him or her while singing or chanting a blessing which invoked the virtues and blessings mentioned above. The child was then lowered into the water and given its first bath.[27]

Thus was the child baptized in the old way, bringing in the blessings of sun and moon, Fire and Water, and the ever-sacred three.

In yet another example of the combination of powerful things, Lady Wilde mentions that a person wishing to cure a toothache performed an interesting ritual that included several magical beliefs and practices. The person seeking the cure must make a vow to God, the Virgin Mary, and, interestingly, to the new moon, that he would never comb his hair on a Friday. He vowed this in remembrance of the relief he would feel should his toothache be cured. In addition, the person promised to fall upon his knees, wherever he might be, and say five prayers of gratitude for his cure whenever he thereafter saw the moon.

This cure is so interesting, combining so many powerful and archaic elements, that I would like to spend a bit of time deciphering it. It uses the sacredness of the moon, especially the new moon, that lovely lamp of the night which represents purity and new beginnings, and being a light in the darkness shows itself to be a sign of God's care for his children. The ritual also uses vows to God, and to the Virgin—whose virtues included purity and the loving concern of a Mother. We can immediately see that the help and loving care of the Higher Beings, the Divine Parents was being called upon, with a request for new beginnings. The promise to say the five prayers of gratitude upon sight of the new moon thereafter not only brings in the magical number of five, but uses the moon with its already mentioned rich symbolism as a trigger for remembering to be grateful.

The person vows to never comb his hair on a Friday, and this seems, at first, rather curious. Why not comb the hair? Although Lady Wilde describes this practice as being done so that the person so healed would retain the "memory of the grace of healing received" until his dying day, the practice itself, especially combined with its other elements, seems essentially a much more archaic one.

The hair aspect is quite possibly related to the old magic of binding and loosening in which strands and threads were used to magically bind and hold, or loosen and free the object of the magic (as mentioned in the section on *Binding*, above). This concept is related, ultimately, to that of the Norns or Fates, who spin and weave the destiny-strands that make up the tapestry of our individual and collective fate. This is a very old belief found in many cultures. Therefore, to comb the hair was, in such a magical/spiritual context, to interfere with the setting of the destiny-strands into the position desired and prayed for. One did not comb the hair because one did not want to interfere with the destiny-strands set into place by the prayers and promises just made.

The next question is "why Friday?" In Ireland, Friday was considered the most unlucky day of the week, as it was the day the faeries and other spirits had the most power and were most liable to spoil things with their spite and malice. But Friday was also, in earlier times, a day sacred to the Goddess. The Scandinavian Goddess Frigga, or Freya, gave her name to this day. Mythologically, she is a complex figure (Frigga and Freya seem to be separate developments of the same Goddess figure) but is ultimately the Great Goddess, mother of the gods, goddess of love and partnerships, giver of fertility, having Sky, Earth, and Underworld aspects. The Scandinavians and Anglo-Saxons who swept down into the British Isles in the early part of the Christian era undoubtedly brought her along with them, and many other bits of their belief system as well.

But why was Friday considered an unlucky day? Possibly because Catholicism did not acknowledge a Goddess, so the day named after her, with her name enshrined within it, became an unlucky one. Or possibly because Catholicism knew Friday as the day upon which Christ was crucified, and it therefore became thought of as a day likely to attract other tragic or unlucky happenings.

So the Irish peasant with the toothache, praying to God, the Virgin, and the new moon, was really weaving a more complex spell than he knew, one which contained traces of far older beliefs and practices.

To reiterate a previous point, all these beliefs and practices may seem like so much superstitious nonsense to us, living as we do in a Rational Age. And on one level, that purely rational one, perhaps they are. But on another level, they are not. They are, rather, attempts to strengthen oneself by intentionally aligning with the Greater Flow of Life.

Energy exists, and connects all. Science is in the process of rediscovering what shamans and healers have known for years: everything is connected in the Web of Life. It is not out of the question, therefore, to assume that hair or nail parings still carry the energetic imprint of their former owner and can serve as a link to him or her; nor that the silver and gold coins in the baby's bath water might—by their color, shape, and metal—provide a magical link to the powers of sun and moon.

The flaws in thinking that turn this into superstition and fearfulness come about when it is assumed that the power of the link is greater than it really is, or that the person being targeted by an ill-wisher is helpless and cannot use the power of his or her own will. Energetically speaking, the power of the link diminishes the longer the "part" is separated from the "whole." In any case, these things, these parts which create the link, are useless to those who don't know how to actually use them.

And we are rarely powerless in any situation. Our own will, intelligence, and resourcefulness, as well as that of our physical and spiritual allies, can help us through just about anything.

Mesmerism

Many accounts of Celtic folk healing demonstrate the use of what the 18th century termed mesmerism, a practice somewhat reminiscent of, and certainly allied to, hypnotism. The word *mesmerism* comes from Anton Mesmer (1734—1815) who developed the theory and wrote about it in a work called *The Influence of the Planets on the Human Body*, which he published in 1766. He postulated the existence of a "magnetic fluid" present in all bodies in the universe, which, similar to the gravitational force, could have affects and influences on other bodies even from a distance.

Mesmer felt that this fluid caused bodies, particularly animal bodies, to act as magnets, with the magnetic forces ebbing and flowing within them. He felt that the body's internal magnetism must be maintained in a state of equilibrium for health to be maintained. Ill-health demonstrated that this state was not being maintained, and could be treated and corrected by application of magnetism.

He developed theories and principles as to how this magnetism worked within the human body, and created treatment strategies based on these principles. For instance, the two sides of the body were of opposite polarities of energy (i.e., one positive, one negative), similar to the arms of a magnet. Likewise, the two arms/hands and the legs/feet were of opposite polarities. The healer used his or her own magnetic energies to adjust those of his or her client.

His theory of animal magnetism, with its principles of positive and negative polarities, foreshadowed the now-documented existence of the body's electromagnetic field, or aura, as well as coming quite close in describing how the body's vital energy operates in the body. This vital energy is called *chi* in the Chinese medical tradition, and in Sanskrit it is termed *prana*. It has also been termed the *Odic force*, and occasionally, *astral light*. The chi/energy moves in and out of the body through the chakras; as it circulates through the body it creates the auric field.

Dion Fortune, occultist, mystic, and magician of early 20th century England, referred to this energy as *elemental energy*, stating that it is the subtle energy component of the physical, elemental realm as differentiated from the astral or other realms and their energies. Thus, it is the Life Force as it manifests through the physical realm.

But Mesmer's theory went deeper than this, especially as it applied to the use of one's inherent animal magnetism as a treatment for those in ill health. When applied, it seems to have included some form of suggestion or hypnotism. In fact, mesmerism has been defined as "hypnotic induction held to involve animal magnetism." It was, therefore, the skilled use of one's "animal magnetism," or vital energy, to entrance, hypnotize, or otherwise deeply influence another person and thus exercise some control over his or her mind and thoughts, and through that means, possibly even his or her physical body.

One of my teachers in the field of energy work once said something that got the whole class laughing. Quoting her own teacher, healer Rosalyn Bruyere, she said, "*Auras are contagious, and the biggest one wins.*" We all laughed, but instantly realized how very true this statement is. Our auras, or energy fields which extend beyond our physical bodies, contain not just our vital energy but also our emotions, thoughts, and indeed, the very "stamp" of our own individual energy pattern. A large personal aura will extend far beyond the person's physical body, and by so doing is capable of penetrating, and thus influencing the auras of other people.

Think of it as someone dropping food coloring into a liquid. The liquid will, to some extent, take on the hue of the food coloring. The more transparent the host fluid, and the more food coloring dropped in, the more the host fluid will be influenced by the food coloring. Similarly, someone with a large aura—full of emotional energy—can influence someone with a smaller aura and less emotional intensity. This is why politicians and evangelists are so successful. It's not just that their words are convincing to our minds, it's that their emotions are convincing to our energy fields. Their strong emotions and convictions have expanded and amplified their auric fields, allowing these emotions and convictions to be projected further, often engulfing and interpenetrating the fields of others, and thus carrying their energetic "messages" directly into the energy fields of those others.

When this happens to us we feel their "force of feeling" and often confuse it, and the accompanying thoughts which may arise, with our own.

It is easy to see how this power, of which we are all capable, can be used and abused. It is abused by those wishing to unduly influence and control others. Yet it can be used wisely and compassionately in a therapeutic setting, to calm and reassure a person and to influence his or her mind and direct it toward self-healing. When doctors or other healers do this, the technique is often referred to as their "bedside manner."

As we read the accounts of the Faery Doctors and healers of old, it is clear that they knew and made use of this and similar techniques, though they most certainly did not call them by any of the same names we use for them today. The ability to reassure, comfort, and occasionally, therapeutically frighten the client was crucial to the healing process, and most certainly this bit of folk psychology was known to these healers. If the client did not possess faith in the healer's abilities, the chances of success were greatly diminished.

This is not to say only clients possessing faith could be cured. Frequently, the healer's influence was capable of prevailing over the client's doubts and misgivings. Once again, it goes back to the concept of "and the biggest one wins."

When a healer uses this technique, he or she is actually *tuning* the client to a different and desired frequency in the hopes that the client will then *entrain* to this frequency, which is one of health rather than sickness.

Entrainment is related to the *Principle of Resonance* and is the process by which a stronger frequency affects a weaker one, causing the weaker to change its vibration and come into alignment with the stronger. Entrainment brings about synchronization of frequency and cycle. This well-known scientific principle appears to be universal, and examples are found in the physical world as well as in the realm of psychology. A classic example of entrainment is when a baby's heartbeat comes into alignment with the frequency of the mother's heartbeat. Another example is the tendency of menstrual cycles of women living in the same household, or sometimes even just the same work environment day after day, to gradually come into alignment, and sometimes coincide.

Interestingly, it has been found that the heart's electromagnetic frequency is greater than that of the brain; so our feelings actually do influence what we think. By the process of entrainment, we really do affect each other's thoughts and feelings. The particular emotional state that generates the highest and therefore strongest electromagnetic frequency has been found to be loving kindness, the strength of which can bring other hearts and minds into resonance with its frequency. This gives us another key to success in our healing work.

Once again, we are brought back around to the power of frequencies and rhythms, as was known and used by the Faery Healers with their songs and chants, sacred numbers and patterns, prayers and love.

END NOTES

1 Wilde, Lady, *Ancient Legends, Mystic Charms & Superstitions of Ireland*, Chatto & Windus, London, 1919, p. 184.

2 Ibid, p. 190.

3 Ibid, p. 199.

4 Ibid.

5 Wood-Martin, W. G., *Traces of the Elder Faiths of Ireland: A Handbook of Irish Pre-Christian Traditions, Vol. 2*, Longmans, Greens, and Co., NY and Bombay, 1902, Vol 2, p. 332.

6 Ibid, p. 332.

7 Wilde, Lady, *Ancient Legends, Mystic Charms & Superstitions of Ireland*, Chatto & Windus, London, 1919, p. 203.

8 Ibid, p. 106.

9 Carmichael, Alexander, *Carmina Gadelica, Vol. 4*, Oliver and Boyd, Edinburgh & London, 1928, p. 166.

10 Wood-Martin, W. G., *Traces of the Elder Faiths of Ireland: A Handbook of Irish Pre-Christian Traditions, Vol. 2*, Longmans, Greens, and Co., N.Y. and Bombay, 1902, p. 190.

11 O'hOgain, Daithi, *Irish Superstitions*, Gill & Macmillan, Ltd., Dublin, 1995, pp. 21, 23, 30.

12 Wilde, Lady, *Ancient Legends, Mystic Charms & Superstitions of Ireland*, Chatto & Windus, London, 1919, p. 124.

13 Ibid, p. 109.

14 Logan, Patrick, *Irish Country Cures*, Sterling Publishing Co. Inc., NY, NY, 1994, p. 46.

15 Yeats, "Irish Witch Doctors," *Fortnightly Review*, 1900.

16 Rees, Alwyn & Brinley, *The Celtic Heritage*, Thames & Hudson, London, 1961, p. 189.

17 Wilde, Lady, *Ancient Legends, Mystic Charms & Superstitions of Ireland*, Chatto & Windus, London, 1919, p. 210.

18 Ibid, p. 128.

19 Ibid, p. 204.

20 Briggs, Katherine, *Fairies in Tradition and Literature*, Routledge, Kegan & Paul, Ltd, London, 1967, p. 106.

21 Wilde, Lady, *Ancient Legends, Mystic Charms & Superstitions of Ireland*, Chatto & Windus, London, 1919, p. 104.

22 Ibid, p. 193.

23 Ibid, p. 203.

24 Ibid.

25 Ibid, p. 204.

26 Ibid, p. 203.

27 Carmichael, Alexander, *Carmina Gadelica, Vol. 3*, Oliver and Boyd, Edinburgh & London, 1928, p. 2.

CHAPTER 5

The Irish Traditions

In this chapter we will examine the Irish healing traditions as evidenced in the collected folklore, and look at some of the beliefs and practices, and especially at that most fascinating of characters, the Faery Doctor.

A VERY BRIEF HISTORY OF MAGICAL HEALERS IN IRELAND

Although in later years, Irish doctors became familiar with the medical information and healing practices of the great Greek and Roman healers (later still, even becoming conversant in Latin), the most ancient mode of healing procedure in Ireland was the religious-medical mode of herb cures, fairy cures, charms, invocations, incantation, and magical ceremonies, quite possibly originating, as we have said previously, with the Druids. Interestingly, during the Christian era priests were held to have the ability to cure, a belief which possibly may have been a continuation of the earlier belief in the healing abilities of the Druids.

Many of these procedures and charms were preserved traditionally by the people and handed down through families, since the profession of physician was hereditary in certain families—the O'Lee, O'Shiel, and the O'Hickey families among them. This accumulated lore was usually handed down from generation to generation in these families in the careful way of oral transmission, hands-on teaching, and example.

Similarly, blacksmiths and millers were held to have power and people sometimes went to them for cures. Those who practiced these professions were seen as powerful because, by virtue of their professions, they held the power of transformation and worked with the very elements of life. Smiths, who worked with fire, water, air, and the ever-powerful iron, transformed the hardness of metal into useful objects by the use of these elements, a quite magical thing to do. Millers likewise transformed hard kernels of grain into useful flour for making bread, the staff of life. Millers used water and water wheels in their profession; thus they worked with not only the life-sustaining power of water, but the *sacred round* of the water wheel which brought in echoes of the circles and cycles of life—the turning Earth, the swirling stars, the wheel of the seasons. Both millers and smiths utilized all of the Four Elements in one way or another, but smiths are predominantly associated with Fire, and millers with Water.

Even within the safekeeping of these blacksmiths, millers, and hereditary physician families the healing lore became fragmented over the course of time, and some of it was lost. By the end of the 19th century with the rise of modern medicine, many of these charms, herbal cures, and folk healing practices—now diffused into the hands of many beyond the original healing families—were regarded simply as so much superstitious quackery, although the more honest of the new doctors were forced to admit the efficacy of at least some of this "quackery."

William Butler Yeats felt that the Irish country people's belief in the faery folk was really a religious belief since faeries are "spiritual and invisible" beings. The people believed the faeries were a race of invisible beings living all around, having a life very similar to human life, and having the ability to take from our human world people and animals as they so desired. Yeats thought that this belief had its priesthood in the Faery Doctors, who were also called Knowledgeable Men and sometimes Cow Doctors since they treat faery-afflicted cattle and other animals as well as people. Women Faery Doctors were sometimes referred to simply as Faery Women, or Wise Women.[1]

These Faery Healers, and indeed, even the more ordinary medicine men and women, were treated with great respect, and it was thought that the women derived their knowledge from the fairies and the spirits of the mountain.[2] In some instances, the line of demarcation between Faery Doctors and herbal healers was a bit indistinct as herbal healers often used charms and Faery Doctors were known to use herbs as well. One of the people interviewed by Yeats and Lady Wilde mentioned that the herbs with which Faery Doctors cured were so natural and normal that you could pick them at all times of the day. An important distinction, however, is that the Faery Doctors alone held the secrets of the magical and mystical uses of these common herbs.

Indeed, the Faery Doctors possessed many secrets which they had learned from the faeries. They were disinclined to talk freely about them as they lived in terror of the faeries who often punished and hurt them when they did talk too freely. Faery Doctors often were good herbalists and able to offer herbal cures for illnesses, but could only work their specific Faery Healings on faery-caused ailments, which they must always first diagnose as such.

Yeats felt that the faery beliefs had blended with the Christian beliefs, though they predated them, and thus were able to exist harmoniously side by side with them.

Traces of the Elder Faiths of Ireland, by W. G. Wood-Martin, mentions that almost every district had its "sybilline dealer in charms," usually an old woman whose skills the local people believed in firmly and frequently utilized.[3]

This book provides a wonderful and very visual depiction of the cottage and gardens of an Irish Wise Woman healer, which I will share with you here.

Over the door to her cottage was nailed a horseshoe to bring good luck. Atop her salt box lay a bunch of fairy flax. Beneath the salt box she kept a bottle of holy water with which to purify the place when necessary, and also to ward off crickets which were thought to be heralds of bad luck. Crickets must be warded off but not killed, lest their comrades avenge their death by invading the closets and eating the woolen clothing.

Within the house, branches of withered yew hung over the bed and the doorway; outside, they hung defensively over the cattle byres as well. The Wise Woman made sure that when her cows gave birth, the protective red woolen thread was tied to the cows' tails, thus ensuring that the cows would not be elf-shot or *overlooked* by the faeries. As for the Wise Woman herself, she was always careful to wear a four-leafed shamrock clover sewn into the folds of her scapular, shamrock being a specific for rendering faeries visible to human sight.

The Wise Woman's garden was a veritable pharmacy. Within its confines grew plants useful as cures for toothache and headache as well as those useful for removing warts and taking motes from the eye. Tansy grew there, as well as bogbane, bugloss, rosenoble, and Solomon's seal. Houseleeks were there, useful for sore eyes, and dandelion, unsurpassed for liver complaints. Comfrey and nettles grew there, both of which had many uses including staunching blood flow. Samphire, useful for heartburn and urinary diseases, grew there too, as did crowfoot whose juice was used to cure warts.

Other medicinal things were kept on hand as well: seal oil for sprains and rheumatism, caragen moss for coughs, and the tongue of a fox to be used as a poultice for extracting thorns.

Also in stock were belladonna, heartsease, ground ivy or mountain sage for heart palpitations or coughs, bog bark or parsley to be boiled in milk for gravel, as well as furze tops and broom which, when combined with caragen moss, made a good remedy for coughs.

Other plants in the garden were there primarily to be used as magical charms.

Poisonous plants were also to be found in this garden: scarlet-berried bryony, and the beautiful henbane, both highly dangerous but nonetheless useful to one wise to the ways of plants.

The pharmacopeia listed here is one that, in skillful hands, is indeed capable of treating a good many diseases and disorders.

Though Wood-Martin wrote during an era that was beginning to take a dim view of the old folk medicines, considering them full of superstitions, abominations, and absurdities, he was forced to admit that many of these "strange sounding" treatments actually did have the desired effect, although he conjectures that some of this might be due to the effect of mind over matter, the power of belief, as well as the chemicals contained in the herbs.[4]

Faery Doctors

It is in the Irish lore that we find the most evidence of, and information about, Faery Healing and Faery Doctors, and folk healing practices among the peasantry.

As has been mentioned, Faery Doctors specialized in treating faery-induced diseases, though often they were excellent herbalists who could also treat a great number of other diseases as well. Faery Doctors were generally women, though many men also were counted amongst their number. Old women in particular were considered to have peculiar mystical and supernatural power. Faery Doctors cured chiefly by charms and incantations, transmitted by tradition through many generations, and by herbs of which they had a surprising and specialized knowledge. It was thought that they learned these things from the spirits of the mountains (which may also refer to the mound-dwelling faeries), or from having been away with the faeries, during which time they received, in particular, this specialized knowledge of herbs and where to find them.

It was well known that faeries were always, but especially at Midsummer, on the lookout for beautiful women to steal. They would take the beautiful women to live with them, usually for seven years, at the end of which the women were considered old and ugly and were returned to Middle-Earth. However, in compensation for their youth and beauty being used up in this way, they were taught all the faery secrets, including the secret magics of herbs and their power over diseases. These women were thereby rendered all powerful as healers and could, with these magics, "kill or save as they chose."

The Faery Doctors kept this knowledge secret, and by tradition, were allowed to pass it on only at their death, and then, only to one of their children, usually the eldest.

Many Faery Doctors worked in private so their mode of practice and prayers was unknown. They had especially great knowledge of the fatal and cursing herbs, and it was known that they should always be consulted before treating sickness when it arose.

Since most of them had lived their entire lives in an area, they knew their clients and were known by them. Because of this they were knowledgeable about their clients' lives, family, and situation. This undoubtedly gave them good psychological insight into the situations brought to them, and it is likely they were aware also of the psychological value of mystery, power, and ritual drama in the healing process since they made good use of all of these.

Faery Doctors were the only ones who could accurately diagnose whether or not a condition was actually faery-caused, or with which of the faery conditions a person was afflicted: Faery Blast, Faery Stroke, or the Evil Eye. This knowledge was critical to affecting a cure.

Their methods were gentle and they did not draw blood, a practice which was offensive to the faeries, who had an aversion to the sight of blood.[5] Nor did they do the purgings or blisterings that were done by the "regular" medical men of that era.

Scientific medicine being what it was in the old days, the common people had a great deal more faith in their Faery Doctors, Wise Women, Faery Women, and Cunning Men—who did not bleed them, purge them, or dispense expensive, often powerfully poisonous medicines to them—than they did in the regular doctors. Although the Faery Doctors and herbal healers were accused of superstitious quackery by their more scientifically educated and oriented contemporaries, the ingredient list of medications prescribed by these good medical men of the 17th, 18th, and 19th centuries is a horrifying list of poisonous and nauseous substances ranging from mercury and antimony to horse-dung and burned owl feathers.[6]

Very often, Faery Healers were precognitive, possessing the Second Sight, or had by some method divined the future, so that when the patient arrived the Faery Doctor already knew what the matter was and had the medicine prepared. This undoubtedly added to their reputations and increased the awe in which they were held.

Quite often, Faery Doctors did things that seemed miraculous. In one instance recorded in the lore, a Faery Doctor was called to help a man who had apparently been faery-struck and was lying unconscious and staring, and almost lifeless. When the Faery Doctor arrived he threw fragrant herbs on the fire (in the manner of incense), and compounded an herbal brew which he used to anoint the person's brow, lips, hands, and then sprinkled the rest of it over the inert body. He told the family to keep silent watch around the man for two hours at which point he would return to finish the cure. The family did as instructed, and by the time the Faery Doctor returned the man had regained consciousness.[7]

Wood-Martin compares the procedures of Irish herb doctors (and he is most likely referring to Faery Doctors) to that of Native American medicine men, and tells us that once the source of the client's pain has been determined, the procedures were exactly the same in both cultures:

> *Sucking acts as cupping-relieves congestion. The Irish 'medicine man' sucks the spot affected by the pain with such severity as to raise blisters, and these often, by the counter-irritation so excited, effect a cure; but if this fails, he next pretends to spit out of his mouth frogs, thorns, stones, or anything the credulity of the sick man or his friends may accept as the origin of the disease.*[8]

Many mysterious rituals were part and parcel of the preparation and administration of the potions of a Faery Doctor.

For instance, secrecy was very important. Most often, the Faery Healers kept their magics, their herbs, and all their methods of preparation deeply secret, gathering the plants alone at night and hiding them in the eaves of their house or another secret place.

Faery Doctors had to pray and chant while they were pulling the special herbs for their cures. They prayed to the faeries, especially the Faery King, Queen, and the "simple among them." They talked and chanted to the plants themselves, sometimes calling them king or queen depending upon the gender of the person to be healed. This sounds very much like they were communicating not only with powers-that-be of the Faery Realm but also with the plant spirits and devas, enlisting the help of their specific power, potency, quality, and magical force.

The healer could often tell whether the person's illness was faery-caused or not by noting the appearance of the plant as he or she gathered it. If the plant had a black leaf, especially folded under or down, or if it had white and withered leaves, the healer knew the illness was "their" (the faeries') doing. If the plant was fresh and green, the illness was not their doing.

Once prepared, the potion must be carried home either by the patient or a friend, taking great care not to ever look behind themselves and making sure that the potion never fell or touched the ground. If it did, it would lose all its power and virtue.

Silence was also important. The potion was not to be shown or talked about to anyone or all the virtue would go out of it. The cure was to be used secretly and alone and then would not fail. When the messenger arrived at the patient's home, he must hand it over to the patient without a word. The patient must swallow it instantly before any other hands touched the cup.

If a potion contained herbs, these must be paid for in silver. But if the cure involved prayers, charms, and incantations, it was never paid for with money but only with gifts given in gratitude or it would lose its power. The Faery Doctors thought that by taking money for the cures they would lose their strength and power.

It was thought that everyone had friends among the faeries, those who would fight with the other faeries who wanted to carry them off or hurt them in other ways.[9] So it is possible that Faery Doctors also prayed for the assistance of the patient's faery friends, which these days we would refer to as Faery Allies.

SOME NOTEWORTHY FAERY DOCTORS
Biddy Early
The Faery Doctor most well known to us is undoubtedly Biddy Early, about whom several books have been written and mention made in many others. Born Bridget Ellen Early Connors (but she went by her mother's maiden name, Early) in 1798 in County Clare, Ireland, she was married several times, had three children, and outlived all her husbands save the last one who was much younger than she. Biddy lived for years in a small cottage just outside Feakle in east County Clare, Ireland. She died in April 1873.

Biddy was very well known in her area as a powerful seer and Faery Healer. She was referred to as the Wise Woman of Clare and people came from far and wide to consult her. It was well known that her powers were from the faeries, and that they helped her with her cures.

There are several versions of how Biddy acquired her powers. One story says that she got them from a changeling baby when she was a young girl working as a house servant. Another story says that she, like many of the other Faery Healer women, had been *away* for seven years, and was given the powers on her return. Yet another version of the story says that she got the powers from her dead son, Tom (or alternately her dead husband or dead brother), who came back to give her the famous magical blue bottle and told her it would provide her a way to make a living (see Note 1 at the end of the chapter). This is interesting in light of the possible connection between faeries and the dead. A more mundane version of this gives the information that her son was given the bottle by some faeries in gratitude for playing hurley with them. They told him to give it to his mother and that she would know what to do with it.

In any case, Biddy was very powerful and well respected. She had a little shed or stable outside of her house, and this is where she would go to consult with her invisible allies, the faeries, about the cures. They would tell her what to do. There was a well beside her house whose waters were said to possess magical powers.

She also had that famous blue bottle, wrapped in her red shawl when not in use, which she used in many ways in conjunction with her healing activities. Sometimes she seemed to use it as a scrying device. She'd shake it around a bit, look into it, and know who was coming to visit her and what was wrong with them. Sometimes she'd walk down the road and greet them before they actually arrived at her home. In addition to her blue bottle she most definitely possessed *The Sight* and seemed to know quite a bit about people, beyond the simple details of their illnesses.

She was very generous and helped most of the people who came to her. If she couldn't help someone she'd tell them so, often sending them on their way with the words, "What ails you has nothing to do with my business." She seems to have cured regular diseases as well as faery-induced ailments, though faery illnesses were her specialty. As is true with all healers and doctors, she didn't like it when people came to her with advanced illnesses as the delay had allowed the disease to progress making it harder and sometimes impossible to heal.

She used a variety of methods in her healing. Sometimes she said holy words and sprinkled holy water to affect a cure. Often she'd make potions—herbal or sometimes just blessed waters—for a person to take home and use, always seeming to know whether or not they'd actually make it home with the bottle intact.

Occasionally, she would tell the person they needed to obtain some Boundary Water to treat their ailment. Boundary Water was water gathered at the boundary of two or three properties or by a boundary wall. She'd advise people to go to the boundary area with a bottle, and if there was a stream nearby, to fill the bottle with water from the stream. If there was no stream, she'd tell them they should collect dew in the bottle. This water was either consumed or rubbed on the sore spot. The leftovers were to be taken to a stream or river and poured into the running water.

Boundaries are borderlands, "in-between" areas. Neither one thing nor the other, they partake of both, and thus are magical. Boundaries encompass such things as seashores (boundaries between Earth and sea), horizons (boundaries between Earth and sky), and twilight (boundaries between day and night); all of which are magical, sacred, and always associated with the Faery Realm.

One of those interviewed about Biddy Early made a curious remark. He said, "There is a cure for all the evil in the world between the two millwheels at Ballylee." When asked what cure that could be, he said that he'd meant it was the moss on the water of the millstream, which could cure all things brought about by "them" save the stroke given by a Faery Queen or Faery Fool, but it could not cure any common ailment. This leads us to wonder if she used this moss in her cures. In addition, it again brings in the magical power of mills, millers, wheels, and water. Yet there is a still deeper layer of meaning here concerning the turning wheels, of time and events, and how those who walk in the spirit realms—the healers—do their work primarily within this realm.

As with other Faery Doctors, Biddy Early refused monetary payment for the magical aspect of her healings, but did accept gifts given in gratitude.

The priests were always after her as they were after other Faery Healers as well. Often, they actively tried to prevent people from consulting her. Priests occasionally did healing work themselves although it was said they really didn't like to have to do it and that some went mad from the effort. So perhaps they didn't like the competition, especially since they considered it to be from an unholy source. Biddy didn't let this bother her or stop her healing work. In fact, she managed without the comforts of the church quite well right up until the end of her life. Then, when she was approaching death, she seems to have decided that maybe she'd better be on the safe side, just in case, so called a priest to her home, received the last rites, and died in the good graces of the Catholic Church.

It is rumored that the priest required her to break the bottle in return for this late-in-life favor. The bottle was never found after her death, and people took this as a sign that she had not passed her powers on to anyone else.

Morough O'Lee

In the library of the Royal Irish Academy there is a manuscript known as the *Book of Hy Brasil*. It dates from the 15th century, is 93 pages in length, and is said to have come from the O'Lee (Mac an Leagh) family, a well-known family of physicians who practiced medicine in the Sligo and Roscommon areas from at least 1400 A.D. onward. This book is associated most especially with a member of that family whose name was Morough O'Lee.

According to an historian of the period, Morough, who lived in Connemara at the end of the 17th century, said that he had been taken away to Hy Brasil for a few days. Hy Brasil, another name for those fabulous and blessed Western Isles, is the same as Tir na nOg, and some versions of the story relate that Morough fell asleep in a faery fort and awakened to find himself in Tir na nOg. There he remained and studied the secrets of Faery Healing for a year. At the end of the year he was allowed to come back, and according to some versions of the story, was gifted with a book that contained the cures for all diseases, with the injunction that he was not to open it for seven years. He arrived home to find that only three days had passed though it had seemed a year to him.

Morough fully intended to honor the faeries' request, but three years later a terrible epidemic swept the countryside. Knowing of the existence of the book, his neighbors begged him to open it and find a cure for them. So open it he did, and was able to heal some of them. Of course, had he waited the entire seven years, he would have had access to the full extent of what the book offered and perhaps he could have helped them all.

Since the actual *Book of Hy Brasil* itself, which contains medical information common to the era, predates Morough O'Lee, it is likely that he did not bring this book back as a gift from the faeries but was familiar with it because it belonged to his family. This does not, however, negate his claims to have learned Faery Healing in Tir na nOg. It is possible that the part of the story concerning the book was a later addition. In any case, Morough seemed to have a talent for healing, and like his O'Lee ancestors was a healer of some renown.[10]

Polly MacGarry

Polly MacGarry's personal story began in a very unusual way. Early one morning a widow went out to check on her cattle and was witness to a strange and silent procession coming up the road from the direction of County Leitrim. It seemed like a funeral procession, and the people in it were carrying a very small coffin. As they passed her, they placed this coffin on the ground and continued up the road, leaving it behind. Because of the strange silence of the procession, the widow knew it was the faery folk she had just seen.

She opened the coffin and found a fine, healthy baby girl inside, dressed in a white and gold silk robe. The widow, whose surname was MacGarry, took the baby home, gave her the name of Polly, and raised her along with the rest of her children.

When Polly was seven she accompanied her mother to a local fair to buy some horses. While there they met a woman from Leitrim who recognized Polly as her long lost daughter and was able to prove this by the existence of a birthmark. Polly declined to go home with her natural mother and stayed with her foster mother and family, eventually marrying one of her foster brothers.

Even when she was young Polly was well known as a Wise Woman and people came to her for help. She not only knew a lot about herbs and potions but like many other

Faery Doctors she always seemed to know about the people who came to her. She was very good at curing the faery-caused ailments because she seemed to know everything the faeries knew. She was especially good at helping women who were trying to have babies. Polly was not only good with people but able to cure animals as well.[11]

Mr. Saggarton/Langan

W. B. Yeats and Lady Gregory interviewed a Faery Healer whom Lady Gregory referred to as Mr. Saggarton, while Yeats, in his writeup of the meeting, referred to him simply as "Langan." Langan recounted his history of Faery Healing, saying that he'd gotten the power from his uncle. He related several of his healing adventures including stories about how the faeries had *touched* and tried to take his wife and several of his children and what he'd done to save them. He offered the further interesting information that there were two distinct classes of faeries. One was large and noble and he called them the Dundonians; the other class was small and spiteful. These he didn't call by name, but he said they had large bellies upon which they carried their bags. Yeats immediately saw in this description a rough correspondence of the Dundonians to the De Danaans and the unnamed ones to the Firbolgs, as the word *Firbolg* means *bag-men*, or *belly-men*.

Langan also mentioned that the faery folk have kings and queens among them, and also one known as the Fool who dressed in strange clothes like a mummer, "but may yet be the wisest of them all." Langan said, "There is a queen in every house and regiment of them (the Faeries). It is of those they steal away that they make queens for as long as they live, or that they are satisfied with them." But to offend the queen was a very serious matter, and Langan added that there was no cure for the "stroke" when it was given by the queen or the Fool.[12]

Mrs. Sheridan

Both Yeats and Lady Gregory interviewed Mrs. Sheridan on more than one occasion. It was Yeats's opinion that Mrs. Sheridan was exceedingly wise in the ways of the faeries and could have been herself a famous Faery Healer had she so desired. She didn't have a reputation for doing cures, like some of the others they interviewed, but she said to them, "I know the cure for anything they can do to you, but it's few I'd tell it to. It was a strange woman came in and told it to me, and I never saw her again. She bid me to spit and to use the spittle, or to take a graineen of dust from the navel, and that's what you should do if anyone you care for gets a cold or a shivering, or they put anything upon him."

As mentioned before, this belief in the power of spittle was widespread in Ireland.

Apparently, Mrs. Sheridan had been *away* several times, and cautiously described a few things she had seen including a fabulous castle-like house, drawbridges, and other things she'd never seen in life nor read about in books since she couldn't read and had never gone to school. She saw fine-looking ladies, one of whom leaned out the window and waved to her, and fancy gentlemen, one of whom invited her to cross the bridge into the manor house, an offer she declined. She saw people she knew but who'd been dead for many years. She saw the death coach itself, and it was driven by one she'd known, now long dead. She told Yeats that she felt the reason the faeries hadn't kept her was because of her disposition. She tended to be cross when she was upset, and she was cross with them while there because they wouldn't let her come back. She could tell the faeries were exasperated with her because of it. Finally they brought her back, and for good.

Her brother had also been a healer. He'd gotten the knowledge of cures from a book that was thrown down before him in the road. He went to England and cured many people, leaving many of the local doctors confused and jealous. Then he decided to go to America. But the doctors had hired some men to shipwreck him. He wasn't drowned but broken to pieces on the rocks and the book was lost along with him. But before this unfortunate episode he'd managed to teach her a great deal out of the book, which was why she knew so much about herbs and was able to do a good many cures. She'd also been a midwife for many years, and was rightfully proud of the fact that she'd never lost a mother or child in her career. She also mentioned that she was a cousin of Mr Saggarton/Langan, and that his uncle from whom he got the power had been *away* for 21 years.

Bridget Ruane

Yeats mentions Bridget Ruane in his *Poets and Dreamers* as the woman who gave him his first knowledge of the healing abilities of certain plants, as some plants seemed to have a natural power and some a very mysterious power. He mentions that Bridget had recently passed on and says, "we may be sure that among the green herbs that cover her grave there are some that are good for every bone in the body and that are very good for a sore heart." This refers, of course, to the story of the Tuatha De Danaan Goddess Airmid and the 365 herbs she found growing on her brother Miach's grave, one herb, it was said, for each nerve in the body.

Carthy of Imlough and Moyra Collum

Lady Gregory and Yeats interviewed a man they refer to as James Mangan. Mr. Mangan related that his mother was a healer and she'd learned cures from an Ulster woman—the women from Ulster being especially noteworthy for their cures. He himself did cures, but he didn't know even half of what his mother had known. The cures he knew he did only for his own family since he thought that doing them for other people would expose him to increased danger. Mangan mentioned a man named Carthy who lived at Imlough; Carthy did cures with charms but no herbs. Carthy used unsalted butter and would kneel down and say his words and charms into it. Then the person used it, presumably rubbing it into his or her sore places.

Mangan also mentioned Moyra Collum, "a great one for doing cures," saying that she was once visited by a little boy whose mother had sent him there to get a remedy for their sick cow. Moyra gave him a bottle and told him to put a drop of its contents into the cow's ear. He did so, and soon after the boy's feet began to hurt him a great deal. At this point, his mother took the bottle into the street and broke it, saying that it was better to lose the cow than the child. The next morning the cow was dead.

A FEW MORE ACCOUNTS OF FAERY DOCTORS AND DOCTORING

One of Lady Wilde's interviewees, Mrs. Creevy, related an interesting experience that had happened to a child in a nearby village. The child had something very wrong with his eyes, and no doctor had been successful at curing him. One night his mother had a dream that she'd gotten out of bed and journeyed to a holy well not far from where she lived. There, she saw a woman dressed in white. The woman gave her some of the well water, which she took home to her son, and it cured his eyes. When the woman woke up next morning, she went off to the well and got the water. Bringing it home, she put it on his eyes. After three applications of the well water, his eyes were healed.

It is interesting to speculate on the possible meaning of this dream. It sounds very much as if the mother had been contacted in her dream by the guardian spirit of the holy well who wished to offer her help in healing the boy.

A woman in County Limerick related that she once had a severe pain in her side that she couldn't stop no matter what she did or what the doctor did for her. Then one day a farmer she knew told her she was a fool to not go see the local Faery Woman who lived two miles away and who could cure her with charms. She decided to do so, and paid the woman a visit. She went three days in a row, and stayed away three days, doing this till her days of treatment numbered nine. The Faery Healer made her reach up and hold on to the branch of an apple tree where she'd swing her back and forth as if she were a child. Then she laid her on the grass and passed her hands over her, while chanting. At the end of the nine visits the woman was cured, and her pain was gone.

PROCEDURES OF A FAERY DOCTOR

Lady Wilde gives us an interesting account of a Faery Doctor at work, most likely taken from the notes of her husband, Dr. William Wilde, who shared her interest in such things. Since it sounds like a personal account, it has been suggested that perhaps Dr. Wilde was himself the patient in this case. And although it describes one, specific, unnamed Faery Doctor at work, the procedures described are probably characteristic of those used by many Faery Doctors, and illustrates the seamless marriage of the medical and magical elements of a cure.

Here's what it would have been like to pay a visit to this Faery Doctor.[13]

When you arrive, the Faery Doctor will have been expecting you, and is therefore awaiting your arrival. He shows you to a seat, then stares fixedly at your face for a while. He is determining whether what ails you is a faery disease or not. After determining that this is the case, he then must determine from which of the three or four major disorders you might be suffering.

He takes up three hazel sticks, each roughly three inches long, and marks each of them with the names of the three major faery disorders: Faery Stroke, Faery Wind or Blast, and the Evil Eye. He then removes his coat, shoes and socks, rolls up his sleeves, and stands up. Facing East, he begins to pray.

When his prayers are done, he places a bowl of pure water by the fireplace. He kneels down and places the three marked hazel rods into the fire. Then he continues his praying, while the hazel rods burn and become black as charcoal. When they have reached this state he stands up and again prays facing East, eyes uplifted and hands crossed. Then he removes the hazel sticks from the fire.

He quickly tosses them into the dish of water and watches them carefully. The moment one of them sinks, he begins a prayer to the sun. Taking the stick out of the water, he declares whether you are afflicted by the Stroke, the Blast, the Dart, or the Evil Eye.

Then he grinds the wet stick into a powder (rendered easier because the stick is so well charred), puts it into a bottle, and pours the water from the dish into the bottle. After you are gone he will bury the other two sticks in the earth. Softly, he utters a prayer or incantation over it, his clasped hands held over the bottle. The words are secret, and if he is a hereditary Faery Doctor, they have been passed down to him through his family.

You are then given your instructions: your bottled potion is to be carried home in silence, and you must not look around on the way home but go straight there. The bottle is never to touch the ground. You are to consume its contents tonight, alone, and in silence.

If none of the rods had sunk to the bottom of the dish, this would mean that your affliction was not faery-caused. The Faery Doctor would then use primarily herbs as a cure—yarrow, vervain, and eyebright being the favorites. Each of these possessed powerful properties known only to the Faery Doctor, and as usual, all the spells, charms, and incantations were kept secret.

Interesting to note in this account are the prayers to the sun, and the fact that prayers are addressed to the East which is the direction of the rising sun. Interesting as well are the use of the primal Elements of Fire and Water in the divinatory ritual, as well as the use of three sticks of hazelwood, which, as we will see in *Chapter 9*, is a wood traditionally linked to the art of divination.

Even the most powerful of the Faery Doctors had no cure for the *Stroke* when it was given by the Faery Queen or the Faery Fool. This fact indicates that these two were considered the most powerful of the Faery Beings.

The Faery Fool is an interesting character. In Ireland he was referred to as the *Amadan* and was so greatly feared that it was bad luck even to mention his name. He usually appeared in the form of a rather stocky and strong man, although he was also known to appear in the guise of an unpleasant looking animal, and was said to be able to change his shape at will. He was most frequently active during the month of June, which is not surprising since the summertime was noted for a high level of faery activity. He was feared because his *touch* was thought to cause very serious illnesses affecting the central nervous system. These disorders grew progressively worse over time and were essentially incurable, except occasionally by the priests.

I would like to end this chapter with a very relevant quote from *The Fairy Faith in Celtic Countries*:

> *Finally, we may say that what medicine-men are to the American Indians, to Polynesians, Australians, Africans, Eskimos, and many other contemporary races, or what mightier magicians of India are to their people, the 'fairy doctors' and 'charmers' of Ireland, Scotland and Man are to the Gaels, and the Dynion Hysbys or 'Wise Men' of Wales, the witches of Cornwall and the seers sorceresses and exorcists of*

Brittany are to the Brythons. These Gaelic and Brythonic magicians and witches, and 'fairy mediums,' almost invariably claim to derive their power from their ability to see and communicate with fairies, spirits and the dead; and they generally say that they are enabled through such spiritual agencies to reveal the past, to foretell the future, to locate lost property, to cast spells upon human beings and upon animals, to remove such spells, to cure fairy strokes and changelings, to perform exorcisms, and to bring people back from Fairyland.[14]

NOTES

1. Although Faery Doctors did not accept money, the gifts they were given by the grateful no doubt contributed to their ability to "make a living" while doing Faery Healing.

END NOTES

1. Yeats, W. B., "Irish Witch Doctors," *Fortnightly Review*, 1900.

2. Wilde, Lady, *Ancient Legends, Mystic Charms & Superstitions of Ireland*, Chatto & Windus, London, 1919, pp. 186-188.

3. Wood-Martin, W. G., *Traces of the Elder Faiths of Ireland: A Handbook of Irish Pre-Christian Traditions*, Longmans, Greens, and Co., NY and Bombay, 1902, p. 176.

4. Ibid, pp. 177-178.

5. Wilde, Lady, *Ancient Legends, Mystic Charms & Superstitions of Ireland*, Chatto & Windus, London, 1919, p. 209.

6. Griggs, Barbara, *Green Pharmacy*, Healing Arts Press, Rochester, VT, 1981, pp. 109-113.

7. Wilde, Lady, *Ancient Legends, Mystic Charms & Superstitions of Ireland*, Chatto & Windus, London, 1919, p. 234.

8. Wood-Martin, W. G., *Traces of the Elder Faiths of Ireland: A Handbook of Irish Pre-Christian Traditions*, Longmans, Greens, and Co., NY and Bombay, 1902, p. 167.

9. Yeats, W. B., "Irish Witch Doctors," *Fortnightly Review*, 1900.

10. Logan, Patrick, *The Old Gods: The Facts About Irish Fairies*, Appletree Press, Belfast, 1981, p. 90.

11. Ibid, pp. 91-92.

12. Yeats, "Irish Witch Doctors," *Fortnightly Review*, 1900.

13. Wilde, Lady, *Ancient Legends, Mystic Charms & Superstitions of Ireland*, Chatto & Windus, London, 1919, pp. 231-232.

14. Evans Wentz, W.Y., *The Fairy Faith in Celtic Countries*, Henry Frowde, Oxford University Press, London, New York, Toronto and Melbourne, 1911, p. 264.

CHAPTER 6

Evidence of Faery Healing Traditions in England, Scotland, Wales, and the Isle of Man

English Traditions

In this chapter we will examine examples of the Faery Healing Tradition as found in England, and documented in the folklore.

In general, such healers were not really distinguished from other healers who dealt with the supernatural, that is, the Evil Eye, witchcraft, and the like. These healers were referred to as Wise Men and Wise Women, conjurers, charmers, sorcerers, but most frequently as either white witches, or Cunning Men. Like their counterparts in Ireland, they frequently inherited their power and knowledge, and came from a *seventh son* or *seventh daughter* type of lineage. They functioned similarly as seers and healers, divining the causes and cures of illness in humans and animals, detecting thieves, finding lost objects, occasionally predicting the future, and in particular, diagnosing supernatural influence including that of witches and faeries in human health and affairs.[1] Yet there were also traditions of Faery Healing and Faery Healers, people who claimed to have been given healing powers, ointments, and powders by the faeries.[2]

In England, the original term for what we now term faeries/fairies was *elf*, due to the Anglo-Saxon linguistic influence. Later, most likely with the Norman invasion, the term faery came to be used as well, and the two were used interchangeably. The early Anglo-Saxon folklore contains many charms for protection against elves and for curing elf-shot, which shows that elves were considered then, as later, to be responsible for at least some human ills.

In 1653 a man in Yorkshire was accused of curing the sick by means of a white powder given to him by the faeries for that purpose. Although this fell under the province of "white" witchcraft (i.e., healing rather than hurting), it was still looked on unfavorably because it was thought that all such powers derived from the devil. This man, however, insisted that he had obtained the white powder from a Faery Woman, not the devil, and even offered to take the judge to the faery hill where he had met the Faery Woman and obtained the powder. The judge declined, but the man must have been persuasive, since he was not convicted.[3]

In this interesting case, the man claims to have encountered the Faery Woman when he was in desperate need, with no way to financially care for his family. Upon learning of his situation, the Faery Woman offered to provide him with a way to get a good living if he would but follow her counsel. He agreed, providing it was a lawful way, and she told him that it would be by doing good and curing the sick. He met her at the arranged time and place, and she led him to a faery hill. They entered the faery hill, and traveling through its rooms they came at last to a great hall where sat the Queen of Faery surrounded by her people. He was introduced, and the Queen told the Faery Woman to give him the white powder and teach him how to use it. He was given a small wooden box of the powder and told to give two or three grains of it to any who were ill and it would heal them. Then he was led out of the faery hall and returned to his home. He used the white powder to great effect, and when the it was gone, he returned to the faery hill, where he was admitted by the Faery Woman and led to the Faery Queen who gave him a fresh supply.

This, unlike so many of the Irish accounts, is a case of the Faeries demonstrating compassion and good will toward a human and gifting him with healing abilities. In this case, unlike the ones in Ireland, the man was not taken away for a while against his will and then given the gift upon his return. He was offered the gift freely and entered the faery hill freely, of his own choosing, to obtain it.

In general, England seems to have entertained a more congenial concept of the Faery Realm than did Scotland and even Ireland, where the faeries were regarded as much more antagonistic and indeed even occasionally malevolent toward humanity in some cases.

Scottish Traditions

In Scotland the faeries were sometimes referred to as the *Sluagh Sidhe* or Faery Host.

An interesting story from the Scottish Faery Healing Tradition is that of Bessie Dunlop of Dalry, Ayrshire. One day when she was taking her cow out to pasture, she was worrying over the fact that her husband, child, and cow were all suffering from various illnesses. Suddenly she beheld an elderly man dressed in grey. He was wearing a black hat and holding a white wand. He introduced himself to her as Thomas. He told her that her husband would get well but that her child and the cow would die. He then walked off and seemed to disappear down a hole which seemed much too small for him. Strangely, things came to pass just as he had predicted.

He appeared to her again and offered her wealth in the form of horses and cattle if she would denounce Christianity. This she refused to do, and he departed somewhat angrily. Surprisingly, he returned to visit her again. This time he told her he would take her into the Faery Realm but that she must swear to secrecy about it and must not speak while she was there. Bessie was very reluctant about all this. While they were walking along discussing it, they came upon four Faery Women and four Faery Men, to whom he introduced her. The faery people were quite friendly to Bessie and asked her to come with them to their realm. Bessie was still worried about this and didn't answer them, so after a while they left in a bit of a huff, apparently indicated by a "hideous, ugly blast of wind," which left Bessie feeling quite ill.

Thomas returned to her and begged her to come with them, explaining much to her about the nature of faeries, but she was still cautious and worried about the consequences so she refused. He told her that she would be well-fed and taken care of, but even this did not convince her to go.

In spite of her refusal Thomas continued to visit her, and she continued to see faeries from time to time, including the Faery Queen. Thomas told her that she had, in fact, met the Faery Queen once before in the person of a rather ordinary-looking woman who'd to come to her room years before when she was confined in childbed.

Thomas began instructing Bessie in ways of curing that he had obviously learned from the faery folk. She practiced the cures that he taught her, and soon her reputation began to grow. She was consulted by many for her cures for both animals and people, and she became well known as one who healed and did no harm. Always, she consulted with Thomas, and he would tell her what to do for each case, giving her procedures, recipes for healing potions, and even telling her where missing items might be found.

Occasionally, Thomas did a bit of future-prediction, speaking through Bessie, and this may have been what ultimately led to her downfall. He predicted that she would be called to account for her dealings with the invisible realm, but that her friends and neighbors would rise up to save her. Unfortunately, the second half of this prediction was incorrect, and she was burned at the stake in 1576.[4]

This unhappy case is interesting in that Bessie learned her faery cures through a deceased human intermediary rather than directly from the faeries themselves. This case is also of interest because it shows yet another link between the faeries and the dead: Thomas was a local man who had died many years previous to his meeting with Bessie.

A similar story is that of Alison Pierson of Byrehill, Fyfe, who was introduced to the faeries by her dead cousin William Sympson. William, who came to her dressed in green and who had been a physician during his lifetime, first came to her when she was sick and alone. Later he taught her the healing arts including, presumably, those which he had learned from the faeries. Like Bessie Dunlop, Alison's good works did not help her case when it came before the courts; she was convicted in 1588 of "haunting and repairing with the good neighbors and the Queen of Elphame" and was executed.

Yet another such story is that of Isobel Haldane who was brought up on witchcraft charges before the magistrates of Perth, Scotland, in 1623, after the death of a child she'd been treating. Isobel confessed to trafficking with the faeries, saying she had been transported from her bed to a hillside that had proven to be a faery hill. She was taken inside the faery hill and kept for three days (a significant number of days) until released by "a man with a gray beard." This man, who sounds suspiciously like Bessie Dunlop's faery contact, later assisted her in her healing work, teaching her techniques, and providing her with information on those who came to her for treatment. She also said that the leader of the faery hosts had advised her to speak of God and to help the poor. But even this did not prevent her from being convicted and executed.

In Scotland as elsewhere, there were many customs, charms, and incantations for keeping the faeries from stealing babies or exchanging them for one of their own. A baby was considered to be at risk from the moment of its birth until it was safely baptized (blessed by the power of water), and thus formally put under the protection of God and his church. This resulted in the creation of interim measures, temporary baptismal blessing ceremonies called *birth baptisms* (mentioned in *Chapter 4*), so that the child might be protected until a regular church baptism could be performed.

Healing Threads recounts a story[5] witnessed by a medical man and recounted to the Caledonian Medical Society by Katherine Whyte Grant. It is similar to one recounted 100 years previously, and describes the details of a custom used to protect the newborn child from the faeries. This was referred to as being "baptized in the ancient manner," and was similar, but not identical, to the procedure recounted previously.

After the child was born, a special baptismal bath was prepared by a seer who was present. A tub of water was set on the hearth and into it were placed three glasses of whiskey, three glasses of wine, and three spoonfuls of salt. Three short swords (probably iron) were laid in the tub. Then all present formed a circle around the hearth, and the child, who'd been in the arms of the seer up till now, was placed in the arms of his next-of-kin. The child was then passed from arm to arm around the circle, ending up in the arms of those serving as godparents. The seer instructed them to wash the baby in the bath. As they did so, one of them said, "I name thee M (the name used was not the one by which the child was actually called), in the presence of these thy godfathers and godmothers, and in the presence of the invisible and all-seeing Father. I pray to him to protect thee from the evil desires of thine enemies and the evil desires of the enemies of thy forefathers." After this, the child was taken in and laid down beside his mother. Then, the child's grandmother, who had a pet deer, milked the deer and the milk was poured into a cup. It was mixed with a few drops of whiskey, a bit of honey, and then fed to the baby. All present then drank to the health of the baby. An oatcake and a drink were sent around to all the neighbors that they might do likewise.

This old ritual demonstrates to us once again the blessing power of water, the protective power of salt and iron, the importance of milk, and the magical power of the number three. The use of deer milk is interesting and makes one wonder if perhaps the deer was a sacred or totemic animal to this family.

In Ireland, Scotland, the Islands, and parts of England as well, the influence of the Norse invaders blended over time with the pre-existing Celtic influence, the result being lore which featured an interesting mixture of faery folk: not only the usual Celtic variety, but also Norse/Teutonic/Scandinavian varieties such as elves, trolls, trows, and wights.

Welsh Traditions

In Wales the Faery Healers were called the *Dynion Hysbys*, which means, literally, "wise men." These were a class of people who were known for their divining, charming, magical, and healing abilities. They were known to work with the aid of the faeries, gaining power from them to perform faery-like magic, yet were also able to counteract faery magic, thereby preventing or healing changelings, strokes, blasts, and the Evil Eye.[6]

The Welsh faery folk were known as the *Tylwyth Teg*, which means the *Fair Folk*. In Glamorganshire they were known as *Bendith Y Mamau* or The Mother's Blessing. There are many stories about them, but the one most directly connected with the healing tradition is about the beautiful Lady of Llyn y Van Vach and the Physicians of Myddfai.

According to legend, this entire family of physicians was descended from the union of a mortal man and a faery woman. This family of physicians existed till the mid 19th century. Their existence and even some of their cures and recipes were documented.

THE PHYSICIANS OF MYDDFAI

In 13th century Wales, there was a famous family of physicians, whose members served the royal court of Wales for centuries. The Physicians of Myddfai, as they were known, were famous for their knowledge, expertise, and efficacy of their cures, which were the subject of a book published in 1821 and entitled *The Physicians of Myddfai*. One of the most interesting things about them was that their ability as healers was traced back to a faery ancestress.

There are several versions of the story. Here is one drawn from *The Physicians of Myddfai*, by John Pughe, 1861.[7]

LEGEND | The Physicians of Myddfai

At the end of the 12th century, near Llanddeusant in Carmarthenshire, there lived a widow and her son. She had some cattle, and in time their number increased and she needed new grazing space for them. So she sent them to graze on the adjoining mountain, called Black Mountain, near a small lake called Llyn y Van Vach, and she sent her son to tend them.

One day, as the young man wandered by the side of the lake, he beheld a maiden sitting on the surface of the lake. She was the most beautiful creature he had ever seen. She sat there upon the unruffled surface of the lake, combing her golden hair, and looking at her reflection in the lake. He was struck with wonder and love, and without thinking, held out his supper of bread and cheese as an offering to her. Presently, she looked up, and beheld him standing there with his hands outstretched and full of his offering and a look of love upon his face. Slowly, she glided toward him. When she reached him, he offered her the bread, and reached out to touch her. She refused both the touch and the bread, saying, "Hard baked is thy bread, tis not easy to catch me." With these words, she dove down into the water and disappeared from his sight.

The youth was sorely disappointed he had not been able to make further acquaintance with this beautiful lady. He returned home and told his mother of what had transpired. She responded that he should, next day, take with him unbaked dough, called "toes," as there must have been some magic connected with the "hard baked" aspect of the bread he had offered that had offended the lady and prevented further communication with her.

By dawn of the next day he was at the lake, hoping to see the beautiful maiden again. He waited many hours, but then, as he was again about to tend to the cattle he saw her. So he offered her the unbaked bread and offered, as well, his heart, and spoke his desire to wed her. But she refused him again, saying, "Unbaked is thy bread! I will not have thee."

But she smiled at him before she vanished beneath the waves and that gave him hope. So, again taking his mother's advice, he was at the lakeshore by the next dawn, this time with a loaf of bread but slightly baked. The lady was not there, and as the morning turned to midday, she did not appear. The afternoon wore on, and the lad haunted the lakeshore anxiously, but still she did not appear. At length, the sun was setting and the lad, preparing to depart for home, cast one final, sad glance at the lake. To his surprise, he saw cattle were walking along the surface of the lake. And to his great delight, he saw that the maiden was following the cattle. He ran to meet her, offering her the slightly baked bread and asked again if she would consent to be his bride. She smiled at him and consented, but only on the condition that he never strike her. For if he should strike her three "causeless" blows, leave him she must, and forever.

Of course he assured her that such a thing would never happen. And at this moment of great happiness, she slipped her hand from his and dove back into the lake, returning with her father and sister. But now the lad was confused, because the two maidens were identical in appearance and he could not tell them apart. As he pondered this, their father told him that he would give his consent to his daughter's marriage only if the lad could tell which of the maidens was his beloved. So he studied them carefully, and just as he was about to give up in despair one of them moved her foot forward slightly. This caught the lad's attention, and looking carefully at the foot and the shoe, he noted a familiar peculiarity in the shoe tie. Boldly, he took the maiden's hand and said, "This is she."

Her father then approved the match, and promised a dowry of sheep, goats, cattle, and horses, all of which came forth magically from the lake as the maiden counted them out. But all this, her father said, was on the condition that the young man be a kind and faithful husband to his daughter. If ever he should prove unkind and strike her three times without cause, the maiden would return to her home in the lake, taking the dowry back with her.

So the two were married. For many years they lived happily together near the village of Myddfai, and in time she gave birth to three sons. But then, as always seems to happen in these stories, the husband grew impatient, embarrassed, and angry at his wife, and forgetting his promise tapped her upon the arm. This happened two times, and each time she reminded him of his promise. So he was watchful with himself and they lived many more years in peacefulness. But then one day it happened again. She looked at him sadly, though with love, and told him that their marriage contract was broken and that she must leave him. She made her way back to their home. She called all the animals by name, and then made her way to the lake, all the animals following behind her. No words could persuade her to stay.

But she did return. Her sons, disconsolate at the loss of their mother, took to haunting the shores of Llyn y Van Vach in hopes of catching glimpse of her. One day, their mother did come to them, and speaking to Rhiwallon, the eldest, told him that his destiny was to be a healer for the pains and diseases of mankind. She gifted him with a bag containing recipes for medicines, instructions for their use, and instructions for the preservation of health. She told him that if he strictly adhered to these things he and his descendants would be, for many generations, counted among the most skillful physicians in the country. She promised her sons she would come to them again when they most needed her counsel, then she disappeared. She came to them again, and taught them the healing secrets of the herbs and plants growing throughout the countryside.

Just as she had foretold, her son and his descendants became famous physicians, and physicians to the local nobility. At length, the Physicians wrote down their cures for the benefit of posterity.

This family of physicians existed for many centuries, the last of the line passing away in the 1840s.

The Physicians of Myddfai represent a healing tradition whose origin stretches far into the past, perhaps back to Druidic times, yet they continued to exist and heal well into historic times. It is exciting to think that their knowledge and cures may be representative of some very archaic practices.

It should be noted that, although in Irish Faery Healing Tradition Faery Doctors are said to cure primarily faery-induced ailments, in the case of the Welsh Physicians of Myddfai, the Faery Ancestress gifted them with the secrets of healing *all* human illness and pain rather than just specifically faery-induced illness. This represents a difference from the Irish Faery Doctoring Tradition.

Manx Traditions

On the Isle of Man, faeries were known variously as the *Mooinjer veggey* or "Little People," the *Guillyn veggey* or "Little Boys," the "Little Fellas," or sometimes as "The Middle World Men." The term *Ferrishyn* seems to have been used as well, though it may have been a later word and a corrupted form of the English "faery."[8]

It should come as no surprise to find that the Isle of Man also had its Faery Doctoring Traditions. In *Manx Worthies* author A. W. Moore tells us that on the Isle of Man, there were men and women who had become quite skilled in the practice of healing. They used herbal remedies, occasionally accompanied by charms and incantations, to cure diseases, including those induced by faeries, witches, and sorcerers. This power was said to be hereditary; but in order for the power and lore to be passed down intact, it was necessary that they be passed man to woman, woman to man, and so on.[9]

He mentions one of these families, the Tears family of Ballawhane, and relates a short tale of the most famous of that family which includes a description of one man, referring to him as a "seer." He notes that this man was said to be the most powerful of all such practitioners and was the one called in when all the others had failed. The messenger sent to request his presence on these occasions was under strict injunctions not to eat, drink, or tell anyone else of his mission. The recovery was said to begin the moment the messenger stated the case to the seer. Many marvelous stories were told of the cures attributed to him.

As we can see, there is great similarity in the Faery Healing Traditions of each of these countries and areas.

END NOTES

1. Simpson, Jacqueline and Steve Roud, *A Dictionary of English Folkore*, Oxford University Press, Oxford, 2000, p. 86.

2. Ibid, p. 116.

3. Briggs, Katherine, *An Encyclopedia of Faeries*, Pantheon Books, NY, 1976, pp. 409, 410.

4. Murray, Margaret, *The Witch Cult in Western Europe, Appendix I*, Oxford, at the Clarendon Press, 1921.

5. Beith, Mary, *Healing Threads*, Polygon, Edinburgh, 1995, pp. 98-99.

6. Evans Wentz, W. Y., *The Fairy Faith in Celtic Countries*, Henry Frowde, Oxford University Press, London, New York, Toronto and Melbourne, 1911, p. 253.

7. Pughe, John, *The Physicians of Myddfai*, published for the Welsh MSS Society, Llandovery, D. J. Roderic, London, England, Longman & Co; 1861. Facsimile reprint of the English translation by Llanderch Publishers, Felinfach, Wales, 1993, pp. xxi-xxviii.

8. Evans Wentz, W. Y., *The Fairy Faith in Celtic Countries*, Henry Frowde, Oxford University Press, London, New York, Toronto and Melbourne, 1911, p. 117.

9. Moore, A.W., & M.A. Douglas, compilers, *Manx WorthiesÑor Biographies of Notable Manx Men and Women, Vol. II*, S.K. Broadbent & Co, Ltd.; Victoria St., Isle of Man, 1901, pp.161-162.

CHAPTER 7

Faeries and Witches

In many instances found in literature and folklore there is a connection drawn between faeries and witches. We find this particularly in accounts of the witchcraft trials. In the accounts of these trials, some of the accused occasionally confessed to associating with the faeries. Faeries were sometimes thought to act as familiar spirits for witches. In the north of England, some of the accused confessed to consorting with faeries rather than the devil. This did not, however, seem to result in much clemency from the witch-hunters or the courts. In fact, admitting to interacting with the faeries was considered almost a sure sign of witchcraft.

John Walsh of Dorset, accused of witchcraft in 1566, confessed to consulting with the faeries. He did this, he said, at both midday and midnight. He said that there were three kinds of faeries: black, white, and green; and that the black were the worst.[1] This is interestingly similar to the three kinds of witches—black, grey, and white—who were held, by tradition, to exist. Black witches were considered the worst, working their malevolence on man and beast. White witches were the beneficial Wise Women and Wise Men whose healing work was a great service to humanity. Grey witches did good or evil as they saw fit.[2] Perhaps we may assume that the black, white, and green kinds of faeries worked similarly; with the green ones, perhaps, being related to plants and healing.

Now perhaps it should be noted that people being tortured to confess—as was quite frequently the case in witchcraft investigations—are very likely to confess to just about anything, especially to that which their torturers suggest they *should* confess. Inquisitors were well known for offering painful "suggestions" as to the behaviors of which they thought the accused were guilty, thus encouraging confession of those behaviors.

There is, however, the curious case of Isobel Gowdie of Auldearn, Scotland, who simply gave herself up to the authorities in 1662, confessed to being a witch, to consorting with faeries, and to other nefarious, illegal activities—all without benefit of prior accusation, much less torture.

Scholars of the witch trials have puzzled over this case for years. Young, beautiful, under no suspicion at all, and knowing what fate surely awaited her, why did she do this? Truly, we will never know. In any case, her unsolicited testimony, not influenced by torture or by her accusers' expectations, is a fascinating account of her "witchly" experiences. It includes such interesting activities as entering the Faery Realm and visiting with its inhabitants, meeting the Faery King and Queen, observing the faery cattle, and shapeshifting into various animal shapes (particularly that of a hare), along with the more-to-be-expected malicious activities such as causing illness and death to people and cattle.

Particularly noteworthy among the remarkable things Isobel shared with the court are descriptions of her experiences within the Faery Realm, which offer several details commonly associated with the faery experience. The Faery Realm was located inside a hill, which opened for Isobel and the others of her coven to enter. Once inside they found themselves at the entrance to a large, "fair" hall which was bright as day. Isobel was frightened by several large elf-bulls who were "routing and skoyling" near the entrance to this hall. Inside the hall were the King and Queen of Faery. Isobel reported that the Queen wore white linens and white and brown clothes, and that the King was "well favored and broad faced." She feasted with the faeries who gave her a generous amount of food, more than she could eat.

The reference to the faery hall being "bright as day" is quite interesting and accords with other accounts of the Faery Realm as being a place of light, although it is within the Earth.

We have already mentioned Bessie Dunlop of Dalry, a Scottish healer who, although she never visited the Faery Realm itself, saw and spoke with faeries and was instructed in the healing arts by the spirit of a man who had clear connections to the Faery Realm. Although Bessie did good work in her village, she was eventually convicted and executed for witchcraft simply because she had converse with the world of faeries and spirits.

It seems appropriate, at this point, to define what is meant by the word *witch*. *Witch* is a word that has been used for the past several hundred years to mean a person, usually but not always a woman, who possesses magical powers derived from a pact with the devil or his minions, and who uses these powers to do evil, causing harm to humans, crops, and cattle. Whether this is an accurate definition of the word witch or not is something that has been argued strenuously by those of the Neo-Pagan revival of the last 50 years, who have reclaimed the word to refer to an Earth-honoring, wholistic spiritual practice with core elements that may date back thousands of years and possibly to the shamanistic and magical practices of the cave dwellers of Europe. These core elements, or fragments of them, were carried forward in time by various Pagan religions, as well as secretly within certain families. Traces of them can still be found in folklore and faery tales.

Witches were accused of worshiping and consorting with the devil, known as Satan or Lucifer, who was supposedly the antithesis of God and the author of all evil. In actuality, the Christian figure of the devil is an interesting conflation of several other figures and concepts.

The word *devi* is itself related to the Sanskrit *deva*, which is translated as *Shining One*, and is understood to meant an "organizing intelligence" type of spiritual being. Mythologically, the word *deva* was used to refer to the gods and goddesses who were the "organizing intelligences" of the nature realm, and is still used in modern Theosophy to mean such.

Satan was originally the Hebrew *Saitan*, or adversary. This does not inherently imply evil; the concept is more akin to that of the *worthy adversary* who keeps one on one's toes by his challenges and opposition. In the early Hebrew Scriptures, Satan was simply an adversary, one of any number of angelic beings God might send to offer specific difficult challenges to humans, for purposes known only to the Divine Mind.[3]

Lucifer means, quite literally, *light bearer*. In old Gnostic lore, Lucifer is the *Light of God*—this term representing God's spiritual spark which imparts the intelligence of mind—who falls to the Earth and into the Earth, imbuing substance with Spirit. Thus Lucifer *bears* the *light* of God—mind and intelligence—to Earth.

Combining myth, metaphor, and science, Lucifer may be seen as the consciousness of the star spark that spun off from the solar parent and evolved over eons into our familiar planet Earth. This spark, the "star within the Earth," is now the consciousness (i.e., mind and intelligence) of the stellar, fiery hot, planetary core and heart, and source (along with the sun) of all conscious life on and in the planet. (See Notes at end of chapter.)

Although Lucifer is scripturally referred to as "he," please understand that this energy is androgynous as masculine and feminine polarities do not exist at such a primal core level of being; they come into being in a later phase of evolutionary development.

Along with the legends of Lucifer being cast out of heaven and into hell, one is reminded again of the Irish legends concerning the angels who fell to Earth and became the faeries.

The devil was said to have horns and was often depicted in animal form. As many scholars have noted, this ties him to the old Horned God of many Pagan cultures who was an embodiment of the raw, virile, masculine, life-and-death power connected with the animal realm, a power which encompassed both the hunter and the hunted. Artistic renderings of the old Knights Templar descriptions of Baphomet, a "devilish idol" associated with the Templars and whom they were accused by the Church of worshiping, shows a black, horned goat-headed figure, winged, but with human hands, phallus erect, and with a candle or torch between his horns. This depiction brings together the themes of the masculine life-giving animal power and the Light of God—spirit, mind, and intelligence. In addition, the Baphomet figure has female breasts, which makes for an interesting and androgynous figure. Baphomet contains male and female, animal and human, darkness and light—symbols of the polarities inherent in physical, earthly life.

The devil that the witches were accused of honoring has come down to us clothed in the garb of the Christian inquisitors. Even so, there appear to be some genuine, archaic, Pagan survivals and truths included among his garments, truths about whose significance the inquisitors may have had little idea.

The word witch derives from the Old English *wicca* (masc.) meaning wizard or sorcerer, and *wicce* (fem.) meaning witch or sorceress. The complete etymology of the word witch is complex and far from certain, but it seems to derive from the earlier Germanic *wikkjaz*, meaning necromancer (one who knows how to waken the dead). In addition, the etymology suggests a relationship with a variety of Proto Indo-European root words, including *weg*, which means to be strong and lively; *weik*, which has to do with consecratory activities, yet also with bending and pliability; and *weid*, meaning "to see, to know." Related words may be the English *wit*, knowledge, the Old High German *wizzan*, to know, the Latin *videre*, to see (seeing and knowing are often connected), and the Old High German *wih*, holy. There are additional strands of etymology that bring in meanings of bending, shaping, twisting, and divination.[4]

Carlo Ginzburg, in his classic work *Ecstasies: Deciphering the Witches' Sabbath*, has given good evidence for the survival into medieval times (in the Celtic, Slavic, and Mediterranean areas) of a very archaic strata of European magical beliefs relating to Goddess worship, healing, shapeshifting, and shamanic type night battles between the Friulian *benandanti*, or "good doers," and the *malandanti*, or evil witches and sorcerers who were thought to steal the fertility of the flock and field.

Much like the Faery Doctors, whose faery-given abilities to heal did not interfere with their fervent Catholicism, the benandanti insisted that their nightly spirit battles did not interfere with their ability to be good Christians. Since they were battling the powers of evil, they considered themselves to be very religious indeed. The Inquisition, however, was not convinced.

The malandanti and benandanti had their Celtic counterparts in the practitioners of *cronachadh* or harming and *beannachadh* or blessing. The former cursed others with illness, ill-luck, and particularly the Evil Eye, while the latter helped and healed.

What interests us here primarily, however, is that the malandanti were accused of things nearly identical to what the spiteful faeries or Unseeley Court were accused of: stealing both fertility and the very essence of the flock and field. And the benandanti, identified as such because they were born with the caul (amniotic sac) still around them, possessed the Second Sight and the ability to "travel in ecstasy" in the Spirit Worlds, just as did many of the Faery Healers of the Celtic traditions, who were likewise known to be seers and healers, especially when born with the caul.

In addition to the night-*battling* benandanti who were primarily men, there were night-*riding* benandanti who were almost always women. On certain nights they rode in silent procession along with the spirits of the dead, lead by the goddess or "blessed woman," whose name varied with the locality.[5]

These similarities are very interesting indeed. In fact, the night-riding benandanti of Italy are but one example of night-riding, ecstatic, spiritual journeying found in old European folk traditions. Legends of night-riding beings—humans, animals, deities—point clearly back to an ancient European shamanic folk tradition of traveling in spirit, similar to what is practiced even today in cultures whose shamanic traditions are still intact.

The most well known of the night-riders were, of course, the witches, who, it was said, always "flew" to their sabbats riding brooms, poles, fennel stalks, animals, or in the shape of animals. They had their amazing and vivid experiences, and then flew back home again.

Similarly, in lands with Teutonic influence in their heritage it was known that the Wild Hunt rode forth during the winter months, sweeping and howling its way through the stormy night skies. The Hunt was said to be lead by a god—either Herne, Odin, Gwyn ap Nudd, depending upon the location—and/or a goddess—Frau Holda, Perchta, Berta. They were the Lord and Lady of the Wild Hunt. Interestingly, at least one of these gods, Gwyn ap Nudd, is also said to be the King of the Faeries. The Hunt swept through the skies gathering up the souls of the dead—and occasionally souls of the living who happened to be in the wrong place at the wrong time—and what was left from the old tide of life so that the new tide could begin. Those in the train of the Lord and Lady were sometimes said to be the souls of the dead, the ancestors, witch women, or sometimes a pack of white (or black) dogs with red eyes or ears, this last a description quite typical of Otherwordly beasts.

Many of the inquisitors questioning those accused of witchcraft believed that the witches quite literally flew through the air, though a few were convinced that the witches flew only in their imaginations. Witches supposedly employed various *flying ointments* to help them fly, the recipes presumably given to them by the devil or his assistants. These ointments were composed of various noxious-seeming and poisonous ingredients, but also, interestingly, of herbs with varying degrees of hallucinogenic properties.

The belief that witches could fly was a curiously literal evolution of an earlier statement to the contrary by the Church. The famous and oft-quoted *Canon Episcopi* of the 10th century stated that there were certain "wicked women, perverted by the devil, and seduced by illusions and phantasms of demons," who believed themselves to able fly through the night, certain nights of the year, with Diana, goddess of the pagans. This statement says clearly that the women who believed they did this were *deluded*, that is, they did not literally fly, but only *imagined* they did so. What a curious turnabout it was for the Church, six centuries later, to insist that the women actually did, quite literally, fly through the air!

To return to the subject of the benandanti, it is also of interest to note that they went forth to their night battles and gatherings on the four Ember Days, that is, *four times a year*, at times that corresponded with the sowing and/or harvesting of the crops. These Ember Days had been fixed by the Church in the early 11th century to correspond with earlier Pagan festivals having to do with the seasonal sowing and harvesting cycle of the year. These times correspond approximately with the equinoxes and solstices, which, as seasonal markers were the rough, functional equivalent (though not the same as) of the Quarter Days so beloved of the Celts.

The relationship of these quarter or solstice/equinox days, the traces of Goddess worship, and the benandanti's battles to preserve the sowing, harvesting, and fertility of the land from the effects of harmful beings, would seem to indicate that what is really going on here has to do with the various spirits of the land and with the land's cycle of fertility.

This brings us back around again to faeries and fairies, who were intimately connected with the powers within the land, the natural features of the land, as well as the vitality and fertility of the land.

The etymology of the word faery/fairy is also quite interesting. The Old English *fairy*, meaning an enchanted Being (or place, for instance fairyland), comes directly from the Old French word of the same meaning, *fairie*, and its relatives, *fee, feie, fae*, all of which derive from the Latin *fatum*, fate, and *Fata*, the name of goddess of fate. Interestingly, the Proto-Indo European root of fate, *bha*, has meanings which involve speaking, announcing, and prophesying, and also relates to the Greek *phos*, meaning light. This last is quite interesting in that the Theosophical psychics of the early 20th century reported that they often perceived faeries as spheres of light which would then condense down into a more recognizable humanoid-type shape.

It should be noted here that the folklore presents evidence of several interesting similarities between witches and faeries. Both witches and faeries were said to be fond of gathering for revels at the time of the full moon, were accused of being allied with the devil, of stealing animals and unbaptized children, were capable of shapeshifting, and were repelled by salt and iron. In addition, witches were thought to gather on the four Quarter Days, while faeries were thought to *flit* or change residence on those same days. Interestingly, in King James I of England's book about witches, *Daemonologie*, Diana, the goddess of witches, is also mentioned as being "Queen of the Faeries."

Diana has a long history as the goddess of the witches, under her Roman name of Diana and the many other names (including Artemis, Herodias, Aradia, and Habondia) by which she was known in other lands. As mentioned above regarding the *Canon Episcopi*, there are legends of Diana, under various of her many names, leading a procession of the souls of the dead, or, alternatively, a procession of the spirits of living women. They follow her silently through the night, obeying whatever orders she might given them, learning from her the virtues of herbs and healing, how to dissolve spells, and to find things which had been stolen. Charles Godfrey Leland's classic work, *Aradia, the Gospel of the Witches*, gives us the important piece of information, taken from Italian witch lore, that Diana had a brother who was none other than Lucifer, the "light-bearer," bearer of God's light, or perhaps, a god of light himself.

Much harm and distortion has come about due to a mistranslation of a biblical Old Testament verse that in the King James and subsequent versions is rendered as "Thou shalt not suffer a *witch* to live." The actual meaning of the word in question was more akin to *poisoner*, and the verse therefore, should have, read, "Thou shalt not suffer a poisoner to live." Before and during the era this translation was made, witches were thought to deal in herbal poisons; in the minds of the translators, the two—witch and poisoner—may well have been synonymous. In addition, the translators were working under the patronage of King James of England who was very much against witches since he was convinced that they had targeted him for death. One can see, therefore, how such a confused mistranslation came about.

But although there was much distortion and misconception about the power, influence, technicalities, and extent of witchcraft, there must have been a kernel of truth behind some, though certainly not all, of the accusations. There were, and still are, people who used their power to ill-wish others and their knowledge of herbs to poison and hurt, just as there were those who helped, healed, and blessed (it is unlikely, however, that the majority of people accused and executed for witchcraft had anything at all to do with the so-called "Black Arts.")

This is true of the world of subtle beings as well. Lady Wilde mentions an Irish belief that the bad faeries taught their evil magic to the witch women.

Not all beings in the universe are sweet, kind, friendly, and have the best interests of humans at the top of their list of priorities. Indeed, their first priority might be, as is frequently our own, their own food and survival. While this may not currently be a popular opinion about Spirit Beings in some schools of metaphysical thought, it has, through time, proven true nonetheless; and these facts must be taken into consideration in any study of witches, faeries, or other Otherworldly Beings.

In an attempt to illuminate this difference between spirits, W. B. Yeats put it succinctly in his piece *Witches, Fairy Doctors*: "Witches and fairy doctors receive their power from opposite dynasties; the witch from evil spirits and her own malignant will; the fairy doctor from the fairies, and a something—a temperament—that is born with him or her. The first is always feared and hated. The second is gone to for advice and is never worse than mischievous."[6]

So it would seem that what we are presented with in the case of the benandanti and malandanti, the Seeley and Unseeley Courts of Faery, and the poisoning-spiteful and helpful-healing witches, is that *both* types existed, because power is neutral and can be used equally for benefit or for harm, depending upon the will of the user. This is the nature of the polarity/duality that characterizes life as it manifests on the physical plane. Whether or not we should use the word *witch* as a label for the harm-doers is a completely separate question.

NOTES

1. However, Lucifer may also be seen simply as the being who brings God's light of mind and intelligence to Earth. Lucifer was the Roman name for the planet Venus which, when it was seen in the predawn skies was known as the *Morning Star*. As the morning star, Venus/Lucifer appeared before dawn and was the herald of the day's light and warmth. Venus was the third brightest object in the sky, second only to the sun and moon, and thus was very significant to the ancients, who were nothing if not sky-watchers. Theologically and mythologically, Venus was the Roman goddess of love and beauty, and thus desire and heart, all of which link her with the faery realm and Diana, Goddess of the Pagans, whose "brother" or male counterpart was Lucifer. Luciferian legends are interesting but complex; we only touch briefly upon them here.

END NOTES

1. Hole, Christina, *Witchcraft in England*, B. T., Batsford Ltd, London, Charles Scribner's Sons, NY, 1947, p. 69.

2. Clarkson, Rosetta, *Golden Age of Herbs & Herbalists*, Dover Publications, Inc, NY, NY, 1972, p. 261.

3. Pagels, Elaine, *The Origin of Satan*, Vintage Books, Random House, Inc, NY, 1995, p. 41.

4. Johnson, Thomas K. (a.k.a. Nicholas Gander), private conversation.

5. Ginzburg, Carlo, *Ecstasies: Deciphering the WitchesÕ Sabbath*, Penguin Books USA, NY, NY, 1992, pp.14, 93.

6. Yeats, W. B., "Witches, Fairy Doctors," *Irish Fairy and Folk Tales*, Boni and Liveright, Inc., NY, NY, 1918, p. 156.

PART II

Making the Cure

CHAPTER 8

Faery-Induced Ailments and Their Cures

It was thought that the faeries did many things that disturbed and frightened humans. They stole babies. They took away nursing mothers to nurse their own faery babies, often leaving some "thing" in place of the baby, or leaving the person physically present but weak, wan, and often deathly ill. They harmed cattle, and took the *essence* from milk and butter. In addition, faeries were responsible for causing certain ailments.

The possibility of having one's child stolen, and a faery child, or changeling (who was, without fail, wizened, ugly, and bad tempered) left in the child's place, was especially frightening. A whole medley of practices—from placing a hot coal beneath the cradle, to sewing a bit of the always-protective iron into the child's gown—existed to prevent this distressing occurrence.

There were likewise many practices and procedures for getting the stolen child back again. Most of them involved somehow frightening or threatening the changeling and making use of the things faeries found abhorrent, such as iron and fire, until the changeling's true family reclaimed it and returned the "real" human child. Sometimes, however, these strategies were taken to very desperate lengths, such as when it was advised that the changeling child be put into the fireplace, in hopes that its faery parents would come to rescue it and return the human child.[1] It is very sad to think of the children who were killed by such desperate measures.

That the changeling phenomenon was known in the Germanic countries as well as the Celtic is evidenced in folklore and writings. No less an authority than the famed Martin Luther wrote, in 1540, that he had personally met, seen, and touched a changeling himself, observing its behaviors, which he found contrary to a normal child's behaviors and reactions. He felt the child was only a "piece of flesh" with no soul and should be drowned, or failing that, an exorcism should be performed.[2] These are rather extreme sentiments but not out of keeping with how these unfortunate children were regarded.

The changeling phenomenon has never been adequately explained. Some authorities feel that the babies people described as changelings were just human babies grown suddenly very sick. This may well have been true in many cases, perhaps even in most cases. But it is hard to understand how a person used to living close to nature and its accompanying harsh realities of sickness and death would fail to recognize his or her own child simply because the child's appearance may have altered by falling suddenly ill. Nor does it explain the instances where the cure is performed and the real child is returned. So, just as with all the other faery-induced situations and illnesses, changelings remain a mysterious and unexplained phenomena.

Fairy-caused Ailments

Ailments thought to be inflicted by faeries included paralysis, slipped discs, and anything that twisted or deformed the body; these were supposedly due to faery blows being administered for one reason or another. For more minor offenses against the faeries people might be afflicted with cramps or bruises, especially small round ones clustered together. These were said to come from being pinched by faery fingers. Consumption was thought to come from either being taken away to the faery mounds every night, or else from feeling a compulsive need to go to the faery mounds every night—an activity that deprived the person of sleep and therefore left them constantly tired. In addition, wasting diseases such as tuberculosis were often blamed on faeries, although perhaps more frequently on witches. Skin diseases, including impetigo, were considered to be caused by the faeries as were lice. Sometimes barrenness or difficult childbirth was blamed on the faeries, but this was also blamed on witches.

The folklore record names a few major diseases (and several minor disorders) that were caused by the faeries, and also gives us some information about how these ailments were diagnosed and treated by the Faery Healers. Let us now examine these diseases and the techniques that were used to treat them.

FAERY BLAST

Also referred to as Faery Wind, this condition came on suddenly under specific conditions and was characterized by depression and low, or complete lack of vitality. It was dealt with by the use of blast-water, of which we will say more, below.

It was known that the faery hosts often traveled in whirlwinds which swirled up dust, grasses, leaves, and other things in their path. Swirling wind of this kind was known as the Faery Wind. It was believed that the faeries traveling in this swirling wind were capable of striking anything and anyone that lay in their path. When this happened it was referred to as the Faery Blast, and the person blasted presented immediate and quite striking symptoms. The victim might fall down unconscious or sick upon the spot, or find their health changing dramatically from one day to the next. Having seen a whirlwind pass about the same time, the person would attribute their sudden illness to the faeries. In some cases the person recovered equally quickly, which was also seen as further evidence of faery influence.[3]

Dr. Patrick Logan, writing of this in his wonderful book, *The Old Gods: The Facts About Irish Fairies*, offers the idea that Faery Blast victims might have been suffering from sudden seizures of one kind or another—unexplainable to the common folk and the medical understanding of the time. He suggests that the Faery Blast might have been anything from simple heat stroke or loss of salt in sweat on hot days (the time during which Faery Blast seemed most likely to occur), to hysteria from seeing the whirlwind and worrying about the faeries, or even more serious conditions such as meningitis or hemorrhage.[4]

The cure for Faery Blast was for *blast-water* to be poured over the victim by a Faery Doctor while saying, "In the name of the saint with the sword, who has strength before God and stands at his right hand." Lady Wilde says that great care had to be taken that no part of the water was profaned, and what was left of it had to be poured on the fire.[5] This cure used the always sacred powers of water and fire as St. Michael, who is the Archangel of Fire, is the "saint with the sword," and the leftover blast-water was "offered to the fire."

FAERY STROKE

Closely related to Faery Blast but much more serious was the Faery Stroke. This term was used for the sudden occurrence or attack of a serious disease, one from which the person was not known to have previously suffered. The disease was always serious, dramatic, and debilitating, often with seizures or sudden severe pain, fever, or infection. Dr. Logan suspects that Faery Stroke may well have been epilepsy or perhaps osteomyelitis. When Faery Stroke occurred in young children, especially young girls, they often seemed to pine and wither away for no apparent reason. It was thought that this happened because the faeries wanted them; in the case of young girls, it was thought that they were desired as brides by some of the faery chiefs or princes.

When a child was faery-struck, the remedy given was often a drink of the juice of twelve foxglove leaves. Today we know that foxglove affects the heart. It is the source of the heart drug digitalis and can be quite dangerous if used wrongly. The use of foxglove for Faery Stroke suggests that the healers knew that it affected the heart, knew it was strong medicine, and thus used it to cure a sad and pining heart. Foxglove was also administered in this manner to cure fevers.

Lady Wilde gives a very old and potent charm that was used to great effect in case of a suspected Faery Stroke. Three rows of salt were placed on a table in three lines, three equal measures to each row. The person doing the cure then enclosed the rows of salt with his arms, leaning his head down over them while saying the Lord's Prayer three times over each row, nine times in all. He then took the hand of the faery-struck person, and over the hand recited the following: "By the power of the Father and of the Son, and of the Holy Spirit, let this disease disappear, and the spell of the evil spirits be broken. I adjure, I command you to leave this man (naming him). In the name of God I pray. In the name of Christ I adjure. In the name of the Spirit of God I command and compel you to go back and leave this man free. Amen. Amen."

Please note all the magical threes present in this cure:

Three rows of salt, in
Three lines on the table.
Three equal measures in each row

This is nine. Then,

Three Lord's prayers recited over each row.

Again equaling nine. And then,

The invocation of the Holy Trinity.

This is three again as there are three persons in the Trinity. Also notice the commands are also three in number:

That the disease disappear
That the spell of the evil spirits be broken
That the man be left alone.

These three commands are further strengthened by being

prayed
adjured
commanded and compelled

—thrice invoked to occur. And each of them by a separate power of the Trinity:

In the name of God I pray.

In the name of Christ I adjure.
In the name of the Spirit of God I command and compel

The number of the commands, the ways they are conjured, and the beings to which they are addressed give us an additional nine.

The power of the faery-repelling salt, the power of the threes, nines, and twenty-seven, and the power of the Holy Trinity, made this a most potent charm for curing the Faery Stroke.

FAERY DARTS

It was thought that faeries would occasionally shoot their flint-tipped arrows or darts at humans. Being struck by one of these was thought to cause illness, disability, paralysis, or even death. Often this condition was referred to as being "elf shot." If the faery intention was to kill, it must be said that they were pretty poor shots as faery darts seldom killed anyone though they always caused problems of some kind.

Faery darts were usually aimed at feet and hands, especially fingers, and caused joint swelling, redness, and inflammation. Curing this condition required a Faery Doctor who used an elaborate ritual consisting of many prayers and the use of a special salve. This salve, whose herbal ingredients were held secret, was mixed with unsalted butter—which contains fat soluble vitamins that are quite healing to the skin—to make it spreadable. The salve frequently made the skin red. Some of the herbs were obviously irritants; perhaps stinging nettle was part of the recipe. The irritant herb stimulated the circulation, which could have proven helpful in bringing the offending dart to the skin's surface. Application of the salve was followed by the actual extraction of the faery dart, frequently by using a small instrument such as a slender needle to poke around in search of it. When found, it proved to be a tiny bit of something such as a flax seed which was carefully and ostentatiously removed, and then displayed to the victim and his or her family.

A bottle of medicine was made up for the patient, consisting of the water from boiling "sally rods," which were most likely willow twigs, till the brew was strong and bitter. Willow water or tea contains salicylin which is a pain reliever (aspirin is salicylic acid). Dr. Logan is of the opinion that Faery Darts were, in fact, acute rheumatism or arthritis, and that the salve was a counter irritant, which can sometimes actually bring great relief to the condition.[6]

Our modern treatments for arthritis, usually anti-inflammatories and aspirin for pain, really don't offer too much more!

Other Mysterious Evils
THE EVIL EYE

Though not always directly connected with faeries, the Evil Eye (in Irish, *an droch suil*) and its effects must be mentioned here as they were very much dreaded by the people.

The Evil Eye was a look—a glance—that carried such inherent malevolence that it felt like a poison that could wither and blight. When one was suffering from the effect of the Evil Eye, it was said he or she was being "overlooked."

Lady Wilde describes it thus: "…an influence that seems to paralyze intellect and speech, simply by the mere presence in the room of someone who is mystically antipathetic to our nature. For the soul is like a fine-toned harp that vibrates to the slightest external force or movement, and the presence of some persons can radiate around us a divine joy, while others may kill the soul with a sneer or a frown. We call these subtle influences mysteries, but the early races believed them to be spirits, good or evil, as they acted on the nerves or the intellect."[7]

Belief in the Evil Eye is an old belief, so old that it is referred to in the Brehon laws of early Ireland. This belief was not unique to the Celtic lands but was found in many other lands as well.

People were born possessing the Evil Eye though it might not manifest unless circumstances caused it to awaken. Although most who possessed the Evil Eye seemed to also radiate envy, anger, or malice, this was not true of all who had it. People who were otherwise quite respectable and agreeable could simply suffer the misfortune of having been born with the Evil Eye, a situation which then required them to spend their lives trying to avoid exposing it to others, and thus causing inadvertent harm. Often an eyepatch was used to mask the offending eye. Some afflicted with the Evil Eye handled it by averting their eyes when they spoke to others so as not to unintentionally cause misfortune.[8]

It was thought that children conceived before their parents were married and children not validly baptized might be found to have the Evil Eye. It was also believed that if a pregnant woman denied she was pregnant, the baby would be born with the Evil Eye.

May Eve and the first Monday of a Quarter were considered times when the Evil Eye might be particularly powerful, and special care to avoid it was taken at those times of year.

Certain physical characteristics seemed to be associated with the Evil Eye. For instance, people, especially women, with dark, lowering eyebrows were suspect, perhaps because such eyebrows made them look as if they were glaring and ill-tempered. Red hair, though perhaps not associated with the Evil Eye, was also considered to have a malignant influence—so much so that there was a saying about it: "Let not the eye of a red-haired women fall on you."

According to Lady Wilde, the Evil Eye could come into play in several ways. If met with first thing in the morning it would, of course, cause the rest of the day to be unlucky. If someone came by, or came into one's home to rest and stared fixedly at someone or something, it might be that he was giving him the Evil Eye—a fact frequently not known until the offender had departed. Sometimes the bewitching was done by staring fixedly at another through nine fingers (that magical nine again). These things could all be remedied by a counter-charm from a Faery Doctor.

To avoid being suspected of having the Evil Eye it was necessary to say "God bless it" when looking at a child, and "The blessing of God be on you and on all your labors" when passing a farmyard where the cows were ready for milking. If this was not said, it was immediately suspected that it had been intentionally omitted, and that the person omitting it had the desire and perhaps the power to do harm.

People used all the usual protective things—salt, saliva, iron, red thread, and fire—to avert the power of the Evil Eye, and pieces of rock crystal were worn as protective amulets against it. As with other such ills, rowan was considered a powerful and helpful protection.[9]

Infants had to be protected from the Eye by people saying "God bless it" when they picked the infant up. "God bless it" was widely used as a good luck charm because to call down a blessing was a countercharm. Therefore, the virtue of saying "God bless it" when looking at children was that in this way the children accrued so many blessings that it was harder for the faeries to harm them if they were "taken," or for the Evil Eye to have a fatal effect on them.

A person with the Evil Eye could cause affliction of varying degrees of severity. If such a one muttered a verse over a sleeping child, this was fatal and could not be countered; no charm was powerful enough to turn away this evil. If the bewitching was done in the evening when the moon was full and the victim was seated by the fire, it was also fatal.

Once *overlooked*, symptoms were not long in appearing in the afflicted one. Symptoms might be almost anything. Weakness, pain, fits, and swellings arising shortly after the suspected overlooking would be attributed to the Evil Eye, and treated swiftly and appropriately because otherwise, death might occur.

As with the issue of abduction by faeries, the young and beautiful or anything worthy of admiration and positive attention were especially susceptible to the Evil Eye, which seems to be very much associated with jealousy. Not wanting to invoke the jealousy and therefore the Eye, it was nearly automatic to say "God bless it" when referring to those susceptible to the influence of the Eye. Lady Wilde associates the *superstition* of the Evil Eye with the story of Balor, the Fomorian giant of ancient Irish legend whose glance could turn his enemies to stone. Balor's eye acquired this power when he was passing by a place where several Druids were busily concocting a magical spell, boiling up things and chanting, and the steam of their cauldron passed under his eye. It carried with it all the venom and power of their incantation, and caused his "brow" (i.e., eyelid) to grow so enormous that it required four men to lift it when he wanted to use the power of his eye.[10]

In Ireland, if the Evil Eye was even suspected, a Faery Doctor had to be consulted immediately to recite the correct charm or incantation to destroy its malignant and possibly fatal influence. In Scotland, a "skeely woman" or one possessing the *eolas* or "secret knowledge of an infallible cure" was sought out to affect a cure.[11]

In places in Scotland, *silvered water* was occasionally used as a treatment. Silvered water was water into which silver coins had dropped; and it was prepared in a special way. The water had to be taken from certain river pools that held power, such as those under a bridge that led into a churchyard since this was water over which both the living and the dead had passed and was therefore powerfully "liminal." The water had to be carefully lifted out with a wooden ladle, and the silver coins dropped into it as a charm was recited. Then the water was divided into three parts. The afflicted person was given three sips of the water and the rest of it was sprinkled on him or her, and around their fireside. Silvered water combined the cleansing and regenerative power of water with the power of the moon, as the moon's especial metal is silver.[12]

Sometimes a charm invoking the power of the Trinity was recited while the silvered water was being sprinkled on the afflicted one. Then a drop of water was poured behind the fire-flags and another charm was recited which sent the problem back to the one who'd caused it.

Thy strait be on the fire-flags,
Thine ailment on the wicked woman.[13]

Since jealousy was often suspected to be the inspiration for the Evil Eye, sometimes the charms recited addressed that issue:

An eye covered thee,
A mouth spoke thee,
A heart envied thee,
A mind desired thee.[14]

In the Orkney and Shetland Islands special magical waters were used to cure the Evil Eye. This cure was prepared by dropping small pebbles, gathered from the seashore and of different colors, into water. Although a variety of colored pebbles could be used, it was thought that the most potent charms were made if one stone was black, one white, and the remainder red, olive, or green in color.[15]

There was extreme fear about the Evil Eye because its power seemed so great and because it seemed to rob one of one's own self-reliance and leave one in a passive state, receptive to its evil influence. This was terrifying, and undoubtedly initiated a cycle of fear that grew worse over time and could actually result in a person being literally frightened to death.

But the Evil Eye was not without its positive uses. If someone with the Evil Eye looked upon a child while saying "God bless the child," this act prevented the faeries from stealing that child. Presumably, the power moving through the person because he or she possessed the Eye, combined with the power of the blessing was thought to be stronger than faery power.

Related to the idea of the Evil Eye is the concept of the power of "Fascination by Glance," which was thought to be a gift occasionally possessed by the learned and wise. Related to this is the faery glance, which causes one to enter into a death-like trance during which the real body is carried off into the Faery Realm and something else left in its place. This is, of course, quite the same thing that happened to those who were *taken away* by the faeries.

EVIL INFLUENCE

While less terrifying than the Evil Eye, the Evil Influence was nevertheless quite unpleasant. According to Lady Wilde, people could have an "evil influence" which they were able to cast over others. Sometimes this power was related to cursing. Lady Wilde gives a few examples of cursing done by women who would go around a well, sometimes a holy well, backwards on their knees. They took water from the well and poured it out in the devil's name, asking evil to fall upon their intended victim.[16]

Sometimes an evil influence could come upon a person as a result of that person, even quite innocently, having made the faeries angry.

EVIL STROKE

The Evil Stroke is the ability to cause evil by some form of touch. Similar to the Evil Eye, people seemed to just be born with it, but not all born with it were necessarily bad people. Lady Wilde says that those who possessed it did not act from intentional ill will but from necessity, from a force deep within that acted without the person's conscious volition or assent, and often to his or her sincere regret.

The power of the Evil Stroke seemed to afflict people at unpredictable intervals, often seeming to originate from a chance stroke or blow.[17]

This power was, like the Eye, not without its benefits. A touch from the hand of one possessing the Evil Stroke could reduce a ferocious or mad animal to a state of utter tranquility, or cause the animal to back down, cowering in fear and incapable of doing harm.

Once someone had been harmed by the Evil Stroke, the harm could be undone by the one who had caused it. Lady Wilde cites a case where a young man inadvertently caused harm to another man during a sporting event, but he was able to cure it by anointing the injured arm with spittle, and by making the sign of the cross. If the person who had caused the harm could not be found to put things right, then the Faery Doctor must be called to do so, which he did by the use of many charms and much *stroking*.

Invasion by Evil Spirits and Other Bad Luck

There were other behaviors that were felt to simply invite bad luck and evil spirits. These, too, had their various protective and preventative remedies assigned for them.

As we have mentioned, it was considered very unlucky to give away any water, salt, or fire at certain times, particularly while the butter churning was going on. In addition, it was considered quite unlucky to steal or sneak anything from a smith's forge as smiths were considered powerfully magical because they wielded the power of fire to shape iron.

To yawn without making the sign of the cross protectively over the open mouth was thought to invite evil spirits to rush into the body and take up residence.

Other behaviors were thought to avert evil, such as using the left hand to gather up salt and toss it over the right shoulder into the fire. This strange-sounding measure used the protective powers of salt and fire and combined them with a left-right crossing-over motion, bringing together three protective things to form one very protective action.

Another interesting protective measure was used when going on a journey. The traveler picked ten blades of yarrow, gave one away as a tithe to the spirits, but kept the remaining (magical) nine as protection, placing them in the heel of his right stocking before beginning the journey. This was thought to insure that evil spirits, particularly the devil, would have no power over the traveler.[18]

All evil influences, including the Evil Eye to some extent, could be counteracted by saying: "The fruit of your wish be on your own body." Thus, the evil influence was sent back to the sender.[19]

END NOTES

1. Wilde, Lady, *Ancient Legends, Mystic Charms & Superstitions of Ireland*, Chatto & Windus, London, 1919, pp. 201-202, 230.

2. Luther, Martin, *Werke, kritische Gesamtausgabe: Tischreden* (Weimar: Böhlau, 1912-1921), v. 5, p. 9, http://www.pitt.edu/~dash/gerchange.html#GrimmChangelingIsBeaten.

3. Logan, Patrick, *The Old Gods: The Facts About Irish Fairies*, Appletree Press, Belfast, 1981, p. 97.

4. Ibid.

5. Wilde, Lady, *Ancient Legends, Mystic Charms & Superstitions of Ireland*, Chatto & Windus, London, 1919, p. 200.

6. Logan, Patrick, *The Old Gods: The Facts About Irish Fairies*, Appletree Press, Belfast, 1981, p. 89.

7. Wilde, Lady, *Ancient Legends, Mystic Charms & Superstitions of Ireland*, Chatto & Windus, London, 1919, p. 21.

8. Ibid, p. 24.

9. McNeil, F. Marian, *The Silver Bough, Vol. 1*, William MacLellan, 1956, Canongate Classics, Edinburgh, 1989, p. 165.

10. Wilde, Lady, *Ancient Legends, Mystic Charms & Superstitions of Ireland*, Chatto & Windus, London, 1919, p. 23.

11. McNeil, F. Marian, *The Silver Bough, Vol. 1*, William MacLellan, 1956, Canongate Classics, Edinburgh, 1989, p. 165.

12. MacKenzie, Donald A., *Scottish Folk-lore and Folklife*, Blackie & Son, Ltd, London and Glasgow, 1935, pp. 267-268.

13. Carmichael, Alexander, *Carmina Gadelica, Vol. 4*, Oliver and Boyd, Edinburgh & London, 1928, p. 155.

14. McNeil, F. Marian, *The Silver Bough, Vol. 1*, William MacLellan, 1956, Canongate Classics, Edinburgh, 1989, p. 165.

15. Wood-Martin, Robert, *Traces of the Elder Faiths of Ireland: A Handbook of Irish Pre-Christian Traditions, Vol. 1*, Longmans, Greens, and Co., NY and Bombay, 1902, p. 331.

16. Wilde, Lady, *Ancient Legends, Mystic Charms & Superstitions of Ireland*, Chatto & Windus, London, 1919, pp. 71-72.

17. Ibid, p. 228.

18. Ibid, p. 208.

19. Campbell, John Gregorson, *Superstitions of the Highlands and Islands of Scotland*, James MacLehose & Sons, Glasgow, 1900, p. 281.

CHAPTER 9

Faery Herbs: Materia Magic, Materia Medica

Faerylore mentions many plants, herbs, trees, and flowers that are traditionally associated with faeries. In fact, it sometimes seems as if *most* flowers and trees have been associated with faeries at one time or another, and in one way or another. Probably the most well known of these faery trees are, of course, the "Oak, Ash, and Thorn," made famous by Rudyard Kipling's poem, *Puck of Pook's Hill*.[1] Oak trees are immortalized in the old folk saying, "Faery folks are in old oaks." Ash was considered powerful magic against evil forces, and the Thorn is, of course, the hawthorn—the faery tree par excellence.

Our emphasis, however, is on Faery Healing, so we will briefly examine plants traditionally associated with faeries, but focus on plants more specifically associated with Faery Healing, including those used for protection against faery wiles and magic.

Faery plants, both herbs and trees, can be said to fall into two major categories: those that *belong* to the faeries, and those that are protective against faery enchantments.

It is important to remember that the faeries were considered to have great knowledge of herbs. Indeed, the Faery Doctors were said to have acquired their knowledge of herbs from the faeries themselves, including and most especially, the knowledge of plants used to heal faery-induced ailments.

Let us take a look at each of these categories of plants.

Plants Belonging to the Faeries

The first category of faery plants is those which are said to belong to the faeries in some way. This category includes plants that faeries find attractive, such as cowslips and roses; plants that are used by them as articles of furniture, clothing, food, and even vehicles; and plants that are just simply associated with them, such as bluebells, elecampane, and thyme.

Into this first category fall plants such as the common mushroom, which was sometimes called faery table, and cowslips, which are known as fairy cups. Here also we find foxglove—known variously as faery gloves (or folks' gloves), faery thimbles, faery bells—and plants such as mallow, known in Yorkshire as faery cheese, as well as ragwort and cabbage stalks, upon which faeries are sometimes said to ride.

Much of this is quite fanciful and imaginative. Small, bell or bowl shaped flowers are suggestive of cups, thimbles, and the like, and mushrooms resemble tables. If one considers faeries to be tiny, sprightly dwellers-in-the-wild, then it is not hard to imagine them putting these plants to these uses.

Also among the plants said to belong to the faeries are those that are pleasing to them, are used to allow sight of them, or said to be useful in working with them. In this last category are, again, mushrooms—some of which may have hallucinogenic properties—as well as the hawthorn, known to be very sacred to the faeries, and wild thyme, which was one of the ingredients of a magical brew that allowed one to see faeries.

This category also includes a few interesting plants that seem to have the power to enchant humans. Lady Wilde refers to them as "faery grasses." The first of these is *Faud Shaughran*, which means *stray sod* or *wandering sod*. Whoever tread upon it found himself overcome with an irresistible urge to continue traveling on and on through the night, over all kinds of terrain without ever stopping, despite coldness, exhaustion, or sickness. This was accompanied by the sense of flying, with no ability to stop or even change course. The effect was gone by morning, when the traveler generally found himself cold, exhausted, or even bruised and bleeding, and twenty or thirty miles from home. There was another herb, whose name is not given in the lore, that could counteract the effects of *Faud Shaughran*, but only adepts knew how to utilize its powers.[2]

The second of these is called *Fair-Gortha*, which means *hunger-stricken sod*. It was said that if a traveler should happen to accidentally step on this grass he or she was seized with extreme hunger cravings and weakness, which if not attended to in time would cause death.

Here is a summary of the plants belonging to the faeries.

MATERIA MAGICA OF PLANTS BELONGING TO THE FAERIES

Bluebell *(Scilla nutans, Hyacinthus nonscriptus, Rosaceae;* Gaelic: *brog na cubhaig)* Faeries are summoned to their midnight revels and dances by the ringing of bluebells. Bluebells, which are actually wild hyacinths and grow primarily in deeply shaded woodlands, have an aura of danger and death around them. Faery scholar Katharine Briggs says bluebells can cause children and adults to be "pixy led," and can cause children to be taken.[3] It was said also that one who hears the sound of a bluebell ringing, calling faeries to their revels, would soon die. A field of bluebells is especially dangerous as it is intricately interwoven with faery enchantments. The connection of hyacinth with death is most likely from the Greek legend of the hyacinth flower. In this legend, a fair youth named Hyacinth, a favorite of Apollo, was killed accidentally. This fact greatly saddened Apollo, who then caused beautiful blue-purple flowers to arise from Hyacinth's blood. The fresh bulbs of the bluebell are extremely poisonous, perhaps another reason why bluebells are associated with death.

Broom (*Cytisus scoparius, Leguminosae, Papilionaceae;* Gaelic: *bealaidh, bealuidh*) Other common names for this plant are Irish broom, Scotch broom, green broom, broom plant, and genista. When found growing on natural mounds, its yellow flowers are associated with faery enchantments, as the flower's heavy scent has the ability to lull those nearby into a sleepy, magical, trancelike state of consciousness.[4] It was also referred to as the "plant from which the fairies spoke," which may be a reference to the Ballad of Young Tam Lin at the end of which the Faery Queen utters a curse "from out a bush of broom." Broom contains a mild but powerful psychoactive chemical, too much of which can be fatal. As the name would indicate, broom was used to make brooms, and had medicinal uses as well.

Cowslip (*Primula veris major, Primulaceae;* Gaelic: *muisean*) These pretty flowers are loved and protected by the faeries. One of their early names was "Keys of Heaven" and they were sometimes associated with the Virgin Mary and referred to as Our Lady's Keys since she was said to hold the keys to heaven. They were also referred to as herb peter, peterwort, or peterkin, a reference to St. Peter, who was also thought to be in charge of the Keys to Heaven. In pre-Christian times, the Norse Goddess Freya, as ruler of the heavens, was thought to hold the heavenly keys. Given this background, it is not surprising to find that cowslips are said to have the power to unlock hidden treasures. They were called Culvers Keys in Welsh and were said to help one to find hidden faery gold.[5]

Mrs Grieves says they are also called "fairy cups" and are, along with primrose and oxlips, members of the primrose tribe; much of the lore associated with primrose is applicable here as well. Cowslips were thought to protect against evil and were carried by country folk on Beltaine to protect the festivities from threat by witches or other evil forces. The red spots on a cowslip's delicate yellow petals were thought to be the spots of the blood of Christ, or alternately, rubies or fairy favors.

The cowslips tall among her pensioners be;
In their gold coats spots you see;
Those be rubies, fairy favours,

> *In those freckles live their savours.*
> *I must go seek some dewdrops here*
> *And hang a pearl in every cowslip's ear.*
> —William Shakespeare, 'A Midsummer Night's Dream,' Act II, Scene 1

Daisies (*Chrysanthemum leucanthemum, Compositae*; Gaelic: *nòinean*) The tiny field daisies, in particular, were protective plants and were worn in the form of a daisy chain necklace which looked somewhat like a necklace of little suns. The power of the sun was held to bring protection and blessing. Daisy was said to protect children from being kidnapped by the faeries. Daisies were very much associated with children in the Celtic world; in Scotland daisies were referred to as *Bairnwort* (*bairn* meaning child).

Elecampane (*Inula helenium, Compositae*; Gaelic: *eilidh*) Also called elfswort and elfdoc, it was said to be a favorite of faeries and elves and when scattered around the house attracted them, and presumably, their blessings.

Fern (*Pteris aquilina*, or *Filix minor longifolia, Filices*; Gaelic: *raineach*) This plant was also called bracken, or brake fern. In Cornwall, the pixies were especially fond of the fern. It was associated with promises that must be kept, as in the Cornish tale of a young woman accidentally sitting on a fern and then being forced by a faery man to stay and watch over his son for a year. Carrying fern seed gathered on St. John's Eve was said to render one invisible, though this idea might have arisen due to the near invisibility of fern's tiny seeds.[6]

Forget-me-nots (*Myosotis Boraginaceae Latifolia*) These delicate, petite members of the borage family were carried when searching for hidden treasure guarded by faeries or other spirits, and were thought to be associated with prosperity.

Foxglove (*Digitalis Purpurea, Scrophulariaceae*; Gaelic: *lus-nam-ban-sìth*) This is a plant rich in folklore. It was known as fairy bell or fairy glove in Ireland; in England it was known variously as fairy fingers, fairies' petticoat, fairy thimble, and fairy caps, and was also referred to as little folks' glove. Mrs. Grieves says that the name "foxglove" was originally "folks' glove; the glove of the good folk," or fairies, whose favorite haunts were supposed to be in the deep hollows and woodsy dells where the foxglove delights to grow."[7] Planted by the door it was said to invite faeries and faery light. Foxglove belongs to the faeries, yet is also associated with protection against them and other evil influences as well. For instance, if a child was elf-shot, the juice of twelve leaves of foxgloves was supposed to cure the ailment and foxglove juice was used as part of a procedure to determine whether a child was a changeling or the real child.[8]

Heather *(Calluna vulgaris;* Gaelic: *fraoch)* In parts of Scotland stalks of heather were thought to be a faery food.

Mallow *(Malva Rotundifolia,* also *Malva neglecta, Malvaceae;* Gaelic: *Hocas, Lus nam Meall Mòra)* Dwarf mallow was known in Yorkshire as fairy cheese.

Mushrooms *(Fungus campestris esculentus;* Gaelic: *agairg)* The common mushroom was known in Wales as a faery table, and in parts of England as the pixie stool. Mushrooms growing in a ring are said to mark the boundaries of a faery ring, which is a place where the faeries gather to feast and revel.

The most famous mushroom in folklore has got to be the spectacularly beautiful *amanita muscaria.* It was used by Northern shamans to facilitate their shamanic journeying, during which they saw all kinds of things, including, most likely, faeries. This white-spotted, red-capped mushroom, which has found its way into much faery-related artwork, has toxic properties and was also used for the much less glamorous purpose of killing flies and other insects. Amanita usually grows near birch or pine trees.

Pansies *(Viola Odorata, Viola Tricolor, Violaceae;* Gaelic: *sail chuach)* The humble but beautiful pansy is actually a violet and is also known by the endearing folkname "Heart's Ease." It is the sweet-smelling blossom that was used as a love-potion by Oberon, a faery king made famous by Shakespeare's "A Midsummer Night's Dream."

> *Fetch me that flower, the flower I shew'd thee once,*
> *The juice of it on sleeping eyelids laid*
> *Will make or man or woman wildly dote*
> *Upon the next live creature that it sees.*
> —William Shakespeare, 'A Midsummer Night's Dream,' Act 2, Scene 1

Violets were considered effective against evil and witchcraft, but could only be brought into the home in bunches as it was considered unlucky to bring just a solitary blossom.[9]

Peony *(Paeonia officinalis, Ranunculaceae;* Gaelic: *lus a phione)* A necklace made of its seeds was used to protect children from faeries and evil spirits and also as a preventative for convulsions. Sixteen black peony seeds steeped in wine and consumed were used as a specific remedy for nightmares.[10] Interestingly, peony seeds are said to glow faintly in the dark.[11]

Periwinkle *(Vinca major, vinca minor, Apocynaceae;* Gaelic: *faocha)* This plant is called sorcerer's violet in Somerset, but the term seems to mean faeries rather than sorcerers or witches.[12] In Wales it was known as the plant of the dead and was grown primarily on graves. It was considered unlucky to pluck its flowers or uproot it from a grave, as the dead buried there would then appear to the one who did this, giving him miserable and haunted dreams for the next year.[13]

Poppies *(Papaver, Papaveraceae*; Gaelic: *poipin)* Poppies are said to invoke faeries into one's dreams. The delicately beautiful poppy contains opiates and is therefore gently relaxing and sleep-inducing.

Primrose *(Primula vulgaris minor, Primulaceae*: Gaelic: *sobhrag)* According to legend, wearing primroses is a key into the land of Faery but only if worn in proper number. Another legend relates how a young girl found a doorway rock covered in flowers. She touched it with a primrose and it opened, leading into an enchanted castle. Primrose, therefore, seems to not only be a key into Faeryland but to have the power to make the invisible visible. In a similar story, a lost child picking primroses accidentally touched them to a faery rock. The faeries came out, gave her gifts, and showed her the way home. An old miserly man tried to imitate this just to get the gifts, but he took the wrong number of flowers and was never seen again. The significance of number as related to this flower is found in a related belief which says that if the number of primroses in a bouquet is less than thirteen, it must be protected by the inclusion of violets into the bouquet.[14] In Ireland, primroses plucked before sunrise were scattered on the threshold to protect the house from evil spirits. They were also tied in bunches to cows' tails by old women in order to keep away evil and to keep the faeries from stealing the milk and butter.[15] But in some parts of England, primroses are the special property of the faeries.

Ragwort *(Senecio Jacobaea, Compositae*; Gaelic: *Balcaisean)* Along with cabbage stalks and blades of grass and straw, ragwort stems were used by diminutive fairies for transportation, similar to the manner of a witch on her broom. Ragwort was said to belong to the faeries and therefore could not be used against them. This is shown in a story of a man who found beneath a ragwort a treasure left there by a faery. The man tied his red garter to it, to mark the spot, and rushed off to get a spade to dig it up. When he returned later he found red garters tied to all the ragworts in the field, thus saving the faery treasure from human greed.[16]

Roses *(Rosaceae)* Roses have a long history of association with the magical arts. They were worn as protection against the Evil Eye and yet were also said to attract faeries. In the *Ballad of Young Tam Lin*, Janet summons her faery lover by pulling a rose from a bush near a well (i.e., gateway to Faery) in the magical and haunted Carterhaugh Wood. Rosewater was used as part of a recipe for a magical brew that enabled one to see the faeries. Since roses have long been associated with the Goddess, including the Goddess in her Faery Queen aspect, they became connected with the lore of the Blessed Virgin Mary as well. They are beautiful, colorful, sensually aromatic and enticing, yet the sharp thorns command respect as they can be quite painful—very appropriate to a plant representing the Goddess of both life and death. In addition to the beautiful flowers we most commonly think of as roses, it is interesting to note that the apple and the hawthorn—both magically important plants and both important in faery lore—belong to the Rosaceae family.

Scarlet Pimpernel *(Anagallis arvensis, Primulaceae*; Gaelic: *rinn-ruisc, falcaire fiadhain, seamair mhuire)* This tiny beautiful plant was used magically to induce Second Sight and Hearing. Although it also was used medicinally, its narcotic properties make it safe only in the hands of those with proper training and knowledge.

Silverweed *(Potentilla anserina, Rosaceae* Gaelic: *Brisgein)* The yellow flowered *brisgein*, as it was known in Scotland, was thought to be faery food and the property of the Little People; it was thought unwise to uproot it. In spite of this injunction, humans were also known to eat the nutritious root of this plant, particularly in the era before the introduction of the potato. It was also known as white tansy and silver cinquefoil, the silver in the name referring to the silvery, silky hairs on the underside of the leaves.

Toadstools Although technically there is no difference between toadstools and mushrooms, the term *toadstool* has been used traditionally to refer to poisonous mushrooms. Indeed, some mushrooms are deadly poisonous, and some have hallucinogenic properties. The Vikings consumed them; this is probably connected to the Vikings' reputation as "berkerkers." In Celtic lore, the reddish ones are considered as the foods of the gods, as was true with many red plants. Some toadstools/mushrooms associated with the faeries are fly agaric, yellow fairy club, slender elf cap, dune pixie-hood, dryad's saddle, and as mentioned above, the *amanita muscaria* mushroom.

Water Lily *(Nymphaea Alba, Nymphaeaceae*; Gaelic: *duileag bhaite bhàn)* In the Highlands of Scotland it was thought that the faeries used water lily to facilitate their spells, and that it could actually cause one to become faery struck.[17]

Wild Thyme *(Thymus drucei, Labiatae*; Gaelic: *lus an righ)* Wild thyme is part of a recipe for a brew that was consumed to enable one to see the faeries. As found in a manuscript dating back to 1600, the recipe also calls for marigold flowers, hollyhock buds, hazel buds, rose water, and "grass from a faery's throne," all to be infused for three days in sunlight in a base of marigold water and "sallet oyle." The tops of the wild thyme used in this recipe had to be gathered near the side of a faery hill.

To Enable One to See the Fairies:
A pint of sallet oyle and put in into a vial glasse;
and first wash it with rose-water and marygolde water;
the flowers to be gathered towards the east.
Wash it till the oyle becomes white, then put into the glasse,
and then put thereto the budds of hollyhocke,
the flowers of marygolde, the flowers or toppes of wild thyme,
the budds of young hazle,
and the thyme must be gathered near the side of a hill
where fairies use to be;
and take the grasse of a fairy throne;
then all these put into other oyle in the glasse
and sette it to dissolve three dayes in the sunne
and then keep it for thy use.
 -The Bodleian Library (M.S. Ashmole, 1406)

Shakespeare referred to the "bank whereon the wild thyme blows" as the abode of the Faery Queen. Thyme has further magical uses, having been utilized in the past as protection against evil influences (modern science has confirmed its powerful antiviral and antibacterial properties), and to commune with the dead. In Wales, it was planted on graves. It is said that faeries love to both play and rest amid tufts and mounds of sweet-smelling thyme.

I know a bank whereon the wild thyme blows
Where oxlips and the nodding violet grows;
Quite over canopied with lush woodbine,
With sweet musk roses and with Eglantine
There sleeps Titania some time of the nighte
Lull'd in these flowers with dances and delighte
 -William Shakespeare, 'A Midsummer Night's Dream,' Act 2, Scene 2

Wood Anemone (*Anemone nemorosa*; Gaelic: *mead cailleath*) It was fancifully likened to a tent in which, the country-folk said, the faeries nestled for protection.[18] It was also a healing plant, used as a plaster for wounds and for various aches and pains, including headaches and gout. Wood anemone was one of the earliest blooming spring flowers, blossoming in mid-March. Its name, *anemos*, means wind, possibly relating to the spring winds whose force seems to compel the small flowerheads to open.

Note: several of these plants, including foxglove, scarlet pimpernel, and various mushrooms and toadstools, have some very toxic properties. **Do not use internally.** You won't see faeries, you'll just be dead or sick enough to wish you were. Never use an unfamiliar plant without first researching its uses and safety specifications, and/or consulting an expert. Consider yourself warned!

Plants Protective Against Faery Enchantments

If a plant was considered protective against the faeries, it was often considered protective against all other forms of spiritual malice from which one might need protection such as the Evil Eye and witchcraft. Many plants are specified as offering protection against such problems, some of them specific to Faery, others more generalized. The ones most frequently listed as faery protective are St. John's Wort, rowan (also called mountain ash), ash, eyebright, four-leaf clover, fern, gorse, plantain, laurel leaves, and ground ivy.

Into this second category may be placed the entire list of herbs used by Faery Doctors to deal with the faery-caused illnesses of the Stroke, the Blast, and the Dart. Among these herbs, as both Dr. Logan and Lady Wilde attest, yarrow, eyebright, and vervain were the most commonly used and considered the most powerful. All the herbalists and all the Faery Doctors used them.

Lady Wilde lists seven protective plants, which she refers to as "herbs of great power and virtue, used by Faery Doctors."[19] These are ground ivy, vervain, eyebright, groundsel, foxglove, the bark of the elder tree, and the young shoots of the hawthorn. She tells us that nine balls of these herbs were mixed together and taken; and afterward a potion was made of bogwater and salt, boiled in a pot with a piece of money and elf-stone (which will be discussed in the next chapter). Unfortunately, she does not mention for which ailments this interesting potion was used; perhaps it was a "cure-all."

She also lists St. John's Wort, speedwell, mallow, yarrow, and self-help (also known as self-heal) as powerful plants unable to be injured by anything natural or supernatural, and which, along with vervain and eyebright, must be pulled at noon, near the time of the Summer Solstice in order to access their full potency. This demonstrates the belief in the healing power of light, as the Summer Solstice is the time of the greatest amount of light during the course of the year, and noon is the time of the greatest amount of light during the day, especially on and near this day of the year. Thus the pulling of these plants at this time, clearly and powerfully brings in the healing power of light, and thus fire, both of which are considered sacred, protective, and beneficial in the Celtic healing traditions.

In *The Old Gods*, Dr. Patrick Logan lists plantain, polypody of oak, laurel leaves, foxglove, dandelion, ground ivy, but especially, yarrow, eyebright, and vervain as plants associated with Faery Healing. These last three, he says, were used by all Faery Doctors to cure faery diseases.[20]

MATERIA MAGIC OF PLANTS PROTECTIVE AGAINST FAERY AND OTHER ENCHANTMENTS

Bindweed *(Convolvulus arvensis*; Gaelic: *iadh lus)* When burnt at the ends and draped over a cradle, it was said to protect the baby from any harm from the faeries.

Clover *(Trifolium repens, Papilionaceae*; Gaelic: *seamrog)* The trifolium or three-leafed clover becomes the famous lucky shamrock when found with four leaves instead of three. A four-leafed clover may be used to break a faery spell and other evil enchantments. It clears the sight from faery glamors, allowing one to see the faeries, and may be used to penetrate both witches' and faeries' spells, especially if carried or worn in one's hat. It was one of the main ingredients of a protective faery ointment that allowed faeries to be seen and their spells to be broken. It is said to be more magically effective when found rather than sought.[21]

Dandelion *(Taraxacum leontondon,* or *taraxacum officinalis, Compositae*; Gaelic: *Garblus, Caisearbhan)* In Ireland, dandelion was said to be good for any faery disease.[22] Medicinally, it was said to strengthen the heart and was also good for the liver, the health of both of these organs being important to curing most illnesses. In Scotland, the dandelion is called the *bearrnan Bride*, which means the "little notched" of Brigid (St. Brigid, and before her, the Goddess Brigid), the notches referring to the notched or indented edges of the dandelion leaf.

Eyebright *(Euphrasia officinalis, Scrophulariaceae;* Gaelic: *lus nan leac)* It was one of the most commonly used herbs to protect against faeries. Medicinally, it is soothing and healing to the eyes, and is used in modern magical practice to enhance the inner vision—two facts which may be related. Lady Wilde gives it as one of the *seven protective plants*.

Fern *(Pteris aquilina, Filices;* Gaelic: *raineach)* Though some say fern belongs to the faeries, others say it is protective against faeries. The fern, but more often fernseed, is said to render the wearer invisible, which may be related to the tiny size of the seeds.

Flax (*Linum usitatissium, Linaceae;* Gaelic: *l"n*) When green, it was thought to protect against the faeries. Yeats cites a story where a woman was up late spinning and a faery man came to abduct her. However, he couldn't touch her because she was handling green flax, a fact of which she took note. So she kept handling the flax till cock-crow when she knew he would have to leave, and thus saved herself from kidnap. An old woman told Yeats that "no priest would anoint you without a bit of tow (flax)." Flax and tow were used to relieve sudden pains. Heated in a fire, they were used to rub painful spots while an incantation or verse was recited. This cure was thought to be inspired from a Bible story in which Christ used flax and tow, and breathing on it, healed someone. There is another type of flax known as faery flax *(Linum catharticum),* which grew in the mountains and was primarily used as a purgative. Perhaps it was used to purge places of faeries, as well.

Foxglove (*Digitalis Purpurea, Scrophulariaceae;* Gaelic: *lus-nam-ban-s"th, mearacan sidhe*) Foxglove was one of the seven protective plants. Its leaves were said to be efficacious for fairy diseases involving the bones.[23] Its Gaelic name, *mearacan sidhe,* means "faery thimble," while *lus-nam-ban-s"th* means "herb of the faery woman."

Gorse (*Ulex europaeus, Papilionaceae;* Gaelic: *aiteann*) Gorse was also known as furze. This golden-flowered shrub was said to be protective against faeries, and especially in keeping the butter safe from them on May Day. Due to its rather prickly nature, it was considered protective against curses and hexes of all kinds.

Ground Ivy (*Glechoma Hederacea, Labiatae* Gaelic: *athair lus)* This plant belongs to the mint family and is used similarly to plantain. It was hung around the necks of those in danger of being taken.[24] If given to someone captured by the faeries, they could use it to help them escape. In Wales it was used as a protection against sorcery of all kinds. Ground ivy was known as alehoof by the Saxons because they used it to brew their beers, some of which were used medicinally. Ground ivy was one of the seven protective plants.

Groundsel (*Senecio vulgaris, Compositae;* Gaelic: *am bualan*) Groundsel was one of those very useful plants whose effectiveness, gentle action, and variety of uses made it an integral part of the healing materia medica wherever it grew. It was known to be a cooling plant. Groundsel was one of the seven protective plants and its Gaelic name means "a remedy."

Hawthorn shoots (*Crataegus monogyna, Spina alba, Oxyacanthus, Rosaceae;* Gaelic: *sceach gheal)* It is given as one of the seven protective plants although this is surprising considering that hawthorn was so sacred to the faeries. It is interesting to note that hawthorn is a superior heart tonic, still used as such to this day, and the faeries—connected as they are to the natural world—are a "heart connection" for us.

Ivy (*Hedera helix*, or *hedera hibernica*; Gaelic: *iadh shlat thalmhainn*) Ivy was used for the protection of the flocks and milk products. On the Quarter Days girls would pin it on themselves to induce dreams of their future husband. Ivy, woodbine, and rowan were woven together into a wreath and placed under the milk vessels to safeguard against the *essence* of the milk being spirited away. Other magic hoops or wreaths consisted of milkwort, butterwort, dandelion, and marigold—which were made into small wreaths; and trefoil, vervain, St. John's Wort, dill, about which the old rhyme says:

> *Trefoil, vervain, John's Wort and dill,*
> *Hinders witches in their will.*[25]

Laurel (*Prunus laurocerasus*; Gaelic: *cran laoibhreil*) Its leaves were ground up and juiced, then used magically to resist faery power.[26] The plant referred to may have been spurge laurel (*Daphne laureola, Thymelaeaceae*), rather than *prunus laurocerasus*, English laurel. K'Eogh says that the leaves and berries of spurge aid digestion and purge viscous substances. If the leaves are juiced or chewed, they were thought to draw out "phlegmatic and clammy substances from the brain." This may indicate that a clouded brain was thought to be due to faery influence and power.

Mallow (*Malva, neglecta* or *malva vulgaris, Rotundifolia*; Gaelic: *hocas*) Although in some regions mallow was said to belong to the faeries, in others it was said to be protective against faery magic.

Marsh Marigold (*Caltha palustris, Ranunculaceae*; Gaelic: *a chorrach shod, gollan*) This plant, with its bright yellow cup-shaped flowers, was called the "Shrub of Beltaine" as it was very much used at that time for protection against faery power. Garlands were made of it for this reason and placed on door posts and on the cattle. Physically it was an irritant, but was nevertheless used medicinally upon occasion to treat anemia and cure fits. The symptoms of both of these disorders bear similarities to those of faery illnesses.[27] Other names for this plant were kingscups, bull's eyes, and verrucaria..

Marigold (*Calendula officianalis*, or *Chrysanthemum segetum, Compositae*) It is not clear whether the marigold referred to in the lore is the golden orange *Calendula officianalis*, commonly known as Marygold, golds, ruddes, or whether it is the bright yellow to red-gold *Chrysanthemum segetum* which was commonly known as corn marigold and yellow ox-eye. Both are reminiscent of small suns. Marigold was used to make protective wreaths and magical hoops. It was believed to strip a witch or evil worker of his or her will to do evil. Its very name, *marigold*, shows that it was doubly sacred—to both the Virgin Mary and as a representative of the sun. Medicinally, it was used to relieve fevers and spasms (among other things), both of which might be associated with faery-caused maladies.

Marjoram, wild *(Origanum vulgare;* Gaelic: *oragan)* Wild marjoram is actually the same as Greek oregano. Its Gaelic name means "delight of the mountain," and the smell of marjoram is, indeed, intoxicatingly delightful. In Wales, throwing wild marjoram and thyme into a faery ring was said to confuse the faeries.[28]

Milkwort *(Polygala vulgaris, Polygalaceae;* Gaelic: *gluinech)* In Scotland and Ireland, it was used along with other herbs to make magically protective hoops and wreaths.

Mullein *(Verbascum Thapsus, Scrophulariaceae;* Gaelic: *lus mor)* This was the famous *lus-mor*, or liss-more, which means "great herb." It has strong healing powers, and was also used as a magical charm protective against witchcraft, enchantments, and faery wiles. It was said to be the only herb that worked to bring back children who had been taken away.

Oats *(Avena Sativa, Graminaceae;* Gaelic: *coirce)* The common oat, used widely in the British Isles as a food source was, when ground into oatmeal, used in the Islands and Highlands of Scotland as protection against faery wiles. Carried in pockets or sprinkled on the clothes, it discouraged faery approach, particularly at night. There was a precaution needed, however. The oatmeal must be sprinkled with salt, lest the faeries use it as an instrument to gain the essence of the entire crop of oats grown by that particular farmer.[29]

Polypody of oak *(Polypodium vulgare, Polypodiaceae;* Irish Gaelic: *sceamh na crainn)* Also known as Wall Fern and "scum of the tree," polypody of oak is a fern that grows on the oak tree. Dr. Logan says that it was infused in water, boiled to its volume, and drunk as a protection against the faeries.[30] Since it was used medicinally for bowel disorders and to alleviate irritability by cleansing the spleen, one might assume that irritable behavior was a sign of being plagued by the faeries!

Plantain *(Plantago Major;* Gaelic: *cop'og ph'adraig)* Plantain was hung around children's necks to protect them from being abducted by the faeries.[31] It was used in divination and was also known to bring on vivid dreams when consumed as in a tea. Its Gaelic name means "cup of Patrick."

Self-heal *(Prunella Vulgaris Lamiaceae;* Scots Gaelic: *dubhan ceann chosach, dubhanuith)* It was also known as Self-help, Prunella/Brownwort/Brunella, and Heart of the Earth. When used magically, its leaves were placed under one's pillow to ensure quiet sleep—safe, presumably, from faery interruption. Self-heal was one of the most important of the healing herbs. Its Scots Gaelic name means "dark healing plant."

Speedwell *(Veronica chamaedrys, Scrophulariaceae;* Gaelic: *seamar chr'e)* Also called Farewell, goodbye, germander, polychresta herba veronica, and blue eyes, this bright blue flower was sometimes sewn into garments as a protective charm, although there is also an isolated folk belief that if the herb is brought into a family, the mother would die within a year.

St. John's Wort *(Hypericum perforatum, Hypericacea;* Irish Gaelic: *Luibh Eoin Bhaiste)* St. John's Wort is an herb of the sun, fire, and light. It was thought to be very powerful, especially if pulled at noon on the Summer Solstice. A beneficial herb with several medicinal uses, it was used to break faery spells and to cure illness caused by faery darts. In the Highlands, it was thought to be protective against being taken by the faeries while asleep, especially if found rather than sought.

On the Isle of Man, however, the plant was sacred to faeries, and one must avoid stepping on it or else risk being pixy-led by the offended faeries. In Ireland, Scotland, and other of the Celtic countries, St John's Wort, the herb of Midsummer, was potent against spells and the power of faeries, evil spirits, and the devil.

St. John's Wort blooms in mid June near the time of the Summer Solstice, June 21–22, the Christian equivalent of which is the Feast of St. John the Baptist on June 24th, from which the plant derives its name. Its Irish Gaelic name, *Luibh Eoin Bhaiste*, means herb of John the Baptist.

The use of St. John's Wort on Midsummer's Eve enabled one to see the faeries. St. John's Wort was burned on the Midsummer bonfires, along with several other herbs (a simple and early form of smudging), for its protective influence in purifying the air of evil spirits. Modern magical uses include its use in protective incense blends.

It was also used for divination. On St. John's Eve (June 24), young, unmarried women picked it and hung it on their bedroom walls in order to bring dreams of their future husbands. It was also used as a protective amulet, hung in houses and barns, and worn around the neck to keep away ghosts, bad spirits, and evil-doers in general.

"Hypericum" is from the Greek, and means "over an apparition" or "holding power over spirits,"[32] a reference to the belief that this herb was distasteful to evil spirits and that a whiff of it would cause them to flee.[33] In addition, the little black dots on the backs of the flowers and leaves contain a red dye known as Hypericine. This red dye, which readily releases when the plant is infused, may have been yet another reason that this plant was especially sacred, since red was considered the color of life, vitality, and potency.

Trailing Pearlwort (*Sagina procumbens, Caryophyllaceae;* Scots Gaelic: *mothan*) This was one of the most valued faery-protective herbs and was often carried in a small cloth bag worn about the neck for this purpose. Trailing pearlwort was thought to bring relief from labor pains when placed under the right knee of a woman in childbirth. It was traditionally fed to cows to protect both the milk and the calf from faery interference. Placed above the home's doorway, it prevented family members from being spirited away by the faeries, and it was sometimes used to protect against the Evil Eye. Its powers as a protective charm were often enhanced by placing it in a small bag together with an iron nail, thus drawing in iron's faery-prevention powers into the charm. Women used pearlwort as a love charm by plucking nine roots, tying them into a ring, and placing the ring in their mouth. The woman then sought to obtain a kiss from the man she desired. Mothan was also considered to be a specific against the attacks of faery women.[34]

In Scotland, the following charm was recited while plucking the pearlwort:

I will cull the pearlwort
Beneath the fair Sun of Sunday
Beneath the hand of the Virgin,
Who willed it to grow.
While I shall keep the pearlwort,
Without ill mine eye,
Without harm my mouth,
Without grief my heart,
Without guile my death.[35]

Vervain (*Verbena officinalis;* Irish Gaelic: *tronbhod*) Mrs. Grieves tells us that the name Vervain is derived from the Celtic *ferfaen*—from *fer*, to drive away, and *faen*, a stone—and refers to its use for treating kidney stones. Its Latin name *verbena*, meaning "sacred foliage," was used in classical Roman times to refer to altar plants in general, but particularly this species. Known in Scotland as dragon's claw, it was also known simply as verbena. It is one of those odorless, tasteless herbs which were always regarded as magical and Otherworldly. Its Irish name means simply "woody."

Vervain was one of the most powerful and commonly used herbs to protect against faeries—one of the Seven—and was associated with prophecy and visions. It had been sacred to the Druids, who were said to favor it as much as they did mistletoe, using it to adorn their altars and including it in their lustral waters. It was to be gathered during the rising of the dog star, Sirius, at a time when neither sun nor moon could shine upon it;

the Earth must be gifted with honey in return. This timing places the harvesting of vervain between sunset and sunrise during the dark of the moon, sometime during the month of July.[36]

It was spoken of in 16th century England as the *Holy Herb* which was used against enchantments. In medieval Wales it was known as Devil's Bane and harvested after sunset to be used to sprinkle holy water.[37]

Slightly crushed, it was worn in a bag around the neck as a charm against headaches and against the bites of venomous creatures such as snakes and spiders. It was used along with varying combinations of milkwort, butterwort, ivy, dandelion, marigold; trefoil, and St. John's Wort to make protective wreaths or magical hoops, and was also an ingredient in love charms. It was believed to strip a witch of her will.

Lady Wilde mentions a red variety of verbena that was thought to be as potent as St. John's Wort, partly because of its pure and brilliant color.

Yarrow (*Achillea millefolium*; Scots Gaelic: *lus chosgadh na fola*; Irish Gaelic: *athair tal'uin,* also *athair talmhan*) It was used by the skillful women (i.e., Faery Doctors/Healers) and was one of the most commonly used herbs to protect against faeries. It was considered to be the best of the herbs for cures and potions, and was even sewn up in clothes for its virtues.[38] Its healing power was so great that it was referred to as the "herb of seven needs." Its Scots name means "herb that stops bleeding."

It was plucked ceremonially with special incantations, especially on Beltaine Eve and Midsummer, for use in love charms. It was hung in homes to bring luck, and worn in a bag about the neck to bring success, and, interestingly, to aid in the transfer of magical secrets as well. Bridesmaids brought it to weddings for "seven years of love."

It was famous as a divinatory herb. Irish maidens danced around it singing:

Yarrow, yarrow, yarrow,
I bid thee good morrow,
And tell me before tomorrow
Who my true love shall be.

They then slept with it beneath the pillow with confidence that the true lover would appear in their dreams.[39] It was also used in weather divination.

Its fame as a divinatory herb may be linked to one of its physical properties. Yarrow was used internally for eruptive diseases, and aided the eruptions in coming forth onto the skin rather than staying (or going) inward, something which can delay healing with diseases of this nature. This demonstrates that yarrow's ability to bring forth that which was hidden within must have been clearly understood. It doesn't seem too much of a stretch to see how this may have been thought to apply on subtle inner levels as well, and the herb was therefore used in divination.

THE MYSTERY HERB

Lady Wilde mentions that she had been told about a mysterious and powerful herb that grew on the island to the west of Connemara. It was reputed to have great and mystic power, but none would dare to say its name, because its power was so great. It was a divinatory herb, used when knowledge was desired as to whether or not a sick person would recover. In such a case, the sick person's nearest relative must search for and pick the herb just while the sun was rising. Then a specific, ancient incantation had to be chanted. If the herb remained fresh and green the person would recover. But if it withered in the hand during the incantation, it was understood that the person would die.[40]

OTHER HERBS

Lady Wilde mentions the existence of a couple other divinatory herbs, one of which was known simply as "faery plant." The other herb was part of a magical drink called the Bardic potion, which was given to infants at their birth in order to endow them with a sweet and charming voice capable of "swaying the hearts of its hearers," truly a Bardic talent. But only the Bards knew the real secrets of these magical plants. So powerful were these plants considered, and held in such great respect, that none interviewed would reveal their names. So their names and manner of usage remain shrouded in mystery.[41]

The Bardic potion and its primary herb are quite interesting in that they seem to be a direct link back to the Bards and Druids of old, who were not only skillful healers, extremely knowledgeable about plants, but also possessed knowledge of the *Power of Sound*. So here is a connection between herb lore and Druidry—by virtue of the extraordinary assertion that the power of sound can be granted by proper use of a magical herb.

The Lore of Faery Trees

It is with the lore of trees that we really witness the concept of plant spirit beings in European folklore and legend. From the birch, sometimes known as the White Lady, to the Oak Men, the Apple Tree Man, and the Elder Mother, these spirits are much more defined and individualistic than those of most of the plants and herbs at which we have just looked.

MATERIA MAGICA OF FAERY TREES

Alder *(Alnus Glutinosa, Betulaceae*; Gaelic: *feàrn)* Alder is a member of the birch family and is thought to possess mysterious properties and powers to avert evil. The first man sprang from an alder, according to old Irish legend, and the first woman sprang from a mountain ash or rowan. It was said that alder was anciently regarded as a faery tree, able to grant access to the Faery Realms.

As with many other of the magical trees, alder in special locations was often considered too sacred to cut. A man tried to cut a branch from an alder hanging over a saint's holy well, but was twice stopped because he saw a vision of his home afire. Hurrying home, he found his vision had been a delusion. The third time he went ahead and cut the branch, but this time he arrived home to find his house burnt to the ground.[42]

Apple *(Pyrus malus, Pomaceae;* Gaelic: *ubhal, aball)* The old lore said that leaving the last apple of your crop for the Apple Tree Man would ensure a good harvest the following year. The Apple Tree Man is the spirit of the oldest apple tree in the orchard. The old custom of wassailing was intended to thank, honor, but especially *awaken* the spirit of the tree, so that it would produce a bountiful crop of fruit in its next season.

LEGEND | The Apple Tree Man

An interesting legend found in England is that of the Apple Tree Man. He is the spirit of the oldest apple tree in an orchard, the one in which the fertility of the entire orchard is thought to reside.

This belief is reflected in the old custom of wassailing the trees which occurred on Christmas Eve or 12th Night Eve, January 5th—a custom recorded as occurring even into the 19th century.

Wassailing the trees was an English wintertime custom in which people went into the orchards to sing, dance, fire guns, beat sticks together, and otherwise make noise in order to waken the spirit of the trees so they would bear a bountiful crop of fruit. Much of this noisemaking and merriment was particularly directed at the oldest tree in the apple orchard—the Apple Tree Man.

The word *wassail* means "be whole." *Wassailing* means to wish health and wholeness, so to wassail the trees was to wish them good health.

The trees were *toasted* with a song or verse repeated three times. The ceremony consisted of the farmer, his family, and his workers going out into the orchard at night, bringing with them hot cakes and a jug of cider. The cakes were placed as offerings in the boughs of the oldest, most abundantly bearing of the trees. All then drank to the health of the trees, saying or singing something like this:

Here's to thee, old apple-tree!
Whence thou may'st bud, and whence thou may'st blow,
Hats full! Caps full!
Bushel bushel-bags full!
And my pockets full too! Huzza!

This was repeated three times, after which the cider was poured over the tree's roots or flung over the trees of the orchard, while a great deal of noise was made—singing, shouting, banging of pots, guns and pistols fired, and so on. All this was done in order to "wake up" the spirit of the trees in the orchard. It was thought that omitting this ceremony would cause the productive trees to cease bearing fruit.

This custom not only shows that trees were known to have spirits, but it demonstrates a knowledge of the need for a relationship with the trees. This relationship included not only a plea to the tree to wake up and begin working, but also a knowledge that thanks and offerings were necessary for the tree's gifts both given and expected. Robert Herrick, a poet writing in the 17th century, expressed this well in his verse "Ceremonies of Christmas Eve":

Wassaile the trees, that they may beare
You many a Plum and many a Peare:
For more or lesse fruits they will bring,
As you do give them Wassailing.[43]

Apples grew in great profusion in the British Otherworld of Avalon, whose very name means *Island of Apples*. Apples are both the fruit of life and the fruit of death, and frequently associated with the Otherworld in legends.

In many faery legends, the *Silver Branch* which grants entrance to the Otherworlds is an apple branch. In the Irish legend of the *Voyage of Bran, Son of Febal*, Bran is lulled to sleep by mysterious sweet music, and upon awakening, finds beside him a silvery branch bedecked with white and silver flowers. When he takes it up, he is able to see and hear the Faery Realm, and a faery woman sings to him:

> *A branch of the apple-tree from Emain I bring,*
> *Like those one knows;*
> *Twigs of white silver are on it,*
> *Crystal brows with blossoms.*
> *There is a distant isle,*
> *Around which sea-horses glisten;*
> *A fair course against the white-swelling surge*
> *Four feet uphold it.*

Bran is helpless against this magical faery music, and when the branch springs from his hand into hers, he is unable to stop it, and likewise unable to stop himself from immediately abandoning home and setting sail for that "distant isle."[44]

Similarly, a magical silver branch is found in the legend of *Cormac's Adventure in the Land of Promise*. This branch had upon it three golden apples and was given to Cormac by a strange warrior who then vanished. The music of the branch soothed the sick and wounded and could banish grief. In the adventures that followed, Cormac traveled to the *Land of Promise*—the Faery Realm—where he met the strange warrior again. He found him to be none other than Manannan Mac Lir of the Tuatha De Danaan. Manannan gifted Cormac with the silver branch that he was to use and enjoy for the remainder of his life.[45]

An apple rather than an apple branch figures in the story of Cuchulain's journey to study warfare with the mysterious warrior-woman, Scatach. Cuchulain found his way across the confusing *Plain of Ill Luck* by rolling a wheel and tossing an apple before him. He followed where the apple led, and thereby arrived at Scatach's stronghold to begin his training.[46]

In medieval England the apple was a tree of enchantment. Lancelot was sleeping under an apple tree when he was carried away by the four Faery Queens.

Cutting an apple in half crosswise reveals that its core and seeds form a pentacle, which has long been held to be a symbol of magic and protection.

And of course we cannot fail to mention Avalon itself, *Ynis Afallon*, the Isle of Apples, which was the name of the British Otherworld. It was into this Faeryland Paradise that the wounded King Arthur was taken by the three "Queens" or Faery Women after his last battle, in order to be healed of his wounds. This ties in beautifully with the belief that the Faeryland Otherworld was not only the realm of the dead, but also the source of life, healing and regeneration. It ties in, as well, with the legend of the Goddess Morgen who lived with her eight sisters on an island where they practiced the healing arts. It may well have been that Morgen's island and Affalon were one and the same.

Ash (*Fraxinus excelsior, oleaceae;* Irish Gaelic: *craobh uinnseann*) The ash tree's magical properties were quite similar to the rowan, and often it not clear in the lore which tree is actually meant since rowan is sometimes referred to as mountain ash.

Ash was said to be all-powerful against witchcraft. Therefore, branches of it were wreathed around the horns of cattle and children's cradles to protect against evil. In addition, when the dead made attempts to lure humans into their dances, if the humans could but keep hold of an ash branch till out of reach of the ghosts or spirits, they would be safe.

In some areas solitary ash trees were considered so sacred (as were most solitary trees) that they were not cut down even if firewood was scarce. In Somerset, ashen gads were used to protect the cattle against faeries and witches, as was rowan in Scotland. Druids wands were said to be made of ash twigs, and Bards used ash twigs upon which to carve their coelbrens or ogham symbols.

In Wales, the ash tree was considered to be spirit-haunted and was respected, if somewhat avoided. Yet it was considered lucky to have an ash growing on one's property. It was thought that the ash learned the secrets of lovers and whispered them on the wind. Three leaves of ash worn on the breast were thought to induce prophetic dreams. Ash berries brought into the home brought luck and prosperity, and women wore the dried berries to forestall the possibility of bewitchment.[47]

Ash was also known to have healing properties. Weak-limbed children were passed through split ash trees that were then bound up. If the tree grew straight, the child would as well. Ash could be used as a substitute for rowan. In Ireland and Scotland, people were hesitant to cut them for firewood even if they needed the wood, and in some places it was believed that if even a chip of it was burnt on the hearth, the whole house would burn down. In Perthshire, Scotland, there was a sacred ash called the old Bell (Bael) Tree, and it was believed that if even a chip of its wood were burned in any house in the district, that house would be ravaged by fire. There is a similar legend about a sacred elder growing over a saint's well, and another about the alder tree (see above).[48] In England, ash was known to be protective against mischievous spirits, but in Scotland the mountain ash or rowan was known to be much more powerful than the regular ash tree. This was most likely due to its red berries—red having power because it is the color of blood, and thus, life.

Of the Five Great Sacred Trees of Ireland—one planted in each of the five provinces —one was oak, one was yew, but three were ash trees, including the one in the center province of Meath. The Yggdrasil, the World Tree of Scandinavian myth and legend, was also said to be an ash.

Birch *(Betula Alba, Betulaceae;* Irish Gaelic: *beith, beth)* Birch has many associations with the Otherworlds, being associated with death and with the Faery and Spirit Realms. The famous hallucinogenic mushroom *amanita muscaria,* which granted access to the Otherworlds, grew beneath birch trees.

In the old ballad, *The Wife of Usher's Well,* a mother is visited by her recently deceased sons who are wearing birch caps. These caps were made from birches that grew at the "gates o' Paradise" symbolizing, perhaps, her sons' "birth" into the paradisial spirit world.

Birch is also, and primarily, associated with beginnings, and with the purifications and cleansings that often precede beginnings as well. Birch shows itself to be a tree of beginnings as it is often the first tree to grow back in deforested areas. In Scotland, birch was one of the woods used for the fires of Beltaine—which marked the start of summer, the season of life and growth—and it was sometimes used as a living Maypole.

Birch's cleansing and purification associations are shown by the fact that it was used for *ritual beatings*—to cleanse the old (or evil spirits) and allow in the new (good spirits). This ritual cleansing promoted fertility.

The Goddess Brigid's (also St. Brigid) white wand—by which she turned the cold, barren earth green again at her festival—was thought to be birch.

An interesting belief that seems to combine both the cleansing and the Otherworldly aspects of birch was the belief that witches' brooms were made of birch. Brooms were obviously used to sweep and clean, yet witches were thought to use them to fly, a term used to denote travel to the spirit worlds as well as physical flight.

English poet Samuel Coleridge called the birch the "Lady of the Woods," which quite possibly was an old folkname for the tree. In some places birch was known as the White Lady. The tree's gleaming silvery bark was, in old legends, the hallmark of faery.[49]

Blackthorn *(Prunus spinosa;* Gaelic: *preas nan airneag)* Also called the Sloe tree, the blackthorn, because it was a thorn tree, was sacred to the faeries. But it also was considered an unlucky tree and associated with strife and difficulty. Its wood was used for cudgels and shillelaghs.

According to Irish legend it was guarded by faeries known as the Lunantishee who would not allow a stick of it to be cut on November 11th (Martinmas, Old Hallows Eve) or on May 11th (old May Day). To do so brought misfortune.[50] These two occasions are, of course, the old Celtic Feasts of Samhain and Beltaine, when the veil between the worlds was said to be thin. These two feasts mark the beginning and ending of the two major seasons of the old Celtic year, winter and summer, times when the faeries were out and about.

Elder *(Sambucus Nigra, Caprifoliaceae;* Gaelic: *crann troim)* Elder, also known as Bourtree, was beloved of the Sidhe, but in Scotland at least, it was also considered to be a protective tree, second in power only to the rowan in its ability to ward off evil. To these ends it was affixed to stables and byres. In addition, the green juice of elder, when applied to the eyelids, was said to give the Second Sight. When so used on Halloween while standing beneath an elder tree, one could see the faery retinue as it rode by—led by the King or Queen of Faery—as did Janet in the ballad of *Ballad of Tamlin*. A similar belief was held in Denmark where this feat was said to be possible at Midsummer's Eve rather than Halloween.

It was also believed that drinking elderberry wine enabled one to see the faeries. But if a faery had just happened to have used the same cup, the person would then gain a permanent ability to perceive the faeries.

Elder was one of the most powerful of all the trees and had important taboos around its uses. In England, elder wood was never used for a baby's cradle lest the baby be pinched and bruised by the faeries. Before any wood was taken from this tree it was approached cautiously, ritualistically, and its permission asked for the use of its wood.

The tree's spirit was very strong, and the tree itself was thought of as a woman who was called the Elder Mother. She was a powerful being who must not be offended. Akin to this belief is one in which the elder was thought to be inhabited by the faeries. The tree was sometimes thought of as a shelter for faeries hiding from witches, but then again, might also be a witch disguised as a tree.

Since elder juice on the eyelids imparted the Second Sight and the ability to see the faeries, particularly on Samhain and Midsummer, one has to wonder if the Elder Mother is not, perhaps, the Goddess in her aspect of Lady of the Green World or her summer aspect of Faery Queen.

Along with these magical properties, elder was greatly esteemed by the country folk for its medicinal uses. Soothing and refreshing elderflower water was used for eye and skin complaints, burns, bruises, and sprains, while both flowers and berries were made into an infusion for colds and fevers. In Ireland a skin-healing salve was made of elderflowers and bee pollen, particularly useful for chapped skin and rashes.

Hawthorn *(Crataegus oxyacantha, Rosacea;* Gaelic: *sgitheach geal)* Its Gaelic name means "white haw." According to tradition, this tree, which was also called Maytree and whitethorn, originally sprang from lightning. It was therefore revered and endowed with many supernatural attributes and properties. It is the faery tree par excellence, being very sacred to the faeries, particularly when found growing solitary near a faery hill or when the trees were found growing in a ring of three or more. Hawthorn was said to be the faeries' place of camping and resting, especially when it stood in the center of a faery ring. In Irish lore, when hawthorn grows alone near river or stream banks or on faery forts, it is considered to belong to the faeries and cannot be disturbed without incurring their wrath. The faeries do protect their property, as innumerable old Irish stories attest.

Hawthorn wood was used to feed the sacred fires of Brigid at her shrine in Kildare, a fire that was said to burn without producing ash.

It is known as the May Tree because its lovely white flowers blossom near Beltaine/May Day. Thus, associated with the feast of Beltaine, hawthorn corresponds to love, marriage, sexuality, and fertility, and is associated with the Goddess in her spring/summer aspect. It is thought that the tree under which Thomas the Rhymer encountered the Faery Queen was a hawthorn. On May Day a libation of milk was poured over its roots as an offering to the tree, and perhaps to the faeries. On Midsummer's Day, and later, on Old Midsummer's Day (early July), hawthorns were often blessed, adorned, and honored. Hawthorn branches were brought home by those who went "a'Maying" on May Morning. But the branches were hung on the outside of the house, for to bring such a powerful faery tree inside the home invited all the powers of that realm inside as well. This meant that the powers of the Otherworlds, including the power of death, had been invited to enter the home.

It was thought unlucky to use hawthorn as walking stick for journeys, perhaps because from fear that hawthorn's close association with the Faery Realm would cause the stick's user to be pixie-led.

Hawthorn is a member of the rose family and the rose has been associated not only with the Goddess, but is sometimes used to represent the concept of *Center*. It is interesting that this faery tree par excellence is also a powerful heart tonic. Our heart is, in some ways, our center, metaphorically if not strictly physically—as the blood pumped through it travels through veins and capillaries, moving throughout the body carrying life-sustaining oxygen to the body's farthest reaches and back again. Similarly, the heart is sometimes thought to be our emotional center. Our connection with the Faery Realm is likewise heart related: it must be born from a loving *heart-place* within us, and not from mere idle curiosity or a desire to gain the famous *faery gold*.

Hazel (*Corylus avellana*, Betulaceae or Corylaceae; Irish Gaelic: *coll*) Hazel is a tree of many virtues, some of which were so powerful and sacred as to be known only to the most adept of healers. It was said to be powerfully protective against the devil's wiles and was considered lucky as a walking stick for journeys. It was plunged into Midsummer fires till it caught fire, and was then used to singe the cattle's backs as blessing. The hazel sticks so used were then kept safely afterward, and considered to be of great power for driving the cattle to and from watering places. Tying hazel twigs onto a horse's harness was a way of protecting it against faery enchantments

Hazel rods were used for water-witching as well as in divining for lead, gold, and coal, and other minerals as well.[51] In Ireland, Faery Doctors used them to divine faery-caused ailments. In Wales, there was a very specific way that these divining rods were made. The hazel branch had to be cut in a perfect crescent shape and this must be done when the moon was new. The branch had to have nine twigs upon it and be taken from an old hedge.

Hazel and hazelnuts are traditionally associated with prophecy, intuition, inspiration, and divination. In Scotland, the freshly gathered green hazelnuts of autumn were sometimes ground up and made into a milk to be fed to babies. For sickly babies this hazelnut milk was enriched with wild honey. Hazelnuts were gathered in autumn to be used in the Halloween divinations.[52]

In England the hazel was associated with fertility, brides being gifted with a bag of nuts to assure a fruitful marriage. The fertility aspect of the nut-gathering time of year could be overdone and in the past, the Hallowmas nut gathering was said to be as full of liberty and wantonness as the May hawthorn branch gathering. The devil was said to be abroad in the woods at this time of the year and girls were said to meet him there. "So many cratches (crates of nuts), so many cradles," goes the old saying from Somerset.[53]

In Ireland, the hazel was likewise associated with mystical knowledge and wisdom.

In ancient Ireland it was believed that the Boyne and Shannon Rivers had their source in the Otherworld. At the head of these rivers was a fountain or well. Over the well grew nine sacred hazel trees. As these hazel trees produced their beautiful red-purple nuts in due season, the nuts fell into the water below and salmon leapt up to eat them. This caused red spots, reminiscent of the nuts, to appear on the salmon. By eating these nuts the salmon absorbed the powers inherent in them; and anyone who then was able to catch and eat one of these salmon was thereby imbued with great wisdom, insight, inspiration, prophetic, and poetic abilities—all gifts of both the hazelnut and the salmon. This collection of inspirational gifts was often referred to as *Imbas* in Ireland and *Awen* in Wales, both of these words relating to *Inspiration*, or "Fire in the Head." It is not surprising to learn that the Druids made magical wands from hazel wood.

Nuts are such small compact packages of nutrition that it is not hard to see how they came to represent wisdom. As with all seeds, they are small in comparison to the tree that bore them, yet they represent the future of the tree. They quite literally *hold the future*, so it is no wonder they were used for divination. Nuts, along with apples, were used in divinations performed at Samhain.

With the connection to *Awen*, Druids, and the Otherworlds, the hazel was sometimes referred to as the Poet's Tree, Druidry being intimately connected with poetry. The hazel was anciently associated with the Faery Realm as well, allowing entrance into it.[54]

This connection with Druids, poetry, and the Faery Realm reminds us again of the power of sound, of words, of vibration, and the power to create through these means and to bring about change. To receive the *Awen*, the *Imbas*, was to receive enlightenment and the divine frenzy of inspiration, both very much valued in Celtic cultures.

Oak *(Quercus Robur;* Irish Gaelic: *dair)* "Fairy folks are in old oaks" goes the old British saying, indicating that oaks were known to be the habitation of some varieties of faeries. The roots of the oak were thought to extend down into the Faery Realm.[55] In the north of England, oak groves were sometimes thought to be haunted, particularly after sunset, by sinister beings known as the Oak Men. Oaks were thought to be capable of revenge if one of their number was cut down. This revenge was shown by how fast new oak shoots sprang up from the roots of felled oaks. The oak was associated with a vital, virile power, demonstrated by its fast growth.

Oak groves were thought to be haunted in Wales as well, especially at midnight when the spirits of ancient Druids gathered there to celebrate their rites. Sometimes these ancient voices might be heard in the whisper of the oak leaves in the wind, particularly in summer or early autumn.[56]

The oak was venerated by the continental Celts as a tree of divine power. It was associated with lightning, thunder, and the Gaulish thunder god Taranis. It was similarly associated with other powerful "thunder and lightning" gods, such as the Greek Zeus, the Roman Jupiter, the Norse Thor, and the Irish Dagda. Oaks are very much associated with the Druids and it was said that acorns were eaten by the Druids in order to gain prophetic powers. On the oak grew the famous "golden bough" of the Druids, the sacred mistletoe, a fact immortalized by Pliny's account of its careful and ceremonial harvest by the Druids.

Although the oak grows in Scotland and Ireland, and though there are legends of their veneration in those places, the rowan and hazel seem to have figured more prominently in the Druidic rites there.

In Scotland oak was used—along with birch—as one of the woods used for the Beltaine Fire.

Rowan *(Sorbus Aucuparia,* also *Pyrus aucuparia, Rosaceae;* Irish Gaelic: *caorthann)* Also called mountain ash, rowan was held to be protective against faery enchantments and all evil spiritual powers. An old saying (attributed to Janet Leisk of Scotland, 1597) used as a preventative against bewitchment goes:

"Rowan tree and red thread puts witches to their speed."

Or in the old Scots dialect,

"Rowan tree and red threid, gar the witches tyne their speed."

This meaning that rowan and red thread, both full of power, slowed down the witches' ability to do their evil deeds.

The first man sprang from an alder, according to old Irish legend, and the first woman sprang from a mountain ash, or rowan.

Rowan was all-powerful against witchcraft, faeries, and evil influences, including the Evil Eye. Before sunrise on May Morning branches of it were wreathed around children's cradles, the horns of cattle, and butter churns to counteract the evil of witches and faeries. It was particularly important as a protection for "bearing" animals.

Rhys's *Celtic Folklore* mentions that one being held captive and forced to dance in a faery ring could be rescued if two strong men held out a rowan pole for the captive to grasp. If the captive could but grasp the pole and keep hold of it, he or she could be pulled to safety; the faeries could not prevent this because of their aversion to rowan.

Crosses made of its twigs and tied with red thread were made and hung over the doors of houses and barns for protection, as well as being worn on clothing by men in the Highlands. Women of the Highlands made protective necklaces of the berries by stringing them on red thread. Branches of rowan were woven into the roofs of houses to protect them from fire, and used in building boats to protect them from being upset in storms.[57] Sometimes rowan trees were planted by the door of a house to offer additional protection.

Rowan's power may have stemmed from the red color of its berries and from the fact that each rowan berry has a tiny five-pointed star on it opposite the stalk. As has been mentioned, the five-pointed star was regarded as a protective symbol.

In Scandinavia and the British Isles, mystical secrets were believed to have been carved upon this beautiful tree.

Strangely enough, in another of those seeming contradictions, when rowan was found growing within a faery fort or faery ring or by a spring or boulder, it was often thought to be cherished by the faery folk, and humans disturbed it at their own risk. In some parts of Scotland, Rowan was even said to be a favorite of the faery folk, who built their homes amidst its roots.

Willow *(Salix Alba;* Irish Gaelic: *saileòg, sail)* In Ireland, willows were said to uproot themselves by night, and muttering, stalk (and terrify) belated travelers.[58] In Ireland it was thought that they could cause one to break into uncontrollable dancing. Willows were known as the "witch's tree," and witches' brooms were sometimes bound with the flexible willow withes. Willows always grow near a water source and thus are associated with water. The renowned herbalist, Nicolas Culpepper, tells us that "the moon owns the willow," therefore, we can assume that the supple and yielding willow partakes of the lunar qualities of magic, enchantment, femininity, intuition, and the emotional and subconscious realms. Such correspondences also suggest a connection to the subtle, magical realms of Faery.

Yew *(Taxus Baccata;* Irish Gaelic: *ibar, iubhar)* In Scotland, Beltaine fires were sometimes lit in the middle of yew trees, causing them to eventually split in half and look like two trees instead of one.[59] The yew is be associated with the Isle of Iona, whose old name, *Ioua*, meant yew tree. Although most frequently depicted as an ash tree, some think that the Scandinavian World Tree, Yggdrasil, may well have been a yew tree, rather than an ash. Mountain yew, which is actually juniper, was used in Scotland as a fragrant and purifying fumigant, being burned on New Year's Day and sometimes Samhain for purification purposes and to enhance clairvoyance. Yew was also associated with the dead and was planted in graveyards.

END NOTES

1. Briggs, Katherine, *An Encyclopedia of Fairies*, Pantheon Books, NY, 1976, p. 159.
2. Wilde, Lady, *Ancient Legends, Mystic Charms & Superstitions of Ireland*, Chatto & Windus, London, 1919, p. 181.
3. Briggs, Katherine, *Faeries in Tradition and Literature*, Routledge, Kegan & Paul, Ltd, London, 1967, p. 86.
4. Paterson, Helena, *The Celtic Lunar Zodiac*, Charles E. Tuttle & Co, Inc., Rutland, VT, 1992, p. 59.
5. Briggs, Katherine, *Faeries in Tradition and Literature*, Routledge, Kegan & Paul, Ltd, London, 1967, p. 84.
6. Grieves, Mrs., *A Modern Herbal (In Two Volumes)*, Dover Publications, Inc., NY, 1971.
7. Ibid.
8. Wilde, Lady, *Ancient Legends, Mystic Charms & Superstitions of Ireland*, Chatto & Windus, London, 1919, p. 203.
9. Kear, Katherine, *Flower Wisdom: The Definitive Guidebook to the Myth, Magic and Mystery of Flowers*, Thorsons, an imprint of HarperCollins Publishers, London, 2000, p. 166.

10. K'Eogh, John, *Botanalogia universalis Hibernica* (English), An Irish Herbal: the Botanalogia Universalis Hibernica, revised and edited by Michael Scott, Anna Livia Press, Dublin, 1991.

11. Kear, Katherine, *Flower Wisdom: The Definitive Guidebook to the Myth, Magic and Mystery of Flowers*, Thorsons, an imprint of HarperCollins Publishers, London, 2000, p. 107.

12. Briggs, Katherine, *Faeries in Tradition & Literature*, Routledge, Kegan & Paul, Ltd, London, 1967, p. 85.

13. Trevelyan, Marie, *Folklore and Folk-Tales of Wales*, Elliot Stock, London, 1909, Chapter 7.

14. Briggs, Katherine, *Faeries in Tradition & Literature*, Routledge, Kegan & Paul, Ltd, London, 1967, p. 84.

15. Wilde, Lady, *Ancient Legends, Mystic Charms & Superstitions of Ireland*, Chatto & Windus, London, 1919, p. 104.

16. Briggs, *Faeries in Tradition and Literature*, Routledge, Kegan & Paul, Ltd, London, 1967, p. 85.

17. McNeil, F. Marian, *The Silver Bough, Vol. 1*, William MacLellan, 1959, Canongate Classics, Edinburgh, 1989, p. 83.

18. Grieves, Mrs., *A Modern Herbal (In Two Volumes)*, Dover Publications, Inc., NY, 1971.

19. Wilde, Lady, *Ancient Legends, Mystic Charms & Superstitions of Ireland*, Chatto & Windus, London, 1919, p. 182.

20. Logan, Patrick, *The Old Gods: The Facts About Irish Fairies*, Appletree Press, Belfast, 1981, p. 102.

21. Briggs, Katherine, *An Encyclopedia of Faeries*, Pantheon Books, NY, 1976, p. 180.

22. Logan, Patrick, *The Old Gods: The Facts About Irish Fairies*, Appletree Press, Belfast, 1981, p. 102.

23. Ibid.

24. Logan, Patrick, *The Old Gods: The Facts About Irish Fairies* Appletree Press, Belfast, 1981.

25. McNeil, F. Marian, *The Silver Bough, Vol. 1*, William MacLellan, 1959, Canongate Classics, Edinburgh, 1989, p. 82.

26. Logan, Patrick, *The Old Gods: The Facts About Irish Fairies*, Appletree Press, Belfast, 1981.

27. Wilde, Lady, *Ancient Legends, Mystic Charms & Superstitions of Ireland*, Chatto & Windus, London, 1919, p. 106.

28. Trevelyan, Marie, *Folklore and Folk-Tales of Wales*, Elliot Stock, London, 1909, Chapter 7.

29. Campbell, John Gregorson, *Superstitions of the Highlands and Islands of Scotland*, James MacLehose & Sons, Glasgow, 1990, p. 47.

30. Logan, Patrick, *The Old Gods: The Facts About Irish Fairies*, Appletree Press, Belfast, 1981, p. 102.

31. Ibid.

32. Huson, Paul, *Mastering Herbalism*, A Scarborough Book, Stein and Day Publishers, NY, 1975, p. 283.

33. Grieves, Mrs., *A Modern Herbal (In Two Volumes)*, Dover Publications, Inc., NY, 1971.

34. Carmichael Alexander, *Carmina Gadelica, Vol. 4*, Oliver and Boyd, Edinburgh & London, 1928, p. 132.

35. Ibid, p. 135.

36 Huson, Paul, *Mastering Herbalism*, A Scarborough Book, Stein and Day Publishers, NY, 1975, p. 283.

37 Trevelyan, Marie, *Folklore and Folk-Tales of Wales*, Elliot Stock, London, 1909, Chapter 7.

38 Wilde, Lady, *Ancient Legends, Mystic Charms & Superstitions of Ireland*, Chatto & Windus, London, 1919, p. 181.

39 Ibid, p. 104.

40 Ibid, p. 183.

41 Ibid, p. 181-182.

42 Wood-Martin, W. G., *Traces of the Elder Faiths of Ireland, Vol. 2*, Longmans, Greens, and Co., NY and Bombay, 1902, p. 157.

43 Grieves, Mrs., *A Modern Herbal (In Two Volumes)*, Dover Publications, Inc., NY, 1971.

44 Evans Wentz, W.Y., *The Fairy Faith in Celtic Countries*, Henry Frowde, Oxford University Press, London, New York, Toronto and Melbourne, 1911, p. 339.

45 Ibid, p. 342.

46 McNeil, F. Marian, *The Silver Bough, Vol. 1*, William MacLellan, 1959, Canongate Classics, Edinburgh, 1989, p. 79.

47 Trevelyan, Marie, *Folklore and Folk-Tales of Wales*, Elliot Stock, London, 1909, Chapter 8.

48 Briggs, Katherine, *An Encyclopedia of Fairies*, Pantheon Books, NY, 1976.

49 Paterson, Jacqueline Memory, *Tree Wisdom: The Definitive Guidebook to the Myth, Folklore and Healing Power of Trees*, Thorsons, an imprint of HarperCollins Publishers, London, 1996, p. 94.

50 Evans Wentz, W.Y., *The Fairy Faith in Celtic Countries*, Henry Frowde, Oxford University Press, London, New York, Toronto, and Melbourne, 1911, p. 53.

51 McNeil, F. Marian, *The Silver Bough, Vol. 1*, William MacLellan, 1959; Canongate Classics, Edinburgh, 1989, p. 79.

52 Ibid, p. 79.

53 Tongue, R. L., *Somerset Folklore* (County Series VIII), F. L. S., 1965.

54 Paterson, Jacquelyn Memory, *Tree Wisdom: The Definitive Guidebook to the Myth, Folklore and Healing Power of Trees*, Thorsons, an imprint of HarperCollins Publishers, London, 1996, p. 70.

55 Jackson, Nigel Aldcroft, *Call of the Horned Piper*, Capall Bann Publishing, Berks, 1994, p. 54.

56 Trevelyan, Marie, *Folklore and Folk-Tales of Wales*, Elliot Stock, London, 1909.

57 Wilde, Lady, *Ancient Legends, Mystic Charms & Superstitions of Ireland*, Chatto & Windus, London, 1919, p. 127.

58 Tongue, R. L., *Somerset Folklore* (County Series VIII), F.L.S., 1965, p. 26.

59 Briggs, Katherine, *Faeries in Tradition and Literature*, Routledge, Kegan & Paul, Ltd, London, 1967, p. 82.

CHAPTER 10

Faery Stones: Materia Magic, Materia Medica

STONES AND CRYSTALS

Quite often the large standing stones or other stone monuments located throughout the countryside were associated with faeries and were used for healing purposes. Sick children were passed through large holed stones or led beneath a stone archway, sometimes to the accompaniment of elaborate rituals. There are numerous examples of the use of large standing stones for healing and as a cure for barrenness.

Stones, in general, have a long history of use for healing illness and barrenness as well as for divining the outcomes of illness. Many of the large old stones in the British Isles have Druidic, Faery, or god legends attached to them, and it was considered bad luck to try to move them. Smaller healing stones were quite common, such as the *magic stones* dipped in water to avert the Evil Eye or the *stitch-stones* carried to relieve severe pain.

SOME SPECIFIC HEALING STONES

Elf-stones, which we now know to be ancient stone arrowheads, were held to be of great magical value because they were thought to be weapons used by elves and faeries. Usually found near faery hills, elfstone was thought to have great power and virtue. Once removed from the ground, however, it was thought to lose this power if it ever again should touch the Earth. It was a fairly common belief that power could be *grounded* or drained away into the Earth should the powerful object again come in contact with it.

In the Scottish Highlands, several families possessed charm stones that had been passed down through the generations. Some of these healing stones were simple rocks of grey, green, or black, and some were crystal of one sort or another. These magical stones were much treasured and used for healing various ailments. Usually, the stone was dipped into water a prescribed number of times (often the magical number of three); then the water was consumed. Sometimes, the stone itself was touched and a wish was made.

A STONE OF PROPHECY

The famed Highland Seer Kenneth MacKenzie of the Isle of Lewis, who was known as the Brahan Seer, made use of a magical stone. Like many of the seers, he gained his powers as a gift after an encounter with the Land of Faery. One day when he was still a child, he lay down to rest from his labors and fell fast asleep. He may not have known it, but he was on a faery hill, or so the story goes. When he awoke, he found a small white round stone lying on his breast. The stone had a hole in its center, and when he looked through the hole, he found he could see things. He could see the future, and he could see people's motives as well as their actions. Over time, he became well known as a prophet.[1]

STONE WATERS

As mentioned, healing stones were often dipped in water and the water was then consumed. Thus, the stones were seen to *charge* or bless the water, and amplify its healing power. However, sometimes stones were dipped into holy wells, in which case the stone's power was amplified by contact with the power of the well's sacred waters. In either case, the water was then used to bathe the person or the animal. Occasionally the stone was rubbed over the afflicted part of the body, or even the entire body.

Often, bottles of *stone-treated water* were sent out as cures by the keepers or guardians of the stones.

In Wales, the healing power of stones was brought together with the healing power of herbs, and an ointment for healing joint pain was made by pounding flintstone, primroses, and chickweed together.

In parts of Scotland, pieces of white or rose quartz were used to prevent rheumatism and other ailments. These were known as fever stones or *hectic stones*. The stones were put into boiling water; when the water had cooled, it was used to wash arms, legs, and other afflicted parts. Other times, the water was consumed to help cure fevers. It is probable that prayers were said over the stone-blessed water.[2]

In some parts of Scotland, one these hectic stones was referred to as "the white stone of the faeries" from a legend that it had been given to a young boy by a faery one day. The boy had been pouring water on a faery knoll, and a greatly appreciative faery appeared at his side and gifted him with the stone as a reward for providing such refreshment. The faery told the boy that the stone would heal the boy's father of his pain if it was rubbed on the painful part of the body, and the water into which the stone had been dipped was consumed. The stone proved its worth by curing not only the boy's father but others suffering from similar ills as well. The family kept the stone very carefully for several generations, at least until the end of the 19th century when folklorists recorded the story.[3]

STONES FROM HOLY WELLS

Special yellow crystals were found near a holy well near Lough Neagh in Ireland. They were said to have power to avert evil and bring good luck and blessings if the Faery Doctors pronounced certain secret words over them while gathering them. These crystals were said to grow in one night, Midsummer's Eve, and were found in great number scattered for a few miles about the general vicinity of the well.[4]

In some places in Ireland, pilgrims visiting the holy wells gathered the small white stones found on the ground nearby and used them to make their prayers with, piling them up to make monuments between the rounds of their praying. Often the pilgrims heard soft beautiful music, which seemed to rise up from the watery depths of the well itself. Hearing such music delighted the pilgrims greatly, and often they would impulsively laugh and clap in joy. But such a response resulted in a cessation of the magical music, and often caused their piles of prayer stones to come tumbling down as well. When this happened, the pilgrims took it as sign that they should not have laughed while angels were singing, so they knelt down and resumed their prayers in a more reverent manner.[5]

GODSTONES

In ancient Ireland, the dead were often buried with small white stones or pieces of quartz crystal, which were referred to as *godstones*. Sometimes these were on the graves rather than within them. Godstones have also been found in burial sites in Britain, Scotland, the Hebrides, and the Isle of Man, which shows the custom to be a very widespread one. Although no reason has ever been given for this, it is tempting to speculate that, as with the above custom of praying with the stones at the holy wells, these godstones were also prayer stones of some kind. Perhaps they were prayers for the deceased, messages of love to the deceased, or messages sent with the deceased to the gods.[6] Most of the white godstones were smooth, clean, polished, and water-worn, so possibly the intention was to make a connection between death and rebirth—with the smooth, water-cleansed stones representing the necessary preparation for rebirth.

ST. FILLAN'S STONES

In a village in Wales, there existed some strange and curiously shaped stones that were used for both healing and averting evil. They were river stones, and the constant washing of the waters was most likely responsible for their strange shapes. One set of these stones was held to be the property of a St. Fillan, who lived there in the 8th century and founded a nearby monastery. Like many of the old saints and Druids, he had a reputation as a healer and was said to have used a set of stones whose shapes resembled parts of a human body. Much later on these stones passed into the keeping of the owners of a nearby mill where for years they were cared for by the mill owners and their family—the official guardian of the stones always being an elderly woman of the family. She would use the stones to heal by passing or rubbing them over the afflicted body part three times one way, three times the other, and then three times the first way again, while reciting an incantation in Gaelic.

The use of stones this way, the number nine in their usage, and their guardianship by an old woman whose mill-keeping occupation associates her with water and therefore "well-guardians," all show that this particular tradition has its roots in the distant past, and is indeed part of a much older magical healing tradition.[7]

BULLAUNS

Another interesting example of the use of stone in healing is that of bullauns. Bullauns are stone basins of varying sizes and antiquity (and some seem likely to be artificial rather than natural in origin) that contain a hole within them wherein sits a smaller stone. Rainwater tends to gather in such basins, and it is considered very sacred and healing. Generally speaking, bullauns were thought to be useful for specific things, such as eye problems, warts, rheumatism, and the like. Often they were said to be sacred to Brigid.

The presence of the smaller stone within suggests that they may have had a mortar and pestle type usage, and this very sexual connotation definitely suggests a use in fertility magic. Therefore, it is not surprising to find that one of their primary uses was in issues of virility, fertility, and childbirth. But the simple fact of the stones' suggestive shape imbued them with *all* the power inherent in what such a sexual union of opposites holds: the very power to create new life. The rainwater that gathered in bullauns held this magical potency of newness, vitality, and regeneration. Powerful healing magic indeed!

Bullaun water was consumed, rags were dipped in it and applied to sore places, and offerings of various sorts were deposited within it. In Christian times, the water was sometimes collected for use as baptismal water.

Certain hollow stone basins were referred to as "cup and ring" stones and have traditionally been used for a variety of magical purposes including use as a place to leave offerings for the faeries. In the Highlands and Islands of Scotland, milk was poured into such stone basins as offerings to the *gruagach*, the long-haired and sometimes shaggy-haired fairies or spirits who protectively looked after cattle and fields.

Modern science tells us that stones, particularly crystalline stones (and many of the stones used for healing contained a crystalline structure), have various piezo-electric properties relative to expansion and contraction, and that under certain conditions and certain pressures they give off light. Crystals have certain physical properties. They can hold, focus, magnify, and transmit energy. When crystalline stones are boiled in water, certain nutritious minerals may be released. Many other cultures besides the Celts have made use of healing stones, so it is certain that these properties—very useful in the hands of a dedicated healer—were not unknown, even if they were not spelled out as precisely as our modern science has allowed us to spell them out.

END NOTES

1 McNeil, F. Marian, *The Silver Bough, Vol. 1*, William MacLellan, 1959, Canongate Classics, Edinburgh, 1989, p. 96.

2 Beith, Mary, *Healing Threads: Traditional Medicines of the Highlands and Islands of Scotland*, Polygon, Edinburgh, 1995, p. 154.

3 Ibid, pp. 154-155.

4 Wilde, Lady, *Ancient Legends, Mystic Charms & Superstitions of Ireland*, Chatto & Windus, London, 1919, p. 250.

5 Ibid, p. 237.

6 Wood-Martin, W. G., *Traces of the Elder Faiths of Ireland: A Handbook of Irish Pre-Christian Traditions, Vol. 1*, Longmans, Greens, and Co., NY and Bombay, 1902, pp. 329-330.

7 Clarke, David, with Andy Roberts, *Twilight of the Celtic Gods*, Blandford, Cassell PLC, London, 1996, p.64.

PART III

Faery Healing for Today

CHAPTER II

Standing on the Threshold of a New Era

In the preceding chapters, we examined Faery Healing from historical and spiritual perspectives. We learned about the herbs, trees, stones, and other items used, as well as the charms, incantations, and spiritual beliefs that are part of this tradition.

But aside from being an interesting historical study, what does any of this have to do with us here and now as we move into the 21st century? We have the marvels of modern medicine at our fingertips. Who needs herbs, stones, charms and songs? Who needs the faeries, anyhow?

The answer is, *we* do. We all do. We need the faeries in our lives, and we need the Elemental Beings, the nature spirits, the devas, and the angels, as well. For in our rush to materialism, we have, in our minds, depopulated the world of these beings. We have denied their existence, and relegated them to the category of a children's story or a fantasy novel.

But now it is time for us to once again recognize their existence. It is time to reclaim them and re-create a relationship with them. How is it that we can think we can live without our kin, here on the Mother Earth we all share? Why is it that we have chosen such self-imposed isolation from our relatives?

Working with the Faeries

To summarize what we have learned from the old legends, there are seeming contradictions with respect to how faeries were regarded and related to. On the one hand, faeries were feared and people made attempts to placate them. The faeries' very real power, which could be experienced both as beneficial and malignant, was highly respected. On the other hand, some faeries were appreciated as being quite friendly and helpful to humanity, and the legends speak of their kind deeds, and gifts of good luck. Other faery-given gifts included musicianship, seership, and healing powers, including specialized knowledge of herbs for healing.

Legends agree, however, on the fact that what faeries desire most is respect: respect for their persons, their lands, their homes, and their privacy. It is when humans interfere with these things, purposefully or inadvertently, that trouble is the inevitable result. Even in the cases of Faery Doctors—whose healing powers and knowledge was known to come directly from the faeries—it was only when they did something out of the bounds of the terms of their agreement with the faeries that they were beaten or otherwise punished by the faeries. Their mistakes or disobedience were interpreted as a lack of respect. And it is clear from the folklore that many of the Faery Doctors were constantly and fearfully aware of this need to maintain the agreements.

Faeries meting out punishment to humans for lack of respectful behavior is, in essence, a statement of how natural law works. These beings of the subtle realms—so close in many ways to humans, yet in many other ways so different—have been communicating to us for centuries in this way. They have been reminding us of the fact that other realms and other life-forms are part of the Wholeness of Life, and therefore, deserving of respect.

They have also been reminding us that while humans seemingly have the power to do as they will on the earth, this perception is, to some extent, an illusion based on our perception of time scales. These other realms and life-forms are not simply and inherently subject to human whim and arrogance; there WILL be consequences for lack of respectful relationship—sooner or later. These are the messages. Just because we have in these last few centuries rendered ourselves deaf to the voices, this does not change the message these voices have been so implacably communicating.

Given the rising level of human-induced world environmental crises, I am left with the feeling that the actual consequences of human environmental arrogance are beginning to arrive, even as nature—speaking with many voices—continues to transmit her messages in the form of unusual floods, droughts, polar ice cap melting, global warming, and holes in the ozone layer.

My sense of things is, that at this point in time, we are seeking a new and different relationship with the faery folk than that which was experienced by our ancestors and evidenced in the folklore. The rising tide of materialism of the last few hundred years has so successfully sundered us from our psychic sensitivities to the invisible, subtle realms of nature, that we now seek restoration of these faculties of perception—faculties that our ancestors once took for granted. And along with this must come a new type of relationship with the Faer Folk.

As this new millennium dawns, we find ourselves preparing to once again approach the Faery Realm, wishing to open ourselves to exploration of the subtle realms of life and the beings who live therein, and seeking a new and hopefully more cooperative type of relationship with them than humanity has previously experienced. But this time, we approach with knowledge of our past errors. We come with new respect for faeries and the other invisible beings of the subtle realms, realizing them to be fellow travelers on the vast continuum of consciousness that makes up sentient life in the universe.

So what is it that we can do to demonstrate our respect for them, in these days when the rapid disappearance of the wild lands must surely signal violations of faery rights? We cannot, as individuals, put a stop to the worldwide ravaging of the wilderness and the resultant violation of nature's beauty, many ecosystems, the Elemental and Faery Realms, and life's delicate balance, which are occurring in the name of progress.

But a thoughtful assessment of the problem provides, in fact, clues to a possible solution. There is something *big* going on here. The balance has been upset, and can only be restored by a power greater than that possessed by one or two concerned individuals.

The Mother Earth is a huge being; her power is immense beyond imagining. She has her own life, and her own cycles of which we are but a tiny part. Our perspective, as one of the many life-forms inhabiting her body, is bound to be skewed by the fact of our relative smallness.

But though we are small, we are not entirely insignificant. As one of the few Earth creatures so far noted to possess the power of choice, we can exercise that power and make good, honorable, and conscious choices—for ourselves, our children, our Mother Planet, and the future of life itself. We can educate our children and others who cross our path about the power inherent in making honorable and educated choices about how to live on the planet lightly and gracefully, and in right relationship with all our kin. These things may seem simple and basic, but they have power, especially when significant numbers of people are involved. There are, after all, many individual drops of water in an ocean. Having done these things, we then must bow, ultimately, to the greater power and wisdom of our Mother Planet herself, and to the even greater power of the Creator/tress. We must acknowledge these great powers, and come into alignment with them. We must cooperate.

And in order to do these things, we must be listening. We must train ourselves to listen to the subtle voices of the invisible realms of life, including those of our close relatives in the Faery Realm.

Our faery siblings have much to offer us. Their realm holds the mystery of the Primal and Pristine Land, the *template* of our own world. Because they are creatures of the subtle realms of life, a renewed relationship with the faeries is most appropriate as we prepare to move into the much heralded Age of Aquarius. This Age is ruled by the planet Uranus whose influence is said to govern the higher octave of communications, as well as the electro-magnetic frequencies which make up the Web of Life. If we would restore the wasteland our world is becoming, we must attune ourselves, re-tune our frequency, to the Pristine, Primal Land, the original template, and allow ourselves to become Living Bridges, through which the energy of regeneration and restoration can pass from that world into our own.

KINSHIP

I find the concept of *kinship* useful in defining relationship with the Faery Realm. Faeries are our kin; Robert Kirk referred to them as "co-walkers," and other authors have referred to them as "cousins." In my inner travels, I have occasionally come upon some who referred to themselves as my siblings. As by virtue of our physical nature—flesh, blood, bones—we are kin to the animals, we are by virtue of our inner, subtle, etheric nature, kin to the faeries. This relationship allows us, when we are doing our Faery Healing work, to find that place within ourselves that is Faery, and thus tune ourselves, by methods which will be discussed in the next section, to the appropriate frequency.

HOW TO LISTEN

Life is continually giving us feedback, signals, and lessons. For many reasons we tend to be somewhat unconscious of these things, even blocking them out in some cases. Sometimes this is just a matter of overwhelm: there are too many things going on, too much input, and we just can't seem to handle it all. Other times, we simply do not catch the often subtle, messages and signals sent our way, or if we do, we fail to interpret them as messages and teachings.

Once we have realized that life and nature are constantly teaching us, the next realization is in learning how to listen. Just as it is hard to hear someone speak if there is loud music or background noise going on at the same time, it is hard to hear the subtle voices of life and nature if our lives and minds are cluttered with too much mental clutter and background noise.

Perhaps part of the solution lies in learning how to tidy up our minds and keep them uncluttered, so that what comes in to us can be peacefully assessed and comprehended, a task—like other tasks of personal hygiene—needing daily attention. In my own life, I have noted that there are certain signals that tell me I am racing and need to slow down. Losing my car keys or locking myself out of my house or car, for instance, tell me that my mind is racing far beyond my body's ability to keep up with it. If this happens several times within a short period of time, I am being warned that my ability to effectively get from point A to point B is seriously impaired on all levels of my being and life, because my racing mind has managed to leave crucial parts of myself (or my thought processes) behind. Without them, I am at a standstill and sometimes, especially if I don't realize what's going on, a danger to myself and others.

Therefore, self-awareness and learning one's own inner cues is very helpful in learning to listen, and in learning to listen *beyond* the self as well. Once this level of awareness has been achieved, we can then begin to understand the other messages that come our way, things that may not specifically have to do with us personally.

But it is a subtle form of listening we must learn if we are to listen to the often delicate messages of the beings of the inner realms, which category includes the faeries. It is a whole-body affair, a very *inner* listening, rather than a mental thing. It is learning to listen—and see, feel, and sense as well—for the clues and cues, some extremely subtle, that the body gives us while we are experiencing the inner realms through journeywork and imagination.

ABOUT IMAGINATION

Imagination gets a bad rap these days. It is equated with fantasy, with non-reality, with childish nonsense and make-believe.

In actuality, imagination is a crucial human faculty. At its most basic level, it is our *image-making* ability, without which we would be unable to visualize anything, including mundane things like how to get to the grocery store and back again. "Imagination is our structure-creating device for accessing subtle energies. In its highest use, it allows us to access the Gods and Goddesses by creating a mental form or matrix for those subtle energies to flow through to us. The form thus created is then empowered by the energies flowing through; the form seems to take on a life of its own, and the inner images we see act, move and speak in ways that we have not pre-programmed."[1]

What has been termed "creative visualization" is the use of the imagination to create deeply detailed, sensory-enhanced, feeling-level imagery, complete with enough sensory detail that each of the senses is fully, if mentally, engaged in the process. It is about painting pictures with the mind, living pictures that move, have sound, texture, scents, and into which we can step at will. It is good exercise for the imagination to work on these things.

Yet, as vivid as we can make them, they are simply the structures we use to access the energies, not the energies themselves, which is an important distinction to keep in mind.

It is through the power of the imagination that we will, in the exercises that follow, make contact with the Faery Realm. This way of using the imagination is similar to using a muscle—although it may seem difficult at first, over time it gets easier, the results clearer, and our ability to become more secure in interpreting the results grows and strengthens as well.

Once again, we are having to relearn, or at least strengthen, something which our ancestors took for granted. Years of listening to magical tales, lives of the saints, and stories of ancestors and heroes provided them with well-exercised and trained imaginations which we, living in the more passive television era, may not possess.

BODY LANGUAGE

Another human faculty long under-exercised is the ability to understand the messages given to us by our own body. We understand pain, of course, and pleasure—both rather extreme forms of messaging. But what about all those subtle things, such as a gut feeling, a sinking stomach, a fluttering stomach, a rush of energy, a draining of energy, or a generalized but subtle feeling of rightness or wrongness?

I have found it helpful to simply ask my body to show me its signals for yes and no, for what is true for me and false for me. A way to do this is to ask your body to give you indicators for this, and then verify these indicators by making statements that are true and ones that are false, and noting the differences in how your body *feels*. Although this may sound vague and imprecise, over time you will find that it does work, and that you really can develop the ability to understand the true and false cues your body provides. It is very subtle at first. The indicators may be things like a rush of energy or a "good" feeling for *yes*, and a lack of energy, drained, or perhaps agitated feeling for *no*. Some people experience tingling, or a slight tickling on the hands, face, or stomach (amazing how often the stomach tells us things!). One of my friends experiences shoulder pain every time she hears something that is untrue.

Learning to be aware of these body signals is helpful for many reasons, not the least of which is in assessing one's experiences in the Otherworlds and being aware when one is being given a message.

When doing innerwork, we eventually come to a point where we can feel the energies moving through our body as we do the work. Often, we can feel very distinct differences in the qualities of the various energies that flow through us, and in time, we learn how to interpret these energies, and tell the differences between them. These sensations, along with whatever guidance we are receiving from our Faery Allies, guide us as to how to proceed while doing Faery Healing work.

END NOTES

1   McArthur, Margie, *Wisdom of the Elements*, Crossing Press, Freedom, CA, 1998, p. 60.

Sacred Earth: The Living Land and the Web of Life

The land, the Sacred Earth, is the basis of everything. It is, quite literally, the foundation of our experience, the ground of our being. It is the source and root of our physical manifestation as human beings. It is from the land we draw the food, water, and supplies that sustain our lives, and it is back into Earth's embrace we shall go when we have drawn our final breath. Without the land, we are but disembodied spirits having no form into which we might pour ourselves to experience this particular realm of life and being. The land, and physical life in general, grants our spirits/souls the power of self-expression.

Our modern culture and society tends to look upon the land in a very mechanistic way, regarding the Earth as dead and inert, mere *matter*, a "thing" from which resources can be freely extracted and upon which roads and buildings may be placed, as if Earth's sole purpose for existence was to supply us with what need, or we think we need, for our lives.

Yet the roads and buildings are but new and temporary placements upon the Living Land. Beneath the roads and buildings are soil, rocks, pebbles, stones, plant material, roots, fungus, earthworms, nematodes, bacteria, and microorganisms of many kinds. In short, beneath the roads and buildings is *Life*! The teeming power of life itself resides beneath our feet, no matter how hard we try to cover it up and deny it. A dandelion, pushing itself up through a crack in the sidewalk, gives testimony to this fact. We must never forget that the word *matter* comes from the Latin *mater*, which means mother, and it is mothers who give birth to life.

ORDERS OF BEINGS

The Earth itself, and indeed, the universe as well, are composed of many orders of beings—from simple to complex. Each of these life-forms has a subtle, spiritual aspect, as well as the physical manifestation that we apprehend with our senses.

Therefore, there are physical and (usually) visible realms of life and their inhabitants; and there are subtle, (usually) invisible realms of life and their inhabitants. The physical realms are usually tangible, quantifiable, and measurable—even if this means we must use our most technologically advanced equipment to measure them. The subtle realms are best apprehended with our subtle senses of clairvoyance, clairaudience, and clairsentience, using *imagination*—our image-making faculty—as the Key to the Door.

When we look at the physical world, we must realize and remember the existence of the invisible, subtle-energy aspect of it even though we may not be able to see it with our physical eyes. This subtle, energetic Web of Life is made up of the subtle essences and consciousnesses of the many beings involved. These consciousnesses vary in awareness levels, depending on the complexity of the being. The larger and more complex beings are composed of many smaller ones, but it is likely that each possesses some degree of consciousness and awareness. Consciousness pervades the universe whether we acknowledge that fact, or not. In fact, the entire universe may be described as an interconnected Web of Consciousness composed of beings of varying sizes and types to which many different names have been given.

This Web of Life and life-forms should indicate to us that the Earth's primary reason for existence is not to simply supply our personal wants and needs. We are but one part of a vast and complex chain of life-forms, co-existing in varying forms of relationship—often interdependence—with one another. This becomes a bit clearer when we think about the millions of tiny life-forms, such as bacteria, that exist on and within our bodies, and of how our body's organs are made up of millions of tiny cells that are, in their turn, made up of even smaller units of matter, right on down to the sub-atomic level, and all in a complex dance of relationship.

Yet another example is trees, whose respiration cycle gives us the oxygen we need to breathe in order to live, while our respiration cycle allows us to give them the carbon dioxide they need to live.

If you sense a "cycle" happening here, you are correct. There is almost always an energy flow; seldom does the energy go just one direction without some sort of reciprocal movement. This is as true of interactions between subtle energies as it is between physical life-forms. It is as true in relationships on the subtle realms as it is in relationships in the physical realms.

On both physical and energetic levels the Earth is, herself, an enormous, complex being, composed of several layers and kinds of substances, and several corresponding layers and kinds of beings both large and small, whose bodies *are* these layers and substances.

SACRED EARTH

Physically, at the very center of the planet is a liquid crystalline core, which is covered by a molten fiery core. This two-fold center is surrounded by a sizable layer called the mantle upon which rests the crust. Upon the upper level of the crust rests our soil, and all the amazingly diverse and abundant forms of mineral, animal, plant life of both soil and sea. All of which, as we have said, are themselves composed of many, many other smaller life forms, including bacteria, viruses, and fungi.

Spiritually, we would say that the Earth contains many *subtle* beings and consciousnesses within and on her body. These inner beings are the consciousnesses of the core, the mantles, the magma, the earthquake faults, the chemical elements, and all the other forces that live and move within her. On Earth's outer level, the beings are those that ensoul mountains and mountain ranges, forests and trees, rivers, lakes, oceans, land masses, plants, animals, fungi, bacteria, viruses, and all the rest. These are not human-type consciousnesses, but they are consciousnesses all the same.

Prologue to *The Washer at the Ford* by Fiona Macleod

"…Everywhere we see the life of Man in subservient union with the life of Nature; never, in a word, as a sun beset by tributary stars, but as one planet among the innumerous concourse of the sky, nurtured, it may be, by light from other luminaries and other spheres than we know of. That we are intimately at one with Nature is a cosmic truth we are all slowly approaching. It is not only the dog, it is not only the wild beast and the wood-dove, that are our close kindred, but the green tree and the green grass, the blue wave and the flowing wind, the flower of a day and the granite peak of an aeon. And I for one would rather have the wind for comrade, and the white stars and green leaves as my kith and kin, than many a human companion, whose chief claim is the red blood that differs little from the sap in the grass or in the pines, and whose "deathless soul" is, mayhap, no more than a fugitive light blown idly for an hour betwixt dawn and dark. We are woven in one loom, and the Weaver thrids our being with the sweet influences, not only of the Pleiades, but of the living world of which each is no more than a multi-coloured thread: as, in turn, He thrids the wandering wind with the inarticulate cry, the yearning, the passion, the pain, of that bitter clan, the Human."[1]

Land and legends

One of the most important things to remember when looking at the old faery lore and legends is that, in a very real sense, the legends come out of the land. That is to say, people living in lands with similarity of physical characteristics are likely to experience faeries, gods, and Subtle Beings that are quite similar. This is borne out by comparisons of tales of people living in the great forests, people living on the edge of the sea, people living in the desert lands, and people living where rivers and lakes are abundant or scarce. In particular, a comparison of Teutonic and Celtic mythologies and stories provides illustration of this, as both peoples inhabited, at different times, the same great forested northern and western parts of Europe. Even Britain and Ireland were once heavily forested lands. Therefore, it is not surprising that we find quite similar Subtle Beings in the tales of each of these cultures.

What this means to our Faery Healing work is that it is quite important to seek relationship with the beings of *our* land, the land on which we currently find ourselves and call *home*. This is where our work can make a difference.

In addition, it is good to explore the legends of the Subtle Beings connected with our ancestral lands because we are quite likely to find we have some sort of connection or relationship to these beings, as well. We are connected through blood to the ancestors who give us our DNA and therefore the very bodies through which we experience life, but we are also connected through birth and/or nurture to the land in which we live. Both of these connections are very important.

Not only are those ancestral land legends and beings likely to be part of our genetic psychic inheritance, but there is much information in the folklore and legends of those lands which can teach us about Subtle Beings in general, as well as how our ancestors perceived and interacted with them.

Although faeries generally are land-based, it is not unknown for certain types of Faery Beings to attach themselves to a family, work with the family, and even move with the family to a new land. In these cases, they tend to see the family rather than the individual as the entity to be worked with. If the new land bears enough similarity to the old, both physically and energetically, the beings might well be able to make themselves fully at home there, just as their humans have done. This is another reason why it may be helpful to explore the lore and legend of one's ancestral lands.

The Old Gods

At this point, I would like to refer you back to, *Chapter 1*, where we spoke of the way the Greeks and Celts viewed these very same aspects of nature. Rivers, lakes, trees—all were considered to be living, sentient beings composed of body and spirit and possessing names or titles. In addition, there were Divine Beings whose powers included those of vulcanism, earthquake, rain, wind, storms, thunder, lightning, hurricanes, and other such phenomena.

This is quite comparable to the Celtic deities, some of whom were the spirits of locality, but many, such as the Irish Tuatha De Danaan and the Welsh Children of Don, were perhaps, along with the earlier Irish race known as the Fomorians, personifications of the great forces of nature.

The great giant gods—Balor of the Eye, Bran the Blessed, Llyr of the Seas and his son Manannan, Dagda the All Father, Goibniu the Smith, Dian Cecht the Leech, the youthful Angus Og, God of Love, the Great Mothers Dana of Eire and Don of Wales, and Brigid of the Hearth Flame and of Wells—seem to represent the deep powers of nature which create life, shape it, and/or keep it in existence.

If you will recall your Greek mythology, you will remember that the Titans (I find it interesting that William Shakespeare used the name *Titania* for the Faery Queen) were eventually vanquished by the Olympian gods to the realm of Tartarus, the lowest level of the Underworld. This is quite reminiscent of the fate of the Fomorians, who were said to be monstrous beings, huge, misshapen, one-eyed, and sometimes one-legged. Such characteristics mark them as primal powers of creation, rather than as a race of humans.

One cannot help relating these ancient Irish Fomorians to the Titans of Greece who were also primal powers of creation—Elder Gods who were the firstborn children of the Great Goddess Gaia (earth) and her son/consort, Ouranus, (sky). In Greek mythology the Titans were defeated by the Olympian gods and were then secured in the Underworld of Tartarus to keep them from causing further harm, similar to the manner in which the Fomorians were defeated and banished back into the sea by the Tuatha De Danaan.

Metaphorically, this is interesting as it represents the containment of the primal powers after they have participated in the creation of world. These primal powers are so potent that their raw, unbridled energies would have prevented the further development of that which they had helped bring into being, and would have, in fact, destroyed it if not contained. Therefore, so that life could continue to develop, these powers had to be contained, and driven back to their origins in the Underworld or the Sea—both places associated the Otherworld—which was always the earthly source, or "residence" of the powers that bring forth life.

Ancestral Connections

We have speculated in previous chapters on our relationship with the Tuatha: how they may be *our* ancestors, and how we may be related to the Faery Realm, as co-inhabitants of the Earth, as part of the Earth. Here are my thoughts on the nature of this relationship.

The Fomorians and the Tuatha are the Old Gods. The Fomorians are similar to the Titans or star powers living within the Earth and are represented physically by the primal elements such as hydrogen, oxygen, helium, and the others. The Tuatha are similar to the forces such as electro-magnetism, chemical reactions, expansion, contraction, heat, cold, geological and tectonic activity, and gravitational pull that interacted with these primal elements to literally shape the world.

Some scholars interpret the Fomorians as the chaotic, watery, deep Earth forces responsible for the growth of plants, and the Tuatha De Danaans as the earthly or even heavenly forces of the power of light. This is borne out by tales of the Fomorians giving or withholding the secrets of the soil from the Tuatha. Both of these are forces of fertility—water and fire—as plants need both moist soil and the sun's light and warmth in order to grow. But even if we include this interpretation, it simply adds another wondrous layer of meaning to a mix that is already rich with layers of meaning.

Since these Celtic tales were not written down until well into the Christian era, it is not only possible but likely that the original, archetypal stories were, over time, layered with tales of invading tribes, heroes, historic events, and changing religious understanding—thus adding to this rich mix of layers of meaning as the stories underwent a very natural, organic pattern of growth.

The Faery Beings are, as the old tales say, the Tuatha in "diminished" form. In other words, they are a smaller, less powerful, subtle/spiritual order of life than the Tuatha De Danaan, but of an energetic frequency that resonates with them, similar to the way low C, middle C, and high C are related to each other on a piano keyboard. This being the case, the faeries thus mediate the raw, wild power of those primal beings, the Tuatha and the Fomorians, into the subtle aspect of our Mid-Earth realm. We in turn can mediate it from the Faery Realm to our own in a more physical way, by virtue of the fact that our bodies are more dense and physical than those of the faeries.

These Old Gods *are* our ancestors in a very real way. *We* are formed of the earth, the water, the fire, and the air. We also contain within us the forces of expansion and contraction, electricity and magnetism, and therefore partake of the very same physical elements and forces that these deities represent. Yet we also, like these old gods, have a spiritual essence, individuality, awareness, and *consciousness*. No dichotomy here: matter (mother) is a manifestation of Spirit in Substance.

Faery Healing

As has been stated in preceding chapters, when we do Faery Healing we must be aware that we are calling on the energies of many beings and working with the many strands of consciousness which comprise the Web of Life, including its subtle and invisible realms.

Occasionally these beings will reveal to us knowledge of their specific identities, but more frequently, particularly in the case of the less individuated beings, they do not. Sometimes they will simply give us a term that indicates their function.

But they will come forth to perform the functions for which the Divine Intelligence designed them—happy to play their part, do their job in maintaining the Web of Life, and interact with human intelligence in a co-creative, co-healing fashion.

END NOTES

1   Macleod, Fiona, *The Works of Fiona MacLeod, Vol. II; Washer of the Ford: and Other Legendary Moralities*, Patrick Geddes and Colleagues, Edinburgh, Stone & Kimball, Chicago, IL, 1896.

CHAPTER 13

Yesterday's Faery Healing: Assessing the Past

FAERY-CAUSED DISORDERS

In the preceding chapters we looked briefly at faery-caused diseases such as Faery Stroke, Faery Blast, Faery Dart, and at how these disorders were treated by Faery Doctors. But what really was going on in these disorders? What *is* Faery Blast, really? Faery Dart may be easier to figure out as it sounds very much like arthritis or rheumatism; the others are more puzzling.

We have been given some of the physical symptoms accompanying these diagnoses, but probably not enough real information to adequately determine, from this remove in time, what exactly was going on with the victims or by what modern names their conditions might be called today. Dr. Logan offered his own speculations on this in his book *The Old Gods*. He feels that things like paralytic stroke, heat stroke, seizures, and such were the disorders being described.

It is intriguing to look at faery diseases from the perspective of the physical symptoms themselves. Symptoms of the suddenly occurring Faery Blast, such as low vitality, depression, sudden fainting, would seem to suggest a sudden drop in blood pressure or blood sugar levels, while symptoms of Faery Stroke, which was always sudden, serious, and frequently painful or infectious, suggest a severe bacterial or viral infection of one sort or another complete with a raging fever of the type that left one weak and debilitated thereafter.

Faery Dart, on the other hand, with its accompanying joint swelling, redness, and inflammation, sounds very much like arthritis, rheumatism, and the like, just as Dr. Logan has said. But what does not sound quite like mere arthritis is that Faery Dart was also thought to sometimes cause, in addition to the arthritic symptoms, paralysis or death.

Other symptoms mentioned as occurring in concert with faery-caused diseases, such as semi-paralysis, catatonia, and loss of mental powers, sound as if they may relate to high or low blood sugar, high or low blood pressure, and stroke. These symptoms also suggest possible nervous system burnouts or disorders, nervous and/or mental breakdowns, depression, and perhaps even mental illness. Other symptoms are suggestive of various forms of tuberculosis or other wasting-type diseases.

It is interesting to observe the human tendency to give a combination of symptoms a name, and then having named it, think we know what the condition really *is*. Often, treatment protocols are designed by assessing which treatments will ameliorate a given set of symptoms. Sometimes this seems to work, but alleviating the symptoms is not always the same as curing the disorder.

As tempting as it is to look at these faery disorders from the sole perspective of their physical manifestation, we cannot and should not separate them from either their emotional aspect or from the spiritual component that would have been present in the lives of the people.

The role of emotion

Emotions are energies that flow through us. We tend to interpret our experiences through the lens of our belief systems, and our belief systems advise us as to which things about which we need to get excited, nervous, or fearful. Our thoughts and emotions are intricately interwoven, and our interpretations of our experiences reflect this fact.

But it is beyond dispute that emotions cause very physical reactions in the body and that fear is one of the strongest, if not *the* strongest of emotions. And the truth of the matter is that people were *afraid* of the faeries, terribly afraid. Another truth of this matter is that because people really did see, converse with, and have experiences with the faeries, their fear was founded in something that was very real in their lives.

Furthermore, emotion works in such a way that the mere thought of something, or a good scare about it, can often be nearly as bad as the real thing, and can cause the same emotional, and especially physiological reactions as the real thing, which include the release of various body chemicals and all their accompanying physical manifestations and characteristics.

Because emotions are energetic frequencies, experiencing an extreme emotion about a situation can cause a body/emotional remembrance (which does not always include a mental listing) of all the other times and events when that emotion was felt. This makes the situation worse than it really is because we then are reacting emotionally to much more than that which simply lies before us.

This often can work to one's detriment, triggering inappropriately strong emotional states and all the accompanying physiological reactions and responses, some of which, such as catatonia and loss of mental powers, sound suspiciously like those which accompanied the faery-caused disorders.

It would be tempting at this point to conclude that all faery-caused diseases were therefore simply psychosomatic. But again, giving something a name does not really tell us what it is; and the very term *psychosomatic* begs for an accurate definition.

The real point I am trying to make here is that body and mind, thoughts and emotions, are so interwoven as to be well nigh inseparable in most cases—a fact which makes it impossible to state with any real precision exactly what was going on in these cases of faery-induced disorders. We can explain faery disorders from a physiological perspective and from an emotional perspective. We can define and quantify the symptomology. But we really cannot say that we know, definitely, that those suffering from faery diseases were *simply* having strokes, heart attacks, acute viral infections, or nervous breakdowns. It becomes, in fact, much like the old debate: "which came first, the chicken or the egg?" Did the physical symptoms cause the beliefs-based thoughts and emotions to arise, or did the thoughts and emotions cause the physical symptoms? We will never know for sure.

Mystical Experiences

By way of comparison of experiences, it is interesting to take note of historical descriptions of people undergoing visionary experiences. Catholic literature is full of this, and attests to the existence of many altered states of consciousness, including the ecstatic state, in those experiencing visions. During the ecstatic state, the person sees things others do not, and is focused completely on this experience, with rigid, chilly limbs, diminished respiration and circulation, and is often impervious to physical sensation.

The great 16th century Catholic mystic, St. Teresa of Avila, describes the ecstatic state, which she refers to as *trance*, and also a state of spirit flight which she refers to as *transport*, or *rapture*. In trance, there is a gradual loss of the awareness of outward things and sensory impressions, as awareness focuses ever more inwardly upon the object of the trance. Often, the ability to see and hear continues, but these impressions retreat to a very dim, distant part of the consciousness. Always, there is a loss of the ability to move physically.

Transport, rapture, or *flight of the spirit* on the other hand, comes on quite suddenly and unexpectedly, carrying the higher part of the soul swiftly away from the body. So suddenly does it arise, St. Teresa tells us, that there is not even time to collect the thoughts, or help oneself in any way. The perception is that of being carried away, upward, sometimes by a bird or on a cloud, to a destination unknown. Sometimes this feels very physical, and resisting it seems to induce a counter-force to the resistance, which intensifies the feeling of being lifted up physically and borne away. This is often a very frightening experience.

While in this state of consciousness, the person experiences the innerworlds and interacts with beings there; in the case of St. Teresa, this was, of course, God. While within this rapturous state the body is powerless, as if dead, and remains in the same physical position that it was in when the rapture came upon it, while the soul might be either completely entranced or in total possession of its faculties.

St. Teresa is certainly not the only Catholic visionary to have experienced such symptomology. Just within the last century, the children seers at both Fatima and Garabandal had identical experiences.

One cannot help but see the similarities between the description above and the description of those who have interacted with the faeries, including those who have been *taken away* and then brought back again. It is very important to realize that many of the same characteristics demonstrated by those interacting with the Faery Realm are found in accounts of those experiencing other mystical and trance states, and interacting with Divine Beings whose existence is more widely accepted today than is that of faeries.

In other words, those who said they spoke with God, the Virgin, the saints, and angels were held to be saints—blessed and holy—while those who said they spoke with faeries were held to be, at best, unfortunate, ill-fated, often deluded, and perhaps even mad.

Looking at all the above from the perspective of the subtle energies, we may conclude that interaction with an energetic frequency higher than that which humans normally deal can result in altered states of consciousness at best, or a sort of nervous-system or psychic burnout—either temporary or permanent—at worst.

Sometimes those taken by the faeries never really returned.

Soul loss

Another interesting comparison might be drawn between the states induced by interaction with Faery, including the influence of the Evil Eye, and that of the shamanic concepts of soul loss, and soul theft.

In shamanic terms, *soul loss* is a state wherein a fragment or part of the soul departs from the main portion of the soul. It can occur as the result of severe trauma, abuse, or fear. There are varying degrees of soul loss. Sometimes it is just a bit of soul that is lost, in which case the personality is still recognizably normal and functional. Sometimes many bits or fragments are lost and the personality is therefore greatly affected. When soul loss is the result of negative interaction with a stronger being or personality it is referred to as *soul theft*, and this can be either intentional or inadvertent on the part of the stronger personality.

Modern psychology acknowledges and deals with the phenomena of soul loss and dissociation, but uses terminology such as *Dissociative Identity Disorders* to describe them. We all possess the ability to dissociate, and do so from time to time; it is a survival mechanism. In its simplest form it is nothing more than turning our attention away from things we do not wish to see and experience, unpleasant external or even internal realities over which we feel we have no control. It is when an extreme form of this occurs—usually due to trauma—that it becomes clinical and starts acquiring nomenclature and descriptive terminology.

Such an extreme dissociation would be seen by shamans as a very serious condition because the more parts of itself that a soul loses, the more that soul becomes fragmented—its vital essence dispersed and therefore unavailable for actually living and functioning. Over time, this can become life threatening in the sense of not having enough soul left to truly function in life. This is true whether the case is one of soul loss or soul theft. The person so afflicted experiences a sense of being greatly depleted, and pines or withers away.

Once again, the similarities to being taken by the faeries or afflicted by the Evil Eye are quite remarkable.

Faery Doctors

We have also, in past chapters, taken a good look at the Faery Healers—the Faery Doctors, Faery Women, and even the herbal healers. We have, as well, looked at the magical, psychological elements and techniques employed by these healers to affect their cures.

The existence of Faery Healers and Faery Doctors in the Celtic tradition provides a direct link back to a much earlier era of human history. It may be safely said that the Faery Doctors are the direct heirs to a tradition that stretches, in part at least, back to the Druids and even earlier—to the times when a form of what may be called shamanism was practiced among the tribes of people whose descendants ultimately became known as the Celts. Human history is full of magic; all cultures have used it. The Celtic peoples of the

British Isles, whose ancestors are known to have come from the steppes of Eurasia (not too far a remove from the Siberian homelands of traditional shamanism), were no exception.

The dividing line between magic and religion is very thin, if it exists at all, and different societies are likely to draw it in different places in the sand. The techniques used by shamans and Faery Healers fall into a category that I refer to as *Spiritual Technology*. These techniques are used to access powers beyond the physical realm and to interact with non-physical beings. If the methods are known and correctly applied, the technology works no matter which pantheon of gods, spirits, saints, angels, or faeries is called upon. Each of these categories of beings has its own uniquely helpful ability and energy, and each of us must find the pantheon, beings, and belief system that works best for us, knowing, however, that there is but One Source for them all.

And so it is with this knowledge that we may now step forward and move into the future of the Faery Healing Tradition.

PART IV

A Practical Manual for Faery Healing

CHAPTER 14

Faery Healing

What is the work of Faery Healing? Why do we seek to do it? These are valid questions to ask, as we begin this section of the book.

My definition of Faery Healing is this: *Accessing the regenerative and healing powers of the Otherworlds—the Faery Realm, and by extension, the powers of the Elemental and Devic realms, as well as that of the Deep Earth—for purposes of healing work, which is the work of "reconnecting and reweaving into wholeness."* Since the Otherworlds, being the pristine, subtle counterpart of our own, contain the blueprint or template of our own world, they are our prime sources of healing and regenerative energies. These templates are living energies, rather than static forms, active rather than passive, living, relating, interacting, developing, emerging, and becoming, but always pristine and whole.

Our bodies are of the Earth, and nature is the source of our being. While we are alive in these bodies, the Earth, in both its physical and subtle aspects, is the source of all healing and renewal. All traditional cultures have known this; our modern ones seem the first to forget it. The Faery Healers lived in a culture where the spiritual and physical aspects of life were still intimately interwoven. That weaving has been ripped and sundered, in some places and cases, and part of the work of our modern Faery Healing is to weave it back together.

In its broadest sense, Faery Healing is about working with the assistance of Faery Allies to restore balance in unbalanced situations. Frequently, this takes the form of working with not only Faery Allies, but with plant or tree spirits, spirits of the land, and other Spirit Beings as well. The object of the healing work can be a place, a person, a plant, an animal, emotions, the environment, even the Earth herself. Sometimes there is no direct object of the work, and the work is more general, having to do with simply allowing ourselves to be vessels for the rebalancing energies that are coming through, and allowing them to flow forth from us and into the world.

It is important to remember that healing is about a return to health, wholeness, and balance, a process which can be lengthy and take many forms and which may not look like what we think it should. In Faery Healing we seek to access these primal templates of wholeness, and by use of these energies affect change in a manner that is positive and gradual.

Because healing with plants is a complex and demanding subject, our study of Faery Healing will focus less on the medicinal, herbal aspect of Faery Healing than on the magical one. Herbal healing is another study for another day, and one that I encourage you to undertake if you feel called to do so. We will work briefly with the plant world in this book; however, our primary focus will be on learning the spiritual technology necessary to interact with the Earth powers, including the plants, to re-establish a relationship that is mutually beneficial.

Looked at from a larger-than-human perspective, Faery Healing is the practice of re-establishing communication and working relationship with our kin of the subtle realms of the Earth, the Elementals, the Earth Beings, the Faeries, and the "small clans of the Earth's delight," to use Fiona Macleod's charming phrase.

To do Faery Healing we must be prepared to go into the *Heart of the World*, that innerworld place where the Flame of Being burns brightly and connects us all by virtue of the Fire of Life which sparks and blazes within all life.

Faery Healing works in a way in which we, in this era of magic-bullet drugs, are not accustomed. It is not quick and easy. It may not always seem logical. It is not about forcing our will, even our good will and intentions, upon others, whether they be of our own realm or of the subtle realms. It is not about commanding Faery Allies to do our bidding.

There are a few terms that illustrate what Faery Healing for today is all about. These terms are *Reweaving*, *Alliance*, *Attuning*, *Retuning*, and *Bridge-building*. These words describe the heart of what we are really after in this work. Our intention is to *reweave* our connection with the subtle worlds and our kin therein, thus forming *Alliances* with them that may be used to our mutual good. Doing this involves *Attuning* ourselves to their frequency. This allows us to *Build Bridges*, or more accurately, to actually become the Bridges ourselves, Bridges by which the energy from their realm, the Primal Lands, flows into ours. When this occurs, our realm is subtly *Retuned* to its original, primal state of wholeness. At least, this is the goal for which we strive.

The effects we create by our workings are in the spiritual, subtle realms. But if our work is done consistently and on a large enough scale, as with any true magic, effects will begin to manifest into the physical realm—beginning with ourselves and moving outward from there.

There is another term that could be employed here as it describes several of these actions, activities, and functions rather concisely: *mediation*. Mediation is the process of attuning oneself to a specific energy frequency (or state of being), and allowing the energy of that frequency to flow through one and out into the world.

This requires several other skills as well, not the least of which is the ability to get our own "stuff" out of the way so that we can be a clear and dedicated channel for the energies flowing through us.

It is important to realize that as these energies flow through us, they can't help but affect us. We, ourselves, will change and transform because of the energies that we are mediating.

As with any deep inner work, faery work can have the effect of holding up a mirror for us, forcing us to face our own issues and take responsibility for them. It is wise to be aware of this, to be open to it and cooperative with the process, dealing with issues as they arise and seeking help if we have need. This process is not always easy. Indeed, if worked with honestly and consistently, these energies cannot help but bring about change and transformation in our lives as the old, outworn, and unsuitable parts of our inner selves break down, dissolve, and fall away so that new growth and the resultant health can occur. Those unwilling to look in such mirrors should go no further with this work.

This aspect of faery work is so important that the late Margaret Lumley Brown, a contemporary of occultist Dion Fortune and possibly one of the finest mediums of the last century, stated that serious work with the Faery Kingdom should not be undertaken by anyone who is not already at work on themselves. She felt that premature connection with the Faery Realm by one who had not yet undertaken work of balancing the Elements within themselves could lead to an even greater imbalance. In her day, one worked toward this balance in carefully graded degrees within the confines of an established magical lodge. Although it may still be done that way now, it is also possible to do this work on one's own, providing one is scrupulously honest with oneself. Along these lines, it is worthwhile to remember the old saying about an encounter with the faeries leaving one either a poet (inspired) or mad!

Rules of the Work

There are a few basic rules that apply to this kind of work, and as we begin this study we would do well to consider them.

1. The first rule is to be aware of our motivation. We must truly seek within our heart and soul and come up with some sense of *why* want to do this work. Hopefully, the answer will have something to do with *service*, since service to the Hearth-fire of Life and to our fellow beings is always the foremost job of a healer, priest, or priestess.

2. The second and most important rule is that Faery Healing work must be done unconditionally. This means that we cannot allow our own preconceptions, misconceptions, desires, or whatever to get in the way of the work that is being done. When we do this kind of work, we are offering ourselves in service to the Goddess, the Earth, and to the Great Hearth-fire of Life. Most of the time, our small, finite minds simply do not have the Big Picture, though we may occasionally have hints of pieces of it. It is important that once we have prepared carefully and accessed these powerful innerworld forces and agreed to mediate them into our realm, we allow that to happen without getting in the way of the process.

   This is not to say that we surrender our will and become a pawn of any and all energies that wish to move through us. That is not what is meant by working unconditionally. It's more a matter of using discrimination and discernment with the energies we choose to work with in the first place, and only then allowing ourselves to become clear channels, hollow conduits, through which those energies may then freely and unconditionally flow.

3. The third rule is to remember always that we do what we do with love. Love is not the sticky-sweet emotional feeling that is commonly portrayed as such. Love comes from a *true heart,* and a true and loving heart is the key to much within the Faery Realm. We will discuss this in greater depth in *Chapter 19*.

4. The fourth rule, which perhaps should be the first, is that we must approach this work with a high degree of self-awareness and balance. We must have done our spiritual homework with regard to the condition of our own inner being, and our issues. As mentioned above, in the older traditions of magic this was often approached elementally. Students learned to observe and analyze themselves in terms of their own innate balance of the Elemental qualities, getting to know themselves as fiery, watery, airy, or earthy, and getting to know their deficiencies and excesses. In this way, they gained insight into their own minds and souls, and could work on achieving a more balanced state of being. It is important for us to know ourselves in this way. I advise those interested in Faery Healing to undertake some version of this kind of work. Basic instructions are contained in my book, *Wisdom of the Elements: The Sacred Wheel of Earth, Air, Fire, and Water* (Crossing Press, 1998).

Necessary Skills

As we have seen, Faery Healing requires several skills, the development of which must be undertaken if not already possessed.

BEING HOLLOW

Faery Healing, and really any healing work, requires us to be able to allow the energies to move through us. As mentioned in the section above, this is very essential to the work and is definitely a skill to be cultivated. Being hollow relates to *unconditionality*, doing the work "without conditions."

We must be clear channels. We must allow ourselves to be *hollow*, so that the healing and regenerative energies may flow through us easily, and without getting contorted or blemished along the way by something we have, intentionally or unintentionally, put into the mix.

A good visual image to work with here is that of a drinking straw or any other kind of hollow conduit. There must be an openness through which things can easily flow. To take up our image of a drinking straw, if the straw we put into our water glass did previous service in a soft drink, our water is likely to have a strange taste and color because the soft drink residue will have contaminated it. A clean straw preserves the integrity of whatever we are drinking.

When starting a healing session, it is good to first "clean out the works" by becoming hollow, pulling up some energy from the Earth, and allowing it to course through us and out again.

Learning to be hollow is an important key to any of the healing arts. It involves the use of methods such as visualization, sensing, and clear intention, and a fair amount of just plain old practice, as well. In addition, it involves working with our inner guides and helpers, and co-operating in the process of our own inner growth, purification, and transformation. The exercises given in subsequent chapters will provide practice opportunities for working with this technique.

BODY SENSING

One of the most important elements of this practice is that of developing a *body-sense*, that is, learning to recognize the subtle sensing-feeling language of your body, a topic about which we have spoken in previous chapters. Visualization is a fine way to start out in this process, but it should not be mistaken for sensing, and is in no way as important.

In fact, visualization may sometimes get in the way of sensing if we, consciously or unconsciously, tie in our feelings of success in this work with whether or not we get a clear visualization while doing it.

Sensing is what allows us to *feel* ourselves as a hollow tube through which the healing energies of the Otherworlds may flow. It is a subtle art. Many of us need to rediscover our abilities to do it—to slow down and *feel* ourselves, and to notice the subtle nuances of sensing, of *knowing*, as well as the information we are receiving at almost every moment of the day.

With our rapid pace of life many of us don't even know how to slow down. One way to do this is simply to sit quietly and focus on our breathing. Slowly breathe in and out, paying attention to the in-and-out flow, seeking only to make it even and calm. As you do this, form an intention in your mind that as you breathe in and out, you allow everything else but this awareness to flow out of you with the breath.

Do this for a few minutes and establish a rhythm with it; notice how you are feeling. Then, use your imagination to feel yourself breathing in and out, not just through your nose, but also through every pore of your body. Extend your awareness to your pores. Imagine and feel your whole body breathing. Use the exhalation to allow all those things you don't need—your worries, your cares, your fears, your concerns, your discomforts— to simply flow out of you, through your pores, through your nose, through your mouth. They flow out into the surrounding air, and are dispersed into a million tiny pieces, and carried away on a gentle breeze. Use the inhalation to bring in pure, fresh energy to revitalize you.

It is easy and natural to breathe through the nose or mouth; breathing through the pores, however, does require the use of the imagination! Yet it won't take long before you feel, ever so subtly, that you are, indeed, inhaling and exhaling through every pore of your body. This may perhaps be accompanied by a very subtle physical sensation, such as tingling, a heightened awareness of your skin, or a heightened awareness of sensation through the skin. This is a good beginning.

After you have mastered this, practice extending your awareness in other ways as well. As you breathe in, become aware of your aura and feel how it expands beyond the confines of your physical body. Please note that auric field is not flush with the physical body but actually extends out several inches, forming a shape similar to a small cocoon. You exhale, and your aura grows much larger, especially if you "puff it out" with your intention. You inhale, and feel it contracting gently back in. Practice this till you can feel it reasonably well, even if you think that what you feel is *only* in your imagination.

To summarize, body sensing is an ability developed through the practice of slowing down and truly noticing the myriad of subtle energies that influence us, and *register* with the body in a manner which is usually just below the level of our conscious perception. In order to get at this level, things such as relaxation exercises, breathing exercises, and the use of imagination and intention are all helpful. The goal of all of these practices and procedures is to expand our awareness.

Body sensing is actually related to the whole spectrum of inner senses which include inner forms of seeing, hearing, touching, tasting, and smelling. You will quite naturally become more aware of these as you proceed along through these exercises, developing and refining them along your way.

CLEAR INTENTION AND ATTENTION

Clear intention can be as simple as thinking about what it is we intend to do, clearing all else from our mind, and articulating that intention, even if only silently, to ourselves. Clear intention makes use of our powers of choice and will to narrow our focus down to a precise thought, issue, or point.

Although it may be hard for the material-minded to believe, *intention* moves energy, causing the energy to flow toward (i.e., in the direction of) the intention. *Intention* places our *attention* squarely onto something—and our energies follow along as a natural result of this. *Clear intention* moves our energy/attention clearly, and in a more focused way, in the direction of our desired goal.

Yeats mentions that he was told that the emotions of envy or admiration could serve as a conduit to allow the faeries to do harm, which is why people would always say "God bless it" when admiring something or someone beautiful. The blessing seemed to close the conduit, or at least counteract the sheer openness of the connection.

Spoken words have emotional energy behind them; speaking them puts forth that energy and opens a doorway. That energy, if not properly directed, is then available for use or misuse by various spiritual entities. In the case of admiration or jealousy, it was thought that faeries, who were known to be very attracted to beautiful things and people, would be attracted by these words and energies and would use them to their own ends. The blessing, therefore, served as a protection against misuse of the energies, since it imprinted the energies specifically with an intention of blessing and invocation of the Divine.

While we are not so fearful of demons or ill-intentioned faeries lurking over our shoulder these days, it is still worthwhile to do our work within an *attitude of blessing*.

PRACTICE

Practice makes perfect; it also allows for ease of energy flow. Repeated use of these exercises and meditations will set up subtle energetic pathways for the energy to travel along, a scaffolding or framework of energy lines, so to speak. With practice and over time, these pathways become progressively easier for our attention to locate and our energy to follow. It is somewhat similar to a pathway formed by repeated travels through a grassy meadow, in which the grass over which we travel is flattened down by our footsteps till it becomes, over time, a well-worn path.

THE MAGICAL JOURNAL

While not absolutely necessary, it is extremely helpful to write down your magical and innerworld experiences for future contemplation and learning. I have found much value in doing this through the years. Often I will come upon information that I had forgotten, but which provides me with another strand of my work or adds the final piece to a puzzle on which I've been working. Sometimes my journal will remind me of a useful technique, or bring back to mind an image from an inner landscape that provides an impetus for a whole new round of workings.

I suggest you obtain a notebook to use as a magical journal for recording the results of your inner workings and exercises, as well as any symbols or images you have obtained in these workings. The journal does not have to be fancy or expensive, but it should be dedicated solely to this purpose. Be faithful in your record keeping.

Chapter 15

The Tools of Healing: Some Foundational Techniques

How to Begin

The first steps in learning Faery Healing are to acquire a few very basic techniques and tools that will allow us to adjust our energies and state of consciousness, thereby enabling us to work in the innerworlds. These techniques, and practical exercises for them, are the subject of this chapter.

The reader should be aware that the Faery Healing techniques and methods offered herein are a unique mix of old and new. No claims are made that these ways of doing things are the exact ways used by traditional Faery Healers of the past or present. No claims are made that this material is "ancient and archaic," or brought forward in its fullness from times past.

What is offered is new; it will partake of new understandings of magic and energy, and will, when appropriate, partake as well of the old, time-honored ways and means. This is the way we must proceed, since much of the old cultural ways are diminished or gone completely. In addition, many of us do not live in our ancient homelands or in societies with intact traditional cultures. Some of what is offered here may be viewed as a contemporary evolution of the older ways—based on newer perceptions and understandings.

The use of these methods will facilitate that fluidity of consciousness which allows interaction and relationship with the Faery Realm. This, in turn, enables us to create a partnership with our Faery Allies for purposes of healing and growth.

Several structures for the work will be provided. Structure seems to have a bad reputation these days; many see it as something which *confines*, thus denying freedom, spontaneity, and creativity. Yet structures are necessary and valuable. Without the physical structure of our skeleton upon which the rest of our physical being is built, we could not stand erect, walk, or move. Structure provides a framework or *container* in which growth may occur.

The structures provided herein for use in innerwork are for exactly the same purpose. Structure provides a pattern along which the energies organize themselves as they flow, and by which they may be accessed. Since organization of information is central to understanding and using it, the use of these structures will also aid in understanding our experiences in the Faery Realm. By making use of these structures we can access our Faery Allies, communicate with them, and work under their guidance in our Faery Healing work.

So without further ado, let us begin learning these techniques. These tools, as you will see, enable us be about the business of *Reweaving, Alliance, Attuning, Retuning,* and *Bridge-building*.

Tools of the Trade
Journeywork

The single most important tool/technique we will be using in this work is journeywork, also referred to as inner journeying, inner plane journeying, or pathworking. This latter term is more strictly applied to Qabalistic work, but has come to be used in a wider context in recent years.

Inner plane journeys are, quite literally, inner journeys: guided visualization and meditations done for the purposes of learning the landscapes of the inner realms as well as gaining access to the teachers, teachings, and transformations that await us there.

Journeywork is quite useful in Faery Healing as it gives us a tool for finding our Faery Allies, for receiving guidance and inspiration in our work, and really, for actually *doing* the work itself. Visualization creates inner pathways that allow our consciousness and our energies to travel when and where they have need.

Journeys are best performed within a sacred space of some kind, an area where the energies have been cleared, the space delineated as "sacred" by virtue of declaration of intent and an orientation to the Directional powers. This may be done either formally or informally. General instructions for this will be given in the section on the *Sacred Circle*, (see page 200). Grounding and centering exercises, as well as a general induction for the purpose of relaxation, are often quite helpful in preparing for the journey, especially if one is new to journeywork. Such preparatory techniques train the mind and body to relax, and to prepare to alter and deepen the consciousness.

If the journey is to be done in a group setting, usually one person will act as a facilitator. One can also record the journeys found in this book and use them by oneself if no one else is available to act as facilitator (see Note at the end of the chapter 1).

Journeywork Guidelines

There are some general guidelines concerning journeywork that are wise to observe.

1. Get yourself into a physically comfortable position. It's hard to relax into the experience if you are uncomfortable.

2. Allow yourself to become as fully relaxed, mentally and physically, as possible while still remaining awake. Methods for doing this involve performing simple relaxation exercises which focus attention on each body part in turn, consciously relaxing it, proceeding from feet to head. This should be accompanied by slow, deep breathing. The suggestion should be made that as the body/mind relaxes, the consciousness becomes more keenly aware and able to follow along on the journey.

3. Listen to the facilitator and allow yourself to visualize clearly and follow the images in the journey as they arise.

4. Make no attempt to interpret or judge the images and messages that come to you. Simply receive them. If an interpretation is presented along with the image or message, accept it in a non-judgmental way, but put off thinking about it till later.

5. When the suggestion to return is given, finish up anything you may in the middle of doing (such as conversing with a being) as rapidly as you can, and follow the suggestion. Follow the return instructions as given, and allow yourself time to settle back into your body before attempting to open your eyes, or to sit or stand up.

6. If you are new at journeywork and are doing the journeys on your own, tape recording them is highly recommended, until you learn how to get in and out of the inner realms with ease. At this point, you may be able to simply read the journey, noting instructions and imagery and allowing them to form an outline or pathway in your mind. Then close your eyes, and go.

7. When returning from a journey, it is important to reorient yourself to the Directions as a way of reestablishing yourself in this realm. It is also wise to do something physical, to signal to yourself that you have truly returned, and will now function in this physical realm. This *something* can be as simple as taking in a deep breath and letting it out as you open your eyes, blinking your eyes a few times, stamping your foot, or another technique of your own choosing. Deciding to do this and then implementing your decision serve important, self-training functions.

8. Record your experiences in your Magical Journal.

Some Journeyworking Rules of the Road

Before beginning your journey, please make sure that you have done the proper relaxation and grounding work. This will not only give you a good *grounding cord* to keep you attached to the Earth and thus actually able to do your work with out floating away, but will greatly aid you in returning quickly when your work is finished. It will also help *loosen* you up for innerwork, making it easier to do this kind of traveling.

Once you are securely anchored by your grounding exercises, you must request protection and guidance from your Spirit Allies, including your Faery Allies and Guides, as well as state clearly (inwardly) your intention for undertaking the journey. This intention will set your course, so to speak. As you will recall, your *intention* directs your *attention* to a focus, and your energy then follows.

Aim yourself at a particular location or destination within the Faery Realm, follow the instructions to get there, and set yourself specific parameters and guidelines such as for time spent, signals for returning, and the like, and then you will have created a safe way to travel and return. If you do not have a clear reason for your journey, you may find yourself wandering. If you feel like you have no real reason other than exploration, then state that as your intention for the journey.

GROUNDING

Grounding is the term used for connecting our own personal energy field into that of the Earth's. This is done by the use of our intention, and sometimes with the help of visualization. All of us have no doubt heard and even used terms like ungrounded, disconnected, spaced out, floating, and the like. These refer to states of consciousness where our essential energy is disconnected from that of the Earth. When this happens, it is as if we are not plugged into our energy source; our consciousness literally *is* floating, disconnected, adrift, not anchored or secure. Our Earth is our home, and we were designed to be constantly connected to her energetically as well as physically. Gravity keeps us physically connected, but it is our intention and state of consciousness, as well as our lifestyle (food, sleep, general state of health), that keeps us either connected or disconnected from Earth's energy field. And believe it or not, when one is well grounded it makes spiritual travel in the subtle worlds much easier.

Paradoxical as it may sound, good grounding during spiritual work allows us to float freely in the Otherworlds. Just as a ship's anchor allows the ship to float on the sea's surface without drifting too far away, the energy cord which connects us to Earth's core provides anchoring for us, allowing us to work in the spiritual worlds without floating away into fruitless drifting and distraction. It also provides a connection by which we may access and draw up into ourselves potent energies from the Earth, a fact that makes it indispensable in Faery Healing.

Grounding 101

There are a few very basic principles that are applicable to ALL methods and procedures of grounding. Simply stated, it helps if you are, as with journeying, in a physically comfortable position, though this is not always possible for all occasions when you feel grounding to be a necessity.

Secondly, no matter what visualizations you are using, your breath is probably the single most important tool for grounding that you possess. Controlling your rate of breathing, the spacing of your breaths, is crucial; combining these with visualization and autosuggestion provides you with a spectacularly effective tool for realigning your consciousness. I learned the power of breathing techniques by making use of them during both childbirth and dental work experiences—the true tests!

Some Grounding Techniques

Here are a few basic grounding and centering techniques that may be used in your Faery Healing and other spiritual workings.

GROUNDING | Beginning Level

The Cord of Light

Sitting in a comfortable position, close your eyes, and spend a few moments breathing deeply, getting yourself relaxed. Pay attention to your breath as it moves in and out of you. After a while, move your attention to your body, and feel it sitting on the chair, the floor, or the cushion. Put your attention on your root chakra, which is located roughly between the tailbone and pubic area. Feel a cord of light grow downward from this area of your body, through the floor, and into the Earth. Feel this cord of light move effortlessly through the layers of earth, dirt, pebbles, and stones, going deeper and ever deeper downward into the Earth. You are aware of it reaching down, as if it were being pulled by a magnet. Downward the cord grows and goes, through the Earth's crustal layer, through the mantle and intermediate layers, and into the core layers, where it joins and anchors itself into the fiery heart of the Earth.

THE TOOLS OF HEALING | 195

With your grounding cord firmly anchored into Earth's heart, you breathe deeply, allowing the energy of the deep heart of the Earth to move upward through the cord, through the layers of Earth's core, mantle, and crust, and into your body. As you do this repeatedly, you feel Earth energy filling your body completely, beginning at the root chakra, spilling down into your legs and feet, and moving upward into your upper body. You feel it particularly strongly in the area of your own heart, and you realize that your heart and that of the Earth's are joined in love. Once you have established this connection, you can feel that the energy from Earth's heart continues to move upward and into your body without further effort on your part. You are, in fact, so full of this energy, that you place your hands on the floor to feed the excess back into the Earth....

Now thoroughly grounded, you may open your eyes, and begin whatever ceremony or magical work you wish.

Be sure to record your grounding experiences in your Magical Journal, at least the first few times and thereafter, if anything unusual occurs.

Growing Roots

Sitting in a comfortable position, close your eyes and spend a few moments breathing deeply, getting yourself relaxed. Pay attention to your breath as it moves in and out of you. After a while, move your attention to your body, and feel it sitting on the chair, the floor, or the cushion. Put your attention on your root chakra. Feel a tendril of energy begin to grow downward from this area of your body, through the floor, and into the Earth. Simultaneously, feel other, smaller tendrils of energy emerging from the soles of your feet, and growing downward in to the Earth. These energy tendrils push themselves down into the Earth, moving effortlessly through the layers of earth, dirt, pebbles, stones, going deeper and ever deeper downward into the Earth. As they grow downward, you are aware that they are growing thicker and sturdier, till they resemble the roots of a tree. You are aware of them growing, twisting, twining, but ever downward, through layers of soil, sand, and pebbles. They continue twining their way deeper and deeper, through Earth's many layers, until they push themselves down into the very core layer, where they grow into the fiery heart of Earth, merging with it.

With your roots now firmly anchored embedded into the heart of the Earth, you breathe deeply, allowing the energy of the deep heart of the Earth to move upward through the roots, pushing through the layers of Earth, upward, and into your body. As you breathe this into yourself several times, you feel the Earth's energy moving into your body and filling it completely, beginning at the root and foot chakras, moving upward into your upper body, chest, arms, and head. You feel it particularly strongly in the area of your own heart, and you realize that your heart and that of the Earth's are joined in love. Once you have established this connection, you can feel the energy from Earth's Heart continuing to move upward into your body without further effort on your part. You are, in fact, so full of this energy, that you place your hands on the floor to feed the excess back into the Earth.

Now thoroughly grounded, you may open your eyes, and begin your ceremony or magical working.

GROUNDING | Intermediate Level

Becoming a Tree
Sitting in a comfortable position, close your eyes and spend a few moments breathing deeply, getting yourself relaxed. Pay attention to your breath as it moves in and out of you. After a while, move your attention to your body, and feel it sitting on the chair, the floor, the cushion, or whatever. Put your attention on your root chakra. Feel a tendril of energy begin to grow downward from this area of your body, through the floor, and into the Earth. Simultaneously, feel other, smaller tendrils of energy emerging from the soles of your feet, and growing downward into the Earth. These energy tendrils push themselves down into the Earth, moving effortlessly through the layers of earth, dirt, pebbles, stones, sprouting additional tinier tendrils as they descend, going deeper and ever deeper downward into the Earth. As they grow downward, you are aware that they are growing thicker, and sturdier, till they resemble the roots of a tree. You are aware of them growing, twisting, twining, but ever downward, through layers of soil, sand, and pebbles. They continue twining their way deeper and deeper, through Earth's many layers, until they push themselves down into the very core layer, where they grow into the fiery heart of Earth, merging with it.

With your roots now firmly anchored embedded into the heart of the Earth, you breathe deeply, allowing the energy of the deep heart of the Earth to move upward through the roots, pushing through the layers of Earth, upward, and into your body. As you breathe this into yourself, several times, you feel the Earth's energy moving into your body—the trunk of your tree—and filling it completely, beginning at the root chakra, and foot chakras, and moving upward into your upper body, back, and chest. You feel this energy particularly strongly in the area of your own heart, and you realize that your heart and that of the Earth's are joined in love. Once you have established this connection, you can feel that the energy from Earth's heart continues to move upward and into your body without further effort on your part. The energy continues to move upward, into your upraised arms, your neck and your head, through your crown chakra and above, and these parts of you seem to have branched out toward the sky, as if reaching up for the moon, sun, and stars. You are, in fact, so full of this energy, that the excess spills out from the tips of your branches, and falls in lovely cascade down to the Earth again, and the Earth absorbs it gratefully....

You are now completely connected to the Earth's energy; and when you wish, you may open your eyes, and begin your ceremony or magical working.

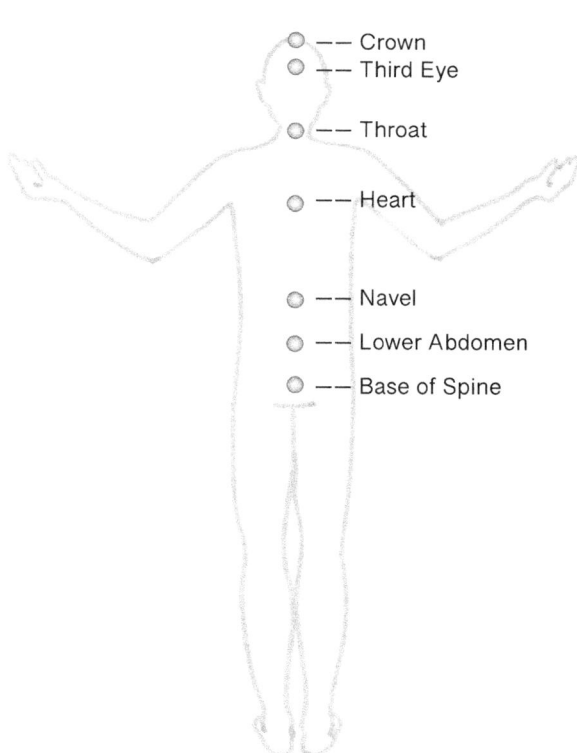

Chakra Points

Grounding 102

The following is a more complex and advanced exercise, and has the advantage of not only connecting you with the above and below, but also of giving you practice at running energy through your body and beyond your body, something which will become essential when you actually begin doing healing work.

This exercise, *Star Showering*, is more complex than the preceding ones, and is designed to expand your awareness, bringing in more levels of being and Spirit Beings at one time. It's good practice, after the previous ones have been mastered, for getting used to both running energy through your body and for noticing what it feels like to do so.

GROUNDING | Advanced Level

Star Showering

Close your eyes, and allow yourself to become still and quiet, and your breathing to become slow and regular. Take a deep breath, and as you do, you feel roots beginning to grow from the soles of your feet and from your root chakra. Keep your attention on these roots and as you exhale allow the exhalation to carry your roots down into the Earth. Allow your consciousness to accompany the roots as they go down... As you descend into the Earth, you become aware of the life within the Earth, the many beings and many spirits who live in the many layers of Earth's crust—and you greet them... As you continue to descend, you become aware of other realms, and other beings. Give your greetings to these beings also. Extend your roots down, deeper and deeper, till you come to the fiery heart of the Earth, and the iron crystal core within it. Anchor your roots here.

As you inhale, feel energy from Earth's heart moving into your roots and beginning to move upward... Once again, your awareness and attention follow the energies as they flow, ever upward, through the layers of Earth. Again, you meet, and greet many beings along the way... Allow the energy to flow upward through your roots, and into your body, starting with your feet, then moving into your legs, torso, chest, arms and head... Feel yourself to be filled with this energy. With every breath you take, more Earth-heart energy fills your body. And with every exhaled breath, you feel the departure of energies that are no longer useful to you.

Now feel this energy from your roots as it runs upward through your chakras. It comes in at your feet but also at your root chakra... Place your attention on it, and feel the energy spiraling up your chakras from root to crown... Feel the energy moving out of you at the crown chakra and spiraling upward into the sky and beyond... Feel it, follow it, as it spirals upward encountering and passing through the moon. Spend a few moments communing with the moon, giving your greetings and love... Notice how you feel when communing with the moon... Feel the energy continue spiraling outward, encountering and passing through the sun... Give greetings and love to the sun. Spend a moment feeling what it feels like to commune with the sun...

Passing through the sun, you feel the energy continuing now into the great vast depths of space....Greet the stars as you come to them—as you travel with the energy as it spirals along the curving arm of our home galaxy, the Milky Way Galaxy, to the very center of the galaxy. Feel the burst of energy as you connect with, and go into, this great source. Spend some time being with this, feeling, noticing, communing...

Now you become aware that the energy is flowing downward, to you, through you... spiraling now the opposite direction on the arm of the galaxy. Your awareness follows this energy, and you feel it flow downward, past the stars, through the sun, the moon, toward the Earth... downward... and into your body, passing through your body and into the Earth. As it passes through your body, notice how it combines with the Earth energy already there.

You can feel how the energy spirals both upward and downward at the same time. Feel the Sky-Earth energy exchange happening through you as you simultaneously "feed" Earth energy to the sky, and sky energy to the Earth. You are a conduit, therefore this energy runs through you, leaving a plentiful residue to feed you as well. You can feel how you are related to both Earth and sky.

Spread your arms, hold them out from your body and parallel the ground so that your body forms a star shape, and shower sky energy into the Earth. Lift your arms to the sky and radiate Earth energy to the sky. You, as human, act as a bridge between the Earth and star energies, since by your heritage you partake of both. When you are finished, slowly lower your arms, and prepare to begin your magical working.[1]

Be sure to record your journey in your Magical Journal.

𝒯HE SACRED CIRCLE

We will be making use of the Sacred Circle as one of our basic tools. A circle divided into parts and representing the world, cosmos, or universe is familiar to many spiritual traditions worldwide. Let us begin with a brief and basic description of the circle as we intend to use it, which will include the Four Directions, and the directions of Above and Below as well, thus bringing together the vertical and horizontal perspectives mentioned in preceding chapters.

The wheel or circle is a representation of the world, not just the planet upon which we live but the world as we perceive it. Because our physical beings have a front, back, and sides, we are able to perceive four basic directions. As we observe this it is immediately obvious that our awareness of it comes from the point of Center—we are the Center of our own circle. We look out from the Center to all directions. Therefore, a circle is our first way of truly orienting ourselves to our surroundings, and as such, is a remarkably good way to orient ourselves to any surroundings in which we find ourselves, including the inner realms.

Wheel of the Four Elements and Directions

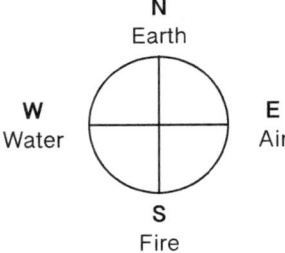

CASTING THE CIRCLE: CREATING SACRED SPACE

As with journeywork, when doing healing or any magical work it is advantageous to work in a safe and sacred space. Creating sacred space is a way of setting aside a working area, protecting it, and infusing it with positive and protective energies.

Such a sacred space is quite simple to establish. One need only use imagination and intention, and occasionally sage or other incense, to clear the space of unwanted energies.

I often envision sweeping the unwanted energies out of the working space, and then mentally send them to the Underworld for composting. After this, bring the attention to the Directions—East, South, West, North, Above, and Below, each in turn—and the powers that reside there, and ask for their presence, help, and protection. Remember to give thanks for these, as well. At the end of the working, it is customary to thank these beings again, and dissolve the sacred space by the use of the imagination and will.

The Directions and the Elements

We have spoken previously of the Four Elements and how they correspond with the Four Directions. By way of a brief recap, see the table below for a summary of these and other correspondences.[2]

The Four Elements and Four Directions

Element	AIR	FIRE	WATER	EARTH
Direction	EAST (NE to SE)	SOUTH (SE to SW)	WEST (SW to NW)	NORTH (NW to NE)
Part of Cycle	Beginning	Growth	Ripeness / Harvest	Ending
Season	Spring	Summer	Fall	Winter
Time of Day	Morning	Midday	Evening	Night
Qualities	Beginning / Origination / Sowing	Blossoming / Creativity / Growth	Nourishment / Fulfillment / Harvesting	Silence / Sleep / Darkness / Death / Renewal
Elemental Spirit	Sylph	Salamander	Undine	Gnome
Magical Tools	Sword / Dagger / Blade	Wand / Spear / Staff	Cauldron / Chalice / Cup / Bowl	Pentacle / Mirror / Shield
Solar Festival	Spring Equinox	Summer Solstice	Autumn Equinox	Winter Solstice
Fire Festival	Imbolc / Brigid	Beltane / May Eve	Lughnasadh / Lammas	Samhain / All Hallows

The Cross-Quarters

Mention must also be made of the cross-quarter points that fall between the four major compass points, creating the directions of Northwest, Northeast, Southeast, Southwest. On the Celtic Wheel of the Year these correspond to the old Quarter Days of Samhain, Imbolc or Brigid, Beltaine, and Lughnasadh, about which we have previously spoken (see Note 2 at the end of the chapter). These were very important days to the early Celtic people of the British Isles. Beltaine marked the beginning of summer, and Samhain the end of it, and these determined the times when the cattle and sheep must be taken out to summer pasture, and brought back in again to winter quarters. These two festivals were most likely first determined by the rising and setting of the constellation of the Pleiades, though later they were set to certain calendar dates. Imbolc seems to have marked the start of spring and the beginning of lambing season, and thus plentiful milk, while Lughnasadh marked the start of autumn and was the time of the first harvest and also a time of tribal gatherings for purposes of games of strength and skill, the marketing of wares, and the finding of mates.

The essential thing to note about these festivals in terms of their position on the Wheel is that falling between the major compass points as they do, they mark what I like to call the *Marriage Points* between the Four Elements: the place where Water meets Earth, Earth meets Air, Air meets Fire, and Fire meets Earth. These are points of great energy, creativity, and transformation, where it is possible for something entirely new to emerge, born from the marriage of these elements. This is something to be aware of as you travel in the innerworlds of this Wheel. For more information on this, see my book *Wisdom of the Elements.*

These marriage points may be thought of as being similar to the borderlands and border times so important in faery lore. They are places where one thing meets and gives way to another, with the threshold, border, or boundary becoming indistinct as one thing (or energy, or state of being) merges into another. Indeed, the threshold itself may be seen as a line that both divides and unites the two things.

Realizing the relationship between the borderlands and the elements, seasons, and festivals can help us understand why these festivals were traditionally held to be times when contact with the Otherworlds was highly likely.

Working with the Circle

In working with the circle, you may use as many layers of meaning as you wish or is necessary for a given working. Sometimes you will just be observing the seasonal festival;

sometimes you may wish to add the elemental significance for greater understanding of the seasonal energies. Sometimes, you may wish to add the borderlands aspect to the mix, to more easily journey into the Otherworlds.

JOURNEY | Feeling the Directions and Their Powers

Using the method outlined above, create a Sacred Circle for yourself. Be sure to include bringing your awareness to the Upperworld and Underworld as well as the Middleworld of the Four Directions. Be aware that the Center is within all realms.

When you have done this, bring your awareness to the Center of the circle as if you were standing there. As you "stand" in the Center, move your awareness to the East, and feel and think about the directional attributes, correspondences, and Elements given in the chart on page 201. Feel the power of the East as it flows in through the Eastern Gateway of the circle, to the Center, and into you where you stand.

Now move your awareness to the South, and feel and think about the directional attributes, correspondences, and Elements given in the chart on page 201. Feel the power of the South as it flows in through the Southern Gateway of the circle, to the Center, and into you where you stand.

Now move your awareness to the West, and feel and think about the directional attributes, correspondences, and Elements given in the chart on page 201. Feel the power of the West as it flows in through the Western Gateway of the circle, to the Center, and into you where you stand.

Move your awareness to the North, and feel and think about the directional attributes, correspondences and Elements given in the chart above. Feel the Power of the North as it flows in through the Northern Gateway of the circle, to the Center, and into you where you stand.

Be aware of the power of the Upperworld above you, as you think about the powers of the Sky Beings, the Star Beings, the Angelic Beings, and the High Gods. Feel these powers flow down from the sky and into you.

Be aware of the power of the Underworld beneath you, as you think about the powers inherent in the land beneath your feet, and the Underworld God and Goddess, and all the beings who reside within the land. Feel these Underworld powers as they flow up and into you.

Be aware of yourself as the Center point of all of this, and breathe it all in to yourself, very consciously, one direction at a time. Hold this inside of you, then slowly exhale, and let them all flow forth from you.

When this is done, take in another breath, then breathe out slowly, allowing the breath to bring your awareness back to the present time and place, and back to your ordinary reality.

Be sure to record your journey in your Magical Journal.

APPLYING THE ELEMENTS IN HEALING WORK

It is interesting to see how these primal Four Elements can apply to the spiritual technology of Faery Healing.

The Element of Air is used when we learn and use correct breathing techniques, as well as when we make use of the imagination—our image-making faculty—as a tool for focusing our awareness/consciousness on the inner realms of existence. Such use creates a gateway into those realms. Where there is attention, there is energy, as energy follows our attention (i.e., conscious awareness). The senses of *hearing* and *smelling* correspond with this Element.

The Element of Fire is used when we recognize the divine spark—the Fire of Life, the Flame of Being—and use it in our work. This work also includes self-care, and the feeding and tending of our own inner fires both physical and spiritual. Fire is also used when we focus our intention and will on something. The sense of *sight* corresponds to this Element, as it is about learning about how to see and feel on the inner levels.

The Element of Water is used when we utilize the power of rhythms and flowing: cycles, energy movements, blessing, cleansing, and dissolving. Blessed and empowered vessels of water can be used for healing purposes and for special anointings. Recall all those Water Ladies who bring healing: mermaids with herbal knowledge, the Faery Mother of the Physicians of Myddfai; damsels who guard wells; and faeries or other beings who guard holy wells. Water is also used when we work magically with Earth's waters, such as lakes, rivers, oceans, ponds, and streams. *Sensation* and *emotion* correspond with this Element.

The Element of Earth is used when we use the power of structure, number, and substance—physical things such as plants and stones—for healing purposes. Grounding exercises might also fall into this category. The senses of *taste* and *touch* correspond to this Element.

Elemental Correspondences

Element	AIR	FIRE	WATER	EARTH
Body System	Respiratory Eliminative Nervous	Digestive Cardiovascular (heart and lungs, mix of fire and air)	Circulatory Lymph Kidney (cleansing systems)	Skeletal (structural system)
Basic Mode	Brings energies in and moves them out	Movement of energies by use of will	Movement of energies for nourishment and cleansing purposes	Foundational energies which provide framework for all else
Magical Function	Use of the breath to induce altered states	Use of intention and will to travel inworld and to direct energies	Use of sensing abilities to feel differing nuances and streams of subtle energies	Use of structure to create and hold patterns, feeling the energies as they move through the body
Healing Uses	Blowing things away—the power of sound and chant to change vibrational frequencies	Using flame for focus—power of color for healing and nourishment, fire of will, creativity, passion	Using water to dilute, dissolve, cleanse, and bless	Using physical objects such as stones or plants to hold energies; creation and breakdown of energetic patterns

THREE REALMS AND FOUR DIRECTIONS

In our work within the Faery Realm we will make use of the Three Realms as well as the Four Directions.

We have previously mentioned the Three Worlds of Underworld, Middleworld, and Upperworld. These correspond to the roots of the World Tree, the trunk of the World Tree, and the branches of the World Tree.

About the Three Realms

In many spiritual traditions, the Underworld was seen as the realm of the dead, that is, as a spiritual realm where the dead reside. Yet since it is also the place from which new life rises up and springs forth upon the Earth, the Underworld was also seen as a place where death was transformed into life—a place of regeneration.

The Underworld is home to the many, many beings who comprise the inner being of the Earth. Through the ages these beings have manifested as giants, dwarves, dragons, and magical serpents, the latter of which are sometimes referred to as *vouivre*, or *wyverns* (which means dragons). European folklore is full of stories about them. Frequently, they are associated with caves, grottos, and Underworld chambers of various kinds. Often they are said to be guarding treasures.

These are the Earth spirit energies: the various beings small and large who are the beings of the inner Earth—not only the caves or grottos where they reside, but the actual strata of the land itself.

In faery work, we primarily make use of the Underworld and Middleworld, though upon occasion it is appropriate to work with the beings and powers of the Upperworld who are often referred to as the angelic, archangelic, star, or deity powers. Actually, there is a harmonic resonance between the Upperworld and the Underworld, in that the Upperworlds are the homes of the Star Powers/Beings, and the Underworlds contain these Star Powers as they are found within the Earth.

We will explore each of these worlds in more depth in the next chapter.

We have also made previous mention of the Four Directions, which give us access into the world of Elements and Elemental Beings. Most of us are aware, however vaguely, of these directions of East, South, West, and North, even if it is only how they are used within our mundane reality. This will be treated in greater depth, and from the perspective of their use in Faery Healing, in the chapters that follow.

SHAPESHIFTING

This wonderfully mysterious and magical sounding word refers, as one might suppose, to the ability to shift our shape, when working magically. But it does not refer to our physical shape, except, perhaps, in the advanced magical and shamanic traditions of native peoples (including the very old European native magical traditions), a subject we will not be delving into here.

Rather, it is our inner being that is shifting its *shape*. By virtue of practices, exercises, and journeys, our consciousness and awareness become less rigid, more fluid, and thus more easily able to flow in and out of different states of consciousness—different inner *shapes*. This inner fluidity allows us to flow beyond our physical bodies and into other realms. It allows us to flow into the land, gaining an awareness of what is there. It allows us to blend energies with our animal and Faery Allies, merging consciousness with them for purposes of communication and alliance—techniques necessary for our work of

Reweaving, Alliance, Attuning, Retuning, and *Bridge-building.* The ability to shapeshift allows us to "Enter the Shimmering," flowing in and out of different states of consciousness with relative ease.

All this is not nearly as complicated as it sounds, though it does require practice. The simple act of repeatedly doing these exercises will, over time, result in a loosening of some of the rigid internal structures which we use to define a black-and-white world, and allow us to flow into the more expanded, fluid states necessary for such innerwork, including Faery Healing.

It should be unnecessary to state, though I will state it nevertheless, that work of this kind—that is, work that alters consciousness and accesses innerworlds—is better not attempted by those with psychological or mental imbalances. The imbalances must be resolved before such work is undertaken. This is just common sense. The same warning applies to doing this work while taking psycho-active or consciousness-altering drugs (see Note 3 at the end of the chapter). In a word, DON'T. Your results may not be what you had in mind. Consider yourself warned.

Doing work with the Four Directions, using a Sacred Circle, praying, and meditating—all these things are fine. But please do not do the depth-level work unless you truly know you are up to it. Show that you honor and care for yourself by respecting your limits and working within them. Only in this way will you make spiritual progress.

Shapeshifting Exercise

Do research on an animal to which you feel drawn. It might be wise to start with your cat, dog, or other pet. Study the animal, the way it moves, how it sleeps, its habits and habitats. Feel into it, and try to imagine what it would be like to be covered in its fur, feathers, or fins. Feel more deeply and try to imagine what it would be like to see through its eyes, hear with its ears, feel with its skin, taste with its tongue, and walk with its feet. Finally, breathe slowly and deeply, in and out, and with each breath allow your consciousness to become very fluid and flowing, or perhaps like swirling mist. From this loosened, misty state, try to flow or slip into the animal's body, your spirit alongside its spirit, and see, feel, hear, and walk, crawl, or fly with the animal.

Record your experiences, and think about them, seeing what you have learned. Then choose another animal and repeat this exercise. You may repeat this exercise several times, evaluating your experiences as you go along.

Next, you may choose to do this with a plant or tree. What would it be like to be a plant, rooted into the ground, pushing forth through the Earth's surface and out into the sun, sprouting leaves, flowers, fruit, swaying in the wind and rain? Again, make careful record of your experiences. After several such exercises with a variety of life-forms, you will begin to get a sense of not only their differences and similarities, but a sense of how shapeshifting itself works.

It is important, however, to come fully back into oneself after these exercises! Traditionally, having something to eat or drink afterward is considered a good way of grounding oneself back into this mundane reality. Be sure to record the results of your shapeshifting practice in your Magical Journal.

There will be more about shapeshifting in *Chapter 21.*

The Faery Altar and the Faery Hearth

In working with the faeries, you may want to create a special altar. This is optional, and a nice touch, but not strictly necessary to the work by any means. Such an altar can serve as a reminder of your connection with and dedication to Faery Healing work.

On your Faery Altar, which may be draped in a simple green cloth, you will have a representation of the Faery Hearth. The Flame of Being is the Fire of Life which blazes brightly in all worlds, realms, and beings. Every living being contains a spark of this fire. Within the Faery Realm, this fire burns in the Faery Hearth, which is at the Center of the Faery Realm. On your altar a special candle is used to represent the Faery Hearth and its flame. The candle should go in the exact center of your altar. Around it you may place objects that represent the Four Treasures of the Tuatha De Danaan: the sword, the spear, the cauldron, and the stone. These may be quite simple and inexpensive representations. The altar may be adorned with rocks, stones, and seasonal plants or flowers as you wish.

This altar and Faery Hearth may be used as a focal point while you do your Faery Healing work. As stated above this is not strictly necessary; however, it is pleasing to work with such beauty before you.

Here are some suggestions for creating and dedicating such an altar:

1. Find a suitable space in your home for the altar. This can be a dresser top, a windowsill, a bedside table or other small table, a bookshelf, or even a bit of floor space in the corner of a room which is off the beaten track and which will afford you a bit of privacy when you wish to work there.

2. The altar itself need only contain a few items, the most important of which are a bowl of water, a stone, a feather, a flower, leaf or small branch, and the center candle

to represent your Faery Hearth. These items are representations of the Four Elements and the Four Treasures of the Tuatha De Danaan. I often use a feather to represent Finias/Air; objects more representative of a blade such as small sharp kyanite crystals are also good, but remember, nothing made of iron.

3. The altar may also contain, if you desire, items that remind you of your connection with Faery: special stones, flowers, even pictorial representations such as greeting cards with pictures of faeries. As I said, these are all optional to the work, but pleasing aesthetically and helpful to the imagination.

4. The focus should be on simplicity and beauty. Don't make it too cluttered.

5. When you are finished constructing your altar, dedicate it to the work with a simple blessing and ritual. For example, call on the powers of the Four Directions/Elements and the Center, call on the Faery King and Queen and your Faery Allies. State your intention to dedicate this altar to the work of Faery Healing. Ask them to bestow their blessings and protection on your altar and your work.

As stated above, your center candle will serve as a representation of the Faery Hearth. The Faery Hearth is the Fire of Life—the Flame of Being at the heart of all life—as it burns within the Faery Realm.

This representation of the power of life's spark is truly the Center of your circle for Faery workings. It is the most important part of your Faery Altar, and belongs in its exact center. In fact, if you have nothing else on your altar, or decide not to have an altar at all, please do use the Faery Hearth candle when you do Faery Work.

The Flame of Being burns in all the worlds, and so connects them all. By use of this fire, you may enter Faery, travel through it, and access the other worlds as well, if need be. It is recommended that before you do this, however, you first learn the other techniques presented, and practice them well, before taking this shortcut.

In addition, this Faery Hearth is the place to do all Center-related work, that which has to do with no particular Direction or Element, but has to do with the very core energies of a person or situation.

Faery Healing Allies, Helpers, and Guides

All work is easier when we have helpful, skilled friends present to lend a hand. This is even more true in the realm of spiritual healing. As skilled as we might be, as good at traveling innerworlds as we might be, healing work is more easily and powerfully accomplished with the aid of our innerworld allies. In truth, we cannot do it alone, and to think we can is a rather high degree of arrogance. The error is in thinking that we are ever alone or working solitary when doing healing work. That is simply not how things operate. We are part of a continuum of consciousness, and Spirit Beings are all around us. It is up to us as to whether we acknowledge this and reach out for assistance or not.

THE DIFFERENT KINDS OF HELPERS

Here is a brief listing and description of the kinds of skilled helpers available to us.

Faery Allies, Faery Beings who provide us with a link to the Faery Realm and to the Faery aspect of our own nature. Within this category we include the Old Gods, the Faery Kings and Queens, the Elemental Kings and Queens, fairies, nature spirits, and the Elemental Beings: the sylphs, salamanders, undines, and gnomes.

The Faery Kings and Queens might actually be considered a special category themselves, as they are definitely more distinct and conscious beings than the smaller Faery Beings, and more easy to work with because of it. As sovereigns of the Faery Realm they are akin to deities. One may think of the Faery Queens as the power of the Goddess and the Faery Kings as the power of the God, as these powers are manifest in the Faery Realm.

While in dream-state I have been informed by the Faery King and Queen that in a more localized sense, the Faery Kings and Queens found in local lore are the regional manifestations of the God/Goddess powers, and that they are very frequently linked into certain prominent landscape features within geographical areas. Thus a very prominent mound, mountain, or other such feature in one's local region could well be their residence, and a good place to make contact with them.

Animal Allies, sometimes referred to as power animals. These are animal spirits who represent the energetic frequency of their species. Quite often these animal allies will turn up in our journeywork. They assist us, bringing us the specific and particular gifts of their species, and often protect, guard, and guide us in the innerworlds.

Plant Spirits will occasionally present themselves to us as allies, offering us their unique gifts and energies to be used during the course of a healing or as needed in our work. I've had occasions where this occurred independent of actual physical contact with the plant: the plant spirit simply "showed up" during the course of the healing work, and its unique energy was felt and appreciated by all present.

Spirit Doctors Discarnate humans who were, in life, very skilled in the healing arts, and especially those who have served as Faery Doctors, sometimes choose to assist us.

Angel Allies These are Spirit Beings of the higher realms. At this point we would do well to remember the Irish understanding that the faeries are really angels who, along with Lucifer, fell to and into the Earth after the great war in heaven. This legend holds a great truth within it, and that truth is that faeries and angels are related. Our scientists tell us that our Earth and all upon it are "star stuff," that is, everything in our universe is made from the same stuff that makes up the stars. In traditional magical thought and practice the angelic realm is related to the realm of the stars and planets. Stellar and planetary bodies are thought to be ensouled by the high consciousnesses we term angels. Therefore, those angels who fell to Earth and became the faeries are, in a very real way, "Earth Angels," that is, angelic consciousness within the planetary body. Consequently, a resonance exists between those of Earth and those of sky. Angels and faeries *are* related. Similar to what has been said about faeries and the Faery Kings and Queens, certain angelic beings are larger and possess more individuality and awareness than others, and these are the ones with which it is preferable to work.

Once again, all of this sounds more complex than it really is in actual practice. While it is helpful to know names and categories of these various beings, if we remember to ask for assistance, much of the necessary movement of energies between the various beings and levels is taken care of for us while we are doing our end of the work.

CELTIC DEITIES OF HEALING

Although I have referenced them in the Faery Allies category above, here is a bit more information on the Pagan Celtic deities of healing. When Christianity became the predominant religion, it was God the Father, Son, and Holy Ghost—along with the Virgin Mother Mary, St. Michael, St. Brigid, St. Columba, and many of the other favorite saints and angels—who were invoked instead of these.

When considering Celtic deities associated with healing, it is important to remember that most of them had other associations as well; they were not solely deities of healing. The following list is not exhaustive; it is meant to inspire your own research.

Because true healing arises from the balancing and reconciliation of the apparent opposites—active and passive, being and becoming, fire and water—Celtic healing deities were usually associated with those critical elements of life and well-being, fire and water. Consequently, we find healing deities associated with the sun, as well as with wells, rivers, and springs, especially hot mineral springs. The carvings, statuary, and artifacts found at these places tend to include symbolism that refers to fire and water—solar images, water vessels, and the like.

It is primarily, though certainly not exclusively, goddesses and feminine Spirit Beings that are affiliated with Celtic healing sites. Celtic healing goddesses often were associated with fertility as well as healing and regeneration. Thus they were very often connected with sacred water sources such as holy wells, springs, and hot springs, because water was associated with both fertility and healing—the cleansing of illness and subsequent return of good health.

GODDESSES

Brigid was the Celtic goddess in whose lore many of these correspondences may be found. Her name means High One or Exalted One. She was said to be a protector of women in childbirth, and was associated with the welfare of livestock. Her festival, February 1st, is associated with the lambing season. There is much Fire symbolism in the stories of St. Brigid, many of which are thought to derive from the older, Pagan stories of the Goddess Brigid, who was sometimes addressed as the "golden, sparkling flame." According to legend a perpetual fire burned in her precinct at Kildare (which means Church of the Oak). This fire was tended by nineteen priestesses—similar to the Vestal Virgins of Rome. Like many other holy fires of legend, it was said to burn without producing ash. The nineteen priestesses cared for the fire for nineteen nights, but it was thought that Brigid herself tended the flame on the twentieth night. When Christianity came to be the religion of the land, it was St. Brigid who was honored and Christian nuns who tended the flame.

Brigid was a Triple Goddess: she was sometimes said to have two sisters also named Brigid. She/they were matrons of healing, of poetry—with which seership was connected—and of crafts, particularly those associated with Fire, such as metal-smithing and perhaps pottery.[3] In addition, the legends show Brigid to be associated with that borderlands/liminality/threshold state which clearly link her to the Otherworlds, including Faery. Her association with these liminal states is shown in her St. Brigid legends by the fact that she was born at sunrise and while her mother was straddling a threshold. It is shown in her Goddess legends by the fact that she was of the Tuatha De Danann, yet married to a Fomorian.

Brigid is associated with Water as well as Fire, and many healing wells are sacred to her throughout the British Isles. Places where water emerges from the Earth are always considered thresholds between the worlds—the Underworld and Middleworld in this case. As a goddess of healing associated with seership and liminal states of being, she is uniquely suited to be the especial Matron Goddess of Faery Healing.

Airmid was the Irish goddess best known as an herbalist and may therefore be associated with these green gifts of the earth. Airmid was the daughter of the Tuatha De Danaan physician Dian Cecht; her brother Miach was a skilled healer whose powers exceeded those of his father. Airmid's association with herbalism is illustrated in the story of her discovery of the 365 healing herbs growing upon her murdered brother's grave—one herb to cure illnesses of each of the 365 nerves of the human body, as well as one for each and every day of the year. She gathered these carefully in her cloak, but unfortunately her jealous father mixed them up so that their applications would not be known. I like to think that Airmid, wise healer that she was, already knew these herbs and their uses and had them firmly in her heart and mind before her father mixed them.

Airmid is also associated with the healing powers of water and sound. At the Second Battle of Moytura her father placed healing herbs into the Well of Slaine, and Airmid, her brothers, and her father chanted incantations over the well to empower it. These waters were then used to heal dead and wounded warriors.

Aine was considered the Queen of the Faeries in the area of southern Ireland known as Munster, where she was quite popular. She is thought to be a regional version of Anu, in whose honor two local mountains—the Paps of Anu—were named. Quite likely Anu is the same being as the great Celtic Mother Goddess Danu, for whom several rivers in Europe are named and who was known in Ireland as Dana. Aine's lore links her with Earth, Air, Fire, and Water. The two mountains were thought to be her breasts; she had a home in a special hill named Cnoc Aine (Aine's Hill), and was thought to have created the enchanted lake known as Lough Gur over which she sometimes appeared in the shape of a faery whirlwind.[4] Aine is very much associated with the sun, and was also known as the wife of the sea god Manannan MacLir from whose bed she arose every morning.[5] She was worshiped at the Summer Solstice, at which time people lit torches of hay upon her hill of Cnoc Aine, carried them around the hill in a counterclockwise direction, and conveyed them home, bearing them aloft through their fields while waving the blessed fire over livestock and crops. Not surprisingly, Aine is also linked with the fertility of the land.

Because of her associations with Fire and Water, she was also associated with healing. It was believed that she regulated the vital spark of life's fire, which, like the sun's daily traversal of the sky, circulated through the body every 24 hours. If bloodletting occurred on her sacred days, which were the Friday, Saturday, and Sunday prior to Lughnasadh, it was thought the sacred life spark would flow out from the body and the patient would die.[6] Aine is therefore associated with both the life-giving sun itself, and the sun's power in the human body, through which the spark was thought to travel by means of the blood. These folkloric remains point to the fact that in days past there must have been a full, rich tradition of healing in which Aine—as the spark of life, the sun-spark within the blood—played a significant part.

Morgen, the British goddess, was known as a skilled herbal healer. She lived with her eight sisters on a holy isle reached only by traveling on the Otherworld Sea. This island may well have been the prototype for the legend of the mystic Otherworld Isle of Apples known as Avalon. Apples were the Celtic fruit of life, death, and immortality. Morgen dwelt on this isle with her sisters, practicing the arts of healing, and was the ruler of the island—which was also known as the Fortunate Isle. Morgen was sometimes said to be a daughter of the island's king, Avallach, whose name is derived from the Celtic word *Abal* which means *apple*.

According to the *Vita Merlini* (*Life of Merlin*) by Geoffrey of Monmouth, King Arthur was taken to her isle to be healed after his last battle. In other accounts, Morgen was one of the three queens who came in a barge to fetch him to their isle of healing.

As mentioned in preceding chapters, Morgen has also come down to us in somewhat different form as the Morgan le Fey of the Arthurian tales.

The name *Morgen* itself is thought by some to mean *sea-borne*, as in one who comes from the sea, while other scholars say that it is related to the Irish *Morrigan*, meaning *Great Queen*.

Sirona (or *Tsirona*) was a Gallic goddess of healing venerated in continental Europe in places from Austria and Germany to Brittany. The name Sirona may come from the Celtic *seren*, meaning star, which may have meant she was originally a star goddess, or may have meant that she was like a light in the darkness. Many sites have been found, usually in conjunction with natural springs, at which statuary and inscriptions indicate that Sirona was venerated as a goddess of healing, fertility, and renewal. In some of these places she was honored with a male partner, Grannos or Belenos, but some places are dedicated to her alone.

Sul or Sulis was a British goddess called Sulis Minerva by the occupying Roman forces since they considered her cognate to their own goddess Minerva. She was the deity honored at hot mineral springs near the river Avon, in a location that later became known as Bath. When the Romans came, they constructed a large temple, complete with bath-buildings, an altar, and a reservoir for the water. The word Sul seems to be related to the Irish word *suil*, meaning "eye," and the Welsh *heol*, meaning sun; the sun was sometimes seen to be the "eye of the sky." It is not surprising that the sun, considered feminine by the Celts, should be connected with spring water which flowed, hot and healing, from the Earth.

Coventina was the goddess of a healing spring located at Carrawburgh, Northumberland, in Northern Britain. The number of votive offerings, altars, and statuary to be found there indicates that this was an important healing spring.

Sequana was the goddess of the River Seine, in France. She was honored particularly at the river's source, where the water came up from the ground, a place which became known as the Springs of Sequana. A great healing sanctuary was built there.

Rhiannon was an important Welsh goddess who figured prominently in the Mabinogian. While not a healing goddess per se, she possessed birds who sang so sweetly that the sick were lulled into a healing sleep and the dead were brought back to life.

GODS

Apollo Vindos was an important Greek god whose worship was widespread. Altars to this Gaulish healing deity have been found in many areas of France, including some at healing springs. Apollo was associated with light, warmth, music, prophecy, and healing waters, and was petitioned especially for the healing of eye problems. His Gaulish name may have been Vindos maq Noudens. Vindos appears to come from the ProtoCeltic root word *vin*, meaning "white," and thus related to the Irish *fin* or *fionn*, and the Welsh *wyn*, or *wen*. This may well link him to the sun and its healing powers, although, because white was a color often associated with death, a stronger case might be made for a link to the Otherworlds—the Land of Faery and the Land of the Dead. He may also be related to Gwynn ap Nudd, the Welsh King of the Faeries who was considered to be the Lord of the Land of Death and of the Underworld, and who resided within Glastonbury Tor.

Especially noteworthy is the fact that the altars sacred to Vindos were found at healing springs, since springs were seen as gateways to the Underworld, and the Underworld was seen as the source of life and regeneration, as well as death. Thus, Apollo Vindos, whose help was invoked at healing springs, was an extremely important healing deity, definitely connected with Water, possibly with Fire, and quite likely with the Faery and Underworlds and all their power.

Nodens is a British god whose name shows him to be related to the Irish Nuada and the Welsh Nudd (and therefore father of Gwynn, mentioned above). He was honored as a god of healing at a sanctuary at Lydney, near the River Severn in Gloucestershire. The impressive sanctuary contained bath facilities and guest houses, similiar to the shrine of Sulis in Britain. There was also a building which may have been a dormitory used for sacred sleep. Sacred sleep, wherein healing dreams and visions might occur, was often used as part of the therapeutic process in healing sanctuaries throughout the classical world.

Belenus or Belenos, whose name means *the shining one,* is associated with thermal healing springs in Northern Italy. He may be the same as the Welsh God Beli. He is often found with his feminine counterpart, **Belisama** *(the most shining one)*, and is sometimes associated with the Greek Apollo. Occasionally he is found paired with one of the healing goddesses such as Sirona. Belenus is associated with the power of the sun, heat, and warmth as is another Gaulish god, Grannus, whose name is similar to the Irish *grian*, meaning sun.

Grannus seems to have been a healing deity of great renown. His name is found in inscriptions from the upper reaches of the Danube to places as far away as Sweden, Switzerland, and Scotland. He, too, shared the characteristics of Apollo. Like Belenus, he is often found paired with the healing goddess Sirona, as well as with other, more localized goddesses of healing.

Dian Cecht, whose name means *vehement power*, was the Irish god of healing, the magician-physician of the Tuatha De Danaan. In the Irish tales, he is associated with the Cauldron of Regeneration, which had been brought up from a lake in Ireland and given to the giant Welsh god Bran, son of Llyr. The cauldron itself figures prominently in the Welsh Mabinogian tale of Branwen, which recounts a war between Wales and Ireland wherein the Irish used the cauldron to bring their dead warriors back to life.

We find Dian Cecht doing something rather similar at the second battle of Moytura where the Well of Slaine was used instead of a cauldron. Dian Cecht put a great many healing herbs into the well, and he, along with his sons and daughter, chanted incantations and spells over it. The Tuatha dead and wounded were placed into the well and brought forth alive and well.

Lugh was an Irish god who was "equally skilled in all arts" including healing. This is not surprising since he came from quite a family of healers. His grandfather Dian Cecht, mentioned just above, was the Tuatha De Danaan physician of great renown. Dian Cecht's sons Miach and Octriuil and his daughter Airmid—Lugh's uncles and aunt—were also well known healers.

Goibniu, was an Irish god better known as the Smith of the Tuatha De Danaan. He brewed an ale which preserved the gods from the infirmities of old age, disease, and death. Therefore, he might be said to be the patron deity of healing brews, including medicinal tinctures, teas, and ales.

Issues in Healing—Life, Death, and Our Correct Role

When doing healing work it is important to realize that we are not saviors, nor rescuers. We are not heroic figures of this or any other kind. We are merely channelers, mediators, and bridges of energy working for the greatest good of the person or other entity, something which is determined not by us, but rather by Spirit in conjunction with the Greater Self of the person or entity itself. We do not do this healing work alone, so there is no place for grandiosity and self-importance. We work with the assistance of our Faery Allies, Guides, Spirit Helpers, and Spirit Doctors.

Spiritual healing traditions teach that such healing should not be done without the consent of the person for whom the work is to be done. This is good advice. It is not our place as healers to override the will of others, to say nothing of the larger, possibly karmic implications that might be part of an illness. Therefore, if possible, always ask permission. If this is not possible, then send forth the healing energy in a way that will allow the person to refuse it if he or she so chooses. One way to do this is to call out to the person's Higher or Greater Self and make the offering of the healing energy, to be taken or not as desired. Working unconditionally, with the assistance of our Faery Allies, for the greatest good possible, automatically brings much of this into play, though it is always good to state one's intentions clearly.

Along these lines, it is important to know that healing does not always mean regaining physical health. This is one of those issues that most people in the healing arts find hard to handle, but it is true nonetheless. Once again, the Greater Self is in charge, and knows what is best; our job is to render energetic assistance, and of course, the greatest power of all, love.

SAFETY ISSUES

It is essential to remember that we are merely the channels or vessels for the energy that comes to us from our allies. With the help of these allies and intermediaries, we can modulate the energy flow—raising or lowering it as seems appropriate, or as they deem appropriate.

After we have allowed the energy to flow through us, after our energy has touched and interacted with someone ill, we need to allow ourselves to be cleansed and retuned to our own frequency. After healing sessions, it is advisable to wash our hands with cold, running water, visualizing unwanted energies flowing off, away, and down into the Earth to the Underworld for recycling. Sometimes smudging with sage, lavender, or frankincense can be helpful as well.

If we do not attend to the cleansing, it is possible to suffer from energetic contamination wherein we find we have inadvertently taken on the symptoms of the person with whom we have just worked. If we do not attend to the retuning it is possible to suffer from the psychic equivalent of the "bends," that rather uncomfortable and often life-threatening syndrome known to scuba divers who stay underwater too long, or come up too fast. If these things occur, attend to yourself as soon as possible with grounding exercises, bathing, smudging, laying on the earth to let the energies adjust themselves, and of course, calling on your allies for help.

HEALING THE HEALER

An important issue in healing work is keeping ourselves healthy while doing it. Those unfamiliar with working with energy sometimes inadvertently take on the problems or energies they are working with, as we have just mentioned.

There are a few ways to prevent this from happening. Making sure one is properly grounded while doing the work is quite important. Asking for the help of our allies, instead of thinking we can do it all by ourselves, is another, as is regular use of cleansing techniques such as smudging and the hand washing mentioned above. Maintaining our own health by proper food, exercise, and sleep is essential. Another is not taking on healing jobs beyond our level of expertise or energy. And finally, it is very important to remember to allow any negative energies to flow through us and out into the Earth rather than holding on to them—which keeps them within our own energy field and can lead to problems later on. The Earth is quite good at absorbing and detoxifying them.

NOTES

1. To those who pay attention to such things, the journeys in this book may seem a bit over-punctuated. The reason for this is quite simple. Generally speaking, punctuation has to do with pauses in the narrative, so that the reader will be able to make sense of what he/she is reading. Journeywork is full of pauses—much more so than the regular text—because time must be allowed for the journeyer to see, feel, and experience the words just read or spoken. Therefore, I have added commas and periods—in places where they might not normally occur—to indicate these "pause places." A comma indicates just a slight pause, a period is a longer one, while several periods indicate a much longer pause. As always, these are merely suggestions; feel free to use them or not as seems right to you.

2. We call them the cross-quarter days, yet our ancestors called them the Quarter Days. This reversal is most likely due to the fact that in our modern awareness of the year the solstices and equinoxes are used to mark the quarters.

3. I am not referring to drugs prescribed by physicians in order to rebalance brain chemistry, but rather to casual, recreational, and often irresponsible drug use.

END NOTES

1 McArthur, Margie, *Wisdom of the Elements*, Crossing Press, Freedom, CA, 1998.

2 Ibid.

3 In *Mythic Ireland* (p. 230), Michael Dames relates that Brigid-the-Smith (the Goddess Brigid, in her form as Underworld Goddess) lived within the sacred mound of Croghan Hill, and was said to make vessels and pots of every kind, including "the sacred cauldrons from which the future was poured." This "future" included the River Shannon, and is one of those interesting associations which illustrate the theme of water as a Divine Gift, and the significance of Water and Fire as the Elements of life.

4 Dames, Michael, *Mythic Ireland*, Thames & Hudson, Ltd., London, 1992, p. 73.

5 Ibid, p. 69.

6 Matthews, Caitlin & John, *Encyclopedia of Celtic Wisdom*, Element Books, Ltd; Shaftesbury, Dorset, 1994, pp. 283-284; and Wood-Martin, W. G., *Traces of the Elder Faiths of Ireland: A Handbook of Irish Pre-Christian Traditions*, Longmans, Greens, Co. NY and Bombay, 1902, *Vol. I*, pp. 357-358.

CHAPTER 16

The Cosmology of the Faery Realm

STRETCHING THE SUBTLE SENSES AND THE IMAGINATION

In working with faery energy we will be navigating the subtle, inner realms of the Earth. Therefore, before beginning to work with Faery Healing, it is advisable to have a reasonably reliable map of the terrain and a familiarity with the inhabitants who may be encountered.

The first thing to be encountered is, of course, the Sacred Land itself, and this we have already discussed in *Chapter 12*. It is within the Sacred Land that we find the Faery Realm. Our study of Faery Healing will encompass techniques for moving into that subtle dimension of the Sacred Land.

These realms are best apprehended with our subtle senses and our imagination, and the techniques given below offer instruction and practice in the use of these subtle senses. Here are a few exercises with which to begin your travels within the Sacred Land.

> **EXERCISE** | **Stretching the Subtle Senses**
>
> Find a place outdoors on the Earth where you feel comfortable doing your spiritual work. Spend time sitting there, looking at and feeling the Earth beneath you, the sky above you, and the plants, trees, and animals around you. Notice the information your physical senses bring in to you.
>
> While continuing to practice the grounding exercises in the preceding chapter, add these to your repertoire as well.
>
> 1. While you are doing your grounding, make sure you do not rush through the steps. Spend extra time and awareness on actually sensing and feeling your body as you sit upon the Earth.

2. As you grow your roots, extend your consciousness downward following the roots as they grow down, and really notice both the feeling of your roots and how it feels to move downward through the layers and strata of the Earth as you pass through them.

3. When you have rooted into the Earth's core, carefully bring your awareness back up to the surface, again noting and feeling everything as you move through it.

4. Repeat the above exercise, but this time bring your awareness upward, focusing on your spinal cord as your tree trunk.

5. Go skyward, extending your consciousness up in to the Upperworld, passing clouds, moon, sun, planets, and moving off and out into the galaxy. Take time to notice all of these as you move through space. If you are having trouble noticing and feeling these, *imagine* it instead, and create pictures in your mind of how it would look.

The One

Now let us move into a bit of theology as well as a cosmology, if you will, both of which will prove useful in navigating these subtle inner realms.

The Divine Force is a vast, impersonal force that is essentially unknowable except as it manifests itself through its wondrous creation, the universe in which we live, move, and have our being. The way in which I visualize this manifestation taking place is best described simply as the *One* becoming the *Two*, becoming the *Many*.

The One has throughout time been called by many names, the most descriptive of which are the *Zero* and the *Void*, both of which accurately describe its true nature: that of the *No Thing* which contains the potential for *All Things*. It is *that* from which all else will be eventually birthed.

When this One Power stirs, moves, it becomes the Two, and we then have the presence of Creative Polarity—the feminine and masculine, the Goddess and the God. From this Divine Creative Polarity, all else is born.

MEDITATION | The One

Light a candle and set it in the center of your working space. Gaze at it for a few moments, calming yourself, and just appreciating the flame's beauty. After a bit, close your eyes, and with your inner vision see the candle flame grow into a larger flame, and continue to grow till it becomes a large fire burning within a huge hearth. Step into the fire, and find yourself traveling downward, descending within the fire into the Underworld. You step out of it and turning, look at it, realizing that this Flame of Life burns on many levels, and within all worlds, and indeed, burns within you, as well.

You feel the Life Force itself in this fire, and your own spark of that force blazes up in response to this awareness. Then you step back into the large fire, into its very center, and you find yourself in the Void, the Zero, the No Thing that is full of the potential of Every Thing... and in this, you simply allow yourself to Be....

After a few moments a movement begins. You feel it almost as a wind. The force of it blows you through the fire and out, and back into an awareness of yourself as a being. You look back at the fire as this wind bears you aloft, and then the wind places you back within the fire, and you find yourself traveling upward on the flame, and back into this world, this time, and the place from which you began your journey. Take a few moments to come back to yourself, and when you feel ready, you may open your eyes.

Be sure to record your journey in your Magical Journal.

Goddess and God

The high powers referred to herein as Goddess and God have been described and named in many ways, but I feel that the most understandable way is that which describes their function. Goddess is that which conceives, gestates, births, and nourishes life; God is that which engenders, protects, and guards life. As may be seen, these functions are present on and within every level of manifestation; indeed, they *cause* manifestation. And bear in mind, that these *functions* and *forces*, are themselves, conscious entities—Goddess and God—although their consciousness is far beyond our own and vast beyond our imagining. This is why we personify and name them.

Both God and Goddess appear in many guises and wear many masks in our world. At a very basic level, they are Earth God or Goddess, Sun God or Goddess, Moon God or Goddess, and Star God or Goddess—the gender assigned to Earth, sun, moon, and stars differing from culture to culture.

She is the Bright Mother who gives birth to all beings. She is the Maiden of Spring, in whose footsteps the very first of the spring flowers sprout forth. She is Lady Abundance (Habondia, meaning abundance, is one of her old names) of Summer, the Harvest Mother of Autumn, and the Cailleach, Crone, or Dark Lady of Winter. He is the Lord of both the animals and the plants. In spring and summer he is the Green Man, who becomes, in late summer and autumn, the Sacrificed King (represented by the grain; John Barleycorn is one of his old names) when he gives his life so that the people may be sustained by him. In winter he is Lord of the Underworld, the Land of Death, and in his role as Lord of the Animals, along with the Dark Lady he leads the Wild Hunt to gather up the souls of the dead, including the slaughtered and hunted animals, and take them to the Underworld where they will rest and be refreshed till the time comes for them to be reborn.

Since these functions/forces/beings are found within every level of manifestation, they are also found within the Faery Realm, where they manifest as Faery King and Queen. In other words, the Faery King and Queen are reflections, or harmonics, within this particular realm of nature called the Faery Realm, of the God and Goddess powers.

The Goddess is very important in the Faery Tradition. As the Faery Queen, she is found in legends such as Thomas the Rhymer, Tam Lin, and many others. She is found as both beautiful maid or queen and as hideous hag. As such, she shows that she represents the powers of both life and death; she creates and she destroys.

In her guise of the creating/destroying Faery Queen, she shows herself to be the Dark Goddess of the Underworld who births life into form, destroys the form when its time is done, and then regenerates life by birthing it into form once again. Thus, she is the power of transformation.

In Faery Healing, we work with the Goddess as Faery Queen, but also as the Goddess of the Land and Underworld, as it is her gifts of transformation, wholeness, and healing which we seek.

CEREMONY | Acknowledging the Divine Presence

You will need a votive candle, two other candles, votive or taper, and some matches for this small ceremony. Before you light the candle, hold the match in your hand and pause before you strike it, thinking of the mystery of fire and how it relates to the spark of life. Then, as you strike the match and bring forth the fire, light the candle as you speak the words of the first paragraph, below.

> *By the power of the Ancient Providence,*
> *Which was forever, and is forever,*
> *All knowing, wise, loving and becoming,*
> *Which is male and female, Goddess and God,*

> *Do I light this candle, Symbol of the All-encompassing,*
> *Ever-becoming Presence.*

Pause for a moment as you say these words, and think about their meaning. Then take another match, light it from the first candle, and use it to light the other two candles as you say:

> *From the One comes the Two,*
> *I give greetings and honor*
> *To the Goddess and the God,*
> *Our Mother and our Father.*[1]

Spend a few moments reflecting on the meaning of the beings and concepts of this ceremony. When you are finished, give thanks, and put out your candles.

The Three Realms

Our world may be looked at from two very basic and complementary perspectives. These are horizontal and vertical. The horizontal worldview encompasses that which is all around us—the circle of the world, the four primary directions of right, left, front, and back, also referred to as East, West, North, South. The vertical worldview brings in the perspectives of up and down. All of these perspectives exist relative to us, human beings, standing in an upright position, upon the surface of the Earth.

Both of these perspectives are valuable, but it is the vertical one that I wish to focus on at the moment as it provides us with a way of looking at things that is quite useful in working with the subtle worlds such as Faery.

This vertical perspective has been recognized and worked with in many spiritual traditions. In Christianity, we find it in the ideas of heaven, earth, and hell. In many of the old Pagan traditions, we find it in the form of the concept of the World Tree whose roots are in the Underworld, whose trunk is in this, the Middle or Surface World, and whose branches and leaves are in the Upperworld.

This useful perspective gives us a way of accessing the Three Worlds of Upperworld, Middleworld, and Underworld, just as the horizontal perspective of the Four Directions allows us access into the world of the Four Elements and Elemental Beings.

The Middleworld (sometimes called Middle Earth) is the spiritual dimension of this everyday world of humans, animals, plants, and stones, while the Upperworld is the realm of the Old Gods, the Angelic Beings, and the Star Powers. The Underworld, as we have previously emphasized, is the realm of the Star Powers within the Earth, the Dark Goddess and God, and all the rich deep powers of both destruction and creation.

Some of the older magical traditions refer to the three rays of power, love, and wisdom, and these seem to correspond to the Three Realms: power with the Underworld, wisdom with the Upperworld, and love with the Middleworld.

The Upperworld can be thought of as the place of the great wisdom of the Star Powers. The Underworld can be thought of as the place of the great creative power of these Star Powers within the Earth. The Middleworld is the meeting place of the two, the place of their marriage and manifestation, and thus a place of relationship and love.

It is only with love that power and knowledge may be used wisely. Without love, knowledge never becomes wisdom, but remains cold, dry, and intellectual, while without knowledge/wisdom and love, power has no direction and is easily abused. All three are necessary in order for balance, harmony, and healing to occur.

The Three Realms

Realm	UNDERWORLD	MIDDLEWORLD	UPPERWORLD
Region	Sea	Earth	Sky
Ray	Power	Love	Wisdom
Great Tree	Roots	Trunk	Branches
Beings	Earth Strata Rocks, Minerals, Metals Titanic Powers (fault-zones, magma zones, nuclear fires, hearth-fire) Ancestors Underworld Star Powers	Humans and other Animals Plants and Trees Soil and Soil Life-forms Stones Weather Beings Elemental Sovereigns	Sun Moon Planet Stars Atmosphere Air Currents Clouds
Spirit Beings	Giants Titans Dragon Forces Earth Forces Ancestors Deities	Fairies, Faeries Devas Elementals Nature Spirits Animal Spirits Stone Spirits	Deities Angels Archangels
Deities	Dark God/dess	Nature God/dess Faery God/desses Faery King and Queen	Galactic God/dess Star God/dess

The Four Directions

In the last chapter, we made a beginning in understanding the Four Directions and their corresponding Elements. In this chapter, we will look at them with regard to how they relate to the general cosmology of the Faery Realm.

How are the Four Directions and Elemental energies found in the Faery Realm? They are found as the Four Faery Cities or Convocations, the legendary Gorias, Finias, Murias and Falias, as mentioned in the *Second Battle of Moytura*. The four cities, the four treasures or gifts, and how these can be utilized in Faery Work will be addressed in the following chapters. For now, it is enough to know that each of the Directions may be used as a gateway to the faery city or Convocation of that Direction, and thus to the treasures and wisdom it contains.

The Four Directions and Elements are also found as the "small clans of Earth's delight," the Elemental spirits known as the sylphs, salamanders, undines, and gnomes. These particular spirits encompass several other classes of spirits, and all are often considered part of the Fairy/Faery Realm. Functionally, they have to do with building and maintenance of plant life on both a physical and etheric level, as well as with the growth of plants and the fertility of the land in general. In addition, they have to do with the other things that are part of the planetary life system, such as the waterways and oceans and the atmosphere and the winds. There are many names and classifications of these beings (brownies, leprechauns, selkies, etc.) apart from the four general categories given above, but detailed information about them is not within the scope of this book. Please see the *Suggested Readings* section.

We find the Four again with regard to the Upperworlds when we consider that there are Four Great Powers, also referred to as *Archangels*, who are said to be the Guardians and Keepers of East, South, West and North. These Archangels are Raphael, Michael, Gabriel, and Uriel, respectively. These angels, particularly Michael, were quite important to our Celtic Christian ancestors, and there is evidence to suggest that when Christianity took root, Michael took on at least part of the role previously belonging to the Celtic God, Lugh.[2]

In esoteric tradition, the Archangels are known to be heavenly powers and may be equated with the Star Beings and/or the spirits of the planets (in times past, all heavenly bodies were referred to as stars). Traditionally, they have evidenced quite an interest in the Earth realm and often have interacted with humans. This is illustrated in some very old legends concerning the "Watchers," who are mentioned in the Bible as the Nephilim (and known in other Middle Eastern cultures by other names), and were said to have descended to Earth with their unique gifts to help a very young humanity evolve.

Among these Star Beings, these Watchers (who numbered more than the four), was one who became the especial regent of this planet Earth, and who was known variously as Lumiel, Lucifer, the Lightbearer, and Son of the Morning Star. The Watchers both bestowed their gifts on humanity, and continue to help humanity when called upon; the form in which they are most popularly known currently is that of the *Archangels*, which, contrary to prevailing neo-Pagan thought, is not a strictly Christian concept. Some pagans think of them as gods. Either way, they are beings of immense power whose spheres of influence include both heaven and Earth.[3] The Underworld Beings—the Old Gods—are their deep Earthly manifestation; while the faeries are their Middleworld echoes and resonances.

As has been mentioned, the Irish legends that state that the faeries are fallen angels, are quite relevant in this regard.

One way of looking at the Four Directions/Elements with regard to the Faery Realm is to use the model of the Three Realms of Upperworld, Middleworld, and Underworld because the pattern of "Four and Center" reiterates on each of these three levels. The Upperworld contains the Archangelic Powers, as mentioned just above. The Middleworld contains the Faery Beings including the Elemental fairies, and the Underworld contains some aspects of the Faery Realm and the Faery Beings, as well as the vast, huge InnerEarth Beings, who swirl, flow, glow, and crystallize. In one sense, both Middleworld and Underworld beings may be considered as "expressions" of the heavenly, Archangelic Beings and their powers.

In the next chapter, we will begin a practical application of these ideas as we learn to enter and travel within the Faery Realm.

END NOTES

1 McArthur, Margie, *Wisdom of the Elements*, Crossing Press, Freedom, CA, 1998, p. 154.

2 Lethbridge, T. C., *Witches*, Citadel Press, Inc., Secauscus, NJ, 1972.

3 Howard, Michael & Nigel Jackson, *The Pillars of Tubal Cain*, Capall Bann, Berks, 2000, and Huson, Paul, *Mastering Witchcraft*, Berkeley Windhover Books, Berkeley Publishing Corp, NY, NY, 1970, by special arrangement with G. P. Putnam's Sons, NY, NY.

CHAPTER 17

Traveling within the Faery Realm

Gateways to Faery

There are many ways to access the Faery Realm. Since the Faery Realm is found within the land, any natural feature may be used as a way to go within the land, in vision and imagination, and gain access to the realm of Faery. According to tradition, there have been hills, bushes, and trees associated with entering the Faery Realm. Faeries have seemed to appear to humans from out of lakes, rivers, trees, and mounds. Therefore, any of these may be used as entrances to the Faery Realm, as can the music of the rushing bubbling of a river, the crashing of the ocean's waves and the whisper of the wind in the trees. Each of these gateways makes use of our powers of visualization, feeling, sensing, and believing.

But in truth, *imagination*—our wonderful ability to create and work with mental images—is the true Gateway to Faery, for without it, none of the others will function.

By far the most simple and easy way to enter the Faery Realm is to simply "enter the land." This exercise of imagination and visualization may be done by closing one's eyes, stilling one's consciousness, focusing one's awareness on the Earth beneath one's feet and visualizing an opening appearing in the ground, which one then enters by stepping or falling into it, and quite simply, passing downward.

Other ways of entry into Faery are to imagine oneself diving down into a pool of water, or passing through a doorway that leads into a faery mound, hill, tree, or perhaps stepping onto a cluster of tree roots, growing small and sinking down between them and thus into the land.

The most important thing to remember is the concept of the borderlands. The places mentioned above are all places that are boundaries and borders between one thing and another—land and sea, Upperworld and Underworld, and the like. Because of this, they can all serve as boundaries, interfaces, and gateways between our outerworld, and the innerworld which is the world of Faery.

We will develop and work with a few of these for the purposes of this book. But please remember that these are imaginative structures we are building with our powers of mind and vision, something anyone can do on his or her own. As you work with the faeries of your own land, it is likely you will find your own ways of access, perhaps different from these. If that happens, please develop and use them.

Traveling the Three Worlds

In previous chapters we have made reference to the Three Worlds—the Upperworld, Middleworld and Underworld. There are several ways to apprehend these worlds and several ways to travel into and within them.

TRAVELING ON THE GREAT TREE

The worlds may be pictured in the time-honored, traditional shamanic sense of the Great Tree, or World Tree, where the roots correspond to the Underworld, the trunk to our realm, the Middleworld, and the branches to the sky realm, or Upperworld.

The Great Tree is useful in Faery Work as it allows us to not only enter the land, but to travel into all three realms, moving in and out of not just the Faery Realm but also the Underworld and Upperworlds, interacting with the beings of all of these places.

I have found this very necessary in my healing work. There are times when you need allies much more powerful than your animal or Faery Allies. At times like these it is wise to invoke the Upperworld Beings—the angels, gods, and goddesses. Often it may be necessary to work with the Underworld Beings, such as the Dark Goddess. In addition, one will often find that there is psychic garbage of some kind to be dealt with; the beings of both Underworld and Upperworld are very accepting of this. They simply "compost" it into its basic energetic components, which dissolves its previous patterning, thus purifying it and making the energies available for future use.

Journey on the Great Tree

The following journey is quite long, and is divided into three parts. The first time through you may wish to do each part separately, returning at the end of each part to the "here and now" place from which you began. When you have done this, do the entire journey all the way through to get a feel for moving up and down the Great Tree and from one realm to another. Be sure and allow yourself time and space for the interaction with the various beings you will meet in each realm. This last aspect of the journey is not fully scripted below since it is something which must just *happen*!

For this and all the journeys that follow, please remember to begin by grounding, creating sacred space, and orienting yourself to the Directions by bringing your attention to the East, South, West, North, Above and Below and the spirit powers that reside within them. Your Faery Altar will be the Center point—metaphorically if not always physically—of your sacred space. At the conclusion of your journey or your working, conclude by once again affirming these Directions, giving thanks to the beings who have helped you, and extinguishing your candle.

JOURNEY | On the Great Tree

Part One

Light a candle and set it down in the center of your working space.

You focus on the flame of your center candle, and find yourself passing through to the innerworlds. You still see the flame, but now it appears to glow within the heart of a hollow in the trunk of an enormous tree. You go inside the hollow, and find the space there to be large and cavelike... The cave is glowing with the light of the flame, which seems to emerge from the ground itself, and which burns without fuel. Though the flames appear to reach upward into the body of the tree, the tree is not burned, but seems enlivened by the fire. As you gaze upward, following the flame, you extend your consciousness upward into the tree trunk, and you find yourself traveling upward through the wood and the sap, moving upward into the branches, where your consciousness spreads out into the branches and branchlets that are like many fingers on a hand. You can feel how the branches themselves reach upward, extending their energies and awareness into the sky, reaching toward the sun by day, and the moon and stars by night, communing with them, and becoming wise... If you so desire, you extend your awareness skyward along the energy pathways of the branches, reaching up and out to moon, the sun and the many Star Beings in the sky... After a while, you withdraw your consciousness from the sky realm, pulling it down the branches, through the tree trunk, and back into yourself as you stand within the tree cave.

Part Two

Standing in the tree cave, you look around at the cave's edges, and your attention is drawn to the very large root system of the tree, the thick, rough cords of which are woven into and around the cave's circumference, as well as lying in clumps on the cave's floor, disappearing down into the Earth. You move over to one of the huge, gnarled roots and touch it with your foot. As you do this, the land beneath your feet begins to crumble and give way, and you find yourself falling down into the root structure of the tree, and falling beyond, down into the Earth. You move downward through tangles of roots and layers of soil and pebbles, emerging finally, through a tangle of branchlike roots, and falling down onto the ground beneath it.

You are within a forest that is lit by a green-gold light. Above, you see a soft bluish grey sky, almost opalescent in color, and lit by an unseen light. The tree from which you have fallen is above you, seeming to hang suspended from the sky, stretching upward as far as you can see. Around you are small bushes, trees, plants, tiny flowers, and fallen logs. There are leaves scattered on the ground.

You move over to one of the fallen logs, and sit down. You hear a soft noise behind you, and turning, see that there are several Faery Beings of various sizes, shapes, and appearances observing you with curiosity. They almost blend in with the forest as they resemble it— seeming to be made of, or clad in, leaves, twigs, grasses, and small flowers. You spend some time simply looking at them, noticing their appearances, feeling their energies, just as they are doing with you... Finally, you feel as if something is required of you, so you reach into your pocket and pull out what you find there. It is a small pennywhistle, and you put it up to your mouth and begin to blow upon it. A melody seems to emerge from it, a strange and magical tune. The faeries draw closer, smiling, nodding, tapping feet in time to the music. They take hands, and begin to dance around you as you play... whirling around you, faster and faster... till the music reaches a loud crescendo... and then falls back down into soft, slow notes... and ends. Wonderingly, you bring the pennywhistle down from your mouth and look at it, this musical instrument which seems to play itself.

The Faery Beings move toward you now, reaching out with their hands, touching you, stroking your hair, your skin, and your clothing, with the greatest of curiosity. One of them fingers a piece of jewelry you are wearing, and you take it off, and give it to him as a gift. The faery seems quite delighted with this, and moves away, the others following, to have a closer look at it, and try it on...

At this moment, a breeze springs up...and the green-gold light of this place seems to grow brighter and brighter... till you can no longer see the trees and the faeries... You feel yourself lifted up by the breeze... and borne aloft by it... traveling through the greengold light to the tree which hangs from the sky... and into its dangling roots... and upward, upward... moving through the tree trunk... till you find yourself once again within the tree cave... and standing before the fire which burns in its center.

Part Three

You stand before the fire in the tree cave, and gaze into its depths. As you watch, the fire grows smaller, and seems to contract inward on itself until it becomes a glowing circle of light on the floor of the tree cave... This circle of light seems to burn into the soil... and this burning creates a circular opening—like a well that reaches deep into the Earth. The glowing fire is now the rim of the well.

You step closer to the well with the glowing ring of fire around it, and look down into it....You see nothing but darkness, so you lean in closer, to get a better look... Losing your balance, you fall down into the well, and find yourself tumbling head over heels downward into the Earth... Through the layers of soil, sand, and rock you fall, passing easily through them all as you continue downward into the depths of the Earth... Down you go... deeper and deeper... into the Earth... until finally you come to rest in a pool of water within a large cave.

The cave glows with a dim light, the source of which cannot be seen... You climb out of the pool of water, and look around at the cave in which you find yourself... Jewels gleam in the rock walls... and you notice a large throne-shaped rock just beyond the pool of water. As you gaze at this crystal-studded throne, you notice that there is someone seated in it, someone so still and unmoving, that at first you are not sure if she is really there... A woman of mature years, cloaked in deep blue and purple, gazes back at you from the depths of the rock throne. Her long dark hair, streaked with silver, peaks out from beneath her hood.

After a while, she lifts her hand slightly, and with barely perceptible movement, gestures for you to come closer... You draw closer to her... and stand before the rock throne, gazing at her with great awe. She lays her hand upon your shoulder, and you look into her eyes, which are like deep pools of water. As you gaze into her eyes, you feel as if you taken into them... moving through them into a place which is vast... and deep... like the depths of star-studded space... and yet, paradoxically, as deep as the fiery heart of the deepest Earth... But though you see and feel these things, you know that both of them are Her... and your soul slips into a silent communion with this Great Goddess....

After a long while, your consciousness returns from these far places... and you find yourself standing before her. In your hand, you find a gift for her, and silently, you hand it to her... She takes it from you... and nods her head... and you know it is time for you to go. You walk back toward the pool of water, and step into it. You dive down into its depths, and swim deep into star-filled waters... At length, you see an opening before you, and swim toward it... It looks to be a ring of glowing light... As you swim through it, you emerge from the waters... and find yourself climbing out into a tree cave which glows with a soft green-gold light...

There is an opening that leads out of the tree cave. You walk through it... and as you do, you find yourself passing through the web of dimensions... and back into this one... and find that you have come back to this realm... this time... and to a room where you know a candle burns on a Faery Altar, the place from which you began your journey...You allow yourself a few moments to return completely, and when you are ready, you open your eyes.

Be sure to record your journey in your Magical Journal.

Years ago, I began to note an interesting paradox that seemed to occur in my personal work in the Innerworlds. Often, I would journey quite deeply into the Underworld, interact with beings, and do inner work. Yet I inevitably felt that, for some unknown reason, my work was simultaneously bringing me into contact with higher realms. Over time, I learned that this is one of the interesting paradoxes of working "in-world." Quite often, the *deeper* you go, the *higher* you go. This interesting phenomena seems to work on the principle of *Resonance*, and is yet another illustration of the seeming paradox of how things seem to reverse themselves, or "run backwards," in the Faery Realm and the Underworld.

The Great Tree obviously has many uses as it gives access to all the realms. Here are just some of the ways in which it may be utilized.

Ways in Which the Great Tree Journey May Be Used

Upperworld. As given in the journey above, extend your consciousness upward into the branches and beyond, reaching out to the Sky and Star Beings. They are Wise Elders, and seeders of new life streams. If you choose, you may ask them to share their wisdom with you. When you are finished, carefully pull your awareness back down from the Upperworld, into the branches, into the trunk, and back to normal awareness, using the methods above.

Middleworld. Merge consciousness with the Great Tree, touching into the life within it, and thereby, into all trees. Feel into the life within trees, both physical and subtle, including the elemental life, and the fire within the molecules.

This journey can be used to access the healing powers of nature, particularly of trees, as well as the nature spirits, especially tree spirits. When inside the tree cave, allow yourself to become aware of the Life Force of the tree and the flow of energy (and nutrient containing sap) up and down the tree. From here, you can move into the very cells themselves, finding the fiery heart within each cell. This corresponds to both the star fires and the Underworld fires, so the journey may be used to make deeper contact with these, as well as with all the life-forms whose lives are interrelated with that of the tree—insects, animals, birds, fungi, plants, mosses, lichens, and the like.

Underworld. Traveling down through the Earth can lead one straight into the Faery Realm, as well as into the realm of the Dark Goddess. One can also use this journey to become aware of the consciousnesses of the InnerEarth Beings—the dragons, earth-serpents, and giants.

Occasionally the faeries will instruct you on how to use the Great Tree. This might be something like gathering leaves, bark, or root scrapings, the energies of which will be used in a medicine. Then again, knowing the faeries, it might be something completely different....

These three journeys can be used to link the energies of the worlds together, bringing star energy down to the Earth, the Faery Realm, and/or the Underworld, and Underworld, Faery or Earth energy up to stars. This is an advanced form of *Relinking-Reweaving*, and is done only when directed, but often it will simply happen during the course of the journey. When this happens be aware that you are part of the process, as the energy is moving through your body and most particularly, through your loving, human heart.

The Star Showering exercise in *Chapter 15* showed how the energy ascends, descends, and is looped through the human body at mid-body/heart level, to be *mixed and transformed* and then showered out through the hands to flow out into the world. This is the same process that happens when you are called upon to do the *Relinking-Reweaving* referred to above.

More on the Great Tree

For me, one of the most remarkable things about the Great Tree is the shape it makes. It is a shape that keeps recurring for me, in both my spiritual work and my dreams.

While it is true that a tree's roots reach into the Underworld and its branches reach into the Upperworlds, it is also true that the curve of the root structure is not entirely straight downward, but more like a many-fingered open hand. Some of the roots seem to curve back upward in place, while a portion of the tree's crown of

The Great Tree

branches droop downward due to gravity. More importantly, there is an energetic loop between the roots and crown of a tree. The energy moves up from the Underworld, through the root system and into the trunk. It moves up the trunk and out the branches. It fountains out of the top into the sky, and some of it continues upward, but much of it is drawn back down again.

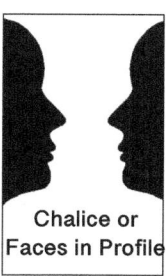

Chalice or Faces in Profile

This is exactly the shape made by the *human tree*—the human body and its auric field. It is also the shape of the energy pattern of Earth's magnetic grid. Seen one-dimensionally it makes the shape of a chalice and also of two faces seen in profile gazing at each other, a symbol commonly used to indicate lovers.

Reduced to its simplest terms, the shape is very simple and profound, and composed of two of life's most basic shapes: a sphere or circle bisected by a straight line. The sphere or circle is feminine; the straight line is masculine. Together, they represent the union of complementary opposites. This constitutes wholeness, and gives rise to creation. Interestingly, it is quite similar to the shape of the Greek letter *phi*, which is the root of the Greek *philo*, which means *love*.

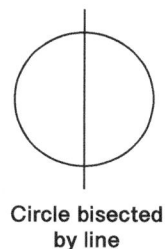

Circle bisected by line

To add to these interesting correspondences, this shape, this *phi*, is also mathematically representative of the Golden Mean, that geometric measure from which life energy spirals out from the still Center or Void into manifestation. The Golden Mean is also the geometric proportion that defines the conjunction of two interlocking circles or worlds, the center of which forms an ovoid containing a fish-like shape known as the Vesica Pisces. The Vesica Pisces is representative not only of this conjoining of the two (i.e. love), but also of that which is birthed from their union (i.e., life), as well as the Womb which births it.[1]

Phi

Also interesting is the fact that this magnetic energy grid/auric shape is also suggestive of the shape of an upright being with wings, the shape often used in illustrations of angels and faeries.

Healing is the wholeness achieved by the harmonious interaction of complementary opposites; this brings about a creative and complementary balance of energies. Faery Healing is

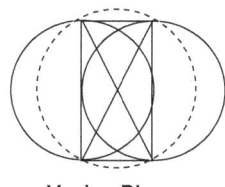

Vesica Pisces

the wholeness achieved by the harmonious interaction of the complementary opposites of the human and Faery Realms.

During the writing of this book, the faeries frequently taught me things while I was in the dream-state. One of the things had to do with wings and the shape we are discussing.

One's dreams are often hard to convey to another, and so it is with this one. But the essential messages of this dream had to do with how the similarity of shape in these things indicated a similarity of energy movement, which was tied into a similarity of function. As the dream ended and I awoke, I was aware of how wings are, in essence, an extension of the heart-lung energy, as well as a means of moving that energy. It may be argued that faeries don't have lungs, but the point is, that there is "something" within the faery body which serves a similar purpose. Instead of air, however, this organ—which is allied with the heart—takes energy into itself from nature and mixes it with the faery's own energy of "faery-ness," then breathes out this mixture of energies into the world by the movement of those wings.

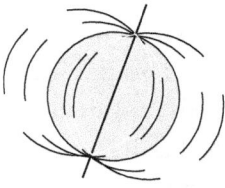

Earth's Magnetic Field

This was a powerful dream; I could feel in my own body what I was being shown, and this feeling continued long after I had awakened.

*T*HE FAERY CITIES

In the old Irish tale, *The Second Battle of Moytura*, the coming of the Tuatha De Danaan to Ireland is described. It is said that they came from four cities in the North, where they had studied the magical arts and become well versed in druidry, sorcery, and occult lore.

These Four Cities were called Finias, Gorias, Murias, and Falias, and were ascribed, in later works, to the Four Directions of East, South, West, and North, respectively. In those cities were four Sages, or Wise Men: Uscias was in Finias, Esras was in Gorias, Semias was in Murias, and Morfessa was in Falias. These Sages were sometimes also described as wizards or poets. Poetry was considered to be the highest art; therefore poets—and true poets were always Druids—were considered to be Sages, that is, well learned and wise.

From these four cities came the four treasures. Some say the Tuatha brought them, though the earliest texts are unclear on this, saying merely that the treasures were from the cities.

Often a question is raised about the actual location of these cities. The passage quoted above says that the Tuatha De Danaan came from "four cities in the North," yet magically speaking we consider them as the Four Directions. The question of their physical location is only really valid if one is considering the issue in an historic sense rather than a mythic one. As to whether the Tuatha can be considered as actual, physical human beings who invaded Ireland centuries ago, an idea which some scholars are seriously considering, that is a question which must be left to scholars and archaeologists. It does not concern us here as we are dealing with the Otherworlds. In this context, the term "North" may have represented that which was mysterious, far away, and "not of this world," similar to the way the Blessed Isles were always "to the West," and the Greeks referred to the Hyperborean lands, and places which were "beyond the North Wind."

Interestingly, the word *tuatha* itself, which is usually understood to mean "tribe (i.e., clan, bloodline, lineage)," or "people of a tribe," has also been translated to mean north. This seems to indicate that the most correct understanding of the word *tuatha* may encompass both meanings—north *and* clan-tribe-bloodline.

Traditionally, North is the direction of winter, darkness, destruction, and death. Mythically, these things must occur before the birth/rebirth of light and life in the spring. Therefore, the "Four Cities in the North" are the dark and mysterious sources of the Otherwordly wisdom whose magical treasures and wisdom were brought "to light" and to our realm by the Tuatha De Danaan, the Clan of the North, our Otherworldly Ancestors.

From Finias in the East was brought the Sword of Nuada, from which none escaped unharmed once it had been drawn from its sheath, and which none could resist. From Gorias in the South was brought the Spear of Lugh, against which no battle was ever sustained. From Murias in the West was brought the Cauldron of the Dagda Mor, from which no company ever went away unsatisfied. From Falias of the North was brought the Stone of Fal, which would cry out from beneath every rightful king.

Magically speaking, these treasures are the tools by which the power of each of these cities or convocations may be safely mediated into this world. As such, the particular powers of these cities are cognate with the four Elemental powers—Air, Fire, Water, and Earth—encountered in traditional magic.

Using material found in Irish oral tradition, author Fiona Macleod gives us a poetic account of this in his work *Iona*:

They had four cities at the four ends of the green diamond that is the world. That in the north was made of earth; that in the east of air; that in the south, of fire; that in the west of water. In the middle of the green diamond that is the world is the Glen of Precious Stones. It is in the shape of a heart, and glows like a ruby, though all stones and gems are there. It is there the Sidhe go to refresh their deathless life.[2]

In *The Little Book of the Great Enchantment,* he continues:

There are four cities that no mortal eye has seen, but that the soul knows; these are Gorias that is in the East, and Finias that is in the South, and Murias that is in the West, and Falias that is in the North. And the symbol of Falias is the stone of death, which is crowned with pale fire. And the symbol of Gorias is the dividing sword. And the symbol of Finias is a spear. And the symbol of Murias is a hollow that is filled with water and fading light.[3]

And again, from *The Divine Adventure:*

Wind comes from the spring star in the east; fire from the summer star in the south; water from the autumn star in the west; wisdom, silence and death from the star in the north.[4]

From these descriptions we may glean the useful information that correlates the Four Cities with the Four Directions and the Four Elements, but more importantly, we gain some beautiful imagery of the Faery Cities that we will visit in the course of our Faery Healing work. These cities may, in fact, become familiar territory, as they may be used quite frequently and in many ways.

By this point you may have noted that there seems to be an inconsistency or even contradiction in the lore quoted above regarding the Directions and the treasures of East and South. Sometimes the convocation of the East is said to be Gorias, and sometimes it is said to be Finias. Sometimes the treasure of Gorias is said to be the Spear of Lugh, and sometimes it is said to be the dividing Sword of Nuada. This seeming contradiction is similar to one in the Western Magical Tradition wherein the sword is sometimes said to be the magical tool of the East (Air), but sometimes it is said to be of the South (Fire). Not surprisingly, Fiona Macleod, whose writings are quoted above, was associated with the primary magical orders of his day, the late 19th and early 20th century, when this confusion was prevalent, and this could be why it is reflected in his writings.

In my book, *Wisdom of the Elements* (Crossing Press, 1998), I explain this discrepancy to the best of my ability (see Note 1 at the end of the chapter). The truth of the matter is that, on a practical, magical level, things seems to work equally well no matter which of these placements is used. Studying the matter, choosing what makes sense and feels right, and then working with it consistently are the most important factors.

In the exercises provided herein, I will go with the Moytura text and use the following correspondences:

East—Finias/Air/Sword of Nuada
South—Gorias/Fire/Spear of Lugh

If this does not feel right to you, please feel free to make the appropriate changes in your own workings.

In the original Irish texts, the word used to describe these places is "cathrachach." It appears to derive from "cathair," which means *city* in both old and modern Irish. A very similar Welsh word is "caer." However, what was meant by the word *city* then is not the same as what is meant now. A *city* was an area enclosed in or banked by stone. It might be a simple stone enclosure, or a fortress, a stronghold, a circular stone fort, perhaps even a castle. Therefore, one may assume that the intended meaning in this instance was that of four different, distinct, and demarcated places, with similarly distinct inhabitants, yet having similarity in that they were located "in the North," and were all places of magical learning.

Because of the difference between the archaic and modern concept of the word *city*, I have chosen to use the word *convocation* to refer to these cities. Convocation means simply a gathering, assembly, or council of beings; we may assume there is purpose or commonality to their assembly. When we go inworld to any of these cities we are going to one of the Convocations; but I will refer to all of them together, and the Glen of Precious Stones, as the Faery Convocation.

The particular imagery used in these journeys, while quite useful in giving us a "visual" and inspiring a "feel" for the particular convocation, is not really a necessity. Imagery itself is a structure for the energy of the place since the place itself is a subtle realm/state of consciousness. Recall, if you will, my comments about structure in *Chapter 15*.

If these images do not work for you, create your own based on the correspondences: the particular Element and Direction, and particular stream, quality, and feel of the energy of the place. In time, you may not need any visual imagery at all because you will have become so attuned to the energetic vibration of each of the cities that quickly calling up the correspondences will tune you to that vibration, allowing you to enter them at will.

Once you have done these journeys and experienced these places, you may repeat the journeys again and again, learning from the Faery King, Faery Queen, and Sage and exploring their realms. In these journeys I have depicted the sages with a specific gender. But in actual working you may find that the sages are not of the gender depicted in the journey; it is also possible that they may appear as either gender but feel to be androgynous.

As all things begin and end from the point of Center, we will start our journey through the Faery Convocation from its Center, the Glen of Precious Stones.

GLEN OF PRECIOUS STONES

> *They had four cities at the four ends of the green diamond that is the world. That in the north was made of earth; that in the east, of air; that in the south, of fire; that in the west, of water. In the middle of the green diamond that is the world is the Glen of Precious Stones. It is in the shape of a heart, and glows like a ruby, though all stones and gems are there. It is there the Sidhe go to refresh their deathless life.*

The Glen of Precious Stones is at the center of the Faery Realm and is the place where the Flame of Life burns within the Faery Hearth. As the place where, as Fiona Macleod says, "the Sidhe go to refresh their deathless life," it is, in fact, the heart center of the Faery Realm, and therefore, the *heart of the heart*. Its counterparts in our physical body are the heart and heart chakra, although since the Flame of Life also burns within each of our cells, each of them is also a little "hearth." The Glen is said to "glow like a ruby, though all the stones and gems are there," and this, too, tells us that it relates to the heart (usually thought of as red)—which is the center, the place where all things begin and end, and where the energies of above, below, and all Four Directions are united.

Work with the Glen of Precious Stones as the center of the Faery Realm for all Center type workings. The Glen is especially powerful because it *is* the Center—the heart/hearth—with the Flame of Life burning in its hearth and the power of the No

Green Diamond of Earth

Thing, the Void, residing within the heart of that flame. The Faery Hearth on your faery altar is the outer representation of this inner reality.

I do much of my Faery Healing work in the Glen, opening the Gateways to the Four Convocations, and inviting the Faery Allies of those Directions to come and assist me.

JOURNEY | To the Glen of Precious Stones

Settling comfortably before your Faery Altar, you light the Faery Hearth candle which is in the center of the altar... As you gaze at this center flame, breathing slowly in and out, you find that you are becoming more relaxed, calm, and serene with each breath. You focus your attention on the candle, then close your eyes, seeing the candle with your inner vision. As you do this, you feel yourself sinking down into the Earth, passing down through the surface layers of soil, sand and clay, and going down, deep, and deeper, into the Earth. The flame you are seeing in your inner vision grows larger and brighter, till finally you see that it is now burning within a large, burnished copper bowl, which sits atop an emerald studded stand. The flame reaches upward as far as the eye can see.

You gaze around, and see that gently rounded walls rise around you, sparkling with many-colored stones and crystals, which glow and gleam with light, now rosy, now ruby red, now shot with sparkles of emerald... You are within the heart-shaped Glen of Precious Stones, which lies at the heart center of the Faery Realm... and before you burns the fire of the Faery Hearth, the Flame of Being and Life as it is found in the Faery Realm.

You gaze into the flames of the Faery Hearth for a few moments, communing with the flame. Then you turn and notice that there are four gateways that lead from the Glen, going off in the Four Directions and leading to the Four Convocations of Finias, Gorias, Murias, and Falias. Each of the gateways is in the form of two slender trees whose branches have grown together and intertwined, forming an arch. Through each of these arched gateways you can see a different landscape...

You turn your attention back to the Glen of Precious Stones, and focus it on the flame within the Faery Hearth. As you watch the flickering of the flames, observing how high the flames reach, you become aware that they somehow seem to extend below the copper bowl and into the ground beneath, a strange thing indeed. You watch the flames, and notice that, although their predominant color is the usual red-gold, there are other colors present within them as well, all the colors of the rainbow, in fact, and these shift, shimmer, and flicker within the main body of the flames, changing hue and intensity as the fire burns. In the very center of this flickering fire you sense a complete stillness, and a consciousness so vast you cannot begin to apprehend it.

You spend a few moments communing with the flames, the stillness, and the vast consciousness... then you slowly withdraw your awareness from the Glen of Precious Stones, and find yourself moving upward through the Earth, and emerging into this time and place, from which you began your journey. When you have completely returned, you may open your eyes.

Be sure to record your journey in your Magical Journal.

Finias in the East

The word "Finias" is from the Celtic fin, which means "white, fair."[5] The Sage of Finias is named Uscias, and the Element is Air. The treasure or magical tool is the sharp, darkness-piercing Sword of Light.

JOURNEY | To Finias

Settling comfortably before your Faery Altar, you light the Faery Hearth candle which is in the center of the altar... As you gaze at this center flame, breathing slowly in and out, you find that you are becoming more relaxed, calm, and serene with each breath. You focus your attention on the candle, then close your eyes, seeing the candle with your inner vision. As you do this, you feel yourself sinking down into the Earth, passing down through the surface layers of soil, sand and clay, and going down, deep, and deeper, into the Earth. The flame you are seeing in your inner vision grows larger and brighter, till finally you see that it is now burning within a large, burnished copper bowl, which sits atop an emerald studded stand. The flame reaches upward as far as the eye can see.

You gaze around, and see that gently rounded walls rise around you, sparkling with many-colored stones and crystals, which glow and gleam with light, now rosy, now ruby red, now shot with sparkles of emerald... You are within the Glen of Precious Stones, which lies at the heart of the Faery Realm, and before you burns the fire of the Faery Hearth, the Flame of Being and Life as it is found in the Faery Realm.

You gaze into the flames of the Faery Hearth for a few moments, communing with the flame. Then you turn and notice that there are four gateways that lead from the Glen, going off in the Four Directions and leading to the Four Convocations of Finias, Gorias, Murias, and Falias. Each of the gateways is in the form of two slender trees whose branches have grown together and intertwined, forming an arch.

You choose the gateway which leads off to the East, whose leaves are a bright, vibrant green, and on whose limbs buds are just beginning to swell. You walk through the gateway and into a small deserted city set high in the mountains. It is chilly, and the wind is blowing. The old buildings seem to flash and gleam with a pale gold light, which casts a sunrise-like glow over everything. Looking around, you notice that what you had thought was a city is really not much more than a very large castle and several surrounding buildings. You are standing within the castle's large central courtyard. From your vantage point, you can see the craggy spires of the surrounding mountains, which stand out starkly against the brilliant sky.

You notice now that a mist has arisen and is filling the courtyard, its silvery greyness diminishing the red-golden glow. Yet, when it has filled the courtyard, the mist itself seems to fill with light. It gathers itself into a swirling, whirling vortex of brightly lit wind. This whirlwind spirals and whirls, and moves, flashing and gleaming across the large courtyard. As it approaches you, it slows... then stops. The vortex changes into a sphere of bright light, and you see, within the sphere, the light seeming to coalesce into the shapes of three beings—a man, a woman, and another person whose gender you cannot immediately determine. These beings step out from the bright light and walk toward you. You see that two of them are wearing rich and royal robes, and realize that these two are the Faery King and Queen of the Eastern Convocation of Finias. As they draw closer, you get a better look at the other person, and see that it is an old man wearing long, golden robes, and carrying a book. This is the Sage of Finias. All three of them are beings of bright, glowing light, and power seems to radiate and stream from them.

The King, Queen, and Sage of Finias stand before you now. The Queen is holding something in her hands, and as you look at it, you see that it is a sheathed sword. The King draws it forth from the sheath and holds it that you may look upon it. It seems to be made of silver and gold; the blade flashes with light in a pattern that resembles a lightning flash, and the hilt is decorated with tiny gems that flash and sparkle. You gaze upon it, and find arising within you a great desire to hold the sword. You look at the King and he nods his assent, so you take the sword in your hands and hold it. As you do so, you feel power flow forth from the sword and into you. You pause for a few moments to experience this....When it is finished, you hand the sword back to the King. You feel different, and you know that something has been transmitted to you, something that it will take some time to fully understand.

The Sage lays his hand upon your shoulder and draws you to one side. He opens the book he is holding, and holds it up that you may see that which is within. You see your name on the page before you, and bend closer to read what is written there... When you are finished, he closes the book.

The King, Queen, and Sage begin to move away from you now, and as they do so, the glowing mist and radiance around them increases until they seem to be encased in a sphere of light. The sphere begins to whirl; you can no longer see the figures inside of it as it whirls away and out of sight. After they have departed, a stillness descends upon the courtyard...

You turn now, and move back toward the gateway that leads into the Glen of Precious Stones. On this side, the tree gateway is set into the wall surrounding the courtyard and is covered with a profusion of tiny, bright green leaves. You walk through the gateway and into the Glen. Once inside the Glen, you pause before the Faery Hearth, and gaze at the flames... You spend a few moments communing with the flames, the stillness, and the vast consciousness... then you slowly withdraw your awareness from the Glen of Precious Stones, and find yourself traveling up through the Earth, coming up through the layers of rock, sand and soil, and emerging into this time and this place, the "now" from which you began your journey....You find yourself in a room where a candle burns... You allow yourself a few moments to completely return, and when you feel ready you open your eyes.

Be sure to record your journey in your Magical Journal.

Gorias in the South

The word "Gorias" is possibly from the Celtic *gor*, heat, which is related to the Indo European *ghara*, meaning heat, brilliance.[6] The Sage of Gorias is named Urias or Esras, and the Element is Fire. The treasure or magical tool is the Spear, which may be seen as a long, thin, sharply pointed piece of wood.

JOURNEY | To Gorias

Settling comfortably before your Faery Altar, you light the Faery Hearth candle which is in the center of the altar... As you gaze at this center flame, breathing slowly in and out, you find that you are becoming more relaxed, calm, and serene with each breath. You focus your attention on the candle, then close your eyes, seeing the candle with your inner vision. As you do this, you feel yourself sinking down into the Earth, passing down through the surface layers of soil, sand and clay, and going down, deep and deeper, into the Earth. The flame you are seeing in your inner vision grows larger and brighter, till finally you see that it is now burning within a large, burnished copper bowl, which sits atop an emerald studded stand. The flame reaches upward as far as the eye can see.

You gaze around, and see that gently rounded walls rise around you, sparkling with many-colored stones and crystals, which glow and gleam with light, now rosy, now ruby red, now shot with sparkles of emerald... You are within the Glen of Precious Stones, which lies at the heart of the Faery Realm, and before you burns the fire of the Faery Hearth, the Flame of Being and Life as it is found in the Faery Realm.

You gaze into the flames of the Faery Hearth for a few moments, communing with the flame. Then you turn and look at the four gateways that lead from the Glen, going off in the Four Directions and leading to the Four Convocations of Finias, Gorias, Murias, and Falias. Each of the gateways is in the form of two slender trees, whose branches have grown together and intertwined, forming an arch.

You choose the Southern Gateway, whose branches are covered with bright green leaves and many roses of many colors, in stages of growth ranging from bud to full flower. You walk through this rose gateway into a bright midday landscape, a verdant plain covered with the thick growth of grasses, plants, and flowers. Toward the center of the plain you see an area where many dark red roses bushes are growing, forming the pattern of a large circle. You walk toward the rose grove circle and enter it. You see that inside the rose grove a fire is set within a small circle of stones. It is burning merrily, and nearby, a wooden spear has been fixed into the ground, a crown of flowers hangs from the tip, fixed there by a thin leather strap.

As you approach the flame, it seems to increase in size, blazing up brightly and high, till its flames seem enormous and almost blinding. As you look upon it, some of the flames resolve into the shapes of three beings, and the Faery King, Queen, and Sage of the Southern Convocation of Gorias step through the fire and begin walking toward you. They seem to radiate a brilliant, glowing light that shimmers in streams from their bodies, surrounding them with a dazzling aura of light.

As they approach you, you see that the King is carrying a spear, similar to the one planted in the ground nearby, but the one he carries sparkles with bright light. The King carries his spear over to the other spear, and places it alongside it, and the two spears seem to melt into each other.

The spear now begins to glow brightly, sparkles of light emanating from it in all directions. You are standing close enough to be bathed in the light coming from the spear...

You look up at the crown of flowers hanging at the spear's tip, and see that the flowers are roses. The crown of roses begins to grow, leaves and vines spilling from the crown, till long tendrils of rose covered vines hang down around the spear. The Faery Queen plucks one of the roses, and hands it to you, and you put it close to your nose to sniff its glorious fragrance. As she does this, you become aware that you hear singing, as if from a distant choir of many voices...

The Sage reaches into the fire, and brings forth a small flame. He approaches you, and very carefully, he places this flame within your heart center. You feel it as it merges with your own inner flame, causing yours to leap up and expand in joy and recognition...

Now the Faery King and Queen place their hands upon their hearts for a moment. Then they place their hands upon your heart, and you feel a great burst of love being transmitted to you. After a while, they remove their hands from you. Then the King, Queen, and Sage move back to the fire, and step into it, merging with the flames, becoming flames, and vanishing from your sight.

You turn now, and walk out of the rose grove and into the grassy, flower-covered meadow, traveling toward the gateway that leads into the Glen of Precious Stones. You pass through the gateway, which on this side is thickly covered with leaves and flowers, and move into the Glen. You pause before the Faery Hearth for a few moments, communing with the flames, the stillness, and the vast consciousness... Then you slowly withdraw your awareness from the Glen of Precious Stones... and find yourself traveling up through the Earth... and emerging into this time and this place, the "now" from which you began your journey... You find that you have returned to a room where a candle burns on an altar before you... You allow yourself a few moments to completely return, and when you feel ready, you open our eyes.

Be sure to record your journey in your Magical Journal.

Murias in the West

The word "Murias" is possibly from the Celtic *muir*, sea, which is related to the Latin *mare*, meaning sea (or bitter sea, referring to the saltiness).[7] The Sage of Murias is named Semias, and the Element is Water. The treasure or magical tool is the Cauldron.

JOURNEY | To Murias

Settling comfortably before your Faery Altar, you light the Faery Hearth candle which is in the center of the altar... As you gaze at this center flame, breathing slowly in and out, you find that you are becoming more relaxed, calm, and serene with each breath. You focus your attention on the candle, then close your eyes, seeing the candle with your inner vision. As you do this, you feel yourself sinking down into the Earth, passing down through the surface layers of soil, sand and clay, and going down, deep, and deeper, into the Earth. The flame you are seeing in your inner vision grows larger and brighter, till finally you see that it is now burning within a large, burnished copper bowl, which sits atop an emerald studded stand. The flame reaches upward as far as the eye can see.

You gaze around, and see that gently rounded walls rise around you, sparkling with many-colored stones and crystals, which glow and gleam with light, now rosy, now ruby red, now shot with sparkles of emerald... You are within the Glen of Precious Stones, which lies at the heart of the Faery Realm, and before you burns the fire of the Faery Hearth, the Flame of Being and Life as it is found in the Faery Realm.

You gaze into the flames of the Faery Hearth for a few moments, communing with the flame. Then you turn and notice that there are four gateways that lead from the Glen, going off in the Four Directions and leading to the Four Convocations of Gorias, Finias, Murias, and Falias. Each of the gateways is in the form of two slender trees, whose branches have grown together and intertwined, forming an arch.

You choose the tree gateway which leads off to the West, and whose branches are covered with bright red-orange rosehips. You walk through the gateway, and onto a sandy seashore at twilight. No sun lights this sky, which is a deep azure rapidly fading into an even deeper turquoise. The first stars begin to appear in the sky, in strange and unfamiliar patterns. The whitecapped waves roll in to the shore, and then, pull themselves back out again, only to rise up and crash forward yet again. You sit on the sand for a while, watching the waves racing in, crashing on the shore, and then ebbing out again... You watch as each wave emerges from the vast moving body of the sea, separates itself into a separate form—a wave—while still joined to the body of the sea... You watch as the wave moves forward as an entity, seemingly on its own, expends its energy and form as it comes crashing to the shore, then ebbs slowly back out and rejoins the great, vast body of the sea. As you watch this happen, again and again, you become aware that this has gone on for countless eons of time, many cycles of the sun and moon, stars and seasons, and that its power has the strength to grind rocks into the sands of time.

From out of the depths of the sea, you see three beings emerge and begin to move toward you. The Faery King, Queen, and Sage of the Western Convocation of Murias rise up and move toward the seashore, walking through the sea foam and waves to the place where you are sitting. They are clothed in the blues, greys, and greens of the sea, their robes draped with seaweeds and shells. The Sage is a woman of mature years, her dark hair streaked with silver, her eyes a glowing and brilliant blue, as blue as the sea on a sunny day. You rise to greet them as they reach the tideline, and you stand there, at the spot where ocean gives way to land.

The Faery Queen is carrying a cup in one hand, the metal of which glints in the fading light. She reaches down as a wave rolls in, and fills the cup with water from the wave. With this water, she begins anointing you, touching head, heart, and shoulders. Each of these places links with the others, and you feel that you have been blessed with the Sign of the Most Sacred Cross. The feeling of the linking moves down into your generative organs, and you become aware of your connections with both your ancestors and your descendants... all of you joined by the amniotic waters of the sea of blood and time.

The Faery King reaches down into the waves and brings up some seaweed. He pulls off a piece of it, and begins feeding it to you. Your mouth is surprised by the seaweed's soft but strong texture, and its salty wet taste. You find yourself filled with a sharp awareness of the sea, and the creatures of the tidal zones who also feed on this seaweed. You feel a kinship with them...

Now the King, Queen, and Sage put their hands over your heart, and you feel something pass into you from them. It is like a wave of the sea. It moves into your heart, and it is carried by your heart's blood throughout your body and being... You feel your cells reaching out for it, absorbing it, utilizing it... This opens up a far memory in you, as you reach back into a distant past, and forward into a far future...

After a while, you become aware of your self again, standing on the shore, with the waves breaking in little eddies around your ankles, the King, Queen, and Sage of Murias standing before you...

They turn and begin to move back into the sea, walking out further and further into the breaking waves. Soon, a great wave comes… covers them… and then you can see them no more…

You turn, and walk back across the sand to the Western Gateway, which on this side seems to be made of a seashells and strands of variously colored seaweeds. You walk through it, and into the Glen of Precious Stones, where you stand before the Faery Hearth for a few moments, communing with the flames, the stillness, and the vast consciousness… Then you slowly withdraw your awareness from the Glen of Precious Stones… and find yourself traveling up through the Earth… and emerging into this time and this place, the "now" from which you began your journey… You find yourself in a room where a candle burns before you… You allow yourself a few moments to completely return, and when you feel ready, you open your eyes.

Be sure to record your journey in your Magical Journal.

Falias in the North

The word "Falias" is from the Celtic *fal*, stone, truth, destiny.[8] The Sage of Falias is named Morfesa, and the Element is Earth. The treasure or magical tool is the Stone.

The word *truth* in this definition is of the upmost importance. Stone is dense, solid, earthy, stable, and reliable. The stone most often associated with the Irish legends is the Lia Fail, or stone of destiny and truth, which would "cry out from beneath every rightful king." These few words convey a mighty reality, and that is that truth, destiny, and authentic kingship (i.e., sovereignty) were all linked with the resolute adamant of stone. Indeed, *truth* was one of the core values of Irish Celtic culture, and the king must be true—without blemish or fault—to be the true king. To be in harmony with truth is the highest of spiritual qualities. The stone, Fal, is representative of these things. As "earth of earth," stone is dense, yet representative of spirit in substance, the starlight within the darkness (as Fiona Macleod says) that is gestated in the Womb of Life, and ultimately, is birthed into being.

JOURNEY | To Falias

Settling comfortably before your Faery Altar, you light the Faery Hearth candle which is in the center of the altar… As you gaze at this center flame, breathing slowly in and out, you find that you are becoming more relaxed, calm, and serene with each breath. You focus your attention on the candle, then close your eyes, seeing the candle with your inner vision. As you do this, you feel yourself sinking down into the Earth, passing down through the surface layers of soil, sand and clay, and going down, deep and deeper, into the Earth. The flame you are seeing in your inner vision grows larger and brighter, till finally you see that it is now burning within a large, burnished copper bowl, which sits atop an emerald studded stand. The flame reaches upward as far as the eye can see.

You gaze around, and see that gently rounded walls rise around you, sparkling with many-colored stones and crystals, which glow and gleam with light, now rosy, now ruby red, now shot with sparkles of emerald... You are within the Glen of Precious Stones, which lies at the heart of the Faery Realm, and before you burns the fire of the Faery Hearth, the Flame of Being and Life as it is found in the Faery Realm.

You gaze into the flames of the Faery Hearth for a few moments, communing with the flame. Then you turn and notice that there are gateways that lead from the Glen, going off in the Four Directions and leading to the Four Convocations of Finias, Gorias, Murias, and Falias. Each of the gateways is in the form of two slender trees, whose branches have grown together and intertwined, forming an arch.

You walk through the Northern Gateway, whose intertwined branches are dry and brown, and covered with sharp thorns, and into a dark, but starlit, night. You are standing on one side of a large, bushy hedge, beyond which lies a tree-covered hillside. To the left you see an opening in the hedge, and as you begin to squeeze through it, you hear rustling in the brush, and can sense that there are wild animals around, hidden in the hedge, the trees, the shrubs, and darkness. As you make your way toward the other end of the hedge, you can see that the ground beyond it is littered with stones which seem to gleam dimly in the darkness. There is one, much larger, tall stone which gleams brighter than the rest; it seems to sparkle and flash with a purple-blue light.

You notice a faint gleam of light coming from an opening in the hillside just before you, and as you turn your attention to this, three beings emerge from inside the mountain, the Faery King, Queen, and Sage of the North Convocation of Falias.

As they approach you notice that the King is tall and sturdy, with dark brown hair and beard, and is wearing a short, dark green cloak under which you can see his rough brown tunic. The Queen is raven haired, with kind eyes, and is wearing a hooded cloak of a brilliant emerald green which covers her from head to foot. The Sage is an old woman with dark skin and a darker cloak. She is barely visible in the dark night aside from her silvery hair, but we can see a small rough cloth bag hangs from the sash at her waist.

Your path converges with theirs at the hedge's outer boundary. The Queen takes your hand, and leads you to the large, sparkling stone. She places your hands on the stone, and as you touch it, you become aware of a humming, a sound, a song, emanating from it, as well as an almost electrical feeling which makes your hands tingle slightly.

The King reaches out his hand and opens it to reveal an acorn. The Sage takes the acorn, then reaches into her bag and brings forth a bone. She touches both the bone and the acorn to the large stone, and they begin to glow with the same blue-purple light as the larger stone. The Sage hands you these two items, but to your surprise, they seem to melt into your hands, and you can feel their essence passing through into your body, and moving deeply into your bones.

Again, you become aware of a humming and singing sound, and now you hear that it is coming not just from the stone, but also from the stars overhead. You listen as the many voices sing a wordless song...

At length, the night falls silent again. The King, Queen, and Sage of Falias place their hands on you in farewell, then turn and walk back toward the faint light which gleams from the opening in the hillside. As they walk away, the standing stone flashes more brightly, its sparks lighting the surrounding area, and illuminating the hillside doorway into the faery mound. The King and Queen pause when they reach the doorway, they turn and smile at you, then step backward into the opening in the mountain. They turn and walk into the inside of the mountain, and are lost to your view.

When they are gone, the sparkles of light from the stone diminish....You turn and make your way through the hedge again, and back to the gate of thorns. You pass through it into the Glen of Precious Stones, where you stand before the Faery Hearth for a few moments, communing with the flames, the stillness, and the vast consciousness... Then you slowly withdraw your awareness from the Glen of Precious Stones... and find yourself traveling up through the Earth... through the layers of rock, sand and soil, and emerging into this time and this place, the "now" from which you began your journey... You find yourself in a room where a candle burns before you... You allow yourself a few moments to completely return, and when you feel ready, you open your eyes.

Be sure to record your journey in your Magical Journal.

ABOUT THE CENTER

Within the Faery Convocation information above, the Glen of Precious Stones marks the Center of the Faery Realm.

At the center of anything and everything is the spark of life; it is from the Center that all proceeds and to it that all returns. The Center can, and does appear in great variety of ways. Sometimes the Center is seen as a tall, pyramidal, often volcanic mountain; it is often seen as fire, or a tall pillar of light whose top and bottom cannot be detected. Sometimes the Center is seen as a single standing stone, a whirling vortex of wind, a beautiful rose, a deep well, or an enormous tree.

All of these ways give us subtly different approaches to the Center, emphasizing one or more of its aspects, which are many, since the Center represents both the No Thing and All Things. All of these ways are valid and useful.

One of my most powerful visions of the Center came in a dream wherein I beheld a circle of trees, within which was a clearing which held an enormous tree radiating forth a vast amount of power. Just above it a circular rainbow gleamed in pearlescent light, and below was a profusion of thick and gnarled roots. As I beheld it, I heard a voice calling me by my "true name." This tree was powerful beyond telling; words on a page cannot begin to describe it.

Another Center image that holds power for me is that of the rose, which retains its mysteries within the spiral of its tightly closed petals, then gently unfurls them to display its full beauty. What a lovely metaphor for the mystery of life manifesting from the point of origin and center. The rose has long been associated with the Goddess, in both her bright and dark forms.

I often use the image of a great, deep well to represent the Center. In Irish legend, the Well of Segais lies in the heart of the Otherworld, and has five streams flowing out of it and into the world. Around it grow the sacred hazel trees; they drop their ripened nuts into the water and the salmon of wisdom leap up to catch them.

The Well of Segais is said to be the source waters of the Boyne or sometimes the Shannon River. What this really means is that rivers—those magical sources of life-sustaining power—must certainly have their sources in the Underworld/Otherworld, since it is the origin of *all* power and life. The five streams flowing out from the well have been said to represent the five senses of seeing, hearing, tasting, touching, and smelling—the outreach into physicality of our innerworld powers of perception and connection.

My favorite Center imagery is that of a fire. It can be a simple fire, even a candle flame, a cheery hearth blaze, or it can be a great, leaping, roaring fire. Fire is a very direct gateway that leads into many worlds. Fire represents the spark of life, and thus it is truly at the center of everything, including the tree, the rose, the whirlwind, the stone, and the well. And within Fire's heart is the infinite speck of stillness, the center within the Center of all things, wherein lies the Void, or the No Thing, from which All Things proceed.

The Glen of Precious Stones, where, as Fiona Macleod says, "the Sidhe go to refresh their deathless life," is a very good image to use in working with the Center of the Faery Realm, as it so clearly represents the heart center—in ways both metaphoric and energetic.

The Glen is said to be in the shape of a heart and to glow like a ruby, though all the other stones are present as well. When I visit the Glen, I am always aware of a distinct green glow surrounding the ruby glow, as well as the rainbow flashes from the other stones.

Upon reflection I realized that the ruby and green glows were related to the heart center (the traditional heart chakra's colors are pink and green), and the other colors were related to the other chakras and their energies—similar to the way that the five rivers flowing from the Well of Segais are representative of the five senses. These sparkling gems represent the innerworld powers both as present within the Center-Origin point, and as they rush outward into manifestation through the rainbow gateways and frequencies of the chakras.

Two ways of traveling within the Faery Realm have now been given: the Great Tree and the Faery Convocations. While they have much in common, each has its unique uses.

The Convocations allow us to access the powers of the subtle Elements, and the beings who reside therein. The Great Tree allows us access to all Three Worlds, including the Four Convocations and its beings, but also the Underworld God, Goddess, the *Inner-Earth* beings, and the high beings above.

Going into the land, a tree, or a hill allows us a special flavor of Faery based on our locale. In this way we get acquainted with the spirits of our own particular locality—an important aspect of the work. To work with our own area in this way is a specific, rather than generalized form of the work, and one which can open us to receiving important instructions from the local Faery Beings relative to the health of the bio-region and what we can do to help.

Giving Back: Offerings to the Faeries and Land Spirits

It has always been customary to leave offerings for the faeries. Milk and cream and sometimes honey were traditional offerings in Wales, Ireland, and England, but sometimes bannocks, cakes, and other food were given.

Be sure that you maintain your part of the relationship you wish to have with the Faery Realm by making offerings of your energy, your love, flower essences, Reiki, and of things such as cookies, milk, cream, and the like. Allow yourself to be part of the reciprocal cycle of energies for each season.

Leave offerings for the faeries as a way of introducing yourself, and inviting them to enter your life. Leave offerings for them when you are asking for their assistance in your work, be it healing or other work. Leave offerings for them when you are out in nature, or picking a plant. Leave offerings for them just to please them, and to show them your love and kinship.

Remember that it is the *toradh* or essence of the food that they consume; therefore the unused material portion should be disposed of rather than consumed.

NOTES

1. As mentioned, this confusion between East and South is not new. Does the sword represent the light of truth and consciousness, or does the spear represent the light of truth and consciousness? Does the spear/wand represent the principle of life and growth, or does the sword represent the principle of life and growth? *Wisdom of the Elements* makes an attempt to explain the reasons for each side of the issue, but the conclusion is, as given above, that both perspectives will work.

END NOTES

1. Poynder, Michael, *The Lost Magic of Christianity: Celtic Essene Connections*, The Collins Press, Cork, 1997, p. 25.
2. Macleod, Fiona (William Sharp), *The Works of Fiona Macleod, Vol. IV, Iona*, William Heineman, Ltd, Long, 1927, p. 202.
3. ———— *Little Book of the Great Enchantment*.
4. ———— *The Works of Fiona Macleod, Vol. IV, The Divine Adventure*, William Heineman, Ltd, Long, 1927.
5. Pennick, Nigel, and Jackson, Nigel,, *The New Celtic Oracle*, Capall Bann Publishing, Berkshire, 1997, p. 167.
6. Ibid, p. 171.
7. Ibid, p. 175.
8. Ibid, p. 179.

CHAPTER 18

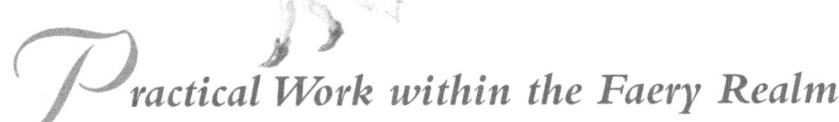

Practical Work within the Faery Realm

The last chapter provided information on means of coming and going in the Faery Realm, and this chapter will offer suggestions for some very practical work which may be done in conjunction with Faery Allies. But before we get to this, two important subjects must be addressed: the gathering of allies, particularly Faery Allies, and faery time, or how time works in the Faery Realm.

Alliance with the Faery Folk

At this point it is time to undertake one of the most important aspects of preparation for Faery Healing work, the acquisition of Faery Allies. These allies make the work possible. If Faery Beings choose to ally themselves with you, they will help you discover how to do the work, and will guide and assist you in doing it. You will find that they gift you with what you need in order to do particular jobs, and they will teach you as you go along.

You may find yourself working with many Faery Allies or perhaps only one. The number is not important. If you approach your healing work with love and sincerity, the beings who wish to help you will draw near; you will be given both who and what you need to do the job.

To find your Faery Ally or Allies, use the journey below. When doing this journey it is possible to discover that Faery Healing is not part of one's path. If this happens to you, please honor it. We all have different strengths and weaknesses, and various gifts. Perhaps the work of healing is not yours to do, or perhaps it is not appropriate at this time in your life. If that proves to be the case, do not be discouraged; you will find your way to your own spiritual work, never fear.

When doing the journey below, you will be asking this very important question, so listen carefully for the answer. If the answer is no, then give thanks for the clarity you've received, and return back to the Middleworld. Know that you may continue to journey to the Faery Realm, communing with the Flame and with the Faery Beings, as often as you wish. If you get the sense that Faery Healing is not appropriate in your life at this time, wait several months and go back and ask again. If the answer is yes, then proceed with the rest of the journey.

JOURNEY | To Find Faery Healing Allies

Settling comfortably before your Faery Altar, you light the Faery Hearth candle which is in the center of the altar... As you gaze at this center flame, breathing slowly in and out, you find that you are becoming more relaxed, calm and serene with each breath. You focus your attention on the candle, then close your eyes, seeing the candle with your inner vision. As you do this, you feel yourself sinking down into the Earth, passing down through the surface layers of soil, sand and clay, and going down, deep, and deeper, into the Earth. The flame you are seeing in your inner vision grows larger and brighter, till finally you see that it is now burning within a large, burnished copper bowl, which sits atop an emerald studded stand. The flame reaches upward as far as the eye can see.

You look around, and you see the sparkling crystal-studded, rounded walls around you. You know that you are within the heart-shaped Glen of Precious Stones, which lies at the heart-center of the Faery Realm, and that the flame before you is that of the Faery Hearth, the Flame of Being and Life as it is found in the Faery Realm.

You spend a few moments gazing into the Fire, appreciating it, communing with it. Since you are here for some very specific reasons, you now speak these into the fire.

First, you ask if the work of Faery Healing is a work that is yours to do, at this time, or even in the future. You still yourself and listen for an answer, which may come in the form of a word, a feeling, an image, or simply an inner sensing.

If the answer feels to be "no," give thanks for the clarity you have received, and after further communing with the Flame, return to your Middleworld the way you have come.

If the answer is "yes," give thanks for this clarity as well. You move to the gateways and open each of them in turn. Returning to the hearth-fire, you now ask that any Faery Healing Allies who are willing to help and guide you in your work now come forth.

After a moment, you are aware of beings who may appear as faeries, animals, or in any way they choose, coming to you through the open gateways. They cluster around you as you stand at the Faery Hearth, and you take note of their appearances, their "feel," and anything else noteworthy.

Now, each of them places one of their hands on one of your shoulders, then places the other hand over one of your hands. As soon as they do this, you feel energy pour into you from their hands, and you feel their hands melt into your own hand, as if your hand and theirs were merging into each other, becoming one. You feel their energy moving through you, and flowing out through your hands. These feelings spread throughout your entire body…

After a bit, this energy transmission feels to be finished….The beings remove their hands from you, and move back a short distance.

You reach into your pocket and find gifts for each of them, which you give to them. They receive the gift… and they look at them with wonder in their eyes… You have an understanding that when you need these Faery Beings for healing work, they will answer your call, because they have chosen to work with you as allies.

Your Faery Healing Allies move back through the gates of the Four Directions, back to their realms. You watch them as they depart… Then you turn your attention back to the Faery Hearth, and give thanks for your allies and the healing gifts they have provided. The Faery Hearth fire blazes up and becomes a gateway, and you step into it… The flames wrap around you, and blaze upward, carrying you up, and through the layers of earth, sand and soil, till you find yourself emerging into this time, this place, the place from which you began the journey… You find that you are in a room where a candle burns… You take a few moments to completely return, and when are ready, you open your eyes.

Be sure to record your journey in your Magical Journal.

You may also do this journey, and the ones to the Convocations, to ask for a Faery God or Goddess to help you in your Faery Healing work. Be advised, however, that they come when they will, and cannot be in any way commanded to appear.

Faery Allies are wonderful. But you must be aware that you have a right to question and refuse advice and information given to you by your Faery Allies, and indeed, any other spirit allies you may have—just as you would information from any other source—if that information or advice doesn't feel quite right to you. Just because we work with spirit allies doesn't mean we give away our self-authority and the right to have doubts and questions. When something simply feels wrong, or if you are in doubt, don't do it, especially if it is something you feel might possibly have detrimental consequences down the road.

Faery Time

Traveling in the Faery Realm brings up, once again, the subject of how time works in this place.

As we have previously mentioned, time seems to run quite differently in the Faery Realm than in our own, and this is because we are interacting with beings whose lifespans and experiences, and thus time perspectives and memories, are very different than our own. But in a sense, because this experience is so very different than our normal human perceptions of time, it allows us to move beyond time and into timelessness, a state of being where everything just *is*, existing in its own time, with no need to equate it to our own "personal" time.

Time is a relative thing in any case. While it seems to exist as part of our physical realm reality, our perceptions and experiences of it are something else again. We can look at a calendar, or the rising and setting of the sun, and mark off the days. This is time. We can look at the geological strata on the face of a cliff, and see another way of measuring time; or perhaps we can contemplate the lifespan of an ant, a bee, or a bacterium, and consider how different our time must be compared to theirs, if they indeed have time perception. Much of what we consider time is simply our own perception and experience of the flow of events. Who has not noticed the phenomena wherein the happy hours fly by, yet the time in the dental chair or a boring classroom drags on endlessly?

When working within the Faery Realm it is important to remember that our human time perceptions are not really relevant because we have entered faery time, which is, to our sense of time, fundamentally a timeless state of being. Since faeries are beings of the subtle innerworlds, their *timeless time* is more akin to stellar time (and stars live a very, very long time) than it is to our earthly solar time.

Because of this, the faeries see us differently than we perceive ourselves. We perceive ourselves as individual beings, but because of their different perspective, they are quite likely to see us as a totality composed of our genetic strands, our ancestry, and soul history.

Past, present, and future take on a different meaning in the innerworlds, and in a practical sense, healing energies may be sent backward in time as easily as forward in time because it is not time itself we focus on, but rather, the energetic threads which weave together to create past, present, and future.

Once again, this sounds more complicated and difficult than it turns out to be in actual practice. It is wise to refrain from trying to think all this out in an exclusively "mental" way, because it is not the mental realm with which we are dealing. Just be aware as you are working that time does not present a barrier to what you do, and that your intention is the important thing. When you are healing, send the energy to the past, present, or future, as your allies and intuition may guide you to do.

JOURNEY | Into the Stars within the Earth

Settling comfortably before your Faery Altar, you light the Faery Hearth candle which is in the center of the altar... As you gaze at this center flame, breathing slowly in and out, you find that you are becoming more relaxed, calm, and serene with each breath. You focus your attention on the candle, then close your eyes, seeing the candle with your inner vision. As you do this, you feel yourself sinking down into the Earth, passing down through the surface layers of soil, sand and clay, and going down, deep and deeper, into the Earth. As you feel yourself sinking downward, you notice that one (or more) of your Faery Allies has joined you, and is descending along with you.

You sink through the layers and levels of the Earth, moving easily through soil, sand, clay, pebbles, passing down, and down, and further down, till at length you come to rest in large cave beside a pool of dark water. You lean over the pool and gaze into its inky depths, and to your surprise, you see what appears to be a reflection of stars within the depths of the pool. Quickly you look above you, but see only the earth and rock of the cave's ceiling there... You turn back to look into the pool of dark water and look again at the stars. Some of them seem to form constellational patterns that appear familiar to you, but other of the patterns are unfamiliar...

As you gaze at the stars in the pool, it seems that the stars are beginning to move... Slowly at first, then a bit faster, they begin to move toward the left in a counterclockwise motion, circling around the pool of water. Their movement creates sparkles and streaks of light in the dark water... And as the stars move, you feel as if you, too, are beginning to move... It feels as though the counterclockwise motion of these swirling stars is pulling you along with it... You feel yourself being drawn backward, in a counterclockwise motion that first circles, then moves into an ever tightening spiral, drawing you inward... You allow yourself to experience this for a moment...

The motion seems to encompass not just space, you now notice, but time as well... Somehow, you feel as if your backward, counterclockwise spiral motion is spiraling you backward in time. Images of your current life flicker before you... and the seasons flash by... You have fleeting images and thoughts of yourself from years past.. and perhaps even from lives before this one...

You continue to be pulled back, spiraling in space and in time, spiraling around and inward, ever deeper inward... And strangely, at the same time you are aware of yourself moving in this inward spiral, you simultaneously feel your beingness both deepening and reaching upward as if you were expanding and contracting at the same time... Inward, yet outward, expanding, yet contracting... Until finally, you expand beyond measure, and contract beyond measure... and all space is one space, and all time is one time, and then... there is no time at all, but only the stillness after movement, the swirling stars in the dark water... and an awareness of your eternal Being... and the presence of your Faery Ally beside you, who seems to be part of you, as is all else...

As you reside in the stillness of this timeless state, you feel both the fullness and emptiness of this state of being... and you are aware of yourself as the One Being...

After a while, you feel your Faery Ally take hold of your hand. This movement gently shakes you from the timeless state of consciousness. You become aware that you are moving again... It feels as if you are moving slowly out from the center point, uncoiling in an outward moving direction, spiraling clockwise... and with this comes a change of awareness... You become aware again of time... and space... as you spiral outward... feeling as if you are being spun into existence once again...

Ever so gradually, you become aware of yourself in a cave... gazing into a pool of dark water, and at the sparkling stars within it, your Faery Ally by your side...

Your Faery Ally pulls on your hand, attracting you away from your fixed gazing into the pool of dark water. Your Faery Ally leads you around the pool to the other side of it, and this movement further breaks your state of reverie... As you reach the opposite side of the pool a winds sweeps through the cave, sweeping you off your feet and lifting you up into the air. You feel yourself rising higher and higher, floating gently upward... Then you begin to spin and spiral as you move to the top of the cave... The dark pool with its sparkling stars is far below you now... You come to the rocky roof of the cave and move through it... continuing to spiral clockwise up through the Earth, through layers of rock, sand, and soil, pushing upward like a seed unfurling itself skyward... till at length you come to the Earth's surface. You push through the crust of the Earth, and as you do so you find that your awareness and consciousness are returning to their normal, waking state of being... You find that you are returning to this time, this place... to a room where a candle burns... You allow yourself a few moments to return completely, and when you feel ready, you open our eyes.

Be sure to record your journey in your Magical Journal.

Practical Work Within the Faery Convocations

Now it is time to look at the kinds of healing and balancing work that can be done within the Faery Realm, and specifically, the Faery Convocations.

When doing this type of working, use one of the entrance journeys found in the preceding chapter. Once you have entered the Faery Realm, move into the specifics of your working by affirming your intention, calling your allies, and finally, opening yourself that the experience may unfold.

GENERAL WORK WITHIN THE FAERY CONVOCATIONS

Using the journeys given in this chapter and the preceding chapters, revisit each of the Convocations in turn, noting again the scenery, the beings, and the general feel of the place. On these journeys, you may make a special point of getting better acquainted with the Sage of each place by asking or just feeling what is to be learned and gained from the particular convocation, both in general, but also specifically with regard to Faery Healing. On other journeys you may do likewise with the Faery King and Faery Queen.

Record the results of these journeys in your Magical Journal.

SEASONAL WORK WITH THE CONVOCATIONS

Seasonal work is practical outerworld work, which might also be said to qualify as Faery Healing work.

In doing the seasonal work, it is important to simply listen to what the land is saying to us, and offer ourselves in service to mediate the energies to accomplish what is necessary for that particular cycle. Listen and learn the songs that want to be sung at each of these times of the year. The land, the river, the ocean, the trees, the plants—each of these will tell you about itself, who it is and what it is doing now. If we learn and sing these songs, we are helping them by contributing our loving energies (in addition to whatever practical things we might do as well, such as environmental cleanups).

Use the seasonal suggestions and one of the following journeys to do this seasonal work at the beginning of each season. If you wish to move into the convocation related to the Element and particular season of the year, use Journey #1. If you wish to do the work from the Glen of Precious Stones, use Journey #2. When you are more experienced, you may wish to utilize the simple Work Suggestion following the journeys.

Brigid/Spring is the time when the nature spirits are waking up and light is returning. The first green things are popping out in some places, the "when" depending, of course, on where you are living. New life is in the belly of the Earth, and is, like all babies, kicking hard, wanting to emerge.
Deities: Brigid, Olwen, the Green Man; all Spring Gods and Goddesses
Powers of: Beginnings, initiation, blooming forth, bursting forth at the end of the Tide of Cleansing

Beltaine/Summer is the time that faeries and nature spirits return in great numbers; they are quite active this time of year. This is a time of renewal, of restoration of plant life, of both the generation and flowering of plants.
Deities: Bel, Aine, all Summer Gods and Goddesses
Powers of: Blossoming, growth

Lughnasadh/Autumn is the time of full growth, harvest, and thanksgiving for the great abundance. Things are at their peak, but about to decline. As this season proceeds, the first harbingers of winter can be felt, even in the midst of the joy of the harvest.
Deities: John Barleycorn, Lugh, the Great Mother as Tailtiu (foster mother of Lugh), the Corn Mother, the Harvest Lady, all Autumn Gods and Goddesses
Powers of: Ripeness, fullness, harvest

Samhain/Winter is the time of endings, the harvest ending, of seeds falling, and of nature preparing to go to sleep for the winter; a time of slow down, and finally, decay. The energies so active on Earth's surface in spring and summer are now moving inward to the inner Earth where things are reversed (as in the Faery Realm). Plant energy moves into the roots, and Earth Mother's root children begin their winter sleep. Things are happening under the surface, within the land, during winter.
Deities: Morrighan, Cerridwen, the Cailleach, the Dark Goddess of the Underworld, the Lord of the Underworld (the Dark God); all Winter Gods and Goddesses
Powers of: Decline, endings, rest, repose, silence

Use each of these seasonal beginnings as an occasion and opportunity to renew the bond, the alliance between humans and nature, humans and the Faery Realm. Draw up Earth energy from Earth's core, and channel it out to the land—as well as to the rivers, lakes, ponds, plants, trees, and rocks. Remember that you, too, are part of it all, not separate. Each of these seasonal energy flows refers to you, as well.

JOURNEY | Seasonal Work #1

You settle comfortably before your Faery Altar, and light the Faery Hearth candle which is in the center of the altar... As you gaze at this center flame, breathing slowly in and out, you find that you are becoming more relaxed, calm, and serene with each breath. You focus your attention on the candle, then close your eyes, seeing the candle with your inner vision. As you do this, you feel yourself sinking down into the Earth, passing down through the surface layers of soil, sand and clay, and going down deep and deeper, and ever deeper, into the Earth.

At length, you find that you have come to rest in a clearing surrounded by trees. In the center of this grove is an enormous tree.

From its base, a mass of gnarled roots sprawl thickly over and into the ground; its wide-spreading branches form a canopy high overhead. There is an opening in the trunk that leads inside the tree's trunk. You walk into this opening and find that you are in a small cave, which is suffused with green golden light. The light seems to radiate from the rough wooden walls of the tree cave. As you observe this, the light seems to swirl toward you, and around you, and it begins to move you, whirling you, spiraling you downward into the ground, through the surface soil, and into the land itself. You pass easily through the many layers of soil and rock, moving downward with the green golden light, which whirls you round and round as it carries you downward. At last you land upon what feels to be soft earth...

You open your eyes and look around. Directly before you burns a fire within a hearth. The hearth is a beautiful large bowl of burnished copper, which rests upon an emerald studded stand. The flame reaches upward as far as the eye can see. You gaze around and see that gently rounded walls rise around you, sparkling with many-colored stones and crystals, which glow and gleam with light, now rosy, now ruby red, now shot with sparkles of emerald.

You realize that you are within the heart-shaped Glen of Precious Stones, which lies at the heart-center of the Faery Realm, standing before the fire of the Faery Hearth. From this Glen, four gateways—formed by the intertwined, arching growth of two slender trees—lead out into the Four Faery Convocations of Finias, Gorias, Murias, and Falias. You turn to look at each of them briefly, and through each arched tree gateway you can see a different landscape... You turn back to the Hearth and gaze into the flames.

You call now upon your Faery Allies, and ask that they be with you here, and assist you. Immediately, they come to you...

With your Faery Allies, you move to the Eastern (or Southern, Western, Northern) Gateway. As you do this, you feel the presence of the Faery hosts of the Shining Ones, the Tuatha De Danaan, and the King, Queen, and Sage of that Convocation, on the other side of the gate. You walk through the tree gateway and enter the landscape of this Convocation. Now you can see the Faery hosts who are there. They crowd around you, welcoming you. You speak to them, telling them what you want to do and you ask for their assistance.

In response, they lead you through the Convocation and to a place where there is a small building, which appears to be a chapel, very unpretentious in appearance... They lead you into the chapel, and up to the simple, unadorned, stone altar. On the altar is a sacred object. The object will be different in each Convocation, but it represents the pure, central power of the Element associated with that Convocation. In Finias you will find a spear of white light, shining brilliantly. In Gorias you will find small lamp, within whose crescent-shaped bowl a small flame burns. In Murias you will find a chalice or a cauldron filled with a sparkling liquid. In Falias you will find a large, beautiful stone, radiating with an inner light.

The Faery hosts surround the altar, and guide you to place your hands upon the object. Your Faery Allies group themselves beside and behind you, and place their hands on you while you do this...

As you look at the object, you can see waves of power emanating from it. You place your hands on the object, close your eyes, and allow yourself to really feel this power. The power moves into your body, permeating it completely. You feel as though the object has melted into your hands. When this happens, you find yourself filled with an awareness of your piece of Earth, the area in which you dwell. You see in your mind images of its contours, its mountains, valleys, rivers, oceans, its plants, and its animals. You feel the power of the sacred object move through your body and out the top of your head. As this happens, you seem to expand and become one with the power as it moves upward, and into the Middleworld. The power radiates upward and outward. It moves into the land, it permeates the land, the trees, the plants, forests, rivers, lakes, streams, and the animals. They are filled with it, till they, too, radiate and blaze with this power…

At length, you feel this process is done…and gradually your awareness returns to the chapel, and to the beings who surround you as you stand at the stone altar. You remove your hands from the object on the altar, and the Faery hosts now lead you from the chapel, through the land, and back to the gateway through which you arrived in their realm. You thank them… they turn and move off. You turn and step through the gateway, and back into the Glen of Precious Stones.

You spend a few moments communing with the fires of the Faery Hearth, and as you gaze within the flames, you see the land above and around you suffused with Spirit, glowing with life and vitality. You find that the green-gold light has begun to swirl around you again. It lifts you up, and swirls around and around, moving upward. You find yourself passing from the Glen of Precious Stones, and upward through layers of soil, roots, and pebbles, till finally you emerge once again upon the surface of the land, finding yourself in the place from which you had begun… You take a moment to return yourself to normal waking consciousness, and then you open your eyes. You are back.

Be sure to record your journey in your Magical Journal.

JOURNEY | Seasonal Work #2

You settle comfortably before your Faery Altar, and light the Faery Hearth candle which is in the center of the altar… As you gaze at this center flame, breathing slowly in and out, you find that you are becoming more relaxed, calm, and serene with each breath. You focus your attention on the candle, then close your eyes, seeing the candle with your inner vision. As you do this, you feel yourself sinking down into the Earth, passing down through the surface layers of soil, sand and clay, and going down, deep, and deeper, ever deeper, into the Earth.

At length, you find that you have come to rest in a clearing surrounded by trees. In the center of this grove is an enormous tree.

From its base, a mass of gnarled roots sprawl thickly over and into the ground; its wide-spreading branches form a canopy high overhead. There is an opening in the trunk which leads inside the tree's trunk. You walk into this opening, and find that you are in a small cave, which is suffused with green golden light. The light seems to radiate from the rough wooden walls of the tree cave. As you observe this, the light seems to swirl toward you, and around you, and it begins to move you, whirling you, spiraling you downward into the ground, through the surface soil, and into the land itself. You pass easily through the many layers of soil and rock, moving downward with the green golden light, which whirls you around and around as it carries you downward. At last you land upon what feels to be soft earth...

You open your eyes and look around. Directly before you burns a fire within a hearth. The hearth is a beautiful large bowl of burnished copper, which rests upon an emerald studded stand. The flame within it reaches upward as far as the eye can see. You gaze around and see the gently rounded walls which rise around you, sparkling with many-colored stones and crystals, which glow and gleam with light, now rosy, now ruby red, now shot with sparkles of emerald.

You realize that you are within the heart-shaped Glen of Precious Stones, which lies at the heart-center of the Faery Realm, standing before the fire of the Faery Hearth. From this Glen, four gateways—formed by the intertwined, arching growth of two slender trees—lead out into the Four Faery Convocations of Finias, Gorias, Murias, and Falias. You turn to look at each of them briefly, and through each arched tree gateway you can see a different landscape... You turn back to the Hearth and gaze into the flames.

You call now upon your Faery Allies, and ask that they be with you here, and assist you. Immediately, they come to you...

Now you move to the Eastern (or Southern, Western, Northern), Gateway and as you do so, you feel the presence of the Faery hosts of the Shining Ones, the Tuatha De Danaan, and the King, Queen, and Sage of that Convocation, on the other side of the gate.

You stand at the threshold of the gateway, and ask them to come in. When you say this, they begin to march through it and into the Glen of Precious Stones, assembling themselves around the Faery Hearth.

When they have all gathered there, you speak to them, telling them what you want to do, and you ask for their assistance. They may have suggestions to offer you, so listen carefully to the answers you are receiving.

Now bring your attention to the Faery Hearth and the flame that burns within. Watch and feel as the flame expands outward, encompassing you and all the beings who stand with you at the hearth. You feel your own inner flame blend with this larger flame, and you feel the inner flame of the other beings do likewise, until you aware of One Flame, which burns in many colors. You feel this flame burning in your heart, and radiating out of you at the same time. Your awareness expands and you allow yourself to be aware of the land around you and above you. As you do this, you feel the One Flame leap outward to encompass the land. You envision all the features of the landscape, and notice how their inner flames are touched and enlivened by the One Flame. You realize that the One Flame carries the energy and imprint of the primal and pristine land of the Faery Convocation within it, and these energies are now being planted and impressed into the land...

You sense when this is accomplished, and simultaneously, you become aware that the Faery hosts are moving back through the gateway, returning to their own realm. The gates grow misty and seem to fade from view. You return your attention to the fire that burns within the Faery Hearth, and as you gaze within it, you see the land above, below, and around you suffused with Spirit, and glowing with life and vitality. You find that the green-gold light has begun to swirl around you again. It lifts you up, and swirls around and around, upward; you find yourself passing from the Glen of Precious Stones, and upward through layers of soil and pebbles, till finally you emerge once again upon the surface of the land, finding yourself in the place from which you had begun... You take a moment to return yourself to normal waking consciousness, and then you open your eyes. You are back.

Be sure to record your journey in your Magical Journal.

Work Suggestion for Each Season

Go into the land, perhaps using one of the journeys given. Listen to the land, the trees, plants, the rivers, or other water source nearby. Listen to and ask to learn the songs of these beings, relevant to this season of spring (summer, autumn, winter), that you may sing them and by so doing lend energy to what they are doing.

Ask if there is anything else you can do to facilitate what is meant to happen next. Clean up any garbage lying nearby.

Bring up energy from the Underworld to help things sprout and grow (or whatever the season calls for), if that is what is asked. Go to the Glen of Precious Stones, tune into the Faery Hearth-fire, bring it up and through you, and into the land. Turn your attention to the East and the Convocation of Finias (Gorias, Murias, Falias). Walk through the Gateway into Finias

(Gorias, Murias, Falias). Go to the "Center" of Finias (Gorias, Murias, Falias), and allow the energy to move through you, and up into the land.

Using the Faery Convocations for Healing

The Four Faery Cities and the Glen of Precious Stones are quite useful in healing work. This fivefold template, complete with tools and elements, is of great value in both assessing the situation at hand and in providing tools with which to do healing work.

Below you will find journeys to each of the Four Cities. These journeys are similar to the ones given in the preceding chapter, but in this case you will interact with the Faery Kings and Queens for the purpose of being empowered with the gifts and treasures of that Convocation. Each of these treasures is actually a unique and powerful healing tool or modality, which can be used in your work.

EMPOWERMENT JOURNEYS TO THE FOUR CONVOCATIONS

Use the journeys below to travel to the Convocations specifically to receive gifts to enable your Faery Healing work.

> **JOURNEY** | **Empowerment Journey to Finias**
>
> Settling comfortably before your Faery Altar, you light the Faery Hearth candle which is in the center of the altar... As you gaze at this center flame, breathing slowly in and out, you find that you are becoming more relaxed, calm, and serene with each breath. You focus your attention on the candle, then close your eyes, seeing the candle with your inner vision. As you do this, you feel yourself sinking down into the Earth, passing down through the layers of soil, sand and rock, and going down, deep and deeper, into the Earth. The flame you are seeing in your inner vision grows larger and brighter, till finally you see that it is now burning within a large, burnished copper bowl, which sits atop an emerald studded stand. The flame reaches upward as far as the eye can see.
>
> You gaze around, and see that gently rounded walls rise around you, sparkling with many-colored stones and crystals, which glow and gleam with light, now rosy, now ruby red, now shot with sparkles of emerald... You are within the Glen of Precious Stones which lies at the heart of the Faery Realm, and before you burns the fire of the Faery Hearth, the Flame of Being and Life as it is found in the Faery Realm.

You gaze into the flames of the Faery Hearth for a few moments, communing with the flame. Then you turn and notice that there are four gateways that lead from the Glen, going off in the Four Directions and leading to the Four Convocations of Finias, Gorias, Murias, and Falias. Each of the gateways is in the form of two slender trees, whose branches have grown together and intertwined, forming an arch.

You choose the gateway which leads off to the East, whose leaves are a bright, vibrant green, and on whose limbs buds are just beginning to swell. You walk through the gateway, and into a small deserted city set high in the mountains. It is chilly, and the wind is blowing. The old buildings seem to flash and gleam with a golden light, which casts a golden red sunrise-like glow over everything. Looking around, you notice that what you had thought was a city is really not much more than a very large castle and several surrounding buildings. You are standing within the castle's large central courtyard. From your vantage point, you can see the craggy spires of the surrounding mountains, which stand out starkly against the brilliant sky.

You notice now that a mist has arisen and is filling the courtyard, its silvery greyness diminishing the red golden glow. Yet, when it has filled the courtyard, the mist itself seems to fill with light. It gathers itself into a swirling, whirling vortex of brightly lit wind. This whirlwind spirals and whirls, and moves, flashing and gleaming across the large courtyard. As it approaches you, it slows... then stops. The vortex changes into a sphere of bright light, and you see, within the sphere, the light seeming to coalesce into the shapes of two beings, a man and a woman. These beings step out from the bright light and walk toward you. You see that they are wearing crowns, and rich and royal robes, and you realize that they are the Faery King and Queen of the Eastern Convocation of Finias. They are beings of glowing, bright light, and power seems to radiate and stream from them.

When they reach you, they stop for a moment, and look at you steadily. Then they reach out their hands to touch you, and you feel yourself whirling and spiraling as if in the vortex, even while you seem to stand there before them. You feel the power of the Element of Air rush through you, whirling through every part of you in little spirals which gather up and blow out of you all that is no longer needed...

As these blow up toward your throat, you feel the energy in your throat center open up... and as the spirals blow and spiral around your heart, you feel your heart center open, that you may speak your truth with conviction and power... As the spirals move through you, cleansing and opening you, you become aware that another power is filling your body, a power that moves through you in spirals, power which pours forth from you through hands, head, and heart... This is the power of Air, and the ability to use the Faery Winds to blow clean that which needs cleansing... This is also the power of sound—speaking, singing, whistling, chanting, and blowing of air to move energy... This also is the power of the treasure of Finias, which is the sword that pierces through darkness and allows in light... and pierces through confusion to allow in truth... You feel this Sword now in your hands, and you know that you can use it to open things and situations that need opening in order to be cleansed, and that you can also use it to cut away that which is no longer needed.

And all the while, the tiny spirals of wind sweep through you like small tornadoes, cleansing, clearing, shearing away, and bringing a sense of regeneration in their wake...

Finally, this process slows down... and after a bit, it feels complete. The wind dies down. The King and Queen move away from you now, and as they do so, the glowing mist gathers around them until they seem to be encased in a glowing sphere of light. The sphere begins to whirl; you can no longer see the figures inside of it as it whirls away and out of sight. After they have departed, a stillness descends upon the courtyard...

You turn and move back toward the gateway which leads into the Glen of Precious Stones. On this side the tree gateway is set into the wall that surrounds the courtyard, and is covered with a profusion of tiny, bright green leaves. You walk through the gateway and into the Glen. Once inside the Glen, you pause before the Faery Hearth, and gaze at the flames... You spend a few moments communing with the flames, the stillness, and the vast consciousness... then you slowly withdraw your awareness from the Glen of Precious Stones... and find yourself traveling up through the Earth... coming up through the layers of rock, sand and soil, and emerging into this time and this place, the "now" from which you began your journey... You find yourself in a room where a candle burns before you... You allow yourself a few moments to completely return... and when you feel ready, you open your eyes.

Be sure to record your journey in your Magical Journal.

JOURNEY | Empowerment Journey to Gorias

Settling comfortably before your Faery Altar, you light the Faery Hearth candle which is in the center of the altar... As you gaze at this center flame, breathing slowly in and out, you find that you are becoming more relaxed, calm, and serene with each breath. You focus your attention on the candle, then close your eyes, seeing the candle with your inner vision. As you do this, you feel yourself sinking down into the Earth, passing down through the layers of soil, sand and rock, and going down, deep and deeper, into the Earth. The flame you are seeing in your inner vision grows larger and brighter, till finally you see that it is now burning within a large, burnished copper bowl, which sits atop an emerald studded stand. The flame reaches upward as far as the eye can see.

You gaze around, and see that gently rounded walls rise around you, sparkling with many-colored stones and crystals, which glow and gleam with light, now rosy, now ruby red, now shot with sparkles of emerald... You are within the Glen of Precious Stones which lies at the heart of the Faery Realm, and before you burns the fire of the Faery Hearth, the Flame of Being and Life as it is found in the Faery Realm.

You gaze into the flames of the Faery Hearth for a few moments, communing with the Flame. Then you turn and notice that there are four gateways that lead from the Glen, going off in the Four Directions and leading to the Four Convocations of Finias, Gorias, Murias, and Falias. Each of the gateways is in the form of two slender trees, whose branches have grown together and intertwined, forming an arch.

You choose the Southern Gateway, whose branches are covered with bright green leaves and many roses of many colors, in stages of growth ranging from bud to full flower. You walk through this rose gateway into a bright midday landscape, a verdant plain covered with a thick growth of grasses, plants, and flowers. Toward the center of the plain you see an area where many dark red roses bushes are growing, forming the pattern of a large circle. You walk toward the rose grove circle and enter it. You see that inside a fire is set within a small circle of stones. It is burning merrily, and nearby, a wooden spear has been fixed into the ground by its sharp point, a crown of flowers hangs from its top, fixed there by a thin leather strap.

As you approach the flame, it seems to increase in size, blazing up brightly and high till its flames seem enormous, and almost blinding. As you look upon it, the flames resolve into a gateway, and the Faery King and Queen of the Southern Convocation of Gorias step out of the gateway, and begin walking toward you. They seem to blaze with a brilliant, glowing light that streams from their bodies in radiant, shimmering ribbons and surrounds them with a dazzling aura of light.

Standing before you, they reach their radiant, bright hands out to you, and touch you upon the head. At their touch, you feel their immense energy and power jolt into your body like a lightning strike, and it begins to course through you with a powerful electric surge. It races through every part of your body, and you feel it especially as it pours out through your hands and fingertips. This is the gift of Gorias, the power of the healing fire, the Faery Fire, and it now flows through you with a special intensity, a gift from the King and Queen.

You feel a need to touch your hands to something, to use this immense power, so you touch the wooden spear that stands nearby… As you do so, you feel the power rush forth from your hands. You can almost see it as it flows in seemingly inexhaustible supply from your hands and into the spear's wooden handle, which instantly shoots upward, roots downward and bursts into leaf, then blossom, then fruit, as you watch… This, also, is the power of the treasure of Gorias, another manifestation of the fire, the power of growth, creativity, and life springing forth. Yet fire both creates and destroys, and you know that this power misused could burn the wooden handle to ash.

You become aware again of the Faery Fire as it circulates throughout your body… nourishing and rekindling your own inner fires… and you open yourself to experience this fully for a few moments… After a while, this feels complete. You look up, and find the Faery King and Queen watching you with a loving smile.

The Faery King and Queen now place their hands upon their hearts for a moment, and then place their hands upon your heart. You feel a great burst of love being transmitted to you from them… After a while, they remove their hands from you… Then the King and Queen move back to the fire, and step into it, merging with the flames… becoming flames… and vanishing from your sight.

You turn now, and walk out of the rose grove and into the grassy, flower-covered meadow, traveling toward the gateway that leads into the Glen of Precious Stones. The gateway on this side is thickly covered with leaves and flowers… You pass through the gateway and into the Glen… You pause before the Faery Hearth for a few moments, communing with the flames, the stillness, and the vast consciousness… Then you slowly withdraw your awareness from the Glen of Precious Stones… and find yourself traveling up through the Earth… through the layers of rock, sand and soil… and emerging into this time and this place… the "now" from which you began your journey… You find yourself in a room where a candle burns before you. You allow yourself a few moments to completely return, and when you feel ready you open your eyes.

Be sure to record your journey in your Magical Journal.

JOURNEY | Empowerment Journey to Murias

Settling comfortably before your Faery Altar, you light the Faery Hearth candle which is in the center of the altar... As you gaze at this center flame, breathing slowly in and out, you find that you are becoming more relaxed, calm, and serene with each breath. You focus your attention on the candle, then close your eyes, seeing the candle with your inner vision. As you do this, you feel yourself sinking down into the Earth, passing down through the layers of soil, sand and rock, and going down, deep and deeper, into the Earth. The flame you are seeing in your inner vision grows larger and brighter, till finally you see that it is now burning within a large, burnished copper bowl, which sits atop an emerald studded stand. The flame reaches upward as far as the eye can see.

You gaze around, and see that gently rounded walls rise around you, sparkling with many-colored stones and crystals, which glow and gleam with light, now rosy, now ruby red, now shot with sparkles of emerald... You are within the Glen of Precious Stones which lies at the heart of the Faery Realm, and before you burns the fire of the faery hearth, the Flame of Being and Life as it is found in the Faery Realm.

You gaze into the flames of the Faery Hearth for a few moments, communing with the flame. Then you turn and notice that there are four gateways that lead from the Glen, going off in the Four Directions and leading to the Four Convocations of Finias, Gorias, Murias, and Falias. Each of the gateways is in the form of two slender trees, whose branches have grown together and intertwined, forming an arch.

You choose the tree gateway which leads off to the West, and whose branches are covered with bright, red-orange rosehips. You walk through it and onto a sandy seashore at twilight. No sun lights this sky, which is a deep azure rapidly fading into an even deeper turquoise. The first stars begin to appear in the sky, in strange and unfamiliar patterns. The whitecapped waves roll in to the shore, and then pull themselves back out again, only to rise up and crash forward yet again... You sit on the sand for a while, watching the waves racing in, crashing on the shore, and then ebbing out again. You watch as each wave emerges from the vast, moving body of the sea, separates itself into a separate form—a wave—while still joined to the body of the sea. You watch as the wave moves forward as an entity, seemingly on its own, expends its energy and form as it comes crashing to the shore, then ebbs slowly back out and rejoins the great vast body of the sea. As you watch this happen, again and again, you become aware that this has gone on for countless eons of time, many cycles of sun and moon, stars and seasons.

From out of the depths of the sea two beings emerge. The Faery King and Queen of the Western Convocation of Murias rise up and move toward the seashore, walking through the sea foam and waves to the place where you are sitting. They are clothed in the blues, greys, and greens of the sea, their robes draped with seaweeds and small shells. The Faery Queen is carrying a cup in one hand, the metal of which glints in the fading light. You rise to greet them as they reach the tideline… The Queen sets the cup down in the sand.

The King and Queen of Murias reach out their hands and touch you, and you are filled with the power of the sea, and of all waters… You feel it flow through you, rushing like a cleansing torrent… The Queen picks the cup up from the sand, and she offers it to you, and you sip from it… then drink down all that is within… As its contents go down inside of you, you are filled with a feeling of healing and well-being… You feel it wash down and through you, flowing through your entire body, through all the tissues and cells, bringing warmth or coolness, as needed, to the different parts of your being… At the same time you become aware that you feel these cleansing waters are flowing over you as well, head to toe, washing and splashing over your body, as if a wave had broken over your head… You feel washed clean, baptized, blessed. As the essence of the water's healing powers sinks down inside your body, it flows along with your blood, to all parts of your body; even joining with the cellular fluid in your cells… There is renewal in this water, there is the love of the mother in this water, and, strangely, there is the sense of time's passages in this water. And everywhere it touches, you are healed, balanced, cleansed, blessed, for these are the waters of healing which cool the burn, chill the anger, and soothe the wounds of mind, body, and heart. These are the waters of time, which flow ever onward bringing change and a new cycle of life.

After a while, you become aware of your self again, standing on the shore, with the waves breaking in little eddies around your ankles, the King and Queen Murias standing before you.

The cup is still in your hands, and as you hand it back to the King and Queen, you know that it is always available to you when you need it. You can use it when you have need of it, to cleanse, to bless, to soothe, to nourish, and to heal…

The King and Queen smile at you… Then they turn and begin to move back into the sea… walking out further and further into the breaking waves. Soon, a great wave comes… it covers them… and then you can see them no more…

You turn, and walk back across the sand to the Western Gateway, which on this side seems to be made of seashells and strands of variously colored seaweeds… You walk through it, and into the Glen of Precious Stones...where you stand before the Faery Hearth for a few moments, communing with the flames, the stillness, and the vast consciousness... Then you slowly withdraw your awareness from the Glen of Precious Stones... and find yourself traveling up through the Earth... through the layers of rock, sand and soil... and emerging into this time and this place... the "now" from which you began your journey... You find yourself in a room where a candle burns before you. You allow yourself a few moments to completely return, and when you feel ready, you open your eyes.

Be sure to record your journey in your Magical Journal.

JOURNEY | Empowerment Journey to Falias

Settling comfortably before your Faery Altar, you light the Faery Hearth candle which is in the center of the altar... As you gaze at this center flame, breathing slowly in and out, you find that you are becoming more relaxed, calm, and serene with each breath. You focus your attention on the candle, then close your eyes, seeing the candle with your inner vision. As you do this, you feel yourself sinking down into the Earth, passing down through the layers of soil, sand and rock, and going down, deep and deeper, into the Earth... The flame you are seeing in your inner vision grows larger and brighter, till finally you see that it is now burning within a large, burnished copper bowl, which sits atop an emerald studded stand. The flame reaches upward as far as the eye can see.

You gaze around, and see that gently rounded walls rise around you, sparkling with many-colored stones and crystals, which glow and gleam with light, now rosy, now ruby red, now shot with sparkles of emerald... You are within the Glen of Precious Stones, which lies at the heart of the Faery Realm, and before you burns the fire of the Faery Hearth, the Flame of Being and Life as it is found in the Faery Realm.

You gaze into the flames of the Faery Hearth for a few moments, communing with the flame. Then you turn and notice that there are four gateways that lead from the Glen, going off in the Four Directions and leading to the Four Convocations of Finias, Gorias, Murias, and Falias. Each of the gateways is in the form of two slender trees, whose branches have grown together and intertwined, forming an arch.

You walk through the Northern Gateway, whose intertwined branches are dry and brown, and covered with sharp thorns, and into a dark, but starlit night. You are standing on one side of a large, bushy hedge, beyond which lies a tree-covered hillside. To the left you see an opening in the hedge, and as you begin to squeeze through it, you hear rustling in the brush, and can sense that there are wild animals around, hidden in the hedge, the trees, the shrubs, and darkness. As you make your way toward the other end of the hedge, you can see that the ground beyond it is littered with stones, which seem to gleam dimly in the darkness. There is one, much larger, tall stone which gleams brighter than the rest; it seems to sparkle and flash with a purple-blue light.

You notice a faint gleam of light coming from an opening in the hillside just before you, and as you turn your attention to this, two beings emerge from inside the mountain, the Faery King and Queen of the Northern Convocation of Falias…

As they approach you notice that the King is tall and sturdy, with dark brown hair and beard, and is wearing a short, dark-green cloak under which you can see his rough brown tunic. The Queen is raven haired, with kind eyes, and is wearing a hooded cloak of a brilliant emerald green which covers her from head to foot.

You see that they are carrying some things with them—antlers, stones, bones, herbs. You walk toward them, and your path converges with theirs at the hedge's outer boundary, beside a small rosebush which has but one small rosebud upon it. As you look at it, this rosebud begins to open and bloom… until it has become a full, mature rose. Then the petals begin to drop off and the center swells itself into a round orangish rosehip. The rosehip continues to swell, then begins to harden. The Faery Queen picks the rosehip from the bush, splits it open with her fingernails, and hands it to you to eat. The Faery King is holding antlers, and now he raises them up to the sides of your head, and presses them into place. The sharp tang of the rosehip is on your tongue, and your head feels heavy with the unaccustomed weight of the antlers. You spend a few moments feeling this, and feeling for the meaning of these gifts which you have been given.

The King and Queen watch and wait while you do this. Then they look at each other for a moment… The King hands you the stones and bones he is carrying, and the Queen hands you the herbs… They bring forth a green tunic, and place it over your shoulders. You know that all of these things are gifts, tools to be used for healing.

As you take each of these gifts in turn, the energy of each seems to move within you, and become part of you. The King and Queen now place their hands upon your head and shoulders, and you feel the power rushing forth from them and into your body. The power that rushes into your body, through flesh, blood, bones, and cells, is one with many strands and flavors to it. It is the power of deep knowing; the power of utilizing the gift of the inner element of Earth, that of working with structures and forms and limitations; it is the power of utilizing for healing and wholeness the gifts of the substance world.

There is a subtle teaching here, too, one that flows into your mind, yet you must open your mind and heart to receive and understand it. The Faery King and Queen tell you that humans are of help and value to the world of Faery. Faeries learn from humans, just as humans learn from faeries. When humans exchange information and energies with faeries, both sides benefit. They need humans, just as humans need them. They do the work that nature has given them to do; yet, their own course of evolution requires a relationship with the other realms and other beings just as does yours. By exchanging energy and gifts with them, humans give them something they need of Earth's physical substance, that they may partake of its essence and learn and grow from it. They give humans the fullness of the subtle aspect of these things, as well as their wisdom and other subtle gifts, that humans may learn and grow.

They appreciate it greatly when humans make the choice to consciously interact with them, when we give them gifts and offerings from our world, when we allow them to touch us and work with and through us, and when we thank them in very substantial ways, such as planting, tending, and watering trees, shrubs, flowers, and herbs. They ask that we be aware that when we work with herbs, stones, and the like, that we are working with them and the gifts they give us, and to be aware of them as we do so.

Now the Faery King and Queen remove their hands from you…

They turn, and walk back toward the faint light which gleams from the opening in the hillside. As they pass the standing stone, it flashes more brightly and its sparks light the surrounding area, illuminating the hillside doorway into the faery mound. The King and Queen pause when they reach the doorway, they turn and smile at you, then step backward into the opening in the mountain. They turn and walk into the inside of the mountain, and are lost to your view.

When they are gone, the sparkles of light from the stone diminish… You turn and make your way to the gate of thorns. You pass through it into the Glen of Precious Stones, where you stand for a few moments before the Faery Hearth, communing with the flames, the stillness, and the vast consciousness. Then you slowly withdraw your awareness from the Glen of

Precious Stones, and find yourself traveling up through the Earth, through the layers of rock, sand and soil, and emerging into this time and this place, the "now" from which you began your journey. You find yourself in a room where a candle burns before you. You allow yourself a few moments to completely return, and when you feel ready, you open your eyes.

Be sure to record your journey in your Magical Journal.

THE TREASURES OF THE FAERY CONVOCATION

Each of the treasures/tools brought from these convocations, presumably by the Tuatha De Danann, can be utilized as a healing tool. The Faery inhabitants of each city, particularly its King, Queen, and Sage, can be invaluable allies in the healing process.

Rather than give exact and specific instructions on how to make use of the energies of each convocation in healing, I will provide you with a list of correspondences, thoughts, and ideas that will help you formulate your own approach. In addition to what is provided below, further information for this is provided in the last chapter of this section.

Finias in the East

Finias is associated with the Element of Air, and therefore, with the mental realm of thoughts and ideas. The tool is the sword/blade. This may be used for cutting energy cords that need cutting, for lancing (on the subtle realms) infected wounds and abscesses, as well as for lancing open and revealing a situation or problem to see its inner aspects. Known as the Sword of Truth, it also represents the "radiance of consciousness," according to Pennick & Jackson's *Celtic Oracle*. Blades, of course, can also be instruments of pain and sacrifice; healing usually involves sacrificing some aspect of the self—often painfully—in order that health and new growth may occur.

Gorias in the South

Gorias is associated with the Element of Fire, and therefore, with the realm of spirit, soul, creativity, and growth, and the faculties of will and intention. The tool is the spear/staff, which represents the power of growth—although spear and staff, like growth, can both hurt and heal. This Staff of Life or Spear of Lugh, which can also take the image of lightning crackling down from the sky, represents the power of dynamic, outwardly moving energy, the projective power of the directed will.

Murias in the West

Murias is associated with the Element of Water, and therefore with the realm of emotion and feeling. The tool is the chalice, cup, cauldron, and all vessels, as well as their fluidic/watery contents. The power of water is the power of the rhythmic tides, and by association, all rhythmic tides and cycles. It is also the power of love and compassion, and the Direction of West brings in the time of fulfillment and harvest. Chalices, cauldrons, and cups hold and contain energies, and water is known to "hold memory." This is the basis of flower essences and other water-based energetic medicines. The Cauldron of Dagda was one of fullness, and of plenty. The Cauldron of Cerridwen was one of transformation, initiation, and regeneration. A vessel can be used to brew potions of healing, nourishment, and magic, as well as being a container from which to drink them and the fruits of whatever we are harvesting. We may also use the cup to drink in the accumulated wisdom of the Otherworlds (always found in the West). No one goes away from the cauldron or cup unsatisfied.

Falias in the North

Falias is associated with the Element of Earth, and therefore with the most dense of the realms, that of the physical, with its attributes of matter, structure, form, and its inherent limits. The tools are the stone and the mirror. The Stone of Destiny, which cried out when the rightful king was upon it, is a stone of *truth*. Stones hold the crystalline power of light. They hold energies and memory and can be used to establish and set a pattern, which can be imprinted into the stone by intention and ritual. Therefore, they lend themselves easily to the making of talismans and amulets that contain patterns of intentions/truth. The mirror, which is used to see situations and truths that need to be seen in order for healing and regeneration to occur, can also be used to see ourselves as others see us.

In *Chapter 19* we will cover another aspect of how the four Directional/Elemental powers may be used in healing.

CHAPTER 19

Coming From a Place of Love

There are some interesting relationships between the nature realm, the faery realm, and our own human emotional energies. It is important to be aware of these as we do this work.

Beauty, Love, Joy, and Gratitude
BEAUTY

It is said that beauty is in the eye of the beholder, and in a sense that is quite true. However, beyond that very subjective definition, a more objective one might state that beauty has to do with an innate, inherent order, symmetry, and harmony which pleases the soul and calls forth feelings of satisfaction, pleasure, and "rightness." When we create beauty—by song, dance, poetry, art, kindness, love, and our loving and kind thoughts and deeds—we are creating a vibration of harmony and order that ripples out and affects what is around it. When we surround ourselves with beauty, especially by spending time out in nature, we are immersing ourselves in its vibration of beauty.

The term "Beauty Path" was used by certain Native American cultures to describe a way of living in which there was a constant awareness of beauty and harmony, and in which actions were first considered and then taken with these principles foremost in the mind. The term is very appropriate for use in relationship to Faery Healing. Much magical work, particularly that having to do with the Faery Realm, may be described as work on the Beauty Path, since its underlying intention is to create harmony, wholeness, right relationship with the other beings (including the faeries and other subtle beings), and thus beauty.

LOVE, JOY, AND GRATITUDE

Unconditional love and deep joy are the currencies of the Faery Realm, and the nature spirit realm as well. As we behold the magnificence of nature, we find gratitude arising within us, born of the recognition and acknowledgment of the beauty and complex mysteries of the natural world. Even when nature presents us with her most terrifying face, there is still an awesome (i.e., that which inspires awe, amazement, and deep reverence) beauty present.

This experience of gratitude opens the heart, allowing us to use it as a vehicle of perception, and to feel the subtle flow of life's energies. By cultivating this, over time we develop our inner senses; that is, we can learn to see, hear, feel and touch, with the heart.

Heart

The heart is very important in faery workings. Faery is a path of the heart. Because of this, the Faery Realm has a sometimes disturbing way of reflecting our own heart back to us. We must be pure of heart and clear of intention to engage seriously with the Faery Realm. If we are not, our impurities and lack of clarity will be mirrored back to us, though it may appear as if they are coming from outside of us rather than from within. Therefore, it is wise to approach the Faery Realm with a pure heart, and a grateful, open heart as well, along with the awareness that our interaction with the Faery Realm is likely to be quite transformative for us, although, perhaps, not always easy.

Green is a color found most abundantly in nature; it is also the color associated traditionally with the heart chakra. Green is found as the middle color of the color spectrum, the middle of the rainbow, and the heart chakra is the middle of our own inner rainbow—our chakra system. Similarly, the world of Faery, long associated with the color green, has been referred to as the Middle Kingdom because it is the place, or "kingdom of being," that is located midway between that of humans and that of gods. Our world, both physical and subtle, is the Middleworld, with the heavens above us, and the Underworld beneath us; so in a sense, we too, are residents of the Middle Kingdom. Interestingly, planet Earth is the *middle* planet of the seven traditionally known planets of the ancient world.

Another color associated with the heart chakra is pink. Pink is a blend of red and white. Red is the color associated with the first chakra whose energies are about grounding, expressing, surviving, and other basic challenges of physical incarnation—the "fire" of earthly life, in a sense. While purple is the color most often associated with the seventh chakra, the chakra that is traditionally held to be the one that connects us to Spirit, white is also sometimes associated with this chakra. Since white is made up of the frequencies of all the other colors combined, it represents wholeness. When observed in a healthy person it is often seen as a beautiful glowing radiance. Therefore, the heart is a place where the most extreme physical and spiritual realities are united; there is no separation between them.

It is interesting to note that it is not just the color green, but also red which is often associated with faeries and the Faery Realm. This is most frequently seen in their clothing and hats, particularly in Ireland. This is suggestive of an association of the faeries with our very physical reality, in spite of the fact that they are held to be creatures of non-substance, or *energy*.

Although we commonly associate the emotion of love with the heart, in some systems of traditional medicine the emotion associated with the heart is joy. Thus, it may be said that both love and joy are associated with the heart. This is an understandable association since love can create joy and joy can inspire love. Joy's opposite, sorrow, is also related to the heart. Tears of both joy and sorrow can cleanse and nourish the heart and soul, giving rise to new growth—the human heart's equivalent of "the greening."

People tend to think of love as just an emotional feeling in the heart, but it is really much more than that. It is a high spiritual power having to do with the forces of attraction and connection. It is the magnet that brings things together, and the glue that keeps them there. Furthermore, it is the power that enables us to "see with the heart." It is when we see with the heart that we are able to see all the links and interconnections that exist among all beings, and this can give rise to compassion.

The opposite of love is not hate, but rather, fear. Fear of some kind is usually what underlies many other negative emotions, especially hatred *(Note: I am not referring to strictly body-based fears, such as those which occur in situations of physical danger, and triggers the 'fight or flight' response)*. Beneath the presenting emotion of fear, hatred, or even anger, is another fear: the fear of being somehow and in some way agonizingly different from others and thus separate and alone—which implies, in essence, that we are somehow inherently wrong and therefore unlovable. This fear arises from our misperceptions wherein we compare our (mistaken) notion of our inferior selves with our (mistaken) notion of the superiority of others...and judge ourselves to be *wrong* or *wanting* in some way. We feel that we are *not enough*: not good enough, not attractive enough, not smart enough, not talented enough, or some other *not enough-ness*. This sense of being *not enough* makes us feel separate, isolated, alone, and ultimately, not deserving of being loved...and thus very miserable indeed.

Even this fear may be traced back to one more primal yet: that very real fear about survival which is linked with the self-preservation instinct. Deep in our cells, we *know* that survival is much harder when we are alone and separate from one another.

Love is an expanded state of being; fear is a contracted one.

As can be seen from this, fear has to do with separation—separation from others, separation from our own inner True Self, separation from the Divine. Sadly, this becomes a self-fulfilling prophecy, for if we perceive ourselves as not good enough, then we have judged, condemned, and separated ourselves from the rest of our kin, and from the flow of life itself.

Therefore, it may be seen that love equals connection, and fear equals separation.

Now what, you may ask, does all or any of this have to do with Faery Healing? The answer is one that ties together the intricate web of correspondences outlined above.

Our modern condition is one of separation and of fear. We have, to a large extent, lost contact with our kin—animal, plant, and faery. We are separated, fearful, and lonely, and this causes us all the suffering that comes along with these kinds of feelings and perceptions because the beings are, in actuality, also parts of our larger self. As has been mentioned in previous chapters, Faery Healing is about healing this rift and reconnecting with our family. Therefore, Faery Healing involves facing the fears, learning compassion, allowing love and (re)connection, and thereby allowing the resulting inner transformations to occur. In the process we, ourselves, become healed. Healing is wholeness. If we are reunited with our kin, we are whole.

Accordingly, the techniques of Faery Healing are designed to foster connection with our kin: our Faery Kin, and our plant, animal, and stone spirit kin as well. As this happens, we acquire a deeper awareness of ourselves as a Larger Being: more complete and whole, in touch with the other parts of our true self. While we may *say* that we are related to the rest of life, often we don't actually *feel* the relationship. We, as humans, are part of a greater being that is Life on Earth—a being of great depth, breadth, and diversity. We cannot be aware of this at every moment any more than we can be aware at every moment of each and every part of our physical body, the flow of our blood, the workings of our digestion, or any other physical process. However, the techniques of Faery Healing do help foster these rare moments of spacious awareness, increase their frequency, and allow us to have the *feeling memory* of them, even when we are not inside those moments.

It is not without a reason that Faery is sometimes referred to as the *Land of the Living Heart*.

Christ tells us that we must "be as little children" to enter the kingdom of God. The natural state of little children is one of awe, joy, wonder, and excitement, although as they grow up the pressures of life often cause them to leave this primal land of joy and forget how to return. It would behoove us all—children of all ages—to remember or to *learn* or how to return to that place, since when we are in this state of being the gateways of the Otherworlds, the Land of the Ever Young, swing open for us with ease.

HEART AS CENTER

In A.E.'s (George Russell) vision, recounted in *Chapter 1*, he beheld luminous beings living within a lake. He felt them to be Elemental Beings. He saw a large being whom he felt to be an Elemental King, seated on a throne beneath which fountained a "lustrous air." The king inhaled this lustrous air and seemed to grow larger and more luminous as he did so. Smaller, paler beings descended through the lake toward the king to be replenished by him. This replenishment was accomplished when they bent forward and touched their lips to the king's heart. This caused them to fill with light, and they soared upward "plumed and radiant."

In yet another vision A.E. beheld smaller beings both disappearing into and emerging from the heart of a Greater Being.

In the last chapter we learned about Fiona Macleod's vision of the Glen of Precious Stones, where "the Sidhe go to refresh their deathless life."

Realizing that the Glen of Precious Stones is the heart center provides us with yet another key to understanding not only these visions but also how the power of the heart is integral to the Faery Realm. It is significant that the power channeled by the Elemental King fountains up from the Underworld, i.e. what we may safely assume to be the heart of Earth. It is significant that the small beings must kiss the king's heart in order to be replenished. It is significant that beings both emerge and disappear into the heart of the Greater Being. In each of these instances, the heart is shown to be the source of life-giving power. In each of these instances, the heart is seen to be a Center—a place of both origin and ending.

And finally, a piece of lore for those herbally inclined: The berries of the hawthorn tree, that most excellent of faery trees, have been esteemed by herbalists of almost every era and place as an efficacious heart tonic.

HAVING A HEART—WHY FAERIES ARE AFRAID OF IRON

It is one of those curiously interesting facts that human blood and plant "blood"—which is known as chlorophyll—share certain basic similarities. On a molecular level both are built in a certain type of ring shape. Human blood contains hemoglobin, the iron-containing substance which carries oxygen from the lungs to the other areas of the body and which gives blood its red color. Chlorophyll, which gives plants their green color, is essentially a *light capturer*; it is the substance in plants which enables them to convert sunlight into chemical energy, a process known as photosynthesis.

Chlorophyll is almost identical chemically to hemoglobin. One of the major differences is that the chlorophyll molecule is built around a magnesium atom, while hemoglobin is built around an iron atom.

Chlorophyll's central element, magnesium, is the eighth most abundant element in the Earth's crust. Magnesium has a hexagonal, crystalline structure and when heated, ignites and burns with an intense white light releasing large amounts of heat. It is frequently found in water of all kinds—fresh, seawater, and mineral waters. Magnesium is necessary for both bones and blood, and for relaxation of both nervous system and muscles. Magnesium is also essential for heart health as it has a regulating effect on irregular heart rhythms, and is, in general, protective to the heart.

The "heme" part of hemoglobin is actually iron. Iron is the fourth most abundant element in the Earth's crust, is found in soils (and is a main contributor to soil coloration), and is a major component of the Earth's core. Iron has a cubic crystalline structure, conducts heat and electricity, and can be both attracted by magnets and magnetized. It is found, in dissolved form, in groundwater and to a lesser extent in seawater. In the human body, iron is found not only in the blood but also in every cell; a shortage of it is life threatening.

Iron, therefore, would seem to be the substance that separates the animal kingdom, or at least the higher animal kingdom, from the plant kingdom (see Note 1 at the end of the chapter). Yet, as we are all aware, the animal kingdom is dependent upon the plant kingdom as much of the animal kingdom, ourselves included, must eat at least some plants in order to survive. Without the chlorophyll-rich plants, there would be no animal life on Earth. Without chlorophyll, there would be no photosynthesis, and thus no life on Earth at all.

Chlorophyll captures sunlight and converts it into a form that plant life finds nourishing. Similar to Lucifer and those fallen angels, chlorophyll brings to Earth the power of light, enabling life to exist. In a way, it might be said that *chlorophyll transforms the power of light into joy, just as iron transforms it into strength.*

Faeries live, move, and have their being within the subtle worlds of nature, most especially the magnesium-rich plant kingdom (and to a lesser extent the mineral kingdom). Faeries live at the heart of the subtle aspect of nature, the primal green heart of nature. Humans, with their red, iron-rich blood, live at the heart of the most physical aspect of nature. Yet the physical and subtle aspects are in constant contact, interface, and relationship with each other, something about which the faeries are very aware, though humans seem to have largely forgotten, or act like they have.

Faeries are said to be afraid of iron, and iron has been used as a charm to protect against them (see Note 2 at the end of the chapter). Many have wondered why this is so, myself included. As I studied the roles of iron and magnesium in nature, it occurred to me that this might be related to that age-old question of why the faeries are afraid of iron.

Perhaps the faeries are afraid of iron because they are afraid of us. Perhaps they are afraid of us because we have forgotten about them. Perhaps our stress-filled lives, always so focused on the "red" first chakra issues of survival that can make us fearful, cause us to broadcast an overly strong red energy frequency, which feels, perhaps, alien and terrifying to them due to its very strength and lack of much in the way of any green or heart frequencies. Do the faeries associate iron with *us*?

Or perhaps they are afraid of the red-blooded animal world because it is harmful to their world. Animals tromp around and, in the case of human animals, destroy faery/fairy habitats and homes. We deny or are oblivious to their very being and existence. In their eyes we are, perhaps, a thoughtlessly invasive species at best and an outrightly destructive one at worst. We have externalized the iron in our blood to make not only implements that serve for our nourishment and good (such as cooking pots), but also weapons that deal destruction and death to the Earth and each other. Iron is the metal of Mars who is a god of vitality and energy, but also and primarily, of war.

As we have mentioned in previous chapters, humans traditionally were quite afraid of faeries. And faeries are known to be afraid of iron, which may, to them perhaps, represent humans—or at least represent and even emphasize the difference between faeries and humans. Are we afraid of the joy they have to offer and the subtle aspect of nature that is their home as much as they are afraid of our brute physicality and strength?

The implications of this line of thought are thought-provoking and intriguing.

Red blood, green blood—red and green are opposite yet complementary colors. They are necessary to each other; they balance each other. So, too, do the physical and subtle realms, the animals and the plants, the humans and the faeries, balance and complement each other and live in interdependent relationship with each other.

When we humans remember our true spiritual natures and our relationship to the rest of life on the planet, and learn to live in right relationship with our kin, perhaps faeries will no longer be frightened of iron, or of us.

NOTES

1. Some plants do possess small amounts of iron, but not as much as does the animal kingdom with its iron-rich blood.
2. It is important to realize that although folk tradition indicates that faeries were afraid of iron and that iron was useful as protection against faery mischief, not all faery lore supports this. The stories of the Tuatha De Danaan make mention of iron weaponry, and the Tuatha even had a smith, Goibniu (in the Welsh stories he is called Govannan) who made their swords and other iron implements. Therefore, it would seem that the folk belief concerning the faeries' dislike of iron refers not to the Tuatha—the Shining Ones—as much as to the smaller faeries/fairies and perhaps the nature spirits..

CHAPTER 20

Brigid's Mantle, Airmid's Cloak

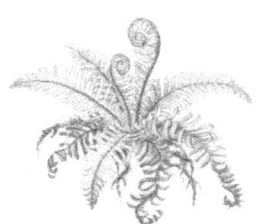

In Ella Young's fabulous book, *Celtic Wonder Tales*, there is a story called "The Earth-shapers." In this story, the great Irish goddess Brigid interests all the other Tuatha De Danaan in visiting a place called Earth, which, she says, "has cried all night because She dreamt of beauty." The Tuatha visit the Earth, and with their divine magic proceed to make the bleak and barren Earth a place of great beauty. Brigid spreads out her mantle and it magically grows, stretching and extending itself, covering the whole Earth, making the Earth green and beautiful and full of living things.

If you will recall from preceding chapters, the story of Airmid tells us of how this goddess found healing herbs growing upon the grave of her slain brother Miach, who had been a brilliant healer. Gathering up these herbs and laying them out on her cloak out in the precise order in which they had grown, Airmid found that there were exactly 365 of them, one for every nerve, joint, and sinew in the human body—a fact which indicated that all human ailments could be healed by these herbs and the proper knowledge of them.[1] But proper knowledge of them was denied to her and those who followed her when her jealous father, the physician Dian Cecht, disturbed the cloak, mixing up the herbs so she would not know their right order and so none but himself would have this special knowledge.

Airmid's cloak represents knowledge of the healing herbs and plants of the Earth. In one sense, her cloak is similar to Brigid's mantle and is like the Earth itself, which provides us all we need for health and healing in the form of the green plants and trees which seem to magically push themselves up through the soil from the Underworld—the source of all life-giving power. But in another sense, Airmid's cloak represents the knowledge and skill we must have to make right use of these gifts.

Dian Cecht kept this power to himself, and later used it in the Second Battle of Moytura when he placed these herbs, "all the herbs that grow in Ireland," into the Well of Slaine (Slaine means *health*). Then he, Airmid, and her brothers chanted incantations over the well to empower it to heal their wounded warriors. Again we are shown that the power of life, the green *spirit-power* of the Earth as represented by "all the herbs of Ireland," can—along with proper knowledge, the life-giving power of water, and magical intention and energies—heal all wounds and bring us back literally from death's door.

Dian Cecht's jealousy may be said to represent the selfishness and impurity of heart that interferes with the ability to become a hollow conduit for the healing power to flow. Although one is still able to channel healing energy, this impurity of heart, which *conditions* the energy, prevents one from knowing that healing is a service to life itself, beyond the facts of who is healed and who channels the healing flow. It also keeps one from flowing along with that greater power which is the infinite wisdom of the Life Force itself.

As has been said before, purity of heart is necessary when working in the Faery Realm; this is true also of any spiritual healing work.

Both Brigid's mantle and Airmid's cloak are powerful symbols of the healing power of the Green World (or "Green Life" as Fiona Macleod referred to it). Yet beneath this medicinal power of herbs flows a power that the great medieval healer Hildegarde of Bingen referred to as the *Veriditas*, or the "greening" power of nature. This is the mystical healing power that is inherent in the green growing things by virtue of the fact that they are channels for the earthly Divine Power, over and above their mere chemical properties.

Journey to the Faery Healing Grove

In this journey you will go to the Faery Healing Grove. This is a place of great magic and power, where many healing modalities are available. Brigid, Morgen, Airmid, Aine, Dana, Belenos, Goibniu, Aengus, Rhiannon, and many other deities are to be found here, as well as Faery Allies, animal allies, plant allies, and other spirits of healing.

> JOURNEY | To the Faery Healing Grove
>
> Settling comfortably before your Faery Altar, you light the Faery Hearth candle that is in the center of the altar... As you gaze at this center flame, breathing slowly in and out, you find that you are becoming more relaxed, calm, and serene with each breath. You focus your attention on the candle, then close your eyes, seeing the candle with your inner vision.
>
> As you watch the candle, you see its flame suddenly flare up, and expand until it has become a wall of flame. You step through the wall of flame, and feel yourself passing through the web of dimensions and into the innerworlds.

On the other side of the wall of flame, a swirling, green-gold mist surrounds you, through which nothing, at first, is visible. As you walk forward, gradually the mist begins to clear, and you find you have come to a riverbank and are standing just before a bridge that crosses a river. Not far beyond the opposite bank you see a grove of trees. You step onto the bridge and walk across it, looking down, as you do so, at the water flowing beneath you. You walk toward where the grove of trees begins, and notice that there is actually a gateway which leads into the grove. This gateway is formed of two trees whose upper branches have intertwined and grown together, forming a portal. This is the Eastern Gateway to this grove.

One of the trees forming the Eastern Gateway is a hazel tree; the other is a hawthorn. Both trees burst into bloom with many lovely small flowers as you watch, but the blossoms rapidly give way to berries in the case of the hawthorn, and nuts in the case of the hazel... Soon the berries begin to shrivel, and then both nuts and berries fall to the ground. As you watch, the whole process begins again...

As you walk through the tree gateway, a hawthorn berry and a hazelnut drop down before you, and you stoop to pick them up, placing them in your pocket. Then you look up and notice that the grove is composed of a grassy clearing within a ring of large, leafy trees of all sorts. The place is very green, and feels vibrant with life. In the exact center of the grove grows an enormous tree.

You can see and feel that there are many beings in this place. There are Faery Gods and Goddesses, Faery Kings and Queens, ordinary faery folk, nature spirits, and devas. There are many realms within this realm, and many doorways into them. You will encounter these beings as you travel to different places within this Faery Healing Grove. But for now, there is a being standing before you, welcoming you into the Faery Healing Grove. This Faery Being has been assigned to guide and help you on this particular expedition.

Your Faery Guide directs your attention over to the immediate right where you see a small, rough cottage. This is the cottage of the Faery Doctor. You may come here at another time for a special visit if you have need or desire.

The Faery Guide takes your hand and leads you to the center of the grove, where grows the Great Tree. You see many beings in and around this Tree, and you see and sense the huge Life Force flowing through it from root to crown... The Tree seems to pulsate with life, it almost glows... You look at the huge mass of gnarled roots, and gaze up into the vast crown of leafy branches, beyond which you see what appears to be a circular, iridescent rainbow set in a pale blue-grey sky... Simultaneously, you hear a voice calling your true name, which you may, or may not, have known up till now... You cannot tell the source of the voice. Is it from within you, or from outside? Is it from the sky, or the Tree, or your soul? As you look at the many branches and branchlets of this Tree, and the many roots, you know that this tree is the Tree of Life, and it is, as well, your family tree. You spend time absorbing this fact, and honoring and communing with the Tree...

You notice that there is an opening, a small doorway, in the trunk of the Tree, from which a golden light seems to glow. You enter this opening and find that you are in a tree cave, and that the golden light is emanating from a small fire that burns in the center of the tree cave. This is the hearth-fire of the Goddess Brigid, goddess of fire and water, light and warmth, hearth-fires and healing wells. She sits nearby, tending the fire, which burns without ash. She looks up at you as you enter, and you move to her, and kneel at her side. She touches your head, and you find that your heart is filling with the deep joy of reunion. You become lost in this bliss and joy, which seems to comes from both deep inside the Tree and deep inside of you at the same time... After a while she touches you again, and you awaken from your reverie. You rise, and walk back out into the Grove.

Your Faery Guide now leads you to the South part of the grove, which is a green verdant plain containing a ring of stones. Within the ring of stones burns a fire with rainbow-colored flames. Near the fire is a pile of bricks and stones. Beyond the fire is a gently flowing stream by which sits a small, beehive-shaped hut made of stone, and covered with patches of turf and grass. This is the "teach an alais," the sweat house, a place of purification, which is known to cure many ills. Aine, guardian of the sacred spark of life, dwells in this part of the grove, and when you return to this place, you may find her here.

From here you walk to the West. There are many small trees, plants, and healing herbs growing in the green fields here, their fragrance drifting through the air like an intoxicating perfume. But the most prominent aspect of the West is a large stone well, which seems to be built up around a spring. There are faeries here, and under the supervision of Airmid they are gathering handfuls of herbs which they bring toward the well and place in heaps nearby... You continue walking, and you come upon many other springs, some hot, some cold. All are healing springs, and are known to heal many different ailments by virtue of the different properties contained within their waters. Beyond the springs you see a small lake, and to one side of the lake, a cottage. This is Airmid's cottage, and when you wish to see her, it is there you must go.

With your Faery Guide, you walk past the springs and the lake. After a bit, you notice that the land beneath your feet has become very irregular, covered with stones and rocks, making the path more difficult to travel. This is the North, and as you continue walking you come to a large hill, a faery mound. This is the Cailleach's Cairn, the entrance to her home that lies within and under the hill; it is also home to many faeries. Just before the mound are several large standing stones of varying shapes, one resembles a chair, while another resembles a bed or table. These also are used for healing purposes, as you will find when you return to this place.

After this circuit of the grove, your guide takes you back through the countryside until you reach the Great Tree, where the Faery Doctor is waiting for you. The Faery Doctor puts his hands upon you, and prays aloud, but in a language which you may or may not understand. He then leads you out into the grove again, your Faery Healing Guide accompanying, to one of the places you have seen—the South, West, or North—for further healing. There, other beings—Faery Deities, Faery Allies, plant, and stone spirits—will join you and be of assistance in your healing process...

When it is done, you give thanks for what you have been so generously given. The Faery Doctor guides you back to the Eastern Gateway. You reach into your pocket and pull out gifts for the Faery Doctor. You are aware that these are the hawthorn berry and the hazelnut you picked up—right in this place—when you entered the grove, but they now look and feel somewhat different... You walk out of the grove through the hawthorn-hazel gateway and toward the bridge. As you walk, you find that within a few steps the swirling green-gold mists have surrounded you again, and as you walk through these mists, you feel yourself returning to your normal, waking state of consciousness, and to an awareness of your physical body as it rests before your Faery Altar. You find yourself returning to this time and place, the place from which you began this journey. Allow yourself a few moments to fully return, and when you are back, you may open your eyes.

Be sure to record your journey in your Magical Journal.

Meeting with Specific Faery Healing Deities

In the journey above, you may well encounter other deities than the ones given within the script of the journey.

But if you do not, and you feel drawn to meet the Faery Healing Deities on an individual basis, please journey to connect with them, referring back to the information about the healing deities as given in *Chapter 15*. Here are instructions for creating such a journey.

Do research on the deities, finding out as much as you can about them in the mythology, folklore, and legends. From your research create inner landscape imagery where you can find them. This might be a specific country, or a specific landscape with certain features connected to their legends. You might create an inner landscape that is by a well or a fire, in a cave, by a mountain, by the seashore, or even in one of the Three Realms. Then travel to meet them in their native element. Use one of the very basic journeys into the Faery Realm, or use the journey above and meet with them in the Great Tree.

The basic elements of a journey are as follows:

- Set up your working place (i.e., your Faery Altar or other place) with needed items.

- When you are ready to begin, take up your matches and prepare to light the Faery Hearth candle by stilling your mind and becoming aware of your own inner flame. This serves as a signal to your psyche that you are about to commence inner work.

- Light your Faery Hearth candle.

- Do some form of grounding and centering exercise to loosen your consciousness and to open you to the inner realms.

- Choose your pathway and enter the Faery Realm.

- Call your Faery Allies to you.

- Ask to be taken to meet the Faery Deity of your choice.

- Take yourself, in vision, to a place where you may find your Faery Deity. This will have been determined previously by your research.

- Speak your intentions, needs, and desire.

- Wait silently for the communication to occur, and remember that such communication may be very subtle and that it may take a few sessions to actually establish contact.

- When you feel finished, thank the beings who've assisted you, and return to the Middleworld using one of the pathways previously given or one you have created yourself.
- Allow yourself time to fully return to ordinary consciousness before opening your eyes.
- Record your journey in your Magical Journal.

Modes of Work

While the main thrust of the message of Faery Healing is about allowing the energy to move through you and out into the world, you will notice that some of the suggestions given here are about *doing* things, such as creating faery medicines, chanting, working with the Elements, color, and the like.

As with almost everything else in life, Faery Healing works in two modes, passive and active. The passive mode is about *being* and occurs when the practitioner, in an open, clear state, is simply allowing the power to flow through him/her and letting the energy and the inner Faery Allies do what they will. They do all the work; the practitioner is simply a conduit for the energy. The active state is about *doing*, and occurs when the practitioner, following intuitive inspiration and faery guidance, brings in things like chanting, color, working with the Elements, making faery medicines, and the like.

As you can see, the *doing* flows forth from the *being*. Sometimes, the *being* part of it is all that is necessary. The *doing* part of it comes into things only when inspired and guided by the allies.

Physical Aspects of Healing

As has been mentioned previously, the physical aspects of Faery Healing are so intertwined with the spiritual aspects, that it is difficult and actually quite unnecessary to separate them. We live in a physical world, but all is imbued with spirit. All outer physical manifestation has its source from the inner, subtle, spiritual worlds.

In this section, we will offer methods to work with physical things such as plants and stones in very simple physical ways, but also in spiritual ways, in conjunction with prayer, blessing, and contact with the plant spirits. We will, as well, learn to utilize procedures that work primarily on an energetic level.

In previous chapters, we have discussed the physical aspects of the Celtic healing tradition, the various herbs and stones used, and how these things were used because they were what surrounded a people who lived close to the land and used what nature had to offer them from their own sacred environs. Unless our physical circumstances were the same, it would be inappropriate for us to try to exactly imitate these ways of healing. This is not to say we cannot use herbs for healing; quite the contrary! But if we wish to do this, we must educate ourselves about them, just as we would about anything else.

Should we wish to use herbs as part of our healing techniques, we could do no better than to start out as Simplers, choosing just a few herbal allies, and learning them quite well, as well as forming a deep and respectful relationship with them and the spirits that dwell within them. Techniques for this will be detailed in a following chapter.

THE ART OF SIMPLING

We are fortunate these days to have the herbs of the world almost at our fingertips. Natural food stores, herb stores, and online herb sellers allow us access to healing plants from far corners of the globe. Our ancestors, no matter from which part of the world they originated, did not have this profusion of choices. They were fairly well limited to what grew around them, whether native or naturalized, and what may have come in on the latest ship, for those who could afford to buy it.

But we must not make the mistake of thinking that the healing herbal pharmacopoeia of our ancestors was thereby limited and impoverished. They practiced the art of herbal healing in a way that has come to be known as *Simpling*. Plainly described, the art of Simpling is the art of knowing, and knowing thoroughly, the many and varied uses of just a few well-chosen plants. When one follows the path of healing by Simpling, not only can a few ordinary, easy-to-find plants be put to a huge variety of uses treating a wide range of symptoms and bodily systems, but the healer is able to form a deeper relationship with the plants used, including a relationship with the spirits of the plants. The healer is therefore able to be guided by these plant spirits, and do healing from this state of consciousness rather than merely from mental knowledge of the plant's medicinal qualities.

That Faery Doctors and Celtic healers practiced Simpling is amply demonstrated in the lore by the many uses to which many common plants were put, including—to name just a few—yarrow, vervain, foxglove, plantain, and mullein.

Let have a look at just a few of these "plants of many uses."

Yarrow was used magically for divination, as a love charm, a good luck charm, a success charm, as a remedy against enchantments, and to protect against faeries. Medicinally, it was used to staunch bleeding and cure headaches, to treat colic, rheumatism, colds, heavy menstruation, to reduce fevers, and to treat many other things. In addition, it was added to mixtures of other herbs to enhance their efficacy. Its neutral-cold energy helped cool heated conditions, reduce swellings, and clear infections, inflammations, and toxins from the body. It was, indeed, one of the most powerful, respected, and well-used herbs in the Celtic healing tradition of the British Isles.

Vervain's reputation as a magical herb goes back to the times of the Druids, and it was esteemed by them at least as much as was mistletoe. It was associated with visions and prophecy, used in love charms and as part of protective magical wreaths, and worn as a necklace amulet to render the wearer invulnerable to harm. Medicinally, it was used to calm the nerves, allay sleeplessness and headache, sore throats, and eyes ailments. It is astringent, which made it good for drying up moist, ulcerous, and scrofulous conditions.

Plantain was used magically for divination. It was wreathed around children's necks to keep them safe from abduction by the faeries. Used medicinally, plantain was similar to yarrow in its ability to cool heated, infected and inflamed conditions, including skin abrasions. It was also used as an antiseptic, for lung conditions, and was good for digestion. Plantain is very rich in vitamins and minerals, and therefore is a quite nutritious addition to the diet.

Mullein was famous as the *Lus mor*, or Great Herb, the only herb that could actually bring back a child that had been taken by the faeries. Medicinally, it was used for many things. Externally it was used for swellings, burns, and ulcers; and internally, for pulmonary and bronchial conditions of all kinds for which it was especially effective.

Foxglove was used magically to treat symptoms of the Evil Eye. It was also used to treat pining, weakened children who were thought to be *away*, as well as being efficacious against elf-shot. The juice of foxglove was part of a procedure used to determine whether a child was a changeling or not. Medicinally, foxglove was a powerful heart tonic from which we derive the modern drug digitalis, which may explain some of its success in treating the weak, pining, pale, and listless whose underlying problem may have been heart-related.

Thus, with the use of just these five plants, many common maladies could be treated.

If you would like to work with these herbs, do research in reputable herb books (see the *Appendices*) to determine which herb is correct for the condition for which you wish to use it. In order to do this, you need to understand the language that plants speak. Plants speak to us in a language of "feeling" and "sensing" and also in terms of hot and cold, wet and dry. Therefore, both the herb and the condition to be addressed may be looked at from the old, time-honored, elemental perspectives of hot-cold-wet-dry.

A cautionary note must be extended concerning foxglove which is much too strong a medicine to be used by the untrained. Plant it in your garden and enjoy the beauty of its faery bells, tune into it spiritually, but do not ingest it.

ELEMENTAL AND ELEMENTARY

With herbal medicines, the conditions of the plant's growth are important to understanding its elemental energies. If it grows primarily in direct sunlight, the plant will possess more of the Fire Element; if it grows mostly in the shade or in very damp ground, it will possess more of the Water Element.

The season in which the plant is harvested also makes a difference. In the spring, plants send forth energy from their roots which causes the stalks, stems, and leaves to grow out again. Thus, spring is a good time to harvest these above-ground parts as they are filled with the vital energies and essences of the particular plant. In summer, plants blossom and produce fruit, and these are the parts that contain the special essences of the plant most powerfully in this season. In autumn, fruit production may continue somewhat, but the focus is on seed production in early autumn, while toward the end of autumn and the beginning of winter the plant's energies move down into the roots to rest and replenish. Autumn is, therefore, a good time to harvest seeds and roots, which are powerful storehouses of the plant's essential energies.

And finally, in working with plants magically it is useful to consider the magical and symbolic aspects of the different parts of the plant. These can be related to the Four Elements.

Air. The aerial parts of the plant—stems, leaves, flowers—are representative of the Element of Air since they are light, move easily in the wind, and show the greatest changes of any part of the plant.

Fire. The seed-pods and seeds and generative organs of the plant are representative of the Element of Fire, as they are the creative power of the plant. They represent its very essence, packed small and tight, ready to unfold when conditions are right, and create "the future." In addition, because they give birth to the seed-bearing fruit, flowers may be said to be linked with the Fire Element as well as associated with the Air Element.

Water. The fruit represents the accumulated wisdom of the plant, harvested, and its essence ready to be assimilated. This links it to the Element of Water, which is the elemental medium of assimilation. In addition, fruit holds seeds; seeds are the plant's offspring, the unborn, the potential, which will come forth in due time, bringing the future.

Earth. The roots, which anchor the plant into the earth, sustain and nourish it, hold its deep wisdom/deep nutrients, and obviously represent the Element of Earth.

Not all plants fall into these tidy categories, of course. Fungi, for instance—our common and not so common mushrooms—are interesting in that they cross the boundaries of the kingdoms of nature. They have cells walls, as do plants, yet lack the ability to move and sway about, as do plants. We tend to think of them as plants, but lacking leaves that photosynthesize sunlight to create food, they are really not quite the same as plants. Their vast underground root system, with its much smaller and manifold fruiting bodies, seems to contain a different balance of the elements. Although their roots link them to the Earth Element, and their fruiting bodies to the Water Element, they contain spores rather than seeds. The spores drift through the air, but the lack of seed seems to indicate that they lack the Element of Fire.

This lack of an Element is curiously reminiscent of some of the old faery lore, which states that faeries are lacking in one of these Classical Four Elements. Thus it would seem that mushrooms are true faery plants, just as folklore would have it.

Meditation to Contact Plant Spirits

Here is a meditation to help you connect with plant spirits. With appropriate modifications it may be used to contact tree spirits or stone spirits. If you are using it to connect with plant or tree spirits, the journey is best done outdoors sitting by the plant or tree because you are then within the aura of the plant. For stones, you may do the journey indoors if you wish. Hold the stone in your hands if it is small enough to do so. An important part of this process is being consciously within the aura of the plant, tree, or stone, as this helps you tune into its spirit.

> **MEDITATION** | **Making Contact with Plants Spirits**
>
> Sitting beside the plant or tree, breathe deeply and slowly, and allow yourself to become completely relaxed. Affirm your intention to make contact with the spirit of the nearby plant or tree. Take the plant or tree in on a sensory level. Open your eyes and look at it. Feel its

texture; smell it; rub it with your fingers and listen to the sound which that makes. If it is an edible plant, take a small taste of it. Then spend some time just being with it, and focusing attention on it.

Close your eyes and become aware of your energy field, your aura. Extend your aura out and your feeling capabilities along with it. Even if you do not feel this happening, imagine it to be so. Visualize the plant in your mind. Allow your aura to flow toward the plant or tree, and to meet and merge with the plant or tree's aura. Open yourself to the information this interaction brings you. Once again, if at first you cannot feel this occurring, trust that it is and imagine it to be so. Be aware that this is a very subtle process, so be mindful of subtle feelings here. Note them; do not make an attempt to analyze, explain, or classify anything at this point.

If you feel the plant opening to you, ask that you be allowed further and deeper communication with it: ask that the spirit of the plant communicate to you in some way. Do not hold any preconceived notions of how this will be. Just ask this politely and wait for a response. Be aware that the response might be quite subtle. It may be a thought, a mental picture, an emotion, an inner sense, or a physical sensation.

When you feel finished, thank the plant and the plant spirit for allowing you this communication; and bring your consciousness back to its normal state. Leave an offering of some kind for the plant.

Be sure your record your experiences in your Magical Journal.

MEDICINAL BREWS—TEAS & INFUSIONS

It is quite simple to make an herb tea, tisane, or infusion. Measure out the amount of herbs needed—a good-sized handful is about right—and place them into a heat-proof, glass quart jar; a canning jar works beautifully for this. Bring water to the boil and pour it over the herbs, filling the jar. Cover the jar with a cloth till it has cooled somewhat, and then screw on the lid. Allow the tisane to steep for at least four hours; overnight is even better. By this process it becomes a medicinal strength infusion rather than just merely a tea.

Be aware that some herbs, such as the dandelion, will be extremely bitter tasting. Resist the temptation to add a non-nutrient such as sugar or artificial sweetener to the infusion. Rather, if the taste is too strong, sip the brew slowly over time, realizing that the taste is part of the healing, and that our life experiences come in many tastes, all of which nourish and build us. On a physical level, dandelion's bitter taste stimulates the liver to release chemicals that help the body purify itself more efficiently, as well as improve digestion.

This very basic process can be infused with faery magic by approaching it in a ceremonial, spiritual way, and this is the next thing that we shall take up.

Guidelines for Making a Magical Brew
The keys to all parts of the process of making a magical brew are consciousness, thankfulness, and of course, intention. I learned this years ago from a very dear friend. Because it illustrates what I am getting at, I would like to share this personal story with you.

Several years ago my friend, Sara, invited me to her house to participate in making an herbal brew to treat a serious disease from which she was suffering. She wanted the herbal remedy making to be a ceremony, but she didn't have any distinct ideas about what it should be like. The best she could come up with was to "bring along whatever you are inspired to bring." Sara was very in tune with the spiritual worlds, and particularly the nature spirit worlds. Despite her serious illness she often spent many hours of the day working in her garden, tending her trees, and meditating in her redwood grove. Although I would have preferred a more structured, defined approach to the ceremony, I knew her well enough to trust that something completely perfect would unfold in our process, and I was not disappointed.

I wondered what I should bring along. I decided my drum would be a good thing, and took it down from its place on the wall. I stood before my crystals and rocks, and a few of them seemed to want to go along. Just as I was about to leave, I got a very strong feeling that my Big Blue Bowl would be needed.

My Big Blue Bowl is quite dear to me. I have had it for more than 25 years. It was used when I created my first herbal preparations and my first batches of bread; it has cracked and been carefully mended more than once. I am very careful with it, and had never taken it out of the house before (except when moving house), so I was quite hesitant when this urge first made itself felt. However, the urge was so overwhelming that I pulled the bowl from the cupboard, wrapped it in a towel, set it carefully in a cardboard box, and secured it safely on the floor of the back seat of my car.

When I arrived at Sara's I found that the other women had experienced similar feelings and urges about what to bring, and as we laid our things on the table, I found that not one item had been duplicated. We had each managed to bring something very essential and unique.

Sara was simply delighted to have the Big Blue Bowl present. She confessed she'd not given any thought at all as to a special bowl in which to mix the herbs, and she pronounced Blue to be perfect for the job.

I placed Blue on the wooden kitchen table and set my rocks around it. The others came and put their objects around Blue, and suddenly the homely kitchen table had become a sacred altar of healing. There were four women and four bags of herbs, so Sara handed the bags of herbs around. Interestingly, each of us felt that our herb's energy reflected an important aspect of our inner being, though we didn't admit this to one another till after the ceremony. One by one, we spoke the words that came to us—words of gratitude for the herb's life and healing powers—as we poured the contents of our bag into Blue. Sara took up the wooden spoon someone had brought along and began mixing the herbs together, praying as she stirred.

We moved to the sink to fill a large stainless steel pot with water. We placed it on the stove and turned on the flame. The herbs were poured into the pot. As we stood around it waiting for it to come to a boil, someone picked up the drum and began beating it. Within a few minutes, I found myself breaking into spontaneous chanting and singing. After a bit, the others joined in. I don't even remember exactly what I said or sang, but I do remember that I was singing to the water, the fire, and the herbs—songs of thanks, of love, and of power.

As the drumming and chanting continued, the energy in the room began to shift and shimmer. Everyone felt the room fill with power as the spirits we invoked gathered round and began working with us. The steady drumbeat guided us deeper into altered consciousness. Time passed, and our chanting voices spun threads of power as water bubbled, herbs simmered, and magic wove around us. I found a wooden spoon in my hand and began stirring the pot, singing directly into the bubbling brew.

Then suddenly, it was finished, and we all knew it. Even the clock told us the herbs had simmered the required number of minutes. The sudden shift in the energy had us all giggling self-consciously as we strained the herbal brew into a large bowl and then into its brown glass bottles. Sara ladled each of us a small cupful and we went outside to sit among the trees and sip. We thanked all the spirits who had helped us, and we knew our rite was ended.

From this rather lengthy account, I wish to extract the following guidelines to help you in the making of your healing brews and potions.

- Gratitude plays a large part in all portions of this operation. Be truly grateful for the plants, the water, the fire, the spirits, and for everything. Each brings precious and unique gifts to the process.

- Awareness/consciousness also plays a large part. Be very aware of the gifts your plants bring, and of the gifts of fire and water. Water extracts the vital elements and makes them more available to us. Fire catalyzes the entire process.

- Realize that time is an important factor. Whether it is the time taken for the water to boil or the herbs to brew, time is a key factor, and an integral part of the process.

- Realize that you can bring true magic to bear by using the power of sound in the form of singing and chanting. This greatly enhances the work being done.

- Realize, as well, that LOVE is needed for all healing work; so let your heart fill with love and gratitude for the object of your healing work, and also for your plants, the water, the fire, your Spirit and Faery Allies, your human allies, the time it takes, the power of sound, and even for being alive in such a magical world as this one we all share.

PERSONAL WELLS OF SLAINE—HEALING BATHS

Sometimes it is more appropriate to bathe in the healing brew than to drink it. This might be the case if one just needs a good relaxing soak as part of the healing, or if, perhaps, the herbs are indicated as being safe for external use but not internal use. Herbal and energetic healing essences can be absorbed quite well through the skin.

In such a case, prepare about two to three quarts of the healing brew in the manner given above. Draw a bath and when the tub is nearly full pour in the healing brew (after first straining the herbs out of it), while praying to the plant spirits whose energies are contained in the brew. Reach your hand into the tub and swirl the waters around in a clockwise spiral to incorporate the healing brew into the bath water, calling on your Faery Allies to help you stir the waters and infuse them with healing energies.

When you disrobe for the bath, make a ritual of the process. As you remove each piece of clothing, remove, as well, your mundane reality, layer by layer, so that when you are ready to step into the healing bath you are nakedly open to the healing process.

Then get into the bath and enjoy it! It's best to simply relax in the bath and meditate on your healing, perhaps even doing prayers and healing journeys, rather than busying your mind with other, more mundane thoughts.

STONES

As has been mentioned in previous chapters, stones were most definitely part of the healing traditions of the Celtic countries, and we can carry this tradition forward in our lives.

Stones have a variety of uses, some of which have already been detailed in previous chapters, and which may be adapted for modern use.

In addition, "holey" stones (stones with holes in them) were held to be sacred and were sometimes used as a device to see into the Otherworlds of Faery. This was done by peering through the hole in the stone. They were also used for protection and healing, particularly for children, the stone being rubbed over the body to absorb the disease. Sometimes these holey stones were referred to as Hag-stones, which links them with the Hag or dark aspect of the Goddess.

The stones you use in healing do not have to be fancy, pretty, expensive crystals. They can be quite common stones, found in the garden, the park, the forest, or on riverbanks. While taking a walk, a stone will often catch your attention, and seem to call out to you. Stones for healing should be selected primarily by *feel*, secondarily by outer characteristics such as color.

Some stones will want to stay with you for a while. Some come to you for a specific purpose or period of time, and then need to be placed back in nature. Some stones may come to you solely to be given away to other people. Only your intuition can give you guidance with regard to these details of your relationship with stones. But please realize that stones have lives of their own, and are not just objects to be collected, put on a shelf, and forgotten.

When a stone has come to you, take some time to connect with it. I have often slept with a stone on the night table beside my bed or under my pillow, or have worn the smaller ones in tiny pouches around my neck when I wanted to really *bond* with it. Feel into your stone, perhaps even journey into it (creating a journey or meditation similar to the one given above for plants), to see what it has to teach you, and how it can be of help to you. Ask the stone spirit to hold and amplify your healing intentions, and to add its unique color, properties, and energetic frequencies to the healing process. Always be sure to give thanks.

One of my particular favorites in the stone world is rose quartz, which was used in Scotland as a *fever stone*. I have found it to be a very soothing *heart stone*, and one that carries the loving energy of the Goddess. Rose quartz is always on my Faery Altar, and I often hold it while journeying to the Faery Realm.

THREAD MAGIC

Threads are used to tie, bind, and secure things magically. Threads may also be used to tie up and constrain an ailment so that it can progress no further. In addition, threads form a link from one thing to another. In healing, threads may be used to link the ailment to the powers and beings of healing. In this sense, it is as if the thread is a pathway for the healing energy to follow. It allows the stronger energy, i.e., the healing energy, to *retune* the unbalanced frequency of the ailment.

Because of these very same qualities, threads can be a versatile tool in Faery Healing, and a useful part of the *reweaving*.

As you can see, threads can be used for both constraining and linking. Both of these, when done as magical actions, require very careful thought, as well as consideration of the possible repercussions.

In this book, we speak often of the Web of Life. I envision this Web sometimes as a delicately spun spider web, glistening in the sunlight or moonlight, or sometimes as a beautifully woven piece of cloth.

The Web of Life is made of threads, threads that connect and link with each other in intricate and delicate ways, ways which are not always obvious or apparent to us. They are the threads of the very structure of life. They are the warp and woof of the weaving of life and destiny, both personal and collective.

These threads may be thought of as the gift or tool of both Center and circumference of the Sacred Circle/Web of Life, as they are what link all together.

We must remember that we are not the Master Weaver of this Web. We are but a part of it—and each part affects every other part. These things are important to keep in mind in all our workings, but especially when we use threads—and their powers of constraining and linking—as a part of our magical practice.

For more information on thread magic and the significance of the different colored threads, please refer back to *Chapter 4*.

Spiritual Aspects of Healing
FAERY HEALING AS ENERGY WORK

In one sense, Faery Healing is a form of energy work, so many of the protocols of energy work will apply. But it is a special form of energy work, a *co-creative* endeavor, wherein the work is done with assistance from the Faery Realm. Using our own subtle senses, we work with the subtle energies of the Faery World, through the intercession of our Faery Allies and helpers, mediating the Primal Wholeness.

As W. B. Yeats has said, "One is constantly hearing that 'the others' must have a mortal among them, for almost everything they do..... The tradition seems to be that, though wisdom comes to us from among spirits, the spirits must get physical power from among us."[2]

BASICS OF SPIRITUAL HEALING

Even science now concedes that the mind and emotions have a powerful influence on the body. The attitudes we hold can have a great effect on our health and well-being. In truth, the body and mental-emotional complex are so interwoven that the mind can be a mighty tool for healing.

Prayer

The power of prayer to affect medical outcomes, the subject of serious scientific research since at least the 1980s, is now being documented. Studies have been done with prayer groups praying for specific health outcomes in specific individuals. The results were quite positive. Prayer does have an effect, whether the person being prayed for is aware of it or not, and whether or not the person doing the praying even knows the person for whom he or she is praying.

Interestingly, similar studies have been done in Europe wherein prayer groups prayed for the growth or non-growth of nonhuman entities such as animals, plants, and even bacteria, thus ruling out the human element of desire or wish fulfillment. In each of these scenarios, the entity—whether human or nonhuman—responded according to the focus of the prayers directed at it.

These studies would seem to demonstrate what we have stated previously: that the power of focused *intention* (i.e., prayer) causes energy to flow in the direction of the object of that focus. As we have observed from the lore, Faery Healers were frequently noted to have prayed during their sessions.

One of the lessons we can take from the above information is that spiritual help—be it from the Divine, guides, angels, or faeries—is always available to us. All we need to do is ask for it, then use our intention and attention to allow it and focus it.

The Energy of Emotions

The way it seems to work is this: Thoughts and emotions generate energy. Energy moves in waves that have two basic aspects: strength and frequency. The strength of the energy can be weak, moderate or strong. The energy's frequency can be rapid, moderate, or slow. The energy itself can be expansive or contractive, or varying degrees of either of these. Emotional energy also has direction; it can move inward or outward.

These variables are affected by three things. The first is how close the facts or details of the situation inspiring the thought or emotion are to us personally. In other words, we will experience stronger emotions, whether positive or negative, about things that directly affect or can affect our loved ones or us. But the other things affecting these variables are intention and will, which are matters of choice. As is indicated by the studies on prayer, if we choose to direct our attention toward something, we think and often *feel* about that thing, and—as we have stated previously—this directs energy toward it.

The energy of emotion has varying qualities to it as well, depending, of course, on

The Energy of Emotions

EMOTION	Frequency	Quality
Love	High	Permeating; fast or slow as appropriate; gentle expansive
Joy	High	Springy; soaring; expansive
Hope	High	Springs and opens up and outward; expansive
Fear	Fast	Too high and too low; contractive
Anger	Fast	Pushy; tight and self-defensive; contractive; sometimes explosive/expansive
Grief	High	Fast or slow
Depression	Low	Slow; inward; contractive

which emotion it is. These are hard to define, although I've made an attempt.

We can use this bit of wisdom for purposes of healing by making positive, healing changes in our own lives. It is important to watch ourselves, to see what affects us and how, and to begin to take responsibility for our reactions. It is important to practice mindfulness and virtue. When we *actively* practice love, compassion, forgiveness, and the like, we are sending forth specific frequencies of energy, and those particular frequencies are healing to ourselves and others.

By opening ourselves to the Faery Realm, by attuning to love and joy, and by living in a manner that creates beauty, we increase the amount of these positive, life-affirming frequencies that exist in our world. Individually, the power we generate doing this is quite significant, but collectively, it is an awesome power. It would therefore serve us well to meet with others of like mind to do healing work, and send forth these healing energies—the power of the group amplifying and multiplying the energies—so that a significant amount of power may be sent forth.

Healing with Energy Tools, Techniques, and Medicines

There are some time-honored energetic tools and techniques of spiritual healing that work with the subtle bodies and the energy field. Some of these have been touched upon in previous chapters in our discussion of the methods of the Faery Doctors. We are fortunate to live in times when many of these are being revitalized and many new ones created.

These energy medicines and techniques work on our subtle bodies and aura. By use of their specific modalities, they create frequency changes that realign imbalanced frequency patterns, causing them to move back into a state of balance and harmony.

Energy Medicines. Some of the most well known of the energy medicines available to us are homeopathic remedies and flower essences.

The subject of how energy medicines work is complex, but the basis of it is that the medium used, such as water, is capable of retaining a *memory* of the plant substance infused in it (an *energy signature* if you will). That *memory* still has potency, although it will work somewhat differently than if one imbibed the actual chemicals found in the plant. Usually only a very tiny amount, perhaps microscopic, of the plant's chemical signature may be present in the medium; sometimes there is no measurable amount at all. Yet homeopathy *does* work, as many through the last few centuries have found.

Many good books are available on homeopathy, flower essences, acupuncture theory, and other ways of working with the body's energy. These books detail the history of these systems, the methods of remedy preparation, lists of various remedies and indications for their correct use, contraindications, and the like. I have used flower remedies for several years, and have found them safe and effective. As with herbalism, these are subjects requiring serious, deep study for anyone wanting to actually practice this form of healing.

A much simpler, more homegrown way of working with energy medicines is in the making of Blessed Waters, a subject that will be dealt with in *Chapter 22*.

Sound Medicine. As was discussed in previous chapters, the power of sound was known and used by Druids and the Faery Doctors. The tones of the scale have specific vibrational frequencies; these have correlations with the chakras, and can have effects on the body-mind complex. Once again, there is much to study on this subject here if one wants to approach it in a professional manner.

My approach is less formal. I sing, chant, or intone the words, sounds, and melodies that come to me when I am working on the land or on a person. Interestingly, this happens for me less often than other, inner, healing adjuncts despite the fact that I am a trained singer.

Colorful Cures. Like sound, colors have specific frequencies, correspondences, and effects. (See chart below.) Books on color therapy detail these specifics. I tend to keep it simple,

The Energy of Colors

COLOR	Temperature	Wavelength/Frequency	Effects
Red	Hot	Longest Wavelength Lowest Frequency Dense	Stimulating Linked strongly to the physical realm
Orange	Very warm	Long Wavelength Slightly Faster Frequency Dense	Stimulating Energetic
Yellow	Warm	Shorter Wavelength Faster Frequency Less Dense	Busy Stimulating, but balancing
Green	Moderate	Medium Wavelength Medium Frequency	Harmonizing Balancing Refreshing Bridge between material and spiritual realms
Blue	Cool	Short Wavelength Fast Frequency Least Dense Diffuse	Expansive Relaxing Calming
Indigo	Cold	Short Wavelength Faster Frequency	More Diffuse Expansive
Violet	Cold	Shortest Wavelength Highest Frequency Very Diffuse	Quite Expansive Least Physical Linked strongly to the spiritual realm

relating the colors to the chakras and classifying them as hot, warm, moderate, cool, and cold, and, fast, medium, slow, and dense to diffuse/expanded. I use color in my healing work only when guided to do so by my allies. The study of color is fascinating, and as any artist will attest, colors affect each other, enhancing or anti-doting one another. This is true about what happens on the energetic level as well. More on the practical, day-to-day use of color as spiritual nutrition will be given in the next chapter.

Sound, color, and frequency or number—all of these things were important and used by Faery Doctors and the Druids before them. Each of these could and should be studied in great depth by those wishing to use them effectively and in a specific manner.

However, in Faery Healing, we work with our allies and allow them and our intuition to guide us. Generally speaking, we stick to simple and very natural ways of doing things rather than complex and modern methods and approaches.

You carry the power of sound with you at all times in your own voice. Bear in mind the power of the Sacred Three in your work. Remember that you are always surrounded by all the colors of the rainbow—present in earth and sky as well as within your own body's chakra system. Remember also that you are always surrounded by the Four Elements:

Fire of sun
Water of dew and rain
Air you breathe
Earth beneath your feet.

Faery Healing is, essentially, the rebalancing and healing of the Spirit by beauty and love—as embodied by our Faery Kin. This is work at a very deep soul level. Please keep this in mind no matter which technique or modality you use. Concentrate on this aspect, rather than on manipulation of the physical realm. If the healing is at all meant to be, the physical means will be revealed to you, and the physical-realm issues will, later on, come into whatever balance they can.

END NOTES

1   Traditional Chinese Medicine teaches that there are 365 acupuncture points on the 12 primary meridians of the human body.

2   Yeats, W. B., "Irish Witch Doctors," *Fortnightly Review,* 1900.

CHAPTER 21

Empowering Yourself to Heal

Nature as Nurture
—Color as Spiritual Sustenance

For most of human history, humans have lived close to nature. It has only been fairly recently that we have so thoroughly isolated ourselves into the sun-proof, scent-proof, sound-proof cubicles of house and office which depend so much upon completely artificial means for lighting, heating, cooling, and air freshening. This unfortunate new trend has served to cut us off from one of our largest sources of nourishment: the colors, scents, and sounds of nature.

There have been many fine books written on color therapy, and I do not intend to go into a long discussion of the principles of general color therapy here. But I do wish to call your attention to how nature gifts us each day with her beautiful colors and gives us an opportunity to feast on them, and thus nourish and replenish our body, mind, soul, emotions, and spirit.

Consider, for instance, the vast blue sky that covers us each day with its lovely azure canopy and each night with its cobalt-midnight beauty, as well as all other variations of blue that occur during the transitions between night and day. Think of the beautiful clouds, white, grey, and black, which travel the skies in many rapidly changing shapes and sizes.

Take note, as well, of the beautiful full spectrum of colors that present themselves at both sunrise and sunset, as the sky moves from one end of the color spectrum to the other. And think about the many shades of green to be seen in forests, fields, or even in the trees and lawns of cities, and the many hued flowers to be seen there as well.

Ponder the beautiful, many-colored crystals which Earth holds within her caves, as well as the countless, simple grey, white, black rocks and stones, found in abundance on the Earth, and on the seashores. And think of the sea itself, which reflects the sky in all its colors and moods.

Each of these colors offers something special to us, and nature nourishes us with them on a constant basis. Most of the time we take these things for granted as we rush through our days and nights.

But I would invite you to slow down and not only enjoy them but partake of them. Realize that these colorful beauties of nature are nourishing you on a very deep level, and consciously breathe the beauty and color into yourself as you behold them. Breathe out your gratitude to them in return.

Various colors have various effects, both physically and psychologically. The so-called *cool* colors of blue, indigo, and violet are calming and peaceful, whereas the *warm* colors of red, orange, and yellow are exciting, and stimulating. Green, which is in the middle of the spectrum, is a bridge between its two ends, and thus is a color of balance and harmony as well as refreshment and revitalization.

Such colorful nutrition is not only good for the soul but nourishing to the body's energy field as well. Our energy field is composed of the colors of the rainbow—each chakra vibrating at a different frequency that corresponds to a different color of the rainbow. We are rainbows—and a microcosm of nature's color spectrum.

In the body, green is one of the colors (along with pink) associated with the body's Center, the heart chakra. As we have previously mentioned, the color green, associated as it is with the plant world, has been consistently associated with the Faery Realm as well. This seems to be telling us that the Green World and the Faery Realm are the Heart of Nature, the Heart of Life, the Bridge between the Deep Fiery Heart of the Earth and the High Starfire Canopy of the Heavens, and do, indeed, comprise what has been poetically called the *Middle Kingdom*.

In addition to the nourishing color aspect, it has been found that natural places produce a large number of negative ions that greatly enhance health, mood, and attitude, and cause feelings of excitement and vitality. Negative ions, or, more accurately, negatively charged ions, are actually oxygen atoms with an extra electron. They are created in nature when enough energy acts upon a molecule of oxygen, nitrogen, carbon dioxide, or even water, in such a way that it causes the molecule to discharge an electron—leaving the molecule with a positive charge. The discharged ion attaches itself to a nearby molecule, which then becomes negatively charged. Rushing, tumbling water, such as is found in waterfalls or the crashing waves of the sea, seems to accelerate this natural process, as does lightning. Negative ions are more plentiful in fresh air than in stale or polluted air. This is yet another way in which we are nurtured by nature.

COLOR BREATHING

The following exercise will help you learn how to breathe color in and out and fill yourself with it, as well as how to access it in your own body so that you can use it for healing. In this way you can—when guided by your intuition and allies—channel color into those you heal or put it into your medicines.

EXERCISE | Chakra and Color Breathing Exercises

Sit quietly, and deep breathe... Grow your roots down and into the ground till they have linked into the Earth's core. Inhale, and bring up the Earth energy from the core and into your body. Feel it moving up your legs, and into your torso, and be aware of your first chakra, the root chakra, which is vibrating at the frequency of *RED*... Just be aware of this, and allow it to be. Breathe in red through your pores; feel red permeate all your cells, and breathe out again.

Move the energy upward to your second chakra, and be aware that the frequency has shifted to that of *ORANGE*. Allow this, and feel it. Breathe in orange through your pores; feel orange permeate all your cells, and breathe out again.

Move the energy upward to your third chakra, your solar plexus, and be aware that it is vibrating at the frequency of *YELLOW*. Allow this, and feel it. Breathe in yellow through your pores; feel yellow permeate all your cells, and breathe out again.

Move the energy upward to your fourth chakra, your heart, and be aware that the frequency has shifted to that of *GREEN*. Allow this, and feel it. Breathe in green through your pores; feel green permeate all your cells, and breathe out again.

Move the energy upward to your fifth chakra, your throat, and be aware that the frequency has shifted to that of *BLUE*. Allow this, and feel it. Breathe in blue through your pores; feel blue permeate all your cells, and breathe out again.

Move the energy upward to your sixth chakra, your third eye, and be aware that the frequency has shifted to that of *INDIGO*. Allow this, and feel it. Breathe in indigo through your pores; feel indigo permeate all your cells, and breathe out again.

Move the energy upward to your seventh chakra, the crown of your head and be aware that the frequency has shifted to that of *VIOLET*. Allow this, and feel it. Breathe in violet through your pores; feel violet permeate all your cells, and breathe out again.

Feel the energy move through the crown of your head in a fountain of rainbow colors. Be aware that directly above you the colors merge and become *WHITE* light, before dividing again and falling down around you on all sides. They create a rainbow around you as they fall down and into the Earth...

Take some time simply being with this experience. When you are finished, slowly bring yourself back to your ordinary waking consciousness, feeling fully nourished by the rainbow of colors which you have breathed in to enhance the rainbow within your own body.

Be sure to record your experiences in your Magical Journal.

Healing sounds of nature

Make a practice of being aware of the sounds of nature. This is not always an easy thing to do, especially if you live in a big city with its own set of sounds. Even our homes, abuzz with the modern sounds of refrigerators and heaters, offer impediment to hearing the sounds of nature. But the sound of the wind in the trees, the sounds of rushing water, pounding surf, birds singing, bees buzzing, the fire crackling in your hearth—all of these bring a nourishment and a primal satisfaction that is incomparable, at least to me.

I recall days as a child living in the Los Angeles area when I would stand at the front door listening to the sound of the wind, which was, to me, so clearly a voice speaking its own language, a language which contained very definite emotional feeling-tones. In those days I could understand what the wind was saying. Often, but not always, it brought me messages from far away places which were dear to me, allowing me to feel the energy of those places, and see them in my mind. Although my ability to do this has lessened over the years, I still try to be open to what the wind has to say. The crackling of fire speaks its own language, as do the splash, gurgle, and rushing sounds made by the various forms of water—rivers, streams, and the sea all having their own distinct voices. Listen to them.

Sun and moon

The sun is our own, local star, and to connect consciously with it is to connect with Star Power. This is the same power that is at the heart of every molecule of life, the great hearth-fire of life, in fact. The moon shines with reflected sunlight and so partakes, in a lesser way, of the power of the stars.

The habit of connecting with the sun and moon may not seem like it is related to Faery Healing, since it is said that in the Land of Faery neither sun nor moon are thought to shine. But the power of the stars is found within the planet as well as outside of it, in the form of the fiery core of the planet—Earth's heart fire—as well as in the spark within the nuclei of every atom. As scientists tell us, all matter is *star stuff*. On an energetic level, this InnerEarth starlight has been referred to as the Earth-Light.

It hardly needs to be pointed out that we, as humans, are quite dependent on the light and energy of the sun for our very lives.

Though living in a realm where neither sun nor moon shine, faeries are known to be out and about during both day and night. The legends tell us that faeries are thought to love the moonlight, and to hold their dances and revels under the magically mysterious light of the full moon.

Making a daily ritual of consciously connecting with these two beings will keep you filled and well charged with the Life Force itself in a very potent way, as will making a conscious connection with the Earth-Light.

You may want to adopt the practice of saying some of the prayers given in *Chapter 2* each day when you first greet sun and moon, and being aware of what they bring to your life, the beauty, the energy, as well as their physiological helpfulness.

EXERCISE | Sun Breathing

Take some time everyday, preferably at dawn, noon, sunset, or all of these, to consciously connect with the sun as a being. Breathe in the sunshine with your breath, and feel it not just upon your skin, but feel it circulating through your entire body, bathing every cell and organ. Send your consciousness out to the sun, expressing your love and gratitude to him/her, and send this out and up to the sun on a beam of energy that comes from your heart. Feel, in return, the warmth and life that the sun provides, and breathe it in. This, as you can see, is cyclical as breath is cyclical—in and out, over and over, for as long as you wish to do the exercise. Three times, seven times, or multiples of these are both good.

EXERCISE | Moon Breathing

This is similar to Sun Breathing but of course done in the moonlight. Take yourself out side in the moonlight during all phases of the moon's cycle and gaze upward at the moon, sending forth your love and gratitude for the moon's beauty, and gifts. Then breathe in the moonlight; draw it down into yourself with several breaths; drink it, breathe it, feel it come into you through every pore of your body, nourishing you, recharging you, the excess flowing out and into the earth on the exhale.

EXERCISE | Earth-Light Breathing

Go down to Earth's core as you would when doing the grounding exercises. Then move your awareness up and into the Realm of Faery, with Earth-light gleaming and glowing green-gold around you. With several breaths, inhale this Earth-light through your skin and your pores, and allow it to recharge you, nourish you, and connect you with the Faery Realm. Allow the excess to flow out and into the Earth on the exhaled breath.

SHAPESHIFTING/MERGING

We have discussed shapeshifting in previous chapters, and have defined it as the ability to shift the state of our *inner shape* from human to non-human consciousness. Tales of another kind of shapeshifting, that of physically changing from one shape to another, are found in many native legends of both America and Europe. Selkies, vampires, and werewolves come to mind here, as do the European witches who were said to assume the forms of cats or hares (or other animals) when they ventured out into the night to their Sabbat revels.

In legend and lore, the faeries themselves are known as great shapeshifters. This is not surprising in that faeries are beings of subtle energy rather than the more solid form of energy of which our physical beings are comprised. Because of this, faeries are not bound to a form; they are more fluid and flowing, able to transmute and transform their shapes as they desire or as they deem necessary.

In my previously mentioned dream about faeries and their wings, the first shape in which the faeries appeared to me was as small, glowing spheres of light. As I watched, these small spheres radiated energy downward, upward, and outward and assumed a butterfly-shaped pattern which was, I realized, the pattern of Earth's magnetic energy grid (see Note 1 at the end of the chapter). These butterfly shapes then rapidly shifted into more recognizably animal and humanoid type beings with heads, arms, legs, and of course, in some of them at least, those wonderful, energy-moving wings.

Faeries appear to us as shapeshifters because they *are* actually shifting their shapes. The shapes in which they present themselves to us may have to do with our personal or cultural expectations and perceptions, which the faeries are capable of mirroring back to us to some extent. Then again, a faery's appearance may have to do with that faery's particular functional aspect, or its wishes and desires of the moment.

As my dream indicated to me, faeries are essentially beings of subtle energy and thus may appear simply as glowing spheres (or other shapes) of light. Because they are alive, they move around, they "breathe" energy in and out, and thus their shape really *can* change—expand and contract—as they perform the life functions of breathing, thinking, feeling, moving, and doing. How we perceive this (light, shapes, or just a feeling) will depend on our natural psychism, as well as on our cultural conditioning and expectations, the function of a given being, and/or the job it is performing or enacting at that moment.

EXERCISE IDEAS

If you have practiced the shapeshifting techniques *Chapter 15*, you will know how to allow this to occur with your Faery Allies should they initiate this process. Please do not attempt to initiate the process yourself. If they feel such a merging is necessary for whatever work you are doing, they will initiate it themselves. Always be careful to return to your human shape at the end of these shapeshifting experiences.

EXERCISE | Shapeshifting Breathing

Here is a breathing exercise which will facilitate loosening, shapeshifting, and merging.

Close your eyes and relax. Take a deep breath and let it out slowly. Breathe in and out slowly and deeply three times, each time becoming more relaxed, and feeling yourself becoming softer, and more open. With each breath you feel your outer boundaries softening, loosening, thinning, becoming more permeable and transparent. Unroll your consciousness into the family cat or dog, or a tree in your back yard, and allow your consciousness to merge with its consciousness. Experience this... Then bring yourself back to an awareness of your own self and body. Resume the slow, in and out, conscious breathing pattern, and with each breath in and out, you feel your own human boundaries forming again, and your auric shell becoming less permeable, and more solid.

EXERCISE | Delving into Your Multi-fold Essence

This exercise gives you access to some of the many parts of the vastness of your being.

Using the above exercise, breathe yourself into a state of looseness once again. Then reach inside yourself till you feel your seed energetic essence, which is located in the vicinity of your heart and which may appear to you as a tiny glowing sphere. As you watch, it changes in size and shape as it radiates and pulses with your breath and thoughts. Move inside of it, and feel the essence of who you are... Find within it the part of you which is of the plant family, and feel your energetic or light body shapeshift in response to this... As your edges dissolve in the process of merging and blending, notice how this feels... Now find that within your essence which is non-human animal, and feel yourself shift again. Search for the part of you that is bird, and find yourself again, shapeshifting. And finally, find the place within you that is Faery, and feel yourself shapeshifting and flowing into your faery self. As you shift into each of these shapes, be very aware of how each of them feels. These will be quite subtle distinctions and feelings; but do notice them, so that later on you may return—by remembering the feeling state—to these states of consciousness, these parts of your essential, multi-fold self.

Remember the importance that the borderlands have in making contact with other realms of being, including Faery. They are places of merging—where one shapeshifts into another. Remember to use them in your workings.

Working with Your Sacred Land
WORKING WITH NATURE IN YOUR AREA

It's not just all in the Old Country you know. Please don't think all the faeries live only in Ireland, Scotland, or any of the other lands from which the previously quoted faery lore originates, or that you cannot do faery work if you are unable to make a pilgrimage to those places.

If you think this you are missing the point. Life is where you are. Nature is where you are. Faeries are where you are. Even if you are in the depths of the most concretized of cities, please remember that the land is beneath the concrete, and that the trees and flowers in your city's landscaping and planter boxes are living creatures with whom you may communicate and make your contact with the natural realm. The fairies and faeries of your land might be different from the ones in Irish folklore, but they are relevant to you because they are *your* "Good Neighbors."

MY GOOD NEIGHBORS

One of my strongest experiences of this was a beautiful Beltaine morning a few years back when the river called me to come and visit. I live in a small city which has a lovely, lazy river flowing through it. The river itself, as it winds through town surrounded on every side by buildings and businesses, is fortunately still in a wild state rather than one of the cement-channeled travesties so beloved of the U.S. Army Corps of Engineers. Yes, there are a few levees here and there, especially near the mouth where it joins the sea, but all in all, the river and riverbed are in a fairly wild state most of the time. This particular Beltaine morning, as I dropped my son at a bus stop near where the river flows through town, the river called to me quite loudly to come pay a visit.

I found a parking place and hiked up the embankment, then down onto the riverbank. Instantly I was in a different world, and almost, a different time. The riverbank was lush with spring plants and flowers; the aroma was tantalizing. I stooped to smell the mugwort and wild fennel, and noticed tiny colorful wild flowers poking themselves up nearby. The river flowed quietly along, bigger from the recent rains than when I'd last visited it. A gentle breeze wafted through, stirring the treetops.

As I took all of this in, I became aware with my subtle senses that everything was shimmering with life and radiance. I could *feel* the plant spirits in their spring-summer vibrancy. I could *feel* faeries hovering around the river and the plants, entering the flood plain and riverbank in increasing numbers, and anxious to begin a new cycle of their work of regeneration, renewal, and restoration. I realized this had to do with it being Beltaine, and I just *knew*, somehow, that they were arriving for the summer. I suddenly remembered that the faeries are known to change residences at the Quarter Days, of which Beltaine is one.

The river was the dominant presence, and I could feel it as a living being. Before I knew what I was doing, I began to sing to the river—a slow and winding song like the river itself, a song of coming to life with this new season, a song of love and appreciation. I did not plan this; it's just what came out of my mouth as if I were merely giving voice to what was already there or what was coming up from the land itself. In a way, I think the river was teaching me her particular song of that particular season.

The song expanded to include the plants and trees growing along the river, and the rocks and stones as well. I felt as though my song were affirming the life of the unique, integral energy of this particular place.

The song expanded again, to include the Faery Beings, and I realized I was singing them back to the river valley, welcoming them in, and singing appreciation for them and all that they are and do. I felt a strong and urgent desire to consciously renew my bonds of alliance with them, and with all the life of this river area. So I did this as my song continued. I think it became part of the singing.

I do not know for how long my song went on, but finally it slowed and stopped of its own accord, and I stood silently gazing at all the life shimmering around me. I realized that the river had given me many messages, one of which was to serve her not only by my singing but also by the very mundane and important task of picking up any trash in the area. My mind filled with images of people coming there in small groups to *be* with the river, picking up the trash, but also allowing the river to teach them her songs in all her various seasons.

Then, with my inner vision, I felt myself taken inside the land and deep into Faery's Inner Realm. I came to the place where the Flame of Being burns within the Faery Hearth...and found myself mediating it—and the Primal Wholeness of the Faery Realm—through my body, up and into the land upon which I stood. I allowed this energy to flow till it tapered off of its own accord.

Finally, I felt myself to be finished and quietly left the riverbank, climbed back up and over the embankment, and went home—with very much to think about.

THE PRIMEVAL PRISTINE LAND AND THE PRIMAL WHOLENESS

We have spoken of the Primeval or Pristine Land and of the Primal Wholeness. What this is, in essence, is the original, undisturbed state of the land as it remains within the subtle, innerworld dimension of the land. It remains there, like an energetic blueprint or template, within the memory of the land. In the Pristine Land, the landscape is undisturbed by human interference. All the plants are native to the specific bio-region and vibrant with health. The native, local animals are there—predator and prey alike—living their natural lives. The waters are clean and clear; the air is clean and clear. The natural system of checks and balances is in perfect working order.

It is this template that we wish to work with, overlaying it on the outer land by use of our imagination, visualization, and mediation of power. This is both *Bridge-building* and *Reweaving*, and is the work of those who may be called *Green Priests and Priestesses*.

LINKING WITH YOUR LAND

When doing spiritual and innerwork, it is important to realize that there are always several levels to the work.

First there is the *mental* level—our information gathering and thoughts on what it is we are doing. Secondly, there is the *emotional* level—how do we feel about it, as our feelings are an important source of energy for our working. Thirdly, there is the *spiritual* work itself—journeying, mediating energy, doing healing, making contact with our inner allies and the deities. Fourth, there is the *practical*, earthy, outerworld level of the work, which has to do with things in this realm, the physical realm.

There is work to be done appropriate to each level. Just as we would not simply meditate on a splinter in our finger and expect it to fall out of its own accord, we also must do our work in a manner appropriate to the level or levels of the problems and issues.

Often a particular working will call for one or more of these in a quite specific way. But when it comes to linking into the land, making contact and working with the local faery folk, I feel the practical level is quite important. Faery lore tells us of faeries offended by work left undone, by untidiness, by disrespect for their special paths and places. This is illustrated in the folklore by mention of such disrespectful acts as the throwing of the footwater (water in which the feet were washed each night before retiring) out the door and onto faery pathways. This has always seemed to me to be quite analogous to the act of polluting and thus seems particularly applicable to the situation of the desecration of our lands today.

One of the ways we can show our local faery folk that we really wish to have a relationship with them is to attend to our local land. First and foremost, do not, in the process of your use of the land, especially for ritual, leave a mess! Ever! Do not pollute the land with your human leavings of paper, plastic, candlewax, and ritual paraphernalia. Secondly, clean up the wild places that are in need of cleaning. Haul away trash. Last of all, its nice to leave biodegradable gifts and offerings for the Faery Folk; foods such as cream, milk, butter, honey, bread, and sweet cakes are traditional. I suspect they like homemade cookies, as well!

When you come upon a place which has been abused by humans, consider it an opportunity to do some good work by cleaning it up as best you can, and then, if it feels appropriate, by attuning it to the Faery Hearth, mediating the Primal Wholeness to the place, and inviting back the resident Faery Beings who may have been forced away by the abuse, pollution, and destruction. Be sure that you call on your own Faery Allies to help you with this process. In terms of the terminology we use in Faery Healing, this is *Retuning*.

Make a practice—daily, weekly, or monthly as it suits your schedule—of working with a natural feature in your landscape: a mountain, river, lake, ocean, field, forest, tree, plant, or whatever you like. Tune in and see what it says to you and what you can do for it. If it makes no requests of you, then just send it blessings and love or perhaps, if it feels appropriate, tune into the Faery Hearth and mediate energy to it from the Pristine Land and the Faery Hearth. You can use *Seasonal Journeys #1 and 2* from "Seasonal Work with the Convocations" found in *Chapter 18* for this purpose, as these are *Mediation* journeys.

Journey to Link into Your Land

This is a journey that you must construct for yourself because only you know where you are. Use what is given here as suggestion and inspiration to fire your mind and feed your imagination. Its purpose is for you to journey into the land where you live right now, to get acquainted with it, and to find out what it wants you to do for it.

Wherever you currently reside, think about how the terrain was before humans were there. You may want to do some research on this and find out about the terrain, the plants, and the animals so that you can form some good imagery as you do this working.

Spend time simply sitting in your backyard or, if you lack a yard, find a fairly quiet, natural place near your home; a city park will do nicely. Sit there quietly and allow the energy of the land to seep up and inside you. Think of what kind of land this was originally, and what it would be in its native state. Then journey into the land to learn what it can teach you.

If you live in an area that was once forested, build in your mind the image of a magnificent forest of tall, healthy, beautiful trees. If you live in a desert area, build an image of the stark beauty of the desert with its startling austerity of cacti, barren and sandy lands, sagebrush, and wild animals. If you live in the plains, visualize it as it once was: wide open, a sea of wild grasses and flowers stretching as far as the eye can see and gently waving in the wind, broken only by gullies and the tree-lined rivers that flow through them. If you live near the coast, visualize the coastal plains and rolling hills, dropping down into sea cliffs or beaches, or river mouths, and the wildly beautiful sea beyond with its waves rushing in and out onto the sandy shores. If you live in the mountains, visualize them covered with their native trees, shrubs, and flowers, peaks touching the sky, a family of mountain beings, caressed by the clouds, winds, and rain.

As you construct your journey, be aware that it is helpful to the imagination to include sensory information. For instance, you will want to answer the following questions:

- How does it look?
- What sounds do you hear?

- Can you feel wind, rain, sunshine?
- Are there any noticeable aromas?
- What is before you, behind you, and to your sides?
- Who is there: plants, animals, or other beings?
- What is above you?
- What is below you?

General Notes About the Beings of Nature

In the world, there are many trees. There are many mountains and mountain ranges. There are several large oceans, and many smaller, inland lakes and seas. There are many, many rivers. Yet all these rivers, mountains, lakes, and oceans are connected with the others of their kind by virtue of the essence of their "river-hood," "mountain-hood," "lake-hood," and the like. This does not detract from their individuality any more than identifying ourselves as human beings detracts from our own individual identities.

This unity is a useful concept to work with magically. In a sense, we may work with a river or forest, yet work with *all* rivers and forests at the same time.

One sleepless night when the spirits were eager to be heard, I found myself pulling the world atlas off the bookshelf and sitting down at the kitchen table with it. I opened it to a picture of the North American continent, and my eyes were drawn to the rivers of the continent. At first I just looked at the big, famous ones—the Mississippi, the Missouri, and the Hudson. Then, I began to notice something. While the Mississippi appears to be the primary major waterway of the North American continent, almost all of the rivers were, somehow, connected....Rivers becoming rivers, becoming streams and creeks, tributaries, big and little.

As I gazed at the map, realizing this, suddenly my perspective shifted, and I was viewing the image of the North American continent as a Living Being, and the river system on it as a Being. This Being, which I began calling the One River, is a winding, flowing Being, with many arms, large and small. These arms are the tributaries which wind their way across the continent, connecting with each other, going underground and into water tables, becoming individualized, yet still are part of the One Being who is River. As River flows across the land, she sustains and nourishes the land, the Continental Being. This is similar, I realized, to how our circulatory system carries our sustaining, nourishing, oxygenated blood in its many tributaries throughout our body.

I closed the atlas and spent time with these thoughts. Later, I realized that the same principle holds true in other part of the Earth, and thought of the Nile in Egypt, the Ganges in India, the Yangtze in China, the Amazon in South America, and the Danube and Volga in Europe. It is not always so much a continental phenomena as I experienced it, as it is a bio-regional one. Either way, I felt it to be an important teaching about how the energy of an area's major river nourishes the land, and is essential to the land's well-being. This is yet another reason that we need to clean our polluted waterways, and restore them to health.

JOURNEY | There Is One River

Settling comfortably before your Faery Altar, you light the Faery Hearth candle that is in the center of the altar... As you gaze at this center flame, breathing slowly in and out, you find that you are becoming more relaxed, calm, and serene with each breath. You focus your attention on the candle, then close your eyes, seeing the candle with your inner vision. As you do this, you feel yourself passing into the inner realms...

At length, you find yourself standing on a seashore, watching the waves break onto the shore... You call to your Faery Allies, and they come to you. As you stand on the shore with your Faery Allies, gazing at the ocean, a breeze begins to blow. You raise your arms up to the sky to enjoy the breeze, and find your arms turning into wings, and your body into that of a bird... You have become a bird, a large bird with great and powerful wings. Opening your wings fully you begin to flap them, catching the wind, and rising high up into the sky. You begin flying toward the North, and your Faery Allies fly along with you...

You fly along, watching the varied landscape pass beneath you, and feeling the air currents which help carry your feathered body... You fly north... continually north... farther and farther north you fly... until you have reached the Far North, as far as you are able to go on this continent. Then you swoop downward, shapeshifting into your human form as you make landfall, your Faery Allies beside you...

You are standing in a cold and frozen land that is covered in snow. There are a few winter-browned plants poking through the snow and small trees nearby, barren of leaves. It feels very fresh and clean here, very wild and primal... Before you, a small spring bubbles out from the Earth and flows toward the south, widening out into a small creek as it goes... This is the place where the One River begins...

You reach into your heart, and pull something out. You find that your hands are now holding a gift for the river. The gift is a small gourd filled with Blessed Water and also with love from your heart for all things wild and natural. As you hold it up, offering it to the Four Directions, you can feel your allies, and the local faeries and nature spirits as well, infuse their blessings into the water contained in the gourd... You hold the gourd of water up to the heavens and bring it back down again, and press it against your heart... Then you pour the water from the gourd into the spring at the place where it has become a creek... As you pour the water, your consciousness merges with the water, and you become a drop of this Blessed Water as it travels downward and merges with the spring...

You flow along, aware of the other droplets of water, and yet part of them at the same time... You are aware of the water spirits, rushing, tumbling, dancing in the drops of water as you flow along to the South... As the creek widens into a river, you are aware of the blessing in the water spreading itself out to encompass the entire width of the river, sharing its blessedness with every droplet of water it encounters, and with every rock and plant and bit of soil as well... As this happens you feel the blessing disseminating and dispersing itself outward through these things, outward farther, and farther yet... till you lose track of how far it has spread...

With your Faery Allies still beside you, flowing in their own drops of water, you continue to flow along, blessing as you flow... The river comes to a place where it spread itself out into arms... and farther on, the arms stretch themselves out into more arms... Your consciousness broadens out again and again, and you spread yourself and your drop of the blessing into all these arms as well...

You become aware that the blessing power as carried by the water blesses, purifies, and revitalizes all it touches, and that the blessing spreads wherever there is the least molecule of the water... Animals and humans come to drink from the rivers, and are blessed... Plants and shrubs growing near the riverbank are blessed... The riverbank itself is blessed as the water flows rapidly along... Water seeps into water tables below the surface of the land, and the water table is blessed, and revitalized... Blessed as well is the soil through which the water has seeped... As the water flows and these things happen, the blessing in the water strengthens, in a way that is almost homeopathic, because the blessing continues to spread and even amplify no matter how small the water molecule becomes, or how widely it is dispersed...

This continues... until you become aware that the drops of water containing the blessings have merged and blended with all the rivers on the continent... and all these rivers, creeks, and streams are approaching their natural outlets at the various coasts of the continent, East, West, and South... As the drops of water flow out into the sea, the drops of Blessed Water merge with the waters of the sea... As they disperse, you lose track of them...

You now feel finished with this Work of Blessing, and find that you are once again becoming a bird... You spread your wings and fly, your Faery Allies once again flying beside you, back to the place where you began this journey... As you come to Earth you find that you are shifting back into your normal human form, as you become aware, once again, of this place, this time, and your body resting comfortably in a room where a candle burns... You are back... You take a few moments to come completely back to yourself, and when you feel ready, you open your eyes.

Be sure to record your journey in your Magical Journal.

FAERY GLENS AND FAERY GARDENS

Because it is so essential to connect with the land when doing faery work, it is advisable to find a place outdoors where you can make the connection with the Realm of Faery. The most convenient, of course, is one's own backyard, and if it is possible to set aside a place for this purpose in one's own yard, the reward is consistent and continual access, as well as the chance to make the spot a place of especial beauty. If no yard space is available, even a carefully tended flowerpot on a deck will do. If even this is impossible, then the nearest place where grass and trees are to be found will work. Privacy is, of course, optimal, if not always possible. But since so much of the work is innerwork with no need for paraphernalia, it is possible for one to simply sit down on a park bench in a city park, tune in, and do some work.

If you are fortunate enough to have a lot of yard space, your options are increased. You may want to consider creating a faery glen and/or a faery garden.

A faery glen is a bit of land that is simply set aside for faery use. The plants grow wildly, untended, in their natural cycle of growth and dying back, and free from threats of pesticides and the family dog. Hopefully, native species will reassert themselves in this area. Such a wild spot is a gift to the Faery Realm, and in times past such a spot was referred to as the *Gudeman's Croft, gudeman* meaning good man or men, and the term being used—euphemistically, as usual—to refer to the faery folk. *Croft* means a small field or farm.

A faery garden is quite different. While both are created to be an attractive invitation for the faeries to enter and take up residence, a faery garden is something created with consciousness, thought, research, and work. To create one, refer to the plant and flower folklore in the preceding chapters and choose plants favored by the faeries. Check out the soil, water, sun, and shade requirements of these plants, choose the ones whose requirements match your locale, and draw up a garden plan. As part of your process sit on the land with your list in hand and ask the faeries what they want planted there. You may be surprised at what they have to say.

Thoughtfully and lovingly plant your garden, and tend it with the strong intention of creating a place of residence for the faeries, nature spirits, devas, birds, bees, and butterflies. This is a place where you can be quite creative, incorporating stones, statuary, benches, pathways, harmonious geometric-shaped patches of plants, color arrangements and the like. It is a place where you can come to relax and be refreshed, but most importantly, it is a place where you come to do your faery work.

This is an ambitious project, and I will confess I have not yet done it myself, though it is on my list of dreams to be realized. However, I do have some lovely faery statuary and a few special faery plants tucked here and there in my yard, as the faeries have directed me! Someday...

NOTES

1. The butterfly-shaped pattern of Earth's magnetic energy grid appears as a butterfly only when seen one- dimensionally; it appears as a bisected sphere when seen three-dimensionally.

Faery Medicines

Creating faery medicines

In this chapter, we will learn the basics of making what I have come to call *faery medicines*. These are made with herbs, flowers, and water, threads and stones, prayers and songs, simple things that our ancestors would have used. And just as the folklore illustrates, these things are made with intention and blessed by our Faery Allies to be used for healing purposes.

They are really quite simple. The tools and techniques for making them are things you have learned in the preceding pages. Only the application is different.

Faery medicines can be made for purposes of assisting physical and spiritual regeneration, or for mental or emotional healing (heart healing). They may also be made for environmental healing.

The making of the faery medicine is a ritual in and of itself. Having decided the particulars about the kind of faery medicine you wish to make, begin each of these medicine-making rituals by creating sacred space, calling in the powers of the Four Directions, the Upperworld and Underworld, and calling on the deities of your choice. As has been mentioned, Brigid, Morgen, and Airmid are all good choices. Tune into the Faery Realm, and call your Faery Allies to assist you in the making of this medicine.

As always, the power of love is of paramount importance in making faery medicines. Open your heart and feel love for all the beings who are helping you, and for the person for whom you are making the remedy.

Always, when making faery medicine, leave gifts and offerings for the faeries in return for the help they are giving you. Such an energy exchange is very important.

MAKING AND WORKING WITH FAERY MEDICINES
BY WATER, BY EARTH, BY FIRE, BY AIR

FAERY MEDICINES | Faery Blessed Waters

Water has a wonderful characteristic that is quite useful in healing. Water has the ability to *hold memory*. In other words, the nature of water is such that it is able to hold the vibration of what is put into it. On a very physical level, this is the quality that allows water to be used to make tea, soup, broth, and such. On a supraphysical (beyond the physical) level, the vibration of the roots, leaves, herbs, flowers, and stones remains in the water, merged and held with the water's molecules, even after the physical substance is removed.

To create Blessed Waters, consider the energies you wish to include in the healing, and pick the time of year, phase of the moon, and time of day of your working accordingly, with respect to the powers of light and dark, hot and cold, waxing and waning, and wet and dry. Pick the day of the week based on the old faery day lore given in *Chapter 4*, or based on the planetary energies of the day.

Day of Week	Planetary Energy
Sunday	Sun
Monday	Moon
Tuesday	Mars
Wednesday	Mercury
Thursday	Jupiter
Friday	Venus
Saturday	Saturn

To make Faery Blessed Waters, start with good, clean water, preferably from a local, natural source such as a well, spring, or river, but even tap water filtered with a very good filter is just fine. Traditionally, the water would have been gathered at or before sunrise, but do the best you can. Fill up a clear glass jar with the water. Thank the water spirits for the water.

Select the herb or herbs you feel are appropriate to the job to be done. It is best if these are either native to your area or grown in your garden, as this brings in the energy of the local beings. Failing this, you may use purchased, dried or fresh herbs. Use a small handful of herbs per quart of water; I seldom make more than a quart at a time, usually less. Tune into the herbs and feel their energies. Thank them, thank the plant spirits and devas, and then place the herbs into the water. Sometimes I use a bowl rather than the jar for this part, and transfer the brew into the jar after it has been stirred.

Using a wooden spoon, mix the herbs in carefully, and begin praying and singing both your intention for the water and your thanks to all these beings, in the manner described in *Chapter 20*. Stir the herbs into the water with a clockwise motion, creating a spiral with your stirring. Feel your Faery Allies next to you, helping you, singing and blessing the mixture in their own special way.

If you intend the medicine for a particular person, it is good to concentrate on them while you are making the medicine, thinking of him or her with love and as restored to health, well-being, and balance.

If you wish, and if it feels right, place three drops of the appropriate flower essence (and you must do your research to determine the correct one) into the water, extending your awareness to the spirit of the particular flower and deva of the species as you do so and giving thanks to them.

Put the lid on your jar, and shake it three, nine, or twenty-seven times. With each shake, affirm with increasing intensity your intention for the water. With the last shake, conclude by saying, "Let it be so!" or "So mote it be!"

Take the jar of herbs and water outside.

Set up a simple altar to the faeries if you wish or use a solitary candle to represent the flame of the Faery Hearth. Strike your match, being aware that you are calling forth the power of Fire, and light the hearth candle. As you do so, take yourself in vision into the realm of Faery using one of the techniques given previously. Tune in to energetic frequency of the Faery Realm and call your Faery Allies to you. See yourself carrying the jar of water and herbs into the Glen of Precious Stones. Set it before the fire of the Faery Hearth and state your intention regarding it. Ask for the blessings of the Faery Realm and the faeries upon it. Feel the power of the flame of the Faery Hearth blaze forth, permeating and infusing the water with its energy.

Now bring yourself and the jar back to this world and set the jar down, preferably on the ground amidst the blades of grass in a place where it can sit undisturbed in the sunlight for a while. Call upon the plant spirits and devas, and your Faery Allies to infuse this medicine with their special blessings of healing. Call upon the sun (and the moon if appropriate) to bless it. Sing or chant as you feel guided and inspired to do so. Remove the jar's lid and once again, stir the water in a clockwise direction three, or nine times.

Cover the jar with a bit of cheesecloth fastened on with a string or rubber band. This will allow air in, but keep out dust and insects. Allow the jar to sit in the sunlight and moonlight for three to nine hours. When the time is finished, go out to retrieve the jar, shake it three more times, and give thanks to all the beings for their help.

If you wish to make Blessed Water without herbs, you may leave the jar outside longer. If you desire to add the power of color to the mix, use a colored jar to make your Blessed Water.

This Blessed Water may now be used in several ways depending upon the purpose for which you have made it. It may be consumed, or it may be used to bathe sore places on the body. It may be poured onto the ground or into a river, lake, stream, or ocean, and in that way spread its blessings.

This technique may be used, with the appropriate modifications, to create Faery Blessed Oils, as well.

FAERY MEDICINES | Faery Blessed Stones

A similar procedure may be followed with the stones you wish to use for Faery Healing. You may begin by gently washing the stone, speaking to it, and asking for its help in the healing work you are undertaking.

Think about the power of stone, the power of Earth, and what this means to the magical medicine you are preparing.

Take the stone outside, and as above, prepare a Faery Altar and light the candle. Go in journey to the Faery Realm, to the Glen of Precious Stones, taking the stone with you. Set the stone before the Faery Hearth and allow the power of the Faery Hearth to infuse the stone with its special energy. In vision, take the stone around to each of the Four Faery Convocations in turn, asking for their special blessings and powers.

Bring the stone and yourself back into this world. Sit for a few moments before your Faery Altar with the stone between your hands, reaffirming your intention for it, blessing and thanking it for its help. If you feel inspired, sing and chant.

Take the stone, and walk around to each of the Four Directions, holding it aloft. Then set it on the altar or the grass where it can lay undisturbed for three days and nights. When the time is up, go out and pick it up, and then spin around nine times clockwise while you are holding it up to the sun.

When you stop, thank all the beings and powers who have helped you.

The stone may now be used in a variety of ways. It can be put into a jar of Blessed Water to amplify the power of both the stone and the water. It may be carried as an amulet of protection. It may be placed into a special bag and worn. It may be buried in the ground or thrown into a body of water to send forth its special powers and blessings. Stones can "hold prayers," as is illustrated by Lady Wilde's account of the women at the holy well piling up white stones as they prayed.

FAERY MEDICINES | Faery Fire

To work with Faery Fire, begin by choosing a candle, preferably beeswax, for your work. If you wish to use a colored candle, red is good for bringing in energy, blue for calming it, green is useful for general healing and bringing in faery and nature energies, black is effective for absorbing illness and negativity, and white is a good all-purpose healing color. Create a Faery Altar outdoors or in a sunny indoors spot. Light your candle and dedicate it to your purpose. For instance, if you wish to use it to assist in the healing of a particular person, dedicate it to their healing, using their name and picturing them as you hold the candle in both hands and project your thoughts and intentions into it.

Let the candle lay in the sunlight on your Faery Altar for no more than five or ten minutes (lest the candle begins to soften and perhaps melt) and ask the power of the sun to bless your candle. Then come stand or sit at your Faery Hearth and tune into the Faery Realm and the Faery Hearth in the Glen of Precious Stones. Holding the candle in both hands, call upon your Faery Allies and the Goddess and God to bless the candle, and to infuse it with healing energy. As you do this, move around the Four Directions to each of the Faery Convocations in turn. Feel the hands of your Faery Allies over your own as you hold the candle, and feel their energy flowing through your hands and into the candle. Feel the green-gold fire of the Faery Realm penetrate and permeate your candle. Dance, sing, or chant as you feel inspired. When you are finished, give thanks to all who have helped you, withdraw from the Realm of Faery, and close your ceremony.

Later, as you burn the candle or give it to the person so that they may burn it, realize that burning releases the power of healing which has been imbued into the candle. The candle may be burned all at once, but it is also nice to use it for only a short time each day, preferably the same time each day, for three or nine days or until it has burned completely down.

FAERY MEDICINES | Faery Winds

Faeries are said to sometimes travel in the whirling winds. The power of Air/Wind is one of movement and change, and it is, in truth, the very breath and rhythmic pulse of life itself. One of my earliest ways of entering the Faery Realm was by noticing that it was but a *pulse-beat* away from this one and learning by experimentation ways to rhythmically "pulse" into it—a method which defies verbal description so I won't attempt it here.

When used in Faery Healing and with the assistance of Faery Allies, the power of Air/Wind can be used to breathe things in and also to blow things out and away. Sometimes, the faeries will seem to breathe *through* you when you are doing this.

The important thing in working with it is to be open to the particular rhythm of the specific situation. Only then can you determine whether that rhythm *feels* healthy or not, and make an attempt to alter it with the aid of your Faery Allies. For instance, if working with someone who is highly stressed and hyperventilating, it is good to get them to breathe with you in a steady, deep, and calming rhythm. While you are doing this, call your Faery Allies to breathe their healing energies through you to the other person.

FAERY HEALING AMULETS AND TALISMANS

Amulets are protective devices; talismans are designed to attract beneficial influences. While not strictly medicines, Faery Healing amulets and talismans can be utilized as part of a treatment program.

FAERY MEDICINES | Creating Faery Healing Amulets and Talismans

If you feel that the healing process would be expedited by the use of one of these devices, then create them in the ceremonial manner described above. Obtain a special piece of paper or parchment and write or draw the appropriate magical symbols, sigils, or words upon it. You can also use a cloth and embroider these markings upon it. The wording can be as simple as "health," "peace of mind," or whatever it is which is being sought. If specific deities, saints, faery helpers, or other beings are being invoked or besought for assistance in the matter, their names or symbols should be included. If you wish to include herbs, review the information in *Chapter 9* and select the ones appropriate to the task at hand.

Create the amulet or talisman in a ceremonial way. Gather your tools, papers, pens, herbs, cloth, ribbons, and whatever else is needed, and settle yourself before your Faery Altar. Create sacred space, light your Faery Hearth candle (which should be placed in a secure candle holder so that it may be left unattended for a time), and take yourself in vision to the Glen of Precious Stones. Speak your intention in the flames of the faery hearth and ask your Allies to come forth to assist you.

Then open your eyes and begin work on your amulet or talisman. Using a small, rectangular piece of cloth, sew up a drawstring bag in which to put the charm. Turn over the top edge of the bag and sew it so that it forms a tube or casing to contain the drawstring. Thread the ribbon through the casing (the use of a safety pin on the end of the ribbon greatly aids this part of the procedure). Turn the pouch right side out and place the charm within it.

If you feel so inclined, you may sing and chant while you are enacting this ceremony. The stating of intentions and calling of allies may be sung rather than said, and it adds powerfully to the magic to sing and chant your intentions *as* you are preparing the amulet and sewing the pouch.

If you have created Blessed Waters as part of the cure, you may want to sprinkle a few drops on your pouch at this time. If you feel directed to do so, use Faery Winds to further empower your charm.

Now re-enter the vision state and take your charm to the Glen. Speak your intention for it into the flames of the Faery Hearth. Still in vision state, arise and physically take your charm around to the Four Directions and ask the powers and beings of each Convocation to bless the charm. Return to the Center and present the charm to the flames of the faery hearth, asking that it be blessed and empowered. When you leave the vision state, leave the charm on your faery altar by your still-burning faery hearth candle for about thirty minutes, or until it feels like it has sufficiently absorbed the energies you have called forth.

When you are finished, thank all the beings who have helped you, and then extinguish the candle. The charm is now ready for use.

IDEAS FOR USING FAERY MEDICINES

As mentioned above faery medicines can be used to assist physical healing and regeneration, as well as the spiritual. They can be used for mental or emotional healing. As every situation must be handled on all the appropriate levels, faery medicines may be used as an adjunct to other healing modalities and other medicines if the situation calls for these.

They may also be made for environmental healing in a manner suggested by the *One River Journey* in the previous chapter.

Faery medicines may also be used for world healing. As I write this, the world is going through a time of great upheaval, disharmony, anger, fear, anguish, and war. While there is much to be done on political and humanitarian levels for these things, working with faery medicines in conjunction with innerwork can also be an important and helpful thing to do during these difficult times.

While meditating recently on the themes of peace, harmony, and balance, I was inspired with an idea for the creation of a Faery Healing medicine for peace. Here are the procedures I used, which you may adapt as you see fit.

Necessary Items

- Choose a flower essence or essential oil that has to do with bringing peace and calmness, creating harmony, and restoring balance (see Note 1 at the end of the chapter). You will only need a few drops of these. If you have access to pure rose oil, add this to the mix as rose brings in heart energy and the loving energy of the Goddess.
- If possible, use a blue bottle or a pink bottle for the medicine. Blue has a very calming and peaceful energy; pink brings in the heart/love vibration.
- Use a small piece of rose quartz (this also brings in the heart/love vibration).
- A medium-sized soup bowl
- A funnel (optional)
- Use good quality water

Procedure

- Gather these materials and proceed as in the instructions given above for the creation of Faery Blessed Waters.
- Hold the rose quartz and the bottles of essences and oils in your hands and pray

over them, giving thanks to the stone spirit and plant spirits, and asking them and the faeries to weave their special magics.

- Place the drops of oil and essences into the bowl of water and stir very gently as given above.

- Pour the mixture into the blue (or pink) bottle and drop the rose quartz stone into it.

- Put the lid on the bottle, and, while continuing with your prayers and songs, shake it gently nine times with your intention clearly in mind.

- In vision, take the bottle to the Glen of Precious Stones and then around to each of the Convocations and ask for the blessings of peace, calm, harmony, and balance on the medicine.

- When this is done, place the bottle outside to sit in the sunshine for several hours till you feel it is "done."

How to Use the Medicine

Outdoors. Sitting outside on the ground, use a stick to draw in the soil a rough map of the parts of the world to be treated with the faery medicine. Speak aloud the names of the places (and/or situations) in need of this medicine, then pour the medicine on those "places" on your map. Do this with prayers, songs, or chants to the Divine and to the spirits of those places, the faeries and angels of those places, that they help bring peace, harmony, and graceful resolution to the problems of those places.

Indoors. Use a bowl of water or one of earth or sand to represent the Earth. Keep this on your altar. Each day for three or nine days sing and pray (as above) over it, adding a bit of the faery medicine to the bowl each time. When all the faery medicine has been added to the bowl, take it outside and pour its contents onto the Earth, affirming your intention.

IN CONCLUSION

It is hoped that the suggestions above stimulate your own ideas for creating faery medicines. Just remember to keep things simple, wholesome, sincere, from the heart, and to always ask for the help and guidance of your Faery Allies.

NOTES

1. I use flower essences from both the Bach Flower selection and the California Flower Essence Society. With regard to essential oils, doTERRA Oils are simply the best, in my opinion.

CHAPTER 23

Reweaving Brigid's Mantle, Restoring Airmid's Cloak

The exercises and visualizations in the preceding chapters have laid the groundwork and given tools for the practice of Faery Healing. A cosmological structure has been established and explored. Helper beings have been contacted and relationships formed. Thus the process of the *Reweaving* and *Alliance* forming has been begun, and will continue to deepen as further work serves to *Build Bridges* and strengthen the *Re-attunement* process.

As with anything else, repeated use of the techniques will bring better and deeper results, as it strengthens both the basic inner structures and also our proficiency.

In this chapter, we will use the structures we have built up and continue into deeper levels of the work. We will learn ways to utilize the energies of the Faery Realm for the healing of self and others. We will learn ways to make ourselves available to the Faery Gods and Goddesses, cooperating with them in the healing work they feel is necessary to be done.

FAERY HEALING TECHNIQUES

The last few chapters have given you a lot of information with regard to the Faery Convocations, the powers of the Four Directions, ways of entering and traveling within Faery, various herbs, and other correspondences.

However, once you have mastered the basics of cosmology and inner travel, the work of Faery Healing can be done with as much simplicity as you like. Pick and choose the methods and images that speak to you, and work with the situation at hand. Remember, this information has been provided to help you do this on your own, not to enslave you to a certain way of doing things. It's the energy that is the important thing. As you practice, gain skill, and learn to *feel* the energies, you will begin to get a sense of what is best used as you progress through healing sessions.

FAERY HEALING FOR YOURSELF

When you work with the Faery Realm, interacting with the beings and mediating the power, those energies move right through your body. Therefore, if you are doing Faery Healing work for another person, you receive some of the benefits yourself.

Sometimes you may want to work solely on yourself. Here is a simple method for doing that.

Read the Self Healing Journey just below. Familiarize yourself with it so that you know the steps and do not need to refer to the written copy. Alternately, you may want to tape record it so that you can play the tape while you journey.

Position yourself comfortably in front of your Faery Hearth. Using the techniques and imagery previously given, create a sacred space, and get yourself relaxed, grounded and centered. Now you are ready to journey.

JOURNEY | Self Healing

Sit before your Faery Altar, and light the Faery Hearth candle. Make yourself comfortable, but not so much so that you will fall asleep. Begin breathing deeply and slowly to relax yourself, and do one of the grounding exercises in the previous chapters, preferably one of the more simple ones.

Focus your attention on your hearth candle and call out to your Faery Allies and your Faery Deities; ask that they come to you and assist you in this journey of self healing which you are undertaking now.

Focused on your hearth candle, you close your eyes. As you focus on the candle with your inner vision, you see it growing larger, and you feel yourself passing down into the Earth. You watch as the hearth candle becomes a large flame that burns within a large, burnished copper bowl. This vessel sits atop an emerald studded stand, and the flame within reaches upward as far as the eye can see.

You find that you are standing before the Faery Hearth in the Glen of Precious Stones. You gaze around, and see the gently rounded walls, sparkling with many-colored stones and crystals which glow and gleam with their rosy and emerald light. Standing before the fire, you commune with it silently for a few moments, then you speak your intention of healing into the flames.

Once again, you call out to your Faery Allies, Gods, and Goddesses, and you feel and see them coming to you.

After you have done this, you move to each of the Four Directions in turn, open the gates of that Direction, and call forth the Faery Healing Beings of that Convocation, again stating your intention. Then you move to the bed of soft grass, flowers, and fragrant herbs that is to one side of the Faery Hearth, and you lay down upon it.

You can feel and see the Faery Healing Helper Beings as they come through the gates to you. They surround you as you lay there, and they begin to work on you… As you feel them working on you, you feel their power flowing into you and through your body, adjusting, fine-tuning, soothing, and strengthening… You lay there, filled with gratitude, and allow them to work on you…

At length, you notice that this work is drawing to a conclusion… When the Faery Beings are done, they begin to withdraw, moving back through their gateways into their convocations. You thank them as they go… When they are gone, you rise and return to stand before the fire of the Faery Hearth. For a few moments, you again commune with the fire, offering your thanks. You reach into your pocket and find a gift there for the faery folk who have helped you, and place it on the ground before the Faery Hearth…

Then you gaze again into the flames of the Faery Hearth where you see a gate of flame opening for you. You step into it, and feel yourself moving upward on the flames, through the Earth, till you find yourself returning to the place and time from which you began your journey, to a room where a candle is burning… Take a few moments to settle in completely, and when you are ready, you open your eyes.

Be sure to record your journey in your Magical Journal.

DOING FAERY HEALING FOR OTHERS

Here is a simple and practical method that may be used to do Faery Healing for another person. For this, you will create the journey for your client, using your experiences from the journey above as well as the guidelines below.

To do a Faery Healing session for another person, start simply by settling your client comfortably, either sitting or lying down as needed or desired. Then settle yourself comfortably and near enough to lay your hands on your client. If your client is on a massage table, you may wish to stand during the session so that you can walk around the table if necessary. If your client is seated, you may want to position yourself in a chair behind him, so you can lay your hands on his head and shoulders. Or you may want to be in front of him, so that you can hold his hands if desired. I've been known to sit on the floor next to my client, in a position that allows me to hold their feet or place my hands on their head. Comfort and ease of movement are the essentials.

Faery Healing Procedure and Journey

- Ground yourself and your client using one of the techniques given.

- Create a sacred space using one of the techniques given.

- If desired, place your hands on the client's head, shoulders, or feet.

- Using one of the suggested techniques or one of your own devising, enter the Faery Realm.

- Call to your Faery Allies and ask them to join you and render assistance to the healing work you are about to do.

- Ask that the spirit helpers and allies of your client join you and help in the healing.

- Ask that the Goddess Brigid (or Airmid, Miach, Morgen, or other gods and goddesses of healing) assist you in this healing work.

- Speaking aloud, take your client and yourself to the Faery Hearth in the Glen of Precious Stones within the Faery Realm.

- You may wish to use the image of the Great Tree to get there, becoming aware of its roots, trunk, and branches, finding the Flame of Being as it burns in the heart of the tree, and uniting your own inner flame with that of the tree.

- There is a soft bed of grass, flowers, and herbs near the hearth upon which you help your client lie down.

- Be aware of the Four Convocations in their respective Directions surrounding the Glen of Precious Stones. Focus your attention on each of them in turn, opening the gateways.

- Bring your attention back to the Center and see there the Great Fire of the Faery Convocation, burning in the Faery Hearth.

- Go up to the fire, acknowledging its power and presence, and speak your intention into it.

- Spend a moment communing with the fire.

- Call forth your Faery Healing Allies to come from their Convocations and assist you; call your client's spirit allies and helpers.

- Return to your client and place your hands on him or her.

- Be aware now that Faery Healing Allies are coming toward you from each of the Four Directions, the Sylph-like Faeries of the East, the Fire Faeries of the South, the Water Faeries and Merfolk of the West, and the Gnomes and Earth Faeries of the North. They each bring the special gifts of their Element. They surround the client and begin to work on or her. Sometimes they will merge with you while doing this, and use your hands.

- While the Faery Allies are working, attune yourself to the Great Fire of the Faery Hearth and to the resonant power of the fiery earth heart beneath you. Bring both of these powers through your body, through your hands, and into your client. Do this both in your vision and in the physical world: feel it happening in your body as you sit or stand there in the physical realm.

- Let the power flow through you as long as it feels necessary. Be aware of the beings working on your client.

- When they have finished, or when you feel the power slow down, suggest to your client that this part of the journey is coming to an end and that he or she will notice that the Faery Allies are withdrawing and returning to their realms.

- Thank the beings who have helped in this healing.

- Bring yourself and your client back to the physical realm and normal waking awareness by using one of the suggested techniques.

REWEAVING BRIGID'S MANTLE

As we go about our journeying, our merging and shapeshifting, and our healing work, we become aware that we are engaged in a process of relinking parts of the world which have become separate. We are bringing them together again in our hearts and minds (which is, in truth, where the separation has actually occurred), and in so doing we are *Reweaving* Brigid's mantle. This *Reweaving* is done by mediating energy from the hearthfire to weave the parts back together into wholeness once again, and includes bringing all the separate parts of ourselves back together again. And though our work may seem tiny in comparison to what is needed, as more and more of us lovingly take it up and do it, it becomes like the leavening in bread dough; and similarly, it will grow and multiply till it has caused an increase. In this way, we affect the future.

When we do this *Reweaving*, the effect occurs on both our internal, personal level and on the outer, transpersonal level—since all is connected.

WEAVING THE FUTURE

While we all know that what we think and do has an impact on our reality and our lives, one day I was powerfully struck with the significance of this common knowledge. I had what, for lack of a better word, I refer to as a *visitation* from the Goddess while I was engaged in the homely task of scrubbing the kitchen floor. Her words to me were quite simple, but deeply meaningful.

She reminded me that every day, with every choice, we are weaving our future. She told me that a vast array of threads present themselves to us every day, threads of many different kinds. There are threads of hatred, violence, greed, fear, doom, and woe, and sometimes these seem like they are the only ones that exist. But there are also threads of love, compassion, generosity, optimism, kindness, and caring. There are threads offered by our animal and plant kin, our human kin, our angel and Faery Kin, by Divine Beings, and by our ancestors. We are not separate from these beings; they are all our kin. The threads they offer are the threads by which we can weave right relationship with All That Is.

She reminded me that the reactions or responses we have to life's events, the mental and emotional states we choose to maintain, and the deeds we do are part of the weaving. We weave the future with the energy of our thoughts and dreams, and we must be more careful in our choice of threads and colors so that we can help to create the balanced, bright, and beautiful future that we so desire for ourselves and our children. These threads we spin and patterns we create with them are energy fields. Fear and chaos, beauty and love—the choice is ours.

"Let the Mothers come forth, in the name of the Mother," she said, "to 're-member' the Wholeness that is, to put the parts back together, that a new aeon may be conceived and brought to birth."

Journeys of Weaving

Here is a journey of *Reweaving* in which we encounter the Dark Goddess in her role of the Weaver of life, death, and destiny. The weaving-spinning aspect of the Goddess is a powerful one and is found in many cultures. In ancient Greece she was Ariadne; in the Northern traditions she was Frau Holde or Perchta; in Wales she was most likely Arianrhod of the spinning Spiral Castle of the North; in Native American tradition she was Spider Woman. In the work of Fiona Macleod, she is referred to as Orchil....

> ....*Orchil, the dim goddess who is under the brown earth, in a vast cavern, where she weaves at two looms. With one hand she weaves life upward through the grass; with the other she weaves death downward through the mould; and the sound of the weaving is Eternity, and the name of it in the green world is Time. And, through all, Orchil weaves the weft of Eternal Beauty, that passeth not, though its soul is Change.*[1]

JOURNEY | Reweaving Brigid's Mantle

Settling comfortably before your Faery Altar, light the Faery Hearth candle. As you gaze at this center flame, breathing slowly in and out, you find that you are becoming more relaxed, calm, and serene with each breath. Focus your attention on the candle, then close your eyes, seeing the candle with your inner vision. As you do this, you feel yourself passing into the inner realms...

You find yourself sitting outdoors in a familiar place in the wilderness. You look around and notice the beauty of the place, and as your gaze returns to what is just in front of you, you notice that a well has seemingly opened up in the Earth a short distance from where you sit. You rise and walk over to the well, and lean over, looking inside.

Suddenly you lose your balance and fall into the well. You find that you are falling down and down, tumbling, not reaching any water, but just falling downward through the Earth, deeper and deeper into the land. Deeper and deeper you continue to fall for what seems like a long time, till at length you come to rest in a large, dimly lit cavern, which glows faintly with green-gold Earth-light that seems to emanate from the walls of the cavern.

Nearby is a woman wearing a dark green cloak and sitting on a stool. You realize that this is the Goddess of the Underworld.

She holds a drop spindle in one hand, and as you watch, she sets it spinning and drops it. Her other hand is held upward, and as you look at her hand you see light from above flowing into it. The light twinkles and sparkles, and you realize it is starlight from the Upperworlds. She gathers the light with her free hand, twisting it into a rough but still sparkling thread, and spins it, using her spindle. As an end of the spun thread drops to the ground, you see that it still sparkles, but that leaves, twigs, and vines are now growing out of it. She spins, and the pile of thread grows, and spreads itself throughout the cavern, the vines growing up the walls and into the roof of the cavern, and out through the top of it to the Middleworld above.

She gives you the spindle, shows you how to use it, and lets you spin for a while. As the starlight moves through your fingers and becomes thread, you become aware of a very faint musical humming or whirring sound. You observe the thread as it tumbles, sparkling, into a pile on the ground, and watch as leaves, flowers, and twigs grow out of it. Some of the twigs seem to be rooting themselves into the floor of the cavern… You pause for a moment, intending to wrap the thread around the spindle's shaft, but the Goddess takes the spindle from you and lays it aside.

She reaches down and picks up a length of the newly spun thread, which looks to be a length of sparkling green vine with many leaves sprouting from it. Pressing it into your hand, she bids you take it up to the Middleworld and plant it there.

Taking the thread, you stand, and begin walking. You are aware that the thread is dragging behind you, and that flowers, leaves, vines, twigs, and even fruit are continuing to grow from it as you walk… As you pass through the center of the cavern, a spiraling vortex of wind arises, seemingly from the heart of the Earth below, rumbling as it rises through the Earth. It begins to blow through the cavern, and whips the thread around and about you, whipping your hair all around you as well. The wind lifts you, and you swirl upward on the vortex, passing through the roof of the cavern, and continuing up through the layers of Earth till you reach the surface, carrying the thread-plant-vine with you.

As you pass through to the surface, the thread keeps moving, and carries you to a place on the Earth where it wants to be planted, and it digs itself into the Earth. You pat the earth down around where it has planted itself, bless it with your love, and watch as it continues to blossom forth into growth of all kinds… Tears of appreciation, awe, and gratitude begin to flow from your eyes and onto the ground, watering the plant.

When this is done, you rise and turn and begin walking across the land, finding that each step brings you closer and closer to a large tree which dominates the area. As you approach the tree, you see that it holds a gateway. You step through the gateway... and back into this realm. You find yourself coming back to your normal state of awareness... as you return to this time and this place. Take a few moments to settle back in... and when you are ready, you may open your eyes.

Be sure to record your journey in your Magical Journal.

REWEAVING BRIGID'S MANTLE, RESTORING AIRMID'S CLOAK —TECHNIQUES FOR HEALING

Below is a list of suggestions of healing modalities that may be used in conjunction with the techniques and journeys above. These may be used for ourselves, for others with whom we are working, for situations, and for the land. By now you will be able to construct a healing journey and incorporate these suggestions, so no journeys will be given here for these things. Remember, the important thing is to clearly affirm your intention for these journeys, and allow your Faery Allies and Faery Gods and Goddesses to guide you through the process.

Getting Rid of Baggage. There are times in life when we find that we are carrying around too much old, inner "junk." We find that the burden has become too heavy and is keeping us from moving forward in life. At times such as these, it is appropriate to enlist the aide of your Faery and Spirit Allies and the Dark Goddess to help you let go of this excess, unneeded energetic baggage. This may be accomplished by journeying with your allies to the Underworld, and asking for help in releasing these energies. Quite often, your allies will help you strip these energies off. These energies will then be handed over to the Dark Goddess for recycling. They are, after all, energetic patterns, and the Dark Goddess is expert at breaking down old patterns so that their energies may be reconfigured and reused.

It is impossible to predict how such a journey will look for every individual reading this book, so I won't try. But a journey such as this can be full of surprises. Sometimes when you try to remove something, it won't allow itself to be removed. This quite likely means that you aren't done with it yet no matter how much you wish you were. If this happens, surrender your desire to have it gone, and simply ask for help in dealing with it. Another kind of surprise that might occur has to do with unexpected things. Since you have gone into these realms affirming your desire to get rid of old burdens that are holding you back, you must allow that you will be taken at your word, and things may happen which you have not imagined nor written into your script. Once again, if you truly seek to have your load lightened, surrender to the process.

Healing the Land. I'm sure that most people reading this book have experienced a desire to help heal our polluted lands. While the outer level work on this is quite important (don't contribute to the pollution and support those who do work to clean it), inner work is very valuable here as well. Go down into the Underworld and connect with the power of the God and Goddess of the Stars within the Earth, the Dark Goddess, and with the giant Earth Beings, most especially the ones with a nourishing energy. Gently pull these energies up through the Earth, very carefully, layer by layer, to replenish and heal that layer. Check in with your intuition quite often while doing this and stop when it feels like you've done as much as you're supposed to do. At some point you may be allowed to move completely up to the surface with these energies; when you do, bring the energy up and out, watching what it does, and visualizing healthy, green growing things springing up in their due season. This can be done along with your seasonal workings if desired.

Faery Convocation Work. Ways in which the elemental powers of the Faery Convocations can be used for replenishing, recharging, and rebuilding our energies are given below. Because these powers are quite strong, it is important that you always do this with the instruction and assistance of your Faery Allies and Faery Healing God or Goddess. While you may decide to work primarily with one of these Convocations in a given situation, be aware that occasionally there may be a need to go to one of the other Convocations to balance the energies of the working. Please ask the guidance of your Faery Allies concerning this as the situation unfolds.

Finias. Use the winds of Finias to blow away that which is no longer needed and which needs to be dispersed. Ask that new inspirations blow your way. Since it is the Eastern Convocation of Finias we are referring to, it could quite likely be old thoughts and energy patterns which get caught up and dispersed in these winds, and new thoughts and the seeds of new patterns which are brought to us. The other power of Finias is that of the blade, whose power of cutting, piercing, lancing can reveal the truth in powerful ways. When you utilize the energy of Finias, be prepared for the truth to be revealed, often starkly.

Gorias. If your inner fire is feeling low and dim, journey to Gorias and the Fire of Gorias to help you relight it. You may also use this fire for purification and healing, which may involve placing yourself within Gorias's Fire to expedite this.

Murias. To refill your inner cauldrons, use the Waters of Murias for healing. Dip yourself into the cauldrons and baths you find in Murias. Your very cells become cauldrons that are filled and nourished by the Waters of Murias.

Falias. Use the Stones of Falias to crystallize and encapsulate harmful influences (including old thought forms) that they may be more easily removed. The Stones of Falias may also be used to encapsulate positive and healing influences and bring them into a situation.

The Problem of Species Extinction

It is always very sad when we hear of a species of plant or animal going extinct. But it is important to realize that the Goddess has her own times and tides with regard to the manifestation of life-forms, and that extinction is a part of the natural and normal evolutionary cycle of life.

That being said, in our lifetimes we have seen this phenomena of species extinction happening with alarmingly increasing frequency. This rate of extinction is, in my opinion, NOT part of the natural, normal cycle, and is due, at least in part, to an abnormal influence of humankind on these beings and their habitats.

Although we as humans are involved and responsible in this matter, its implications are, at the moment, quite beyond our comprehension and will persist beyond our lifespan.

What happens when humankind interferes with the natural cycle of things? Or is humanity's interference with the cycle itself part of a still larger natural cycle?

Pondering this, knowing that we bear some measure of responsibility, many of us wonder what we can do to help.

At the end of our wondering, it becomes a matter of simply doing whatever we can on both outer and inner levels to be of assistance. In the physical world, we should do what we can to slow down the destruction of habitats, and support those who work to maintain and restore them. By way of example, I have a friend who planted much of her backyard in the once-flourishing native plant that provides the primary food source for an endangered species of local butterfly. At the same time, she mounted a local campaign to convince her neighbors to do the same, thus creating a new, albeit small, habitat for the butterfly.

The innerworlds are, as you will remember, the Primal Wholeness, the Pristine Land and they therefore hold the blueprints and prototypes of what manifests in this physical one.

When extinction occurs in our outerworld, some spiritual traditions hold that the creature has not ceased to exist, but that the deva of the species has simply returned to the innerworlds. It is when this happens due to human influence that it tugs at our heartstrings, and causes us to wish there were some way we could help make things better. But what can we do?

The journey that follows is one that might be of help at this time. It revolves around the fact that, ultimately, it is the Goddess of life who, in her wisdom and vast knowledge of the cycles of life, will know how to really use whatever loving assistance we offer.

CARRYING THE FOREST THROUGH TIME

The journey that follows was written by my friend Josephine Dunne, and is used here with her permission.

As priests or priestesses of any spiritual tradition, we have a responsibility to act as unconditional mediators for all beings in our world. One of the many ways that we can be of service to our home, to our Mother Earth, is to carry her children through time. The following vision is a way that we can work with sacred plants to ensure their long-term survival by carrying the inner matrix of the plant through time. You cannot choose the plant; the plant must choose you. Try to do this vision out in nature, on a piece of wild land.

JOURNEY | Carrying the Forest Through Time

Sit comfortably and close your eyes. Using your imagination, see your inner flame burning brightly within you. The Flame of Life burns gently but brightly. As you relax, you become aware that there are beings who are drawn by the brightness of your flame and they inch closer to investigate.

In your inner vision, you stand up and look around you. Out of the corner of your eye, you see many beings hiding and trying to move closer to you. One of them steps before you, a being of the forest and asks you if you are prepared to be of service. When you reply yes, they put their hands over your eyes and tell you to look.

Looking through their hands your vision changes and you become aware of things you had not seen before. The inner light of the plants and trees is very dull, and they all seem to be covered in a dark heaviness. The animals are the same; their inner flames grow weak as they battle against the toxins in their bodies and environment.

The being, a faery, who is working with you, tells you that there is something you can do for the future. It asks you to walk through the meadow or forest and let a plant choose you.

You set off walking, feeling the rich earth beneath your feet as you walk. You pass through tall grasses, bushes, trees, plants, and flowers. One plant in particular seems to stand out to you. As you get closer to it, you can see that plant is struggling to breathe through the polluted air.

Gently and quietly, you scoop up the plant, being very careful not to damage the roots, and hold it close to you. The inner power of the plant, its inner consciousness, surprises you with its vast power and beauty. The Faery Being comes up behind you and urges you to place the plant within you, next to your heart.

As the plant passes into you, a heavy tiredness creeps over you and you lie down to sleep on the soft grass. The earth is warm and soft, moving gently as though you lay on the body of a sleeping mother. The sleep pulls you deeper and deeper until you feel yourself sink down into the earth and the rock.

Deeper and deeper you fall until you become still and silent as you sleep in the rock, deep below the surface of the planet. The seasons come and go, and you sleep. The years pass by and still you sleep. Time has no meaning as you slumber within stone. Your body is heavier and heavier, becoming part of the rock itself. The mother curls around you as you sleep, singing her lullabies of the wind to you as you sleep.

Somewhere in the distance, someone calls your name. The sound echoes through your mind and you struggle to regain your consciousness. The sound gets stronger and stronger until you are urged to move forward. Reaching up, you fight and climb to the surface world, leaving the stillness of the rock behind you.

After a struggle, you emerge out of the darkness and find yourself on the surface and yet it looks very strange. The world has moved on through time as you have slept, and now is the time to replant the children of the Goddess.

You look around for the best place to root the plant. Finding a good spot, you dig with your hands to create a space for the plant to root itself. Placing the plant carefully in the ground, you are overwhelmed with a strange sadness.

Tears begin to fall from your eyes and moisten the ground around the plant. The more you cry, the more the plant is watered. The plant begins to glow with a powerful inner flame, growing beyond its physical boundary until it stretches in all directions.

The inner expression of the plant is a beauty you have not seen before, and you are overwhelmed as the inner consciousness of the plant reaches out to touch you. The earth around the plant changes as it begins to interact with the power of the plant, and you watch in wonder as the land springs to life.

The touch of the plant knocks you off balance and you fall backwards. You fall as though falling off a large cliff, your body tumbling through time as it twists around the directions. You fall and fall, becoming disorientated as the falling becomes faster.

Suddenly you stop, finding yourself sitting back in the patch of land where you first started. You can see all of the beings within the plants and trees all around you as you slowly re-orient yourself.

You remember your inner flame, the Flame of All Being at the edge of the void and when you are ready, you open your eyes.

Be sure to record your journey in your Magical Journal.

Reunion

As you will have realized from reading the last few chapters, the subject of Faery Healing encompasses more than "just faeries." Faeries are a variety of subtle spiritual beings intimately connected with the Earth, the landscape, and the plant kingdom, so what happens to these affects the faeries. Therefore, the larger work of Faery Healing has to do with the health and well-being of the Earth, the landscape, and the plant, and even animal kingdoms as well.

As has been said many times before within these pages, we are all related; we are all kin; what affects one of us affects us all.

In Conclusion

I hope this book has inspired you to seek reunion with your Faery Kin.

Although many of us may be called to reconnect with our Faery Kin, not all of us are called to be Faery Healers. It may be likened to the field of physical health care, where, while it certainly behooves all of us to gain and use basic health-care and health-maintenance knowledge, we are not all called to become doctors.

If you *do* feel called by Faery to do Faery Healing, you must remember and observe the sensible and honorable rules of conduct by which they practiced, as well as the few rules and guidelines that I strongly feel are important and necessary for our era. If you seek help from a Faery Healer, please assure yourself that they are observing these rules:

- Faery Healing uses no particularly shiny, expensive, new agey paraphernalia, but rather, simple and easily available materials; so do not allow yourself to be deceived by those who come calling themselves Faery Healers, bearing glittery wands and expensive potions and crystals.

- Faery Healers are "just folks," so do not allow yourself to be deceived by those with fancy titles or robes of glamour.

- Faery Doctors of the past wouldn't heal without being asked to do so, as they were aware that the seeking of healing is part of a person's healing process and that to interfere with it was inappropriate, and an overstepping of boundaries.

- Faery Doctors, at least the ones who were not also ordinary herbalists, wouldn't heal if it wasn't "any of their business." This means that these particular Faery Doctors would only heal faery or spirit-induced diseases, and not ordinary human ills. The rule here is to "mind your own business" and not act beyond your area of knowledge and guidance. Don't think you can heal anything and everything with your Faery Healing work, because you can't. Stay open to your faery guidance while healing. Be humble and honest, while allowing room for faery surprises.

- Faery Healing is a community service, not a money-making operation. It is, like shamanism, a service performed by a qualified person—for both the health of the general community and the health of individual community members. No money should change hands in the practice of Faery Healing, although occasional non-monetary gifts are allowed in order to keep the energy balanced. Occasionally, very minimal fees may be requested if physical objects such as bottles of herbs change hands, but no money must be charged for the energetic part of the healing work. There are no exceptions to this rule.

- Faery Healing is a vocation, a Calling of the Heart; it is not a career, as careers are intended to support us financially.

In an era when New Age thinking and practices are frequently about the spending and making of money by means of the buying and selling of Spirit and its technologies, remember that the currency of the Faery Realm is an open-hearted love. Faery Healing is not, and has never been, about money. All that glitters is not gold. Learn to discern, lest you be lead astray by faery gold that may later turn to dry leaves and dust....

This book is about opening your connection with the Faery Realm and engaging personally. While it provides structure and guidelines, please remember that the faeries will teach you and that part of that teaching is the transformation of the self, especially the heart.

Heartfelt Faery Blessings on your work. May you be blessed and healed.

END NOTES

1. Macleod, Fiona, *The Works of Fiona Macleod, Vol 11, Washer of the Ford: and Other Legendary Moralities*, Patrick Geddes and Colleagues, Edinburgh, Stone & Kimball, Chicago, 1896.

PART V

Appendices and Bibliography

Appendices

Appendix A
THE FESTIVALS

The four Quarter Days of the Celtic year—referred to in modern Paganism as the Cross-Quarter Days and in Wicca as the Major Sabbats—were the seasonal markers of the Celtic year from a time that significantly pre-dated Christianity. From the surviving literature it would seem that ancient Ireland recognized two seasons of the year, summer and winter, which began on Beltaine (April 30-May1) and Samhain (October 31-November 1) respectively. At some point, the seasons of spring and autumn came to be recognized as well.

The lives of the people revolved around issues relating to their survival, that is, issues of food, shelter, and clothing. Not surprisingly, their seasonal festivals are tied in with these things, celebrating particular times in the cycles of food production (for example, fertilizing the soil, planting, reaping, harvesting, storing, fishing, and gathering seaweed), and the keeping and care of livestock, the making of tools, clothing, fishing nets, household items, and the like. In addition, wells were blessed, and the sacred fires of protection and purification, often called *need-fires*, were kindled. The Quarter Days marked a time of fresh starts: rents were paid, new ventures were undertaken, and auguries were made.

The gods and later the saints—being such a part of the people's everyday life—were intimately involved with these undertakings of life and were therefore a part of the celebrations and activities of the seasonal cycles, their feast days marking important points in the year's calendar of festivals.

Samhain ▪ Winter

The year began with the start of winter at Samhain, October 31-November 1st (the day was reckoned to start at sunset). In more ancient times, this was about the time of the *rising* of the Pleiades in the night sky. In the ancient world the time of the rising of the Pleiades was held to be the time when the Gates of Death were opened. And it *was* most definitely a time of death, as it was the time when cattle herds were culled: those not able to be wintered over, as well as the weak and old, were slaughtered. At Samhain, the veil between this world and the Otherworlds was thin, spirits easily moving from one side of it to the other. Divination practices were common at this time of year.

As night precedes the day, the time of death and darkness at winter precedes the time of life and light at spring. The Celtic year ended and began again at the time of Samhain. Since this was a time of the year when people were already focused on death and the Otherworld, when Catholicism became the dominant religion the Church set the feasts of All Saints (November 1) and All Souls (November 2) at the time of Samhain, of which All Hallow's Eve, October 31st—our Halloween—is a remnant.

Imbolc ∗ Spring

Spring began at Imbolc, January 31st-February 1st. It was also referred to as Oimelc (ewe's milk), the Festival of Brigid, and Candlemas, the latter being the Christian name for a much older observance. Imbolc, a time when the dark of winter is giving way to the light of spring, is the time of the year when lambs (and other young animals) were born. It was, therefore, a time of new life, new milk, new nourishment.

Brigid has been honored at this time of year for a very long time, first as a goddess and later as a saint. She was particularly honored by women, whose rituals at this time of year—recorded by folklorists—involved inviting Brigid back to the world to bring her light, warmth, fertility, and prosperity. A special bed was prepared for her, and omens of future life and prosperity were taken from the evidence of whether or not she was seen to have arrived and slept in her bed.

The feast day of Ireland's patron St. Patrick is March 17th. Its connection with the springlike color green, and its proximity to the spring equinox, seem, perhaps, not coincidental. Following close on is the Christian feast of Easter, whose timing is linked to the lunar cycle and the Spring Equinox—occurring on the first Sunday after the first full moon after the Spring Equinox.

Beltaine ∗ Summer

Beltaine, April 30th-May 1st, marked the beginning of summer, and it was a time of the year associated with growth, flowering, and fertility, and sexual license. Young people would go into the woods "a-Maying" and return, not only with branches of the faery-favored hawthorn with which to decorate house and barn door, but also having observed the time-honored custom of "Greenwood Marriages," that is, having spent the night in the woods making love. When the Puritans came to power in England they looked upon this custom with horror, complaining that, "of the girls who go into the woods, not the least one of them comes home again a virgin." Not surprisingly, the Puritans made these customs illegal.

May and June were the times when the sheep and cattle were taken to their summer pastures or "shielings," where they stayed, tended by the young people, till close to All Hallows Eve.

St. John's Eve, which is actually a celebration of the Summer Solstice and was known also as Midsummer, occurs on June 24th. Both Beltaine (also called May Eve) and Midsummer were times associated with the faeries, as faery power was at its strongest during the warmth of the growth and flowering season of year.

Lughnasadh ▪ Autumn

Lughnasadh (July 31st –August 1st) was, in ancient Ireland, a time of tribal gatherings and games ostensibly in honor of Lugh's foster mother Tailtiu, and founded by him in her honor. It was a time when families visited, goods were sold, games of strength and skill were held, and marriage partners were selected. In more agrarian lands it was associated with the first harvest. In England, it became known by the Christian, Anglo-Saxon name of Lammas, meaning "Loaf-mass," the Catholic Mass held in honor of the loaf of bread baked from the grains of the first harvest. This is an example of the usual Catholic practice of appropriating previously existing Pagan rituals and celebrations. Whether called Lughnasadh or Lammas, it celebrated a time of warmth and abundance.

The important Feast of St. Michael the Archangel falls within this season on September 29th, quite close to the Fall Equinox.

Appendix B
FIONA MACLEOD AND WILLIAM SHARP

The poetic and mystical works of Scottish authoress Fiona Macleod were quite well known to lovers of Celtic revival literature in the late 1800s early 1900s. The public was therefore quite shocked to learn, in 1905, that these works had actually been written by a *man* named William Sharp, recently deceased, rather than a woman named Fiona Macleod.

William Sharp was a Scottish writer whose work encompassed poetry, novels, biographies, and literary criticism. But in addition, he wrote several books of a very different nature under the name Fiona Macleod. These works were lovely, sensitive, poetic, mystical, dreamy, and seemingly from a feminine perspective.

Who was Fiona Macleod? Some have suggested that Fiona was a sub-personality of William Sharp—his inner feminine characteristics taking on an individual persona of its own. Others have suggested that Fiona was William Sharp's gay alter-ego. But since William Sharp was known to be a mystic, and he associated with the mystics and magicians of his day, it is probably more than likely that Fiona was an inner contact who, from time to time, *overshadowed* him and spoke through him. Sharp himself occasionally described her as an "ancestral seeress." Toward the end of his life Sharp attempted to come to terms with the phenomena by referring to a fusion of his psyche and that of Fiona's as an independent third being, whom his wife, Elizabeth, named "Wilfion."

Whatever the actual reality of Wilfion/Fiona/William, the words penned under the name of Fiona Macleod stand on their own as deeply soulful and hauntingly beautiful works of literature.

Appendix C
SUGGESTED READINGS

Note: All the books in the bibliography may be considered part of this Suggested Readings list.

The Celtic Connection

Freeman, Mara, *Kindling the Celtic Spirit: Ancient Traditions to Illumine Your Life*, Harper SanFrancisco, CA, 2001.

Brandon Evans, Tira, *The Green and Burning Tree*, Elder Grove Press, Harrison Hot Springs, British Columbia, 2002.

———, *Portals of the Seasons*, Elder Grove Press, Harrison Hot Springs, British Columbia, 2002.

———, *Healing Waters*, Elder Grove Press, Harrison Hot Springs, British Columbia, 2002.

———, *The Labrythine Way*, Elder Grove Press, Harrison Hot Springs, British Columbia, 2003.

Chakras and Energy Healing

Bruyere, Rosalyn, *Wheels of Light*, Sierra Madre, CA, 1989.

Hunt, Valerie, *Infinite Mind: Science of the Human Vibrations of Consciousness*, Malibu Publishing Co., Malibu, CA, 1989, 1996.

Color Healing

Gardner-Gordon, Joy, *Color and Crystals*, Crossing Press, Freedom, CA, 1988.

Gimbel, Theo, *Healing Through Colour*, Saffron Walden, C.W. Daniel Co Limited, Essex, England, 1980.

———, *Healing with Color and Light*, A Fireside Book, Simon & Schuster, NY, 1994.

Flower Essences
Bach, Edward, M.D., and F. J. Wheeler, *The Back Flower Remedies*, Keats Publishing Inc., New Canaan, CT, 1977, 1979.

Kaminski, Patricia, and Richard Katz, *Flower Essence Repertory*, Flower Essence Society, Nevada City, CA, 1994.

Scheffer, Mechthild, *Bach Flower Therapy: Theory and Practice*, Healing Arts Press, Rochester, VT, 1988.

Wright, Machaelle, *Flower Essences*, Perelandra Ltd., Jeffersonton, VI, 1988.

Medicinal Herbs
Buhner, Stephen Harrod, *Herbal Antibiotics: Natural Alternatives to Treating Drug-Resistant Bacteria*, Storey Books, Pownal, VT, 1999.

———, *The Lost Language of Plants: The Ecological Importance of Plant Medicines to Life on Earth*, Chelsea Green Publishing, White River Junction, VT, 2002.

Griggs, Barbara, *The Green Witch Herbal: Restoring NatureÕs Magic in Home, Health, and Beauty Care*, Healing Arts Press, Rochester, VT, 1994.

Hobbs, Christopher, *Foundations of Health: The Liver and Digestive Herbal,* Botanica Press, Capitola, CA, 1992.

Hoffman, David, *The Complete Illustrated Holistic Herbal*, Element Books, Ltd., Shaftesbury, Dorset, 1996.

Holmes, Peter, *The Energetics of Western Herbs: An Herbal Reference Integrating Western and Oriental Herbal Medicine Traditions (In Two Volumes)*, NatTrop Publishing, Berkeley, CA, 1989, 1993.

Ody, Penelope, *The Complete Medicinal Herbal*, Dorling Kindersley Ltd., London, 1993.

Theiss, Barbara & Peter, *The Family Herbal*, Healing Arts Press, Rochester, VT, 1989.

Wood, Matthew, *Vitalism: The History of Herbalism, Homeopathy, and Flower Essences*, North Atlantic Books, Berkeley, CA, 1992, 2000.

———, *The Book of Herbal Wisdom: Using Plants As Medicines*, North Atlantic Books, Berkeley, CA, 1997.

Tierra, Michael, *Planetary Herbology,* Lotus Press, Santa Fe, NM, 1988.

Tierra, Michael, *The Way of Herbs,* Simon & Schuster, Inc, NY, NY, 1998.

WEB SITES

My Web Sites
Faery Healing: http://www.faeryhealing.com/
Brigid's Hearth: http://brigidshearth.org/
Lady of the Sea: http://ladyofthesea.org/

My Blogs
Writing While Under the Influence of Faeries: http://margiemcarthur.blogspot.com
Musings on the Divine: http://musingsonthedivine.blogspot.com
Path of the Hearthfire: http://pathofthehearthfire.blogspot.com

Celtic Connection Web Sites
Mara Freeman: http://www.celticspirit.org/

Medicinal Herbs
Christopher Hobbs: www.christopherhobbs.com
Michael Tierra: www.planetherbs.com
Rosemary Gladstar: https://scienceandartofherbalism.com/
Mrs. Grieves Herbal: https://www.botanical.com/

Vibrational Healing
Rosalyn Bruyere: http://www.rosalynlbruyere.org/
Joy Gardner: http://www.rmamysteryschool.com/
Flower Essence Society: http://www.fesflowers.com/
Perelandra: http://www.perelandra-ltd.com
doTERRA Oils: http://www.doterra.com

Sound Healing
Vishen Lakhiani: https://blog.mindvalley.com/sound-healing/
Ani Williams - Sound Alchemy: https://aniwilliams.com/
 and https://aniwilliams.com/songaia-sound-medicine/
Jonathon Goldman: https://www.healingsounds.com/

Bibliography

A. E., *The Candle of Vision*, Macmillan, London, 1918.

American Heritage Dictionary of the English Language, Houghton Mifflin Co, Boston & NY, 1992.

Beith, Mary, *Healing Threads*, Polygon, Edinburgh, 1995.

Blamires, Steve, *The Irish Celtic Magical Tradition*, Aquarian Press, an imprint of HarperCollins Publishers, London, 1992.

Bonewits, Ra, *Cosmic Crystals*, Turnstone Press Ltd., Wellingborough, Northhamptonshire, 1983.

Brenneman, Walter L., Jr., and Mary G., *Crossing the Circle at the Holy Wells of Ireland*, The University Press of Virginia, Charlottesville, VA, 1995.

Briggs, Katherine, *An Encyclopedia of Fairies*, Pantheon Books, NY, 1976.

——— *Fairies in Tradition and Literature*, Routledge, Kegan & Paul, Ltd., London, 1967.

——— *The Vanishing People: Fairy Lore and Legends*, Pantheon Books, NY, 1978.

——— *The Anatomy of Puck,* Routledge and Kegan Paul, London, 1959.

Cameron, John, *The Gaelic Names of Plants*, William Blackwood & Sons, Edinburgh, 1883.

Campbell, John Gregorson, *Superstitions of the Highlands and Islands of Scotland*, James MacLehose & Sons, Glasgow, 1900.

Carmichael, Alexander, *Carmina Gadelica, Volumes 1-5,* Oliver and Boyd, Edinburgh & London, 1928.

Clarke, David, with Andy Roberts, *Twilight of the Celtic Gods,* Blandford, Cassell PLC, London, 1996.

Clarkson, Rosetta, *Golden Age of Herbs & Herbalists,* Dover Publications, Inc, NY, NY, 1972.

Cowan, Tom, *Fire in the Head: Shamanism and the Celtic Spirit*, HarperSan Francisco, division of Harper Collins, NY, 1993.

Dames, Michael, *Mythic Ireland*, Thames & Hudson, Ltd., London, 1992.

De Cepeda y Ahumada, Teresa (St. Teresa of Avila), *Relaccion viii. 8 and 10.*

Ellis, Peter Berresford, *The Druids*, William B. Eerdmans Publishing Co., Grand Rapids, MI, 1994.

Evans Wentz, W.Y., *The Fairy Faith in Celtic Countries*, Henry Frowde, Oxford University Press, London, New York, Toronto and Melbourne, 1911.

Ginzburg, Carlo, *Ecstasies: Deciphering the WitchesÕ Sabbath*, Penguin Books USA, NY, NY, 1992.

Green, Miranda, *Celtic Goddesses*, British Museum Press, London, 1995.

———, *Dictionary of Celtic Myth and Legend,* Thames & Hudson, London and NY, 1992.

———, *Gods of the Celts*, Alan Sutton Publishing Ltd., Gloucester, 1986, Barnes & Noble, Totowa, NJ 1986.

Gregory, Lady, *Visions and Beliefs in the West of Ireland*, Colin Smythe, Ltd., Gerrard's Cross, Buckinghamshire, 1970.

Grieves, Mrs., *A Modern Herbal (In Two Volumes)*, Dover Publications, Inc., NY, 1971.

Griggs, Barbara, *Green Pharmacy*, Healing Arts Press, Rochester, VT, 1981.

Grimm, Jacob, *Teutonic Mythology,* James Stallybrass (translator), George Bell and Sons, London, 1883, 1888.

Hoffman, David, *The Wholistic Herbal,* The Findhorn Press, Forres, Scotland, 1983.

Hole, Christina, *Witchcraft in England,* B. T. Batsford Ltd., London, Charles Scribner's Sons, NY, 1947.

Howard, Michael, and Nigel Jackson, *The Pillars of Tubal Cain,* Capall Bann Publishing, Berks, 2000.

Huson, Paul, *Mastering Herbalism,* A Scarborough Book, Stein and Day Publishers, NY, 1975.

Huson, Paul, *Mastering Witchcraft,* Berkeley Windhover Books, Berkeley Publishing Corp, NY, NY, 1970, by special arrangement with G. P. Putnam's Sons, NY, NY.

Jackson, Nigel Aldcroft, *The Call of the Horned Piper,* Capall Bann Publishing, Berks, 1994.

Jayne, Walter Addison, M.D., *The Healing Gods of Ancient Civilizations,* University Books, Inc., New Hyde Park, NY, 1962.

Johnson, Thomas K. (a.k.a. Nicholas Gander), private researcher.

Joyce, P. W., *A Smaller Social History of Ancient Ireland,* Longmans, Green and Co., London, NY & Bombay, M H Gill & Son, Ltd., Dublin, 1908.

Kear, Katherine, *Flower Wisdom: The Definitive Guidebook to the Myth, Magic and Mystery of Flowers,* Thorsons, an imprint of HarperCollins Publishers, London, 2000.

K'Eogh, John, *Botanalogia Universalis Hibernica,* An Irish Herbal: the Botanalogia Universalis Hibernica, revised and edited by Michael Scott, Anna Livia Press, Dublin, 1991.

Lethbridge, T. C., *Witches,* Citadel Press, Inc., Secauscus, NJ 1972.

Logan, Patrick, *Irish Country Cures,* Sterling Publishing Co, Inc, NY, NY, 1994.

———— *The Old Gods: The Facts About Irish Fairies,* Appletree Press, Belfast, 1981.

Luther, Martin, *Werke, kritische Gesamtausgabe: Tischreden* (Weimar: Bohlau, 1912-1921), v. 5, p. 9, http://www.pitt.edu/~dash/gerchange.html#GrimmChangelingIsBeaten.

Macleod, Fiona (William Sharp), *The Works of Fiona Macleod, Vol. IV: Iona: The Divine Adventure,* William Heineman, Ltd., London, 1927.

————, *The Works of Fiona Macleod, Vol. II: Washer of the Ford, and Other Legendary Moralities,* Patrick Geddes and Colleagues, Edinburgh, Stone & Kimball, Chicago, 1896.

MacManus, Diarmuid, A., *The Middle Kingdom,* Max Parrish & Co Ltd., London, 1959.

MacKenzie, Donald A., *Scottish Folk-lore and Folklife,* Blackie & Son, Ltd., London and Glasgow, 1935.

Matthews, Caitlin, *The Celtic Book of the Dead,* St. Martin's Press, NY, NY, 1992.

————, *Elements of the Celtic Tradition,* Element Books Ltd., Dorset, 1989.

————, *Ladies of the Lake,* Aquarian Press, an imprint of Harper Collins, London, 1992.

Matthews, Caitlin & John, *Encyclopaedia of Celtic Wisdom: A Celtic ShamanÕs Source Book,* Element Books, Dorset, 1994.

McArthur, Margie, *Wisdom of the Elements: The Sacred Wheel of Earth, Air, Fire, and Water,* Crossing Press, Freedom, CA, 1998.

McNeil, F. Marian, *The Silver Bough, Vol. 1,* William MacLellan, 1956, Canongate Classics, Edinburgh, 1989.

Moore, A. W., & Douglas, M. A., compilers, *Manx Worthies—or Biographies of Notable Manx Men and Women,* Vol. II, pp. 161-162, S. K. Broadbent & Co., Ltd., Victoria St. Isle of Man, 1901.

Murray, Margaret, *The Witch Cult in Western Europe,* Oxford, at the Clarendon Press, 1921.

O'Cathain, Seamas, *The Festival of Brigit,* DBA Publications, Ltd., Blackrock, Dublin, 1995.

O'hOgain, Daithi, *Irish Superstitions,* Gill & Macmillan, Ltd., Dublin, 1995.

Pagels, Elaine, *The Origin of Satan,* Vintage Books, Random House, Inc., NY, 1995.

Paterson, Helena, *The Celtic Lunar Zodiac,* Charles E. Tuttle & Co., Inc., Rutland, VT, 1992.

Paterson, Jacqueline Memory, *Tree Wisdom: The Definitive Guidebook to the Myth, Folklore and Healing Power of Trees,* Thorsons, an imprint of HarperCollins Publishers, London, 1996.

Pennick, Nigel, and Jackson, Nigel, *The New Celtic Oracle,* Capall Bann, Berkshire, 1997.

Poynder, Michael, *The Lost Magic of Christianity: Celtic Essene Connections,* The Collins Press, Cork, 1997.

Pughe, John, *The Physicians of Myddfai,* published for the Welsh MSS Society, Llandovery, D. J. Roderic, London, Longman & Co.; 1861, facsimile reprint of the English translation by Llanderch Publishers, Felinfach, Wales, 1993.

Rees, Alwyn & Brinley, *The Celtic Heritage,* Thames & Hudson, London, 1961.

Rhys, John, *Celtic Folklore, Welsh and Manx,* Oxford University Press, UK, 1901, Wildwood House, London, 1980.

Simpson, Jacqueline, and Steve Roud, *A Dictionary of English Folklore,* Oxford University Press, Oxford, 2000.

Stewart, R. J., *Mystic Life of Merlin,* Routledge, & Kegan Paul Ltd., London, 1986.

———— *Robert Kirk, Walker Between Worlds,* Element Books, Shaftesbury, Longmead, Dorset, 1990.

———— *The Living World of Faery,* Gothic Image Publications, Glastonbury, 1995.

Tongue, R. L., *Somerset Folklore* (County Series VIII), F. L.S., 1965.

Trevelyan, Marie, *Folklore and folk-tales of Wales,* Elliot Stock, London, 1909.

Webster's Seventh New Collegiate Dictionary, G. & C. Merriam Company, Publishers, Springfield, MA, 1967.

Wheelwright, Edith Grey, *Medicinal Plants and Their History,* Dover Publications, Inc., NY, 1974.

White, Carolyn, *A History of Irish Fairies,* The Mercier Press, Cork & Dublin, 1976.

Wilde, Lady, *Ancient Legends, Mystic Charms & Superstitions of Ireland,* Chatto & Windus, London, 1919.

Wood-Martin, W. G., *Traces of the Elder Faiths of Ireland: A Handbook of Irish Pre-Christian Traditions,* Vols. I and II, Longmans, Greens, and Co., NY and Bombay, 1902.

Wright, Elizabeth, M., *Rustic Speech and Folk-lore,* Oxford University Press, London and NY, 1914.

Yeats, W. B., *Fairy and Folk Tales of the Irish Peasantry,* Walter Scott, London, 1888.

———— *Fortnightly Review,* 1900, 1902.

———— *The Scots Observer,* 1889.

———— *Irish Fairy and Folk Tales,* Boni and Liveright, Inc., NY, NY, 1918.

Index

A

A. E., 10, 20, 22, 286
Air, 7, 12, 14-15, 19-20, 31, 33-34, 43-44, 77, 107, 136, 185, 200-202, 204-205, 209, 213, 225, 236-240, 242, 261, 270-271, 279, 286, 293, 299, 300, 311-313, 321, 325, 330, 351
Aine of Munster, 13, 213-214, 263, 291, 293
Airmid, 10-11, 12, 48, 88, 213, 217, 290, 291, 294, 329, 342
Airmid's cloak, 290-291, 339, 347
All Hallows Eve, 39, 61, 357, 358
Alliance, 183, 191, 206-207, 256, 264, 321, 339
Amanita Muscaria, 127, 129, 144
Amergin, 16, 17
amulet/amulets, 49, 53, 63-64, 118, 136, 280, 298, 333-335
Ana, 12-13, 29
angels/angelic, 7-9, 21, 29, 31, 41, 54, 104, 155, 160, 177, 179, 203, 206, 211, 224, 225-227, 229, 235, 287, 307, 337, 344
animal allies, 206, 210, 229, 291
Anu, 12-13 29, 213
Apollo, 125, 215-216
apple, 6, 13, 90, 129, 139-142, 148, 214
Apple Tree Man, 6, 139, 140
Archangels, 114, 206, 225-227, 358
ash, 123, 131, 140, 143-144, 146, 149-150, 212, 273, 293
attention, 12, 48, 99, 118, 163, 178, 187-189, 192-196, 198, 201, 204, 219, 305, 307-308, 312, 342-343
attuning, 21, 183-184, 191, 207, 309, 322
augury/ auguries, 44, 60, 61, 64-65. *See also* omens

B

Balor, 119, 171
Battle of Moytura, 14, 48, 237, 290
Beltaine, 7, 14, 36, 58, 60-61, 65, 125, 134, 138, 144-146, 149-150, 202, 263, 320, 356, 357, 358
binding, 53, 56, 64, 71
blast-water, 113-114
Blessed Water, 84. 154, 309, 326-327, 330, 332, 333, 335, 337
blessing, 7, 29, 36-37, 39, 54-56, 63, 70. 96-97, 106, 118, 120, 126, 147, 155, 188, 204, 209, 296, 323, 337, 354
bluebells, 123-125
birth baptism, 70, 96
borderlands, 58, 61, 64-65, 84, 202-203, 212, 228, 319
breathing exercises/techniques, 194, 204
bridge-building, 183, 191, 207, 321, 339
Brigid, 11-12, 29, 31, 39-40, 44, 57, 65, 132, 144, 146, 156, 171, 201-202, 211-212, 219, 263, 290-291, 293, 329, 342, 344-345, 347, 357
Brigid's mantle, 290-291, 339, 344-345, 347
British Isles, xii, 2, 5, 11, 18,29, 35, 39, 71, 135, 149, 153, 179, 202, 212, 298 Brittany, 2- 3, 39, 92, 214
broom, 79, 106, 125, 128, 144, 150
bullaun, 52, 156

C

Cailleach, 27, 32, 54, 223, 263,
Cailleach Bheara, 27, 32
caim, 62
cairn, 24, 32, 294
Candlemas, 12, 65, 357
Carmichael, Alexander, 24, 26, 38, 54, 62, 65
Carmina Gadelica, 24, 26, 38, 65
Carthy of Imlough, 89
caul, 106
cauldron, 13-14, 22, 119, 201, 208, 216, 219, 237, 246, 280, 349
Celtic healing, xii, 2, 12, 16, 46-47, 51, 57, 63, 132, 211-212, 298
Celtic people, xii, 30-31, 35, 202
centering, 191, 194, 295. *See also* grounding
chakra/chakras, 62, 73, 197, 199, 240, 253, 283, 288, 311
changeling, 4, 60, 83, 92, 97, 112-113, 126, 298
chants/chanting, 16, 49, 70, 75, 82, 89, 90, 119, 296, 303, 304, 310
charms, xii, xiii, 24, 36, 44-45, 47-52, 56- 64, 66, 77-80, 83, 89, 91, 93, 96, 97, 101, 115-116, 118-121, 135-139, 153, 160, 183, 288, 297, 298
Chretien de Troyes, 13
Christianity, xiv, 7, 9, 12, 24, 26, 30, 54, 62, 95, 211-212, 224, 226, 356
clairvoyance, 150,168
cleanse/cleansing, 35, 38, 40, 54, 119, 135, 144, 204 205, 212, 218, 263
Collum, Moyra, 89
color, 7, 20, 51, 53, 55-57, 72, 120, 136, 138, 143, 149, 186, 205, 215, 283-284, 287, 296, 305, 310-314, 357,
colors of the winds, 27-28
consciousness, 10, 17, 19-22, 47, 58, 82, 104, 125, 162, 168-169, 173, 176-177, 190-194, 204, 206-207, 210-211, 221-222, 228, 233-234, 239, 254, 279, 295-297, 302-304, 315, 317, 328, 359 contagion, 68
Convocations, 226, 237, 239,

241, 253, 258, 262, 269, 279, 323, 337, 339, 342, 343, 348
Creative Polarity, 221
creative visualization, 164
cross-quarters/quarter days, 202, 356
crystals, 47, 50-51, 153, 155, 157, 209, 302, 305, 312
Cunning Men, 46, 81, 93

D

Dagda, 11, 14, 148, 171, 237, 280
daisies, 126
Dana, 12-13, 27, 171, 213, 291
Danu, 12, 27, 213
Dark Goddess, 223, 225, 229, 234, 263, 305, 345, 347, 348
deosil, 24
devas, 15, 17, 19-20, 82, 104, 160, 225, 292, 328, 350
devil, 9, 29, 44, 49, 67, 93, 102-105, 107-108, 121, 136, 138, 147
dew, 25, 39,
Diana, 107-109
Dian Cecht, 10-11, 48, 171, 213, 216-217, 290-291
Dissociative Identity Disorders, 178
divination, 40, 50, 53, 64, 65, 91, 105, 126, 135, 138-139, 147-148, 297-298, 357
Domnu, 12
Don, 10, 12, 15, 27, 171
dragons, 18, 40, 137, 206, 226, 234
Druids, 2, 5, 16-17, 22, 26, 46, 48, 64, 69, 77, 100, 119, 137, 139, 143, 147-148, 153, 156, 178, 236, 298, 310-311
dryads, 17, 19, 129
dwarves, 18, 206

E

Early, Biddy, 83-85
Earth Light, 19, 316-317
elder, xiii, 6, 63, 131, 139, 143, 145
Elder Gods, 18, 171
Elder Mother, 6, 139, 145
elecampane, 126
elemental beings/spirits, 6, 17, 19-20, 22, 31-32, 160, 182, 206, 210, 224-227, 286
elf-shot, 79, 93, 116, 126, 298
elves, 7, 18-19, 93, 97, 126, 153
Ember Days, 107
emotions, 47, 73-74, 175-176, 182, 188, 204, 284, 307-308, 312
entrainment, 74-75
Evil Eye, 37, 54, 60, 63, 81, 90, 93, 97, 106, 117-122, 128, 131, 137, 149, 153, 177-178, 298 evil influences, 36, 45, 122, 126, 130, 149
Evil Stroke, 120-121
Exercises:
  Stretching the Subtle Senses, 220, 221
  Chakra and Color Breathing Exercises, 314-315
  Sun Breathing, 316
  Moon Breathing, 316-317
  Earthlight Breathing, 317
  Shapeshifting Breathing, 318
  Delving into your Multi-fold
    Essence, 318, 319
eyebright, 91, 131, 132

F

Faery Allies, 83, 165, 182-83, 190-191, 193, 206, 209-211, 217, 229, 241, 256-258, 291, 295-296, 304, 307, 318, 322, 325-327, 337, 342-343, 347-348,
Faery altar, 208-209, 230, 233, 240, 294, 295, 305
Faery Blast, 81, 90, 97, 113-114, 131, 174
Faery Blessed Water, 331, 332
Faery Blessed Stones, 332, 333
faery-caused ailments, 87, 90, 112-122, 147
Faery Darts, 116, 131, 136, 174
Faery Doctor, ix, xii, 4, 47-49, 51-52, 55, 57, 59, 62, 69, 74, 77-78, 80-92, 100, 105, 109, 116, 118-119, 121, 123, 131-132, 138, 147, 155, 161, 174, 178, 211, 297, 309-311, 353
faery enchantments, 123, 235, 131-132, 135, 138, 147, 149, 297
Faery Faith, 5, 7, 13
Faery Fire, 333, 334
Faery Fool, 85, 87, 91
faery glance, 120
faery gold, 125, 146, 354
faery hall, 94, 103
Faery Healing Grove, 291-294
Faery Healing Amulets & Talismans, creating, 334, 335
Faery Healing Tradition, xiii, xiv, 2, 46-47, 93-94, 100, 179, 182-189
  necessary skills, 186-189
  rules of, 184-185
Faery Healers, 4, 49, 66, 69, 75, 78, 81-83, 85, 87, 90, 93, 97, 106, 113, 138, 178, 179, 182, 190, 307, 353
faery hearth, 208-209, 240, 295, 321-323, 342-343
faery hill, 93-94, 96, 130, 146, 154
faery host, 94, 96
Faery King, 82, 103, 127, 145, 209, 210-211, 223, 225, 239, 262, 279,
Faery Magic, 35, 53, 97, 134
faery medicines, ix, 206, 296, 329-338
faery mound, 15, 113, 228, 230
Faery Queen, xii, 10, 56, 67, 82, 85, 87, 91, 94-95, 103, 125, 219, 130, 142, 145-146, 171, 209-211, 213, 223, 239, 262, 279
faery ring, 127, 135, 146, 149, 150
Faery Stroke, 81, 90-91, 97, 114-116, 131, 174
faery time, 58, 61, 256, 259
faery trees, 123, 139-150,
  alder, 140, 143, 149
  ash, 123, 131, 140, 143-144, 139, 150
  birch, 127, 139, 140, 144, 148
  elder, xiii, 63, 131, 143, 145
  hawthorn, 123-124, 129, 131, 133-135, 145-147, 286, 357
  hazel, 90, 129, 146-148, 252
  oak, 123, 132, 135, 143, 148,

212
  rowan, 49, 53, 55, 118, 131, 134, 140, 143, 145, 148-150
  willow, 116, 150
  yew, 79, 143-144, 150
Faery Wind. *See* Faery Blast.
Faery Winds, 334
Faery Work, 59, 184, 206, 209, 226, 229, 327-328
Faery Women, 4, 13, 49, 78, 81, 89, 93-95, 137, 142, 178
  Falias, 14, 226, 236-238, 240, 249, 268, 269, 280, 349
Falias, 14, 226, 236-238, 240, 249, 268, 269, 280, 349
fallen angels, 8-9, 21, 29, 104, 227, 287
fern, 126, 131, 132, 135
Finias, 14 209, 226, 236-240, 242, 268, 269, 279, 348
Fire, 11-12, 16-17, 19, 23, 31, 34, 35-38, 43, 47, 50-53, 55, 66, 70, 77-78, 81, 90-91, 112, 114, 118, 121, 132-133, 136, 143, 146-147, 149, 172,183, 185, 200-202, 204-205, 208-209, 211-213, 216, 219, 225, 233, 237-240, 244, 252, 268, 279, 283, 295, 299, 300, 303-304, 311, 315-316, 330, 333, 343, 349
Flame of Life, 208-209, 350
Flame of Being, 183, 204, 208-209, 321, 342
flower essences, viii, 253, 280, 309, 331, 336-338
Fomorians, 12, 171-172
Four Directions, 62, 200-201, 205-207, 209, 224, 226-227, 236-238, 240, 329, 339, 343
Four Elements, 12, 19, 31-34, 62, 78, 200-202, 204, 209, 224, 226, 238, 299, 300-311
Four Faery Cities, 13, 226, 269, 270
four-leaf clover, 131-132
foxglove, 114-115, 124, 126, 131-133, 297-298, 299
four treasures, 14, 22, 208-209, 226, 236
Freya, 71, 125
frith, 60, 64-65
full moon, 25, 61, 108, 316, 357

G
giants, 26, 32, 206, 225, 234
Glen of Precious Stones, 238-241, 251-252, 253, 263, 268, 286, 331-333, 335, 337, 340, 342 Goibniu, 171, 217, 289, 291
Golden Mean, 235
Gorias, 14, 226, 236-240, 244, 279, 349
Grannus, 216
Great Tree of Life, 22, 229, 230, 233, 292-295, 342, *see* World Tree
Greater Self, 217
Great Goddess, 71, 171,
Grimm, Jacob, 18
grounding, 45, 191, 193-199, 204, 208, 218, 220, 230, 283, 295, 317, 340, 342
ground ivy, 79, 131, 132-133
gnomes, 210, 226, 243

H
hair, xiii, 54-55, 60, 68, 70, 72, 117-118, 129 hamadryads, 17
hazel rods/sticks, 90- 91, 147
Hel, 18-19
healing wells, 40-42, 212, 216
heart chakra, 240, 253, 283, 313-314 hearth-fire, 37, 185, 225, 315
herbal healing, 11, 13, 16, 48, 183, 297 Holle, Frau, 32
holy well, 24, 41, 52, 57, 89, 120, 140, 155, 204, 212
hypnotism. *See* mesmerism

I
Imagination, 59, 164-165, 168, 187-188, 200-201, 204, 209, 220, 228, 321, 323
Imbolc, 7, 12, 36, 60, 65, 201, 202, 357
incantations, xii, xiii, 7, 9, 17, 37, 47-49, 61-64, 69-70, 77, 80, 83, 91, 96, 101, 119, 133, 138- 139, 156, 160, 213, 216, 290
incense, 81, 136, 200
innerworld, 183, 185, 189, 207, 210, 228, 233, 252, 253, 259, 312, 350
inquisitors, 102, 105, 107
intention, 116, 155, 183, 186, 187-188, 193, 200, 204-205, 209, 260, 262, 279-280, 282- 283, 302, 307-308, 328-329, 331-333, 335, 337-338, 343, 347
invocations, 28, 31, 77, 115, 188
iron, 37, 45, 47, 50, 77, 96-97, 108, 112, 118, 121, 137, 209, 286-289
Isle of Apples, 13, 142, 214
Isle of Man, 2, 46, 93, 100, 136, 155

J
journeys, 304
  #1, 264-266
  #2, 266-268
  Carrying the Forest Through Time, 350-352
  Empowerment Journey to Falias, 277-279
  Empowerment Journey to Finias, 269-272
  Empowerment Journey to Gorias, 272-274
  Empowerment Journey to Murias, 274-276
  Into the Stars Within the Earth, 260-262
  On the Great Tree, 230-233
  Reweaving Brigid's Mantle, 345-347
  Self Healing, 340-341
  There Is One River, 325-327
  To the Faery Healing Grove, 291-294
  To Find Faery Healing Allies, 257-258
  To Finias, 242-245
  To the Glen of the Precious Stones, 241-242
  To Gorias, 245-247
  To Murias, 247-250
journeying, 106, 127, 191, 194, 305, 322, 344, 347
journeywork, 164, 191-193, 200, 210, 219

K
Kirk, Reverend Robert, 6-8

King Arthur, 13, 22, 142, 214

L
Ladies of the Lake, xiii, 22
Lady Gregory, 2, 87, 89
Lady Wilde, xii, 2, 7-8, 10, 35, 44, 48, 50, 55, 63, 66, 68-69, 70-71, 78, 90, 109, 114-115, 117- 121, 124, 131, 132, 138-139
laying on of hands, 67, 69
Law of Similarities, 64, 68
Leland, Charles Godfrey, 108
liminality, 58, 64, 119, 212-213
Lucifer, 8, 104, 108-109, 211, 227, 287
Lugh, 14, 216-217, 226, 237-239, 263, 279, 358
Lughnasadh, 7, 36, 60, 65, 201-202, 214, 263, 358
Luther, Martin, 112

M
MacGarry, Polly, 86-87
MacKenzie, Kenneth, 154
Macleod, Fiona, 19, 169, 183, 237, 240, 249, 253, 291, 345, 358-359
magic, xii, xiii, 14, 16, 34-35, 42, 49, 52-53, 63-64, 69, 71, 97, 109, 123, 132, 134, 150, 153, 156, 178-179, 183, 185, 190, 237, 280, 290-291, 302-304
magical practices, 5, 63, 66, 104
magnetism, 73, 172
mallow, 124, 127, 131, 134
Mangan, James, 89
Manx traditions, 100-101
Matthews, Caitlin, 3
May Eve, 41, 49, 61, 65, 117, 201, 358
May Day, 35-36, 41, 61, 133, 144, 146. *See also* Beltaine
May Morning, 39, 43, 146, 149
McNeil, F. Marian, 41
medicinal brews, 301-304
Meditations:
  The One, 221-222
  Making Contact with Plant Spirits, 300-301
Mesmer, Anton, 72-73
mesmerism, 47, 69, 72-75
Miach, 10-11, 48, 88, 213, 217, 290, 342
Middleworld, 10, 18, 19, 33, 205-206, 213, 224-225, 227, 229, 233, 256, 283
Midsummer, 36, 42, 61, 80, 126-127, 130, 136, 138, 145-147, 358
Midwinter, 36
Milesians, 13-14, 16-17
milk, 4, 12, 27, 47, 50, 52-53, 60, 79, 97, 112, 128, 134, 137, 146-147, 157, 202, 253, 322, 357 Milky Way, 26-27
moon, 18, 23-27, 30, 32, 48, 49, 61, 65, 70-72, 108-109, 118-119, 137-138, 147, 221-222, 225, 315-316, 330, 332, 357
Morgen, 13, 142, 214, 291, 329, 342
Mr. Saggarton/Langan, 87-88
Mrs. Sheridan, 87-88
Murias, 14, 226, 236-238, 240, 246, 268-269, 280, 349
mushrooms, 123-124, 127, 129, 131, 144, 300
Mythological Theory, 5

N
nail parings, xiii, 54-55, 68, 72
Naturalistic Theory, 5
nature spirits, ix, 15, 17, 19-20, 29, 160, 210, 225, 234, 263, 289, 328 need-fire, 36-37, 356
new moon, 25-26, 70-72
No Thing, 221, 240, 252
Nuada, 11, 48, 216, 237-239

O
Oak Men, 6, 139, 148
oceanids, 17
Old Gods, 14-15, 18, 21-22, 114, 132, 170, 172, 174, 210, 224, 227
O'Lee, Morough, 85-86
omens, 29, 46, 48, 64-66, 357
Opalescent Ones, 10
Otherworlds, xiii, 3-4, 7, 10, 12-13, 19, 23, 38, 43, 56, 58, 141-142, 144, 146-148, 165, 171, 182, 187, 193, 202-203, 212, 214-215, 237, 252, 280, 286, 305, 357

P
Paganism, 24, 26, 30, 356
Physicians of Myddfai, xiii, 2, 97-100, 204
plant spirits, 6, 28, 82, 139, 210, 296-297, 300, 304, 320, 337,
potion/potions, viii, 9, 48, 69, 82-84, 86, 91, 95, 127, 131, 138-139, 280, 303, 353
Primal Wholeness, 307, 321-322, 350
primrose, 56, 125, 128
Principle of Association, 64
Principle of Resonance, 21, 74, 233
Principle of Sympathetic Magic, 64
psychic energy, 8
Psychological Theory, 5-6
Pygmy Theory, 5, 6

Q
Quarter Days, 14, 42, 60, 64-65, 107-108, 134, 202, 219, 320, 356

R
ragwort, 124, 128
rapture, 176-177
Reiki, 253
relaxation exercises, 188, 192
retuning, 53, 183, 191, 207, 306, 322
reweaving, 182-183, 191, 207, 234, 306, 321, 339, 344-345
Rhiannon, 10-11, 215, 291
roses, 123, 128-130
Ruane, Bridget, 88

S
sabbats, 106, 317
Sacred Circle, 191, 200-208, 306
Sacred Three, 311
sacred space, 191, 200-201, 230, 329, 340, 342
saining, 37
saints, xi, 26, 29-31, 53-54, 62, 64, 156, 165, 177, 179, 211, 356
salamanders, 210, 226
saliva, 47, 54-55, 87, 118, 121

salt, 45, 47, 52-53, 79, 96-97, 108, 114-116, 118, 121, 131, 135
Samhain, 7, 36, 55, 58, 60-61, 65, 144-145, 148, 150, 201-202, 263, 356-357
scarlet pimpernel, 129, 131
Scottish traditions, 94
scrying, 84
sea, xiii, 3, 8, 17-19, 21, 24, 32-34, 39, 44, 57-58, 68, 84, 169-171, 225, 228, 246, 312-313, 315, 320, 323
seal-people, xiii, *See* selkies
Second Hearing, 129
Second Sight, 67, 81, 106, 129, 145
secrecy, 47, 61-62, 82, 91, 95
Seeley Court, 9, 109
selkies, xiii, 226, 317
seven protective plants, 131-133
seventh sons, 7-8, 66-67, 93
Shakespeare, William, 126-127, 130, 171
shapeshifting, 103, 105, 108, 206-208, 317-319, 344
Sharp, William, 358-359
Shining Ones, 10, 19, 21, 289
Sidhe, 8, 14-15, 17, 19, 145, 238, 240, 253, 286
silence, 15, 47, 51-52, 61-62, 69, 82, 86, 91, 201, 238, 263
silvered water, 119
silverweed, 129
Simpling, 297
Sirona, 214, 216
smudging, 136, 218
soul loss/theft, 177-178
Spear of Lugh, 14, 22, 237-239, 279
speedwell, ix, x, 131, 136
spells, 9, 19, 91-92, 108, 129, 132, 136
Spirit Allies, 193, 258, 343, 347
Spirit Doctors, 211, 217
spittle. *See* saliva
springs, 22, 38, 58, 212, 214-216, 293-294, 326, 330
Star Powers, 172, 206, 224-225
Stewart, R. J., 19
stinging nettle, 116
St. John's Eve/Day, 36, 43, 61, 126, 136, 358

St. John's Wort, 49, 61, 131, 134, 136, 138
Stone of Destiny, 249, 280
Stone of Fal, 14, 22, 237
stones, 153-157, 160, 204, 208, 305, 328, 332-333
stone waters, 154
stroking, 51, 69, 121
swords, 96, 208, 279, 289
Sword of Light, 242
Sword of Nuada, 14, 22, 237-239
Suillean, ix, x
Sulis, 214-215
summer solstice, 61, 131, 136, 201, 213, 358
sunwise, 24, 37, 41
sylphs, 210, 226
sympathetic magic, 64, 68
sympathy, 55, 56

T
talismans, 63, 280, 334
Thomas the Rhymer, xii, 67, 146, 223
thread, 49, 53-55, 63, 79, 118, 149, 306, 329
Three Realms, 18, 33, 62, 205, 224-225, 227, 229, 253, 295
Three Worlds, 12, 18, 205, 224, 229, 254
throat chakra, 62, 314
Tir na nOg, 3, 21, 85-86
Titans, 18, 32, 171-172, 225
toadstool, 129, 131. *See also* mushrooms
touch, the, 69
trance, 47, 120, 176-177
transference, 48, 55, 68
transport, 176
Tree of Life, *See also* World Tree
Trinity, 49, 51, 54, 57, 62, 70, 115-116, 119
Triple Goddess, 54, 57, 212
Tuatha De Danaan, xi, 10-15, 18, 20-22, 32, 48, 88, 142, 171-172, 208-209, 213, 216-217, 236- 237, 280, 289-290
tuned/tuning, 16, 31, 74

U
Underworld, 13, 15, 18-19, 33, 43, 52, 67, 71, 171, 201, 205-206, 213, 215, 218-219, 223-225, 227-229, 233-235, 252-253, 263, 283, 290, 329, 347-348
undines, 210, 226
Unseeley Court, 9, 106, 109
Upperworld, 18, 33, 205-206, 221, 224-229, 233-235, 253, 263, 286, 290, 329, 347, 348

V
Vanir, 18
vervain, 91, 131-132, 134, 137-138, 297-298
visualization, 164, 186-187, 191, 193-194, 228, 321
vital energy, 8, 73
Void, 33, 221-222, 235, 240, 252, 253

W
Walsh, John, 102
wands, 94, 143-144, 147, 201, 243, 353
wassailing, 140-141
Watchers, 226-227
water, elemental, 12, 31, 33-34, 43, 78, 91, 185, 200-202, 204-205, 212-213, 216, 237, 246, 280, 300, 311
water lily, 129
water wheel, 78, 85
Web of Consciousness, 168
Web of Life, 6, 31, 72, 163, 167-168, 173, 306
well of evil, 42
wells, 12, 24, 38, 40-43, 57, 154, 155, 171, 204, 211-212, 253, 295, 304, 330, 356
Well of Slaine, 213, 216, 290, 304
Welsh traditions, xiii, 2, 97-100
Wentz Evans, W.Y., xii, 2, 5-52
Wheel of the Year, 202
white witches/witchcraft, 93, 102
Wights, 18
Wild Hunt, 106, 223
wild thyme, 124, 129, 130
wind, 15, 17, 24, 27-28, 32, 44, 46, 55, 90, 95, 113, 131, 143, 148, 171, 208, 228, 237, 238,

252, 299, 315, 323-324, 334
Wise Men, 91, 93, 97, 102, 236
Wise Women, 46, 78, 81, 83, 86, 93, 102
witchcraft trials, 102-103
witch women, 9, 106, 109
Wood-Martin, W. G., 44, 79, 80, 82
World Tree, 33, 144, 150, 205, 224, 229

Y

yarrow, 49, 61, 65-66, 91, 121, 131, 138, 297, 298
Yeats, William Butler, xii, 2, 7, 9, 59, 66, 78, 79, 87-89, 109, 133, 188, 307
yew, 79, 143, 150
Yggdrasil, 144, 150
Young, Ella, 32
Yule log, 36

Z

Zero, 221

To order,
or for information about
other titles by
Margie McArthur,
please go to:

http://faeryhealing.com/
faery_store_2.htm

www.ingramcontent.com/pod-product-compliance
Lightning Source LLC
Chambersburg PA
CBHW060417010526
44118CB00017B/2258